Liquid Scripture

Liquid Scripture

The Bible in a Digital World

Jeffrey S. Siker

Fortress Press
Minneapolis

LIQUID SCRIPTURE
The Bible in a Digital World

Cover images, clockwise from top left: Codex Sinaiticus (detail of John 1), used by permission of the British Library; Detail of stained glass window from Stanstead Church, Suffolk, UK; YouVersion (screenshot of John 1); The Gutenberg Bible (detail of John 1), used by permission of the British Library.

Cover design: Pat Pickard

Print ISBN: 978-1-5064-0786-9
eBook ISBN: 978-1-5064-0787-6

The paper used in this publication meets the minimum requirements of American National Standard for Information Sciences — Permanence of Paper for Printed Library Materials, ANSI Z329.48-1984.

Manufactured in the U.S.A.

Contents

Table of Figures

Figures in the Gallery are indicated throughout the text by a G after the figure number.

Preface: From Print to Pixels, 1s and 0s

Yes, it is a press, certainly, but a press from which shall flow in inexhaustible streams the most abundant and most marvelous liquor that has ever flowed to relieve the thirst of men! Through it, God will spread His Word.

—Johannes Gutenberg[1]

These words, attributed to Johannes Gutenberg in his reflection upon the invention of the printing press, ironically could just as easily be applied to the advent of digital media in its many permutations as it was to the printing press. From personal computers to the web to e-readers to email to messaging to Twitter and Facebook to smartphones and tablets of all kinds, the digital age in which we now live has witnessed no less than an inexhaustible torrent of 1s and 0s (that most marvelous liquor) that has ever flowed to relieve (and frustrate) the thirst of millions of people. This torrent shows no signs of abating. Indeed, it is now commonplace to talk about information overload in the extreme, due largely to the capacity of just about anyone to hurl just about anything in writing, image, and sound out into the digital world.

The goal of this book is to trace just one stream amidst the larger flood, the ongoing shift from print Bibles to digital Bibles. While a great deal of attention has been given to the general turn from printed page to pixelated screen, discussion of the "digital turn" in Bibles has been episodic at best. Though it is increasingly impossible to give a full account of digital Bibles with all of their promises and pitfalls, it is possible to address in a relatively comprehensive manner develop-

1. Alphonse de Lamartine, *Memoirs of Celebrated Characters*, vol. 2:287 (New York: Harper & Bros., 1854–56; 3 vols.).

ments in the world of digital Bibles over the last 30 years or so (the last generation), especially since the rise of personal computers in the mid-1980s and their subsequent offspring (smartphones and tablets). As the Bible-app YouVersion loudly proclaims: "The Bible is everywhere."[2] Of course, by the time you read this, there will, no doubt, be something else on the YouVersion home page. By the time you read this, YouVersion may have completely morphed into something else. Digital media makes it so easy to morph.

And so, here is the first paradox. The Bible is supposedly the unchanging Word of God, and yet, all things digital are anything but unchanging. What does it mean to bring the relatively "fixed" Bible into a medium that is utterly transient? For some people, it makes no difference, since the Bible was originally communicated in oral snippets rather than bound together in its current form. For others, however, there is cause for concern since the increasingly digital form of the Bible opens it up to the kind of change that is rather unsettling for sacred scriptures that, somewhat like Jesus himself, are supposed to be—as Hebrews puts it—"the same yesterday, today, and forever" (13:8).

A few years ago, several students in my undergraduate Intro New Testament class at Loyola Marymount University asked if they could use the Bibles they had downloaded on their smartphones, tablets, or laptop computers instead of lugging around the expensive and heavy traditional print study Bible I had asked students to purchase for the class. I thought about it for a moment, calling to mind that I had used various Bible programs on my iPhone, iPad, and MacBook, and so, without much deliberation, I told them they could. Around the same time, I began noticing that church members in different congregations where I teach Bible studies were also coming and pulling out their smartphones rather than opening a traditional print Bible. "Hmmm," I thought, "that's an interesting development." While my undergraduate students have varying understandings and mostly little knowledge of the Bible, especially from an academic perspective, the church members come to study the Bible because they view it as sacred scripture, a sacred text, in one regard or another. What did it mean for them that they could study their scripture in digital or print form? Or did this distinction mean anything in particular?

Katja Rakow, a professor of Religious Studies at Utrecht University

2. https://www.youversion.com.

(in the Netherlands), recently related an experience pertinent to this question. She was doing a study of pastor Joel Osteen's megachurch (Lakewood Church) over a few years, beginning in 2011. At the beginning of her essay "The Bible in the Digital Age,"[3] she recounts how, every Sunday, he invited the worship participants to hold up their Bibles. And then in unison the pastor and congregation recited the following declaration:

> This is my Bible. I am what it says I am. I can do what it says I can do. Today, I will be taught the Word of God. I boldly confess, my mind is alert, my heart is receptive. I will never be the same. I am about to receive the incorruptible, indestructible, ever-living seed of the Word of God. I will never be the same. Never, never, never. I will never be the same. In Jesus' name. Amen.

Clearly, this declaration shows a very high view of the Bible and its authority. But what struck Prof. Rakow was that among the 16,000 people gathered for worship, all holding up their Bibles, she observed a smattering of iPads, iPhones, and e-book readers among the sea of print Bibles of all sorts. A year later, in 2012, as the congregation again declared "This is my Bible," many more of the worshipers were holding aloft their digital Bibles on smartphones, tablets, or e-readers. As she quite poignantly comments: "In that moment of declaration, these electronic devices *became* the Bible. They were not just a technology that enabled its users to read the digital version of the Word of God. For this short moment, the fact became irrelevant that the same device could be used in very different ways besides providing Bible verses." And so, a second paradox emerges: the digital device with a liquid screen "temporarily transforms into a material object with just one function: an object, which attendees lift up while declaring, 'This is my Bible.'"[4] Of course, this very moment of transfiguration, in which the digital device becomes the sacred text, can be shattered in an instant with a text message, a tweet, a Snapchat message, a call, a reminder, or any number of other distractions that break the scripture spell. Still, Rakow's observations resonate strongly with my own experience, more in local Protestant and Roman Catholic congregations than in evangelical megachurches, and not with the same kind of dramatic declaration,

---

3. Katja Rakow, "The Bible in the Digital Age: Negotiating the Limits of 'Bibleness' of Different Bible Media." In *Christianity and the Limits of Materiality*, ed., Minna Opas & Anna Haapalainen (London: Bloomsbury, 2017; forthcoming at the time I completed this book). Emphasis mine. My thanks to Prof. Rakow for sharing this essay with me in advance of its publication.
4. Rakow, "The Bible in the Digital Age."

but with what amounts to a similar sentiment about the sacred text in digital form. And so, from the classroom to the church, and back again, thus began my interest in the use of digital Bibles in both academic and ecclesial contexts.

The goal of this book is to describe and to assess the significant and growing shift from print Bibles to digital Bibles, from print to digital text, image, and sound. As I will spell out in the introductory chapter below, examining this shift involves exploring several facets related to the use of digital Bibles in the life of the Church, on the one hand, and the use of digital Bibles in more academic biblical scholarship, on the other hand. These really are two sides of the same coin, though, in truth, the "two sides" are really a multiplicity of sides with varying degrees of overlap. Many so-called lay readers of the Bible are making increasingly sophisticated use of heavy-duty academic Bible software programs, just as many so-called professional biblical scholars are seeking to communicate with faith communities through various digital social media platforms. While more strictly academic and more strictly pastoral approaches to the Bible certainly continue in the digital domain, there are also many academics and church folks interested in mutual engagement over the biblical text, now in a dazzling array of digital forms. I have often thought of myself as straddling academic and ecclesial worlds, with one foot in the academy (my Professor of New Testament hat) and one foot in the church (my Presbyterian minister—PCUSA—hat, even as I teach in a Roman Catholic setting). It is my conviction that each helps to keep the other both honest and relevant. The academy (and sometimes, the church) reminds us to read the Bible contextually, to remember the ancient contexts in which it was written. Both church and academy also remind us to pay attention to the history of interpretation of the Bible, as it has been the common touchstone for Christians across the ages in myriad contexts all their own. And the church (and sometimes, the academy) reminds us to be self-aware of our own modern contexts in which we interpret and make sense of this sacred text, both for our personal lives of faith and for communities of faith. This book reflects my deep commitment to both worlds, and my goal to address, in an integrated manner, both academic and ecclesial audiences.

I know there are many people who share these same convictions and locate themselves in many of the conversations between ecclesial and academic worlds about the Bible. Similarly, the vast majority of us now live in an increasingly hyperdigitized world, even as we hold on to all

things analog and tangible. We feel naked leaving the house and real-
izing we forgot our smart phones. We no longer use awkward paper
maps while driving, but instead, we let various apps navigate our way
from one place to another (with driverless smartcars now also being
introduced). We love being connected, but also long for the silence and
space that can come with meditating upon a biblical passage without
interruption.

One of the things to which we have grown quite accustomed is the
practice of "googling" just about everything. We can find answers to
virtually any question we have in a matter of seconds thanks to the
internet and various search engines. The published works that I have
referred to in this book have been published in various forms: sometimes only in print, sometimes only in electronic form, and often in
both. One of the downsides of referring readers to web links is that
sometimes web links stop working for a variety of reasons. Fortunately,
web sites can be archived for permanent reference, even if the site
disappears from current use. All of the web links referred to in this
book, both in the text and in the bibliography, have been archived
to https://archive.org/web/ using the "Way Back Machine" internet
Archive. All of the links were active and working when I submitted the
copyedited manuscript in May of 2017. Further, web links can get out
of hand in terms of length. I have at times opted to use the wonderful
program, https://tinyurl.com, which shortens much longer URLs into
more manageable URLs that will redirect readers/users to the site of
the much longer version. A DOI (Digital Object Identifier) is provided
when available.

There are a number of individuals I would like to thank without
whom the writing of this book would not have been possible. At Loyola
Marymount University, my colleagues in the Department of Theological Studies and beyond have been good conversation partners, as usual.
The library staff at LMU has especially gone above and beyond the call
of duty. Melanie Hubbard, the Digital Humanities librarian, has provided valuable help regarding all things digital humanities. She was
also a key facilitator for the summer 2015 Digital Humanities Faculty
Learning Community in which I participated. My colleagues in this FLC
provided stimulating conversation and insights, which I found quite
fruitful. My thanks to each of them: Professors Elizabeth Drummond
and Carla Bittel (History Department), and Dermot Ryan and Stephen
Shepherd (English Department). I also want to thank Dr. Bill Shaules

(who both teaches NT at LMU and works in Diaconate formation for the Archdiocese of Los Angeles) for his insights.

My thanks, further, to Prof. Claudia Setzer, of Manhattan College, a friend and colleague in the field of early Christianity/Judaism and in the history of biblical interpretation. She kindly invited me to give presentations at the Columbia NT Seminar and at Manhattan College in the Fall of 2015. Both of these presentations formed significant parts of the chapters below. Her comments and questions have been most helpful. Professor Michal Beth Dinkler, of Yale Divinity School, also read and commented on various sections of the book, for which I am grateful. My thanks to Ray Waddle, the editor of *Reflections* (a journal of the Yale Divinity School), who kindly gave permission to use part of an essay published there.[5] I am indebted to Prof. Tim Hutchings, of Stockholm University, one of the leading scholars in the field of all things digital religion and digital Bible. He has been a generous conversation partner. Many thanks to John Dyer, Executive Director of Communications and Educational Technology at Dallas Theological Seminary, who provided very helpful comments on the whole book manuscript, and shared some of his unpublished survey work, which was extremely useful. I thank two other conversation partners on this and many other topics over the years, Prof. Mark George and Prof. Pam Eisenbaum, both biblical scholars at Iliff School of Theology in Denver.

My deep thanks to Prof. Robert Kraft, Berg Professor of Religious Studies Emeritus at the University of Pennsylvania. Throughout his long career, Prof. Kraft has been at the forefront of using computers for the study of religious texts from late antiquity. I am honored that he was willing to correspond about his work and memories of developments in the academic use of computers for textual analysis. His comments on chapter 3, the brief history of digital Bibles, were most helpful.

I am especially indebted to Dr. Neil Elliott, the senior editor at Fortress Press with whom I worked on this project. Neil and I first met over 30 years ago in the New Testament PhD program at Princeton Theological Seminary. It has been a joy to be his friend and conversation partner over the years.

I owe a debt of gratitude also to an even older friend, Pat Pickard (nee Stewart!), who has remained a friend since our high school days in Pittsburgh. Pat is a gifted graphic designer, who has articulated a won-

---

5. "Digital Turns and Liquid Scriptures," (Fall 2015), http://reflections.yale.edu/article/new-voyages-church-today-and-tomorrow/digital-turns-and-liquid-scriptures.

derful vision on her website's mission statement: "to rid the world of visual swill"! (See http://www.patpickard.com.) I am so very pleased that she agreed to do the cover design for this book, and I am thankful to Fortress Press for allowing it to grace my work.

My wife, Judy Yates Siker (or RDMJ, as one close friend calls her—the Reverend Doctor Miss Judy) has remained my primary conversation partner on all things pastoral, academic, and personal. Her own long teaching experience as a fellow Bible-geek in both church and university settings has led to invaluable discussions and insights about biblical interpretation, which in turn, has contributed in important ways to this current project on digital Bibles. Her grace and love have been my most precious companions.

Finally, I dedicate this book to Derek, Ursula, Jason (& Prescott), and Jonathan (& Meredith), once children and now adults—each of them amazing in their own ways. They are digital natives all, yet through language (Chinese) and business acumen, baking and analog tattoos, piloting (NetJets) and Ironmanning, the law (from Supreme Court to Latham & Watkins) and the NICU, each manages to integrate quite fully the most human passions. They are all a great source of joy, inspiration, and pride.

1

Introduction: A Transition of Biblical Proportions

It is somewhat of an understatement to observe that developments in computer technology over the last thirty to forty years have been revolutionary. From clunky and bulky first-generation personal computers in the 1980s to the thin-case, touchscreen laptop computers, portable tablets, and smartphones of today, the revolution in both software and hardware development seems to have no end. Digital technology grows more and more powerful with each successive iteration, whether in terms of speed, memory, miniaturization, mobility, integrated multimedia and interactive capacity, data mining, apps upon apps, or even the shift from Web 1.0 to Web 2.0, 3.0, and beyond. Every sphere of digital technology continues to develop at what appears to be warp speed, so that it has become more than just a little difficult to keep up with it all.

These dramatic technological changes have affected virtually and literally every aspect of our daily lives. We feel naked without our smartphones to the ready. We utilize digital devices to do everything from paying our bills to driving our cars to online shopping to tracking down information online to interactive communication and social media of all sorts (messaging, e-mailing, tweeting, facebooking, instagramming, et al.). To say that these devices and technologies have become "ubiquitous" hardly does justice to the word, for it is not just a spatial "everywhere"; it is also a temporal "every moment." As Naomi Baron has noted, through our myriad digital devices, we are "Always On."[1]

The computer age in which we live has also had a dramatic impact on the technology of the Bible. While 2,000 years ago, there was an important technological shift from the scroll to the codex, and some 500 years ago, Gutenberg revolutionized the codex and the book with the invention of the printing press and movable type, the change in technology currently taking place with the emergence of a digital world is having dramatic repercussions that we are just beginning to fathom. And just as the sacred scriptures were the primary focus of scribal activity in the production of Christian biblical codices,[2] and again, the main focus of Gutenberg's printing press,[3] so now, in the digital age, the Bible has been the object of large-scale digital production and transmission.[4]

Print Bibles remain the best-selling physical books year in and year out, but digital versions of the Bible have come to occupy an increasingly greater percentage of the market for Bibles not only in the United States, but worldwide as well. From small Bible study groups, to following the Bible readings in church services, to adopting any of numerous online reading plans for the Bible, it is more and more common to see individuals pull out their smartphones or tablets to read their Bibles, rather than the more traditional old leather-bound print Bibles that have been a mainstay for decades.

The shift to digital Bibles is but one component of an increasingly digital church.[5] Digital media and all that it brings is having a direct

1. Naomi Baron, *Always On: Language in an Online and Mobile World* (New York: Oxford University Press, 2008).

2. See, e.g., Eric G. Turner, *Typology of the Early Codex* (Philadelphia: University of Pennsylvania Press, 1977); Colin H. Roberts and T. C. Skeat, *The Birth of the Codex* (London: Oxford University Press, 1987); Harry Y. Gamble, *Books and Readers in the Early Church: A History of Early Christian Texts* (New Haven: Yale University Press, 1995); and Larry W. Hurtado, "The Early Christian Preference for the Codex," *The Earliest Christian Artifacts: Manuscripts and Christian Origins* (Grand Rapids: Eerdmans, 2006) 43–93.

3. See R. Abel, *The Gutenberg Revolution: A History of Print Culture* (New Brunswick: Transaction, 2011); John Man, *The Gutenberg Revolution: How Printing Changed the Course of History* (London: Bantam Books, 2002); James Thorpe, *The Gutenberg Bible: Landmark in Learning* (Huntington Library Press, 1997); and Stephan Füssel, *Gutenberg and the Impact of Printing* (Burlington, VT: Ashgate, 2005).

4. As but one example, the digital Bible available for free from the app YouVersion has been downloaded on smartphones and other devices over 250 million times worldwide. A Google search for "digital Bible" yields over 50 million hits.

5. See, e.g., M. Brooks, *The Digital Church: How to Use the New Tools of Technological and Communication Revolution for Your Church* (Amazon Digital Services 2013); Jason Caston, *The iChurch Method* (Caston Digital Publishing, 2012); J. Wise, *The Social Church: A Theology of Digital Communication* (Moody Pub-

impact on the life of churches and on the life of faith. Denominations communicate through their official (and unofficial) web pages. Church members blog about every imaginable aspect of church life. Congregations now regularly get the monthly church newsletter as an e-mail attachment. In liturgical contexts, it is increasingly common not to have a weekly paper bulletin with the order for worship; rather, the liturgy appears in scrolling splendor on large flat screens. The words to hymns and the scripture readings for the day also appear in pixelated form, with a computer operator sitting in the choir loft, rather than the more traditional sound person. The development of the internet, smartphones, and multimedia high-speed communication networks of all kinds has resulted in a world that is ever more connected and intertwined. Church communities have developed in virtual space, in online churches, and countless online forums for faith groups.[6] Though the future of such virtual communities is uncertain, they have clearly provided many individuals with a faith connection that has been important and meaningful. And digital Bibles have become an important component of this digital shift.

We might even speak of changes in technology and theology as being "of Biblical Proportions," to use an expression that denotes wide-scale changes in how we live, think, and act—in this case, as a result of technological developments. The pervasive and evolving shift from print Bibles to digital Bibles has taken place on screens of all kinds.[7] As a professor of biblical studies for over 30 years, teaching in a university setting and also teaching actively in various local church settings, I have generally welcomed and benefited from the digital revolution. Over the last several years, however, I have begun to wonder about the significance of the shifting tide away from print Bibles and toward digital Bibles on screens (smartphones, tablets, laptops). This change has been true of both students in my classes and in church groups where I

---

lishers, 2014); and Danielle Zaupan-Jerome, *Connected Toward Communion: The Church and Social Communication in the Digital Age* (Collegeville, MN: Liturgical, 2014).

6. Church blogs attract millions of individuals on a regular basis. For the 300 most popular church blogs, see the "ChurchRelevance" website sponsored by "Ecclesia360," a church website developer that provides content management for thousands of churches, at http://churchrelevance.com/resources/top-church-blogs/.

7. Such shifts were already anticipated with the use of computer technology, for example, in the publication of a scholarly tool way back in 1980 of the *Computer Konkordanz zum Novum Testamentum Graece* (Berlin: Walter de Gruyter, 1980), an imposing physical book that allowed scholars to use a computer-generated concordance of the Greek New Testament (based on the Nestle-Aland 26th edition of the Greek NT). It was, of course, soon displaced by computer programs that could and did do the concordance work of finding words and sequences much more quickly and in a more sophisticated manner than using a physical book.

teach. As we will see, the shift to digital Bibles is truly taking place on a large scale, with Bible publishers and software/web developers trying to keep up with the growing demand, anticipating the next innovation.

It is one thing to notice this transition; it is another to comprehend its significance and to evaluate the pros and cons of this development at the crossroads of religion and technology. Is this change benign? Are there significant new insights that might result from the use of millions of digital Bibles? Are there significant problems of which we are simply unaware that will emerge as this transition to digital religious media continues? In short, to what degree is the transition to digital Bibles (and an increasingly digital church) a blessing, a curse, or both? These are the kinds of questions we will explore in this book.

In the pages that follow (whether you are reading them on paper or screen, I do not know!), I will, on the one hand, be describing the contours of the shift from print Bibles to digital Bibles, while on the other hand, I will also be arguing that this transition in technology is a mixed blessing when it comes to how we read and understand the Bible. After this introduction, chapter 2 presents "Trajectories in Biblical Technology," an exploration of how developments in the production and material form of the Bible have affected its interpretation—from scroll to codex to printing. Chapter 3 looks at "A Brief History of Digital Bibles." Here, we will see that digital Bibles have developed along two basic tracks, one oriented primarily to the academic community and one oriented primarily to the church community. There is, as we shall see, significant overlap as well. Chapter 4, "This is Your Brain on Screens," recounts what we have learned to date about what happens in our brains when we read words on screens as opposed to words on printed pages. We will see that not all screens are created equal, and that, in general, we retain more information when we read words on physical pages of print rather than on virtual pages of pixels. What are the implications of this observation when it comes to reading the Bible? In short, I will argue that screens are fine for surface reading and skimming of texts, but they are not so good for the kind of depth reading (especially meditative reading) that is most encouraged when it comes to the Bible.

In chapter 5, "Survey Says!," we will look at emerging practices in regard to digital Bibles, as seen in a variety of surveys by the American Bible Society, among other studies. Along the way, we will consider what happens when we shift from print Bibles to Bibles "without covers," given their virtual form. Here, we will see how the Bible has morphed into many digital expressions. In part, this is merely an extension of the different kinds of print Bibles that have long been on the shelves, including what can best be called "boutique Bibles." But, as I will argue, there are significant implications for how we read and understand the Bible when the book loses its covers. In part, it results in a loss of knowing the geography, the shape, of the biblical text itself. This is where the notion of "liquid scripture" especially comes into play. When the Bible ceases to be a physical book, not only does it result in a loss of tangibility, it also results in a textual world that is now virtually (literally, virtually!) watered down, so that the contours of the text become diluted and murky.

In chapter 6, we will ask "Is There a Bible in this Church?" This is a play on the influential 1982 book by Stanley Fish, *Is There a Text in this Class?*[8] Beyond losing its covers, the Bible in the digital world has also lost something of its stability as a fixed text. This is another component of the "liquid" character of digital Bibles. To ask if there is a Bible in this church is to ask *which* Bible is in this church, or on this e-reader, or on the web, or on any given screen. The proliferation of different translations, different versions, of the Bible has resulted in something of a Babel of Bibles: NRSV? NIV? NAB? NASB? CEB? TEV? RSV? KJV? NKJV? HCSB? TLB? TNLB? ASV? ESV? And the list goes on. The most widely downloaded Bible app, YouVersion—with over 250,000,000 downloads—boasts over a thousand different versions in over 700 languages. As I will argue, this glut of translation choices, in English alone, has both positive and negative consequences when it comes to the realm of digital Bibles. On the positive side, never have readers been able to be more aware of the importance of translation when it comes to the Bible. It is now rather simple to compare different translations onscreen. The role of translation as the first step of interpretation is more apparent than ever. But on the negative side, the ready availability of so many translations in digital form results in a certain destabilizing of the biblical text. While the Hebrew and Greek original language texts have remained remarkably stable for several generations, the ongoing process of translation, revision, translation, and revision has resulted in such an array of available translations as to be confusing. No longer is there anything "standard" about the Revised

---

8. *Is There a Text in This Class? The Authority of Interpretive Communities* (Cambridge: Harvard University Press, 1982). This book has been extremely influential in the development of Reader Response methods of interpreting texts of all kinds. It helped to shift analysis of Biblical texts away from authorial intent to the history of biblical interpretation and the reception history of the Bible.

Standard Version or the *New* Revised *Standard* Version, or "common" about the *Common* English Bible, or particularly "international" about the New *International* Version. Translation theory has remained relatively stable, but the incredible choices of translation or paraphrase, especially in digital form, raise a serious question about what kind of common Bible is, in fact, in use.[9] If the Bible is the common touchstone for all Christian denominations, it is important to consider the ways in which the easy access to many different digital versions shows the importance of translation, and yet at the same time, undermines what it means to have common scriptures.

In this chapter, we will also ask questions about the role of digital Bibles in the worship life of Christians, both on a corporate and individual level. How have digital Bibles affected the worship experience of congregations? Similarly, how has the explosion of digital Bibles affected devotional reading? "Life.Church," the developers and distributors of YouVersion, claims that having the Bible available on smartphones, for example, leads to greater discipleship. As they state in their promotional screens, "When the Bible is always with you, it becomes a part of your daily life." (www.life.church) What are the practices of various congregations when it comes to the world of digital Bibles? What are pastoral leaders saying and doing in relation to these new forms of Bibles? How do they fit into the larger increasingly digital world of churches? Here, we will find quite a mixed bag of results. While some churches (especially large evangelical Protestant churches with younger congregations) have jumped completely into the digital realm (with pastors saying "Please scroll with me to the following biblical text"!), other churches and denominations prefer the smell of dusty print Bibles, for better and for worse. Beyond taking a look at the function of digital Bibles in liturgical contexts, in this chapter, we will also examine audio Bibles, as well as the important niche world of electronic children's Bibles.

In chapter 7, we will explore "Digital Bibles and Social Media." Given the burgeoning and ubiquitous world of social media across every digital platform (computers, tablets, and especially smartphones), we will take a close look at the role of digital Bibles in four particularly prominent social media programs: Blogs, Twitter, YouTube, and Facebook. How have these social media interfaces affected ways in which we read

---

9. In this context, we will also explore a truly remarkable phenomenon, the "FrankenBible"! See Ted Olsen, "Hacking the Bible" (http://www.christianitytoday.com/ct/2014/march/bible-in-original-geek.html).

and discuss the Bible, for better and for worse? As I will argue, the use of the Bible on Twitter and Facebook typically results in relatively shallow understandings of the Bible, whereas there is far more room for deeper engagement with the Bible via both blogs and YouTube.

In chapter 8, we will take a close look at "The Bible and Computer Programs." There are some wonderful computer-based programs that provide significant tools for engaging in a deeper study of the Bible. Such programs as Logos, Accordance, BibleWorks, and Olive Tree Software, among others, all contain powerful tools for advanced Bible study. Want to do a word study? No problem. Want to compare different translations with the original Hebrew or Greek versions? A click away. Want to read commentaries and Bible dictionaries to gain a deeper understanding of a passage? Just purchase the additional module. Want to see maps and photos of biblical places? Want interactive texts? Want Bible-reading plans and other help? Want to add the writings of Josephus or the Dead Sea Scrolls? It's all there.

And yet, as I will argue, there are also dangers to watch out for in almost all of these Bible programs. Perhaps the most significant issue is that the producers of these various programs understandably want to give their users as much bang for the buck as possible. This has led almost all developers of computer-based Bible study programs to include such relatively dated tools as Matthew Henry's Bible Commentary from 1706. Why do they include it? Because it is in public domain. Why is it in public domain? Because it's *old*! Of course, the Bible is much older still. But most users clicking on such resources as Matthew Henry's commentary are unaware of its original context. They just know it is a resource they can click on. Older resources can certainly be incredibly useful, but users should be as aware as possible of the larger context of what they are reading, not only when it comes to the Bible itself, but also when it comes to resources that seek to explicate the biblical witness. Such larger contexts are not always apparent in the digital domain.

The irony with many digital Bible study helps is that they provide old and often outdated biblical scholarship in the cutting-edge technology of modern digital screens. Every semester, as I give my students instructions on using secondary sources in their exegetical papers, I have to go out of my way to discourage the use of such outdated resources. The students do not really know any better. All they know is that they found it "online!" Cool! No, not cool.

Finally, in chapter 9, we will consider "Biblical Pasts and Digital Futures." Here, we will bring together a more synthetic digest of the blessings and curses that accompany the increasing use of digital Bibles. I will argue for "best practices" and "worst practices" when it comes to the world of digital Bibles. Questions about biblical authority in the digital world and the stability of the biblical text will be among the more important issues here.

Along the way, we will also be considering the relationship between form and content as it relates to the biblical message and the medium of conveying that message. Given the historic authority that books have had, especially since Gutenberg invented moveable type for his printing press, might the very sacred and tangible bookishness of the Bible lend an even greater authority to its content than, say, the biblical narrative in oral form, or in stained glass window form? Does the very medium of the Bible as book become part of the message it communicates and authorizes? It is no accident that the authority of the Bible is paramount within the Protestant tradition (*sola scriptura*), where the Bible is physically present in every pew for the faithful to study and read. By contrast, the authority of the Bible in the Roman Catholic tradition is secondary to the authority of the teaching magisterium, which offers officially sanctioned interpretations of the Bible as part of the tradition, which the teaching authority of the church mediates to the faithful. As the Vatican II document *Dei Verbum* ("Dogmatic Constitution on Divine Revelation," 1965) stated clearly, the Bible means what the teaching authority of the church says it means.[10] No wonder, then, that in Roman Catholic churches, the Bible is not to be found in the pews, but is read aloud from the lectern. These different approaches to the Bible as book illustrate some of the facets involved in correlating the form and function of the Bible, the medium and the message, especially as it relates to the oral and written aspects of the Bible as the Church's Scripture.

As Marshall McLuhan and Walter Ong, S.J., demonstrated in such compelling fashion already a generation ago,[11] important connections exist between form and content, between the medium and the mes-

---

10. "The task of authentically interpreting the word of God, whether written or handed on, has been entrusted exclusively to the living teaching office of the Church" (*Dei Verbum* II.10).

11. Marshal McLuhan, *The Gutenberg Galaxy: The Making of Typographic Man* (Toronto: University of Toronto Press, 1962); *The Medium is the Massage* (New York: Random House, 1967); Walter Ong, *Interfaces of the Word: Studies in the Evolution of Consciousness and Culture* (Ithaca, NY: Cornell University Press, 1977); and especially *Orality and Literacy: The Technologizing of the Word* (London & New York: Methuen, 1982).

sage, between the technological production of words and the meaning of words in varied contexts. The study of the technology of producing the physical Bible has understandably taken a back seat to the study of the content and message of the biblical witness per se, including the growing field of "reception history," the history of biblical interpretation.[12] But just as the biblical narrative serves as a common touchstone for communities of faith, so has the Bible as a material object served in its tangible form as a sacred physical text, a text that has been venerated as the "Holy Bible" in its capacity as a material object that points beyond itself to the Holy God whom the faithful worship. In this respect, the physicality of the Bible as book has functioned as a kind of talisman connecting us to and invoking the divine, whether in the context of a worship service where the "Word of God" processes in liturgical dignity, or in the context of a swearing-in ceremony of a U.S. president who places her/his right hand upon the Bible to take the oath of office. In this way, divine authority and presence is invoked, even divine blessing, as the Bible functions to help sacralize whatever the context is where it is present, from courtroom, to church, to inaugurals, and beyond.[13]

And here we begin to see the blurring of lines between the *content* of the Bible and the physical *form* of the Bible. It is the placing of covers, boundaries, on this sacred book that helps to authorize its contents as the Word of God beyond all other words about God. Even though its contents range far and wide, both in terms of historical context and theological vision, when the words "The Bible" are embossed in gilded lettering on its leather cover and spine, it becomes not just a unified book, but *the Book* of all books. It is no wonder that the Bible continues to be the best-selling book of all time, year after year, version after version, translation after translation.[14]

---

12. See, e.g., Henning Graf Reventlow, *History of Biblical Interpretation*, 4 vols (Leiden: Brill, 2010); James Carleton Paget, et al., eds., *The New Cambridge History of the Bible*, 4 vols (Cambridge: Cambridge University Press, 2013–2015); and especially, the online *EBR, Encyclopedia of the Bible and Its Reception*, ed., Hans-Josef Klauck, et al. (Berlin: Walter de Gruyter, 2009–present), an ongoing comprehensive reference work that grows by some 1,400 newly written articles per year. As of May 2017, fourteen of the projected thirty volumes have been published (http://www.degruyter.com/page/biblical-reception). With each volume weighing in at around 600 pages, the goal for this ambitious project is to publish about 18,000 pages on the history of biblical interpretation.
13. Various presidents have used the symbolism of the Bible quite effectively in such inaugural proceedings. For example, Barack Obama placed his hand on the same Bible used by Abraham Lincoln; and George H. W. Bush placed his hand on what is known as the Washington Bible, used in the inauguration of the first US president. See J. S. Siker, "President Obama, the Bible, and Political Rhetoric," *Political Theology* 13, no.5 (2012): 586–609.
14. See Daniel Radosh, "The Good Book Business," *The New Yorker* (December 18, 2006); http://www.

We forget that the very name "the Bible" derives from the Greek *to biblion,* which means "book"![15] The Bible has existed as a physical bound book, albeit a big book, for well over 1,500 years. But what happens when the Bible loses its covers? What happens when the Bible is simply one additional app on one's smartphone or tablet? What does it mean when the Bible is but one option among hundreds of other books on a Kindle or Nook reader? Does the Bible in digital garb become a more domesticated book than its bound cousin?

Still further questions arise as we ponder what we mean by so presumably clear a word as "text." Given a broad definition of "text," what difference is there between oral/aural "text" and written text, or between medieval stained glass window "text" and other representations of the biblical text in the visual arts? Or in our current digital culture, what might it mean to read the Bible in traditional print text form or as TXT on any number of digital screen devices, or in multimedia form? How does cognition morph and adapt to different articulations of the Bible in such different forms? Or is it all fundamentally the same, regardless of differences?

My goal in this book, then, is to examine how we access, read, and interpret the Bible in an increasingly digital culture. What difference does the shift from print Bibles to digital Bibles of all kinds make for how communities and individuals of faith understand the Bible and its message/s? What difference does it make to read and study the Bible on various screens instead of in physical print form? The ongoing shift from print to digital culture over the last generation provides the fundamental context for this book. The "digital turn," as it has been called,[16] certainly does not mean the end of print, though many agree with Jay David Bolter's assessment that we have entered "the late age of print."[17] While a number of studies have examined some significant differences in how our brains read and comprehend screen pages ver-

---

newyorker.com/magazine/2006/12/18/the-good-book-business. Sales of Bibles are estimated to be between 20–25 million copies each year.

15. The earliest reference to the "Bible" as scripture comes from 2 Clement 14:2, a second-century CE early Christian writing. There the term occurs in the plural, *ta biblia.* See Frederick W. Danker, Walter Bauer, William F. Arndt, and F. Wilbur Gingrich, *Greek-English Lexicon of the New Testament and Other Early Christian Literature,* 3rd ed. (Chicago: University of Chicago Press, 2000), 176, "biblion."

16. See, e.g., Pille Runnel, Pille Pruulmann-Vengerfeldt, Piret Viires, & Marin Laak, eds., *The Digital Turn: User's Practices and Cultural Transformations* (Frankfurt am Main: Peter Lang, 2013); Wim Wester, *The Digital Turn: How the Internet Transforms Our Existence* (Bloomington, IN: AuthorHouse, 2013).

17. Jay David Bolter, *Writing Space: Computers, Hypertext, and the Remediation of Print,* 2nd ed. (Mahwah, NJ and London: Lawrence Erlbaum Associates, 2001) 1–3.

sus print pages,[18] to date, no full-length work has taken a thorough look at how this shift to digital text on screens impacts our reading and understanding of the Bible. Such is my task in the present volume.

18. See especially Naomi Baron, *Words Onscreen: The Fate of Reading in a Digital World* (New York: Oxford University Press, 2015); Maryanne Wolf, *Proust and the Squid: The Story and Science of the Reading Brain* (San Francisco: Harper, 2008); Stanislas Dehaene, *Reading in the Brain: The New Science of How We Read* (London: Penguin, 2010); and Nicholas Carr, *The Shallows: What the Internet is Doing to Our Brains* (New York: W. W. Norton, 2011).

2

Trajectories in Bible Technology

Before we turn our focus to a full discussion of the shift from print to digital technology in publishing and reading the Bible, it will be instructive to pay some attention to earlier technological changes in the production and reading of the biblical text/s from the dawn of ancient writing to the beginnings of the digital world that began to unfold in the late twentieth century. We will see that the form and function of the biblical text go hand in hand, from one technology to the next. The physical forms of texts have had significant implications for how they have been used. Can we trace a trajectory in the correlation of textual form and textual interpretation? Are there discernible patterns in how the technology of text production affects the reading and interpretation of a text? In general, I will argue, the axiom holds that the more sophisticated the technology of text production, the more dependent we have become upon the written text, in whatever form, and the less we have relied on our own memories of the words and stories contained in the text. In short, we have increasingly become experts at exporting our memories onto an external storage medium, from cuneiform tablet, to scroll, to codex, to printed book, and most recently in human history, to hard drives and other digital data storage devices with screens. Part of the goal of this chapter is to explore some of the consequences of downloading our memory, for better and for worse.

Socrates, Writing, and Memory

Debate about exporting our memories goes back at least as far as Socrates in Athens toward the end of the fifth century BCE. According to Plato's dialogue *The Phaedrus* (usually dated around 370 BCE), Socrates fought the advent of the written word, worried that we would no longer truly *know* the words we treasured; instead, we would only know where to *find* the words we treasured in a written text. In this way, our memory of the *actual* words became secondary to our memory *that* the words were contained somewhere, should we not remember them and want to find them. Direct memory became indirect memory. Direct knowledge became indirect knowledge. The risk, as Socrates saw it, was that genuine knowledge would degenerate into mere information. In *The Phaedrus,* Plato has Socrates decrying the invention of writing, which Socrates does by relating the legend of King Thamus and the god Theuth, in which Theuth had invented writing and offered it to Thamus as a tool to help humanity. Theuth told King Thamus that writing would be an aid to memory. But the King thought otherwise. Taking on the voice of King Thamus responding to Theuth, Socrates declares: If people learn writing,

> it will implant forgetfulness in their souls; they will cease to exercise memory because they rely on that which is written, calling things to remembrance no longer from within themselves, but by means of external marks. What you have discovered is a recipe not for memory, but for reminder. And it is no true wisdom that you offer your disciples, but only its semblance, for by telling them of many things without teaching them you will make them seem to know much, while for the most part they know nothing, and as men filled, not with wisdom, but with the conceit of wisdom, they will be a burden to their fellows. (*Phaedrus* 274c–275b)[1]

Socrates's concern with *writing* remains a concern for teachers today in relation to *reading*, namely, that students will engage in passive rather than active reading—passive knowledge, passive learning, rather than having the active ability to generate what they have learned "from within themselves." They remember *that* they have read or learned something, but not exactly *what* they have read or learned. Or as one colleague has aptly put it, too often students (and this includes all of us!) do not so much *drink* from the wellspring of knowledge as they *gar-*

---

1. *The Collected Dialogues of Plato,* ed., Edith Hamilton & Huntington Cairns (Princeton: Princeton University Press, 1973) 520–21.

gle from it! By way of example, I remember when I was an undergraduate at Indiana University (in Bloomington, IN, where many moons ago I double-majored in music and religious studies) that I was taking a course in church history with Professor J. Samuel Preus. In one exam, there was a short-answer question asking, "Who was Ignatius of Loyola?" Given that I have now taught at a Jesuit University for 30 years (Loyola Marymount University, in Los Angeles), it seems especially ironic that my answer then was something like: "Hmmm. I remember *that* I read about him, but I don't remember *what* I read. But I do know there's a University named after him in Chicago!" I received half credit for the answer, which showed the graciousness and good humor of Prof. Preus. Socrates's worry was not unfounded. If we think we know where we can find information that will lead to knowledge, we are less concerned about making such knowledge our own by memorizing it. We seem content enough to know how to *remind* ourselves of something, rather than actually to *know* something. This applies to our knowledge of the Bible as well. Many people have a vague *sense* of what the Bible says about this or that, rather than any genuine *knowledge* of what the Bible says. Hence the oft-repeated phrase: "It's in the Bible somewhere."

While the warning of Socrates had and has merit, especially given how we would all like to have the capacity to remember far more than we do, we cannot, for the life of us, imagine trying to navigate the world without writing, without pen and paper to write down a grocery list, without the ability to write out, and so, save our thoughts, and then, to revise and refine them. We cannot imagine having actually to remember the many phone numbers or mailing addresses (or more likely e-mail addresses) that our smartphones remember for us. No, without consulting so many written records, we do not remember very well. We rely on that which is written to remind us. When it comes to the Bible, we read and reread, listen and listen again, hoping that these words will continue to sink deeper and deeper into our hearts and minds so that as we recall them, we might also be informed and formed by them, both as individuals and as communities of faith.

Our reliance on all things written is not as bad as Socrates feared by a long shot. The capacity to offload our memory allows us to access many more things, at least if we can remember where they are! This offloading/downloading of memory can create more space for us to access more things on the hard drive of our brains. But it can also fool us into thinking that we actually know more than we really do. Knowing *where* to find something is not really the same as knowing the thing itself. Knowing where I can find the poem *The Jabberwocky* is not the same as knowing it by heart, nor does it inspire the same joy to read it as to recite it from memory. Similarly with Lincoln's Gettysburg Address. Similarly with the opening of the U.S. Constitution or the Declaration of Independence. So also with the Bible and anything else that would compete for space in our brains.

We marvel at those who have memorized large sections of the Bible and can recite them at will. By memorizing these texts, they have made the words their own, ready to be recalled and digested anew, to be performed for the edification of others. This is true of the Bible or any lengthy written text. In this regard, I am reminded of a book I first read in High School, Ray Bradbury's classic dystopian novel *Fahrenheit 451* (the temperature at which paper burns). Bradbury describes a world in which the job of firemen is to *burn* books so as to consolidate and control information in the hands of but a few leaders. Reading is not fundamental in the world Bradbury conjures; rather, it is a dangerous entrée to knowledge, and such knowledge can challenge the powers that be. The job of "firemen" in this world is to burn books, not to put fires out. Thus, the most revolutionary act is to read, and toward the end of the novel, the hope of a liberated humanity rests with a group of rebels living on the outskirts of society who have, in fact, *become* the living embodiment of books. They are books personified, as each individual has taken on the task of memorizing a classic text. In the following scene, the protagonist, Montag (who had been a fireman) seeks to join this collective of book-people.

"You want to join us, Montag?"

"Yes."

"What have you to offer?"

"Nothing. I thought I had part of the Book of Ecclesiastes and maybe a little of Revelation, but I haven't even that now."

"The Book of Ecclesiastes would be fine. Where was it?"

"Here." Montag touched his head.

"Ah." Granger smiled and nodded.

"What's wrong? Isn't that all right?" said Montag.

"Better than all right: perfect!" Granger turned to the Reverend. "Do we have a Book of Ecclesiastes?"

"One. A man named Harris in Youngstown."

"Montag." Granger took Montag's shoulder firmly. "Walk carefully. Guard your health. If anything should happen to Harris, you are the Book of Ecclesiastes. See how important you've become in the last minute!"

"But I've forgotten!"

"No, nothing's ever lost. We have ways to shake down your clinkers for you."

"But I've tried to remember!"

"Don't try. It'll come when we need it. All of us have photographic memories, but spend a lifetime learning how to block off the things that are really in there. Simmons here has worked on it for twenty years and now we've got the method down to where we can recall anything that's been read once. Would you like, some day, Montag, to read Plato's Republic?"

"Of course!"

"I am Plato's Republic. Like to read Marcus Aurelius? Mr. Simmons is Marcus. Here we all are, Montag. Aristophanes and Mahatma Gandhi and Gautama Buddha and Confucius and Thomas Love Peacock and Thomas Jefferson and Mr. Lincoln, if you please. We are also Matthew, Mark, Luke, and John." Everyone laughed quietly.

"It can't be," said Montag.

"It is," replied Granger smiling.[2]

This scene literally depicts what Socrates so valued—calling up memory from within oneself. This scene reminds me in some ways of Ezekiel 3:1–3, where God tells the prophet Ezekiel:

"Son of man, eat what is before you; eat this scroll, then go, speak to the house of Israel.' So I opened my mouth and he gave me the scroll to eat. 'Son of man,' he then said to me, 'feed your belly and fill your stomach with this scroll I am giving you.' I ate it, and it was as sweet as honey in my mouth. He said: 'Son of man, go now to the house of Israel, and speak my words to them.'"

Ezekiel eats and literally (or more likely, metaphorically) digests the written words of God so that he might speak God's word to the people of Israel from within himself. He has made the words of God his own. I am also reminded of what the apostle Paul says in Galatians 2:19–20, "I have been crucified with Christ; and it is no longer I who live, but it is Christ who lives in me." The notion that the Spirit of God, the Spirit of Christ, the Word of God, lives inside and animates Paul (at least as he sees it) says a great deal about the fluidity between the external and the internal. Just as Ezekiel eats and digests the words of God written on the scroll, so also Paul is nourished by the indwelling of Christ's Spirit, which is then manifest in Paul's outward writing to the churches he has established along the way. So also in the Gospel of John (14:26),

2. Ray Bradbury, *Fahrenheit 451: A Novel* (New York: Simon & Schuster, 1953) 148–50.

Jesus assures his disciples that "the Holy Spirit, whom the Father will send in my name, will teach you everything, and remind you of all that I have said to you." The Spirit will remind them (*hypomnēsei*) and bring to memory the words that Jesus had spoken. The living word of God animated by the Spirit of God teaches, inspires, comforts.

Many of us do, in fact, know people who have memorized large blocks of the Bible. There are even apps to help people memorize the Bible. My 7-year-old grandson Charlie has Bible memory verses for Sunday School, just as I did when I was a child. But in this age of information overload, oceans and mountains of information, relentless e-mails and text messages, social media on steroids, we are quite literally overwhelmed with information.[3] We are overwhelmed to such a degree that sorting the important from the ephemeral becomes increasingly difficult. As a result, we face ever-growing demands upon our brains, our memories, deciphering quantum sums of information to garner actual knowledge. I would aver that in today's world, Socrates would not be able to get by very well without a smartphone, tablet, and computer of his own! Socrates's challenging question remains, however, about the relationship between memory and reminder, between truly knowing and not quite knowing. The challenge of the present book is to explore how the shift from the Bible as physical book to the Bible as digital data impacts our understanding and appropriation of the Bible. But for now, let us return to a time even before Socrates, to the beginnings of writing technology and the Bible.

From Cuneiform to Scroll, and from Clay to Papyrus

The earliest writing system which contains stories parallel to the Bible is the widespread cuneiform script, coming from the Latin *cuneus* ("wedge") and *forma* ("shape"), referring to the reed stylus that was used to make angled wedges on small wet clay tablets that were later dried. Cuneiform was the script used by several ancient cultures (Sumerian, Assyrian, Akkadian, Babylonian) from around 2500 BCE down through the time of the Babylonian conquest of Judea (586 BCE) and beyond. Most of the over 150,000 cuneiform tablets that survive are business receipts and other administrative records written on

---

3. As of the summer of 2016, for example, Wikipedia (the free online encyclopedia) contained over 5 million articles in English alone, growing at a rate of 800 articles per day. If published in books the size of the Encyclopedia Britannica, it would require an astonishing 2,283 volumes, weighing in at well over 1 million pages. https://atkinsbookshelf.wordpress.com/tag/how-many-pages-would-it-take-to-print-wikipedia/.

small clay tablets. The writing system could accommodate larger narratives, such as the Enuma Elish creation narrative from the ancient Babylonians (a creation story often compared with the biblical account). But, to borrow a very modern parallel in technology, cuneiform tablets were the equivalent of business tweets with a limited amount of text, given the small surface space with which to work. There is no evidence that any of the Bible was written in cuneiform, though various biblical parallels appear in cuneiform texts.

Fig. 2.1. This cuneiform tablet in Irving Finkel's hand casts new light on the shape of the ark. Mesopotamia, ca. 2000 BCE; Musée de Mariemont, Morlanwelz, Belgium.

One of the most well-known is the story of the great flood and Noah's ark, with parallels found in the ancient Epic of Gilgamesh and most recently in the so-called ancient Babylonian "Ark Tablet" that is the subject of Irving Finkel's *The Ark Before Noah*.[4] Finkel, the curator of cuneiform at the British Museum, shows extensive parallels between

4. Irving Finkel, *The Ark Before Noah: Decoding the Story of the Flood* (New York: Anchor, 2015). See also Tikva Frymer-Kensky, "What the Babylonian Flood Stories Can and Cannot Teach Us About the Genesis Flood," *Biblical Archaeology Review* 4, no. 4 (Nov/Dec 1978), http://cojs.org/what-the-babylonian-flood-stories-can-and-cannot-teach-us-about-the-genesis-flood/; and William W. Hallo, The *Bible in the Light of Cuneiform Literature: Scripture in Context III* (Lewiston, NY: Edwin Mellen, 1990).

the Ark Tablet and the biblical account of Noah's ark, including a command from the Mesopotamian god Enki to the Noah-like character Atra-hasis to gather creatures "two by two" for the ark. This tablet, a bit larger than most, shows that somewhat longer narratives could be written. But very few individuals could read, let alone write, such tablets, so they were used mostly by court officials and other high-ranking individuals.

From Cuneiform Tablets to Hebrew and Greek Scrolls

The use of scrolls instead of clay tablets greatly increased the possibilities for writing more extended narratives, poetry, and other kinds of material that had previously been primarily transmitted in oral form from one generation to the next. This was the case, regardless of language—Hebrew, Greek, Latin. To be sure, oral transmission remained primary, as it continued to be the case that only society's elites learned to read or write. The technology of scrolls had been used in Egypt as the primary method for keeping records and writing important narratives since around 3000 BCE. The writing material for scrolls consisted primarily of papyrus, in Greek *papyros* (likely a transliteration from an earlier Egyptian word), from which our English word "paper" derives. The harvesting and use of the papyrus plant to manufacture papyrus rolls made practical sense, given its widespread growth along the fertile Nile River.

The classic description of the manufacturing process and different qualities of papyrus can be found in Pliny the Elder's *Natural History* (xiii, 74–82) from the first century CE. The long stem of the papyrus plant was harvested, peeled, cut to a uniform size, soaked in water, then laid in overlapping parallel horizontal and vertical strips to the desired size, and then pressed together, as the juices of the plant provided a kind of watery glue. The papyrus sheet of "paper" was then dried in the sun, slightly sanded, and then, glued together with other papyrus sheets to the desired length of the roll. Pliny tells us that there was a relatively uniform size to the production of papyrus sheets, and that the typical scroll (or roll) consisted of 20 sheets glued together end to end, to form a roll about 13–15 feet in length, and anywhere from 5–10 inches in width. Just as, today, we open a new ream of paper (typically standardized as 500 sheets of 8 1/2" x 11" paper) for photocopying or use in our printers, so in antiquity, papyrus factories produced readymade rolls of 20 sheets, from which one would cut whatever length was necessary for writing a letter, a business record, or a longer literary work.[5] And just as, today, paper comes in different qualities, so in antiquity, could one purchase different qualities of papyrus. Significantly, scrolls were only written on one side, with the writing on the inside of the scroll to protect it from damage.

Fig. 2.2. Papyrus plant; Kew Gardens, London.

5. See Naphtali Lewis, *Papyrus in Classical Antiquity* (Oxford: Oxford University Press, 1974); Harry Gamble, *Books and Readers in the Early Church: A History of Early Christian Texts* (New Haven: Yale University Press, 1995); and Roger Bagnall, ed., *The Oxford Handbook of Papyrology* (Oxford: Oxford University Press, 2011). See "Papyrus Making 101: at http://www.lib.umich.edu/papyrus_making/lg_strips.html. See also the Duke Papyrus Archive.

Fig. 2.3. A muse reads a papyrus scroll. Attic red-kythos from Boetia, ca. 435-25 BCE. Collection of Samuel Jean de Pozzi, 1919; The Louvre.

Fig. 2.4. Torah scrolls written on animal skin; from a private collection.

Scrolls were not limited to papyrus, even though papyrus was by far the most ubiquitous writing material. Parchment scrolls were also well known. Parchment refers to animal skins, usually sheep or goat, which went through a more complicated process of manufacturing than papyrus. Parchment "paper" was then also cut into sheets and used as a writing surface, initially in scroll form. (The use of lamb or kid skin was called vellum, and was particularly valuable writing material.) Although papyrus rolls were used for the vast majority of writing in the Greco-Roman era (c. 300 BCE–300 CE), parchment rolls were preferred in Jewish circles. For example, of the nearly 1,000 texts that have been found at Qumran (the Dead Sea Scrolls) about 90 percent were written on animal skins (both leather and parchment, which went through different treatments), and only about 10 percent were written on papyrus. The Talmud also stipulates that Torah scrolls should be written on parchment made from the skin of a kosher animal (Tractate Bava Batra 14b and Gittin 54b). There was an eventual shift from using papyrus rolls to parchment rolls. Regardless of whether the rolls were papyrus or parchment, the roll form allowed for continuous reading in an easy format, unrolling one column of text after another. Papyrus and parchment rolls were both portable and very adaptable to whatever size scroll was needed. Scrolls typically contained one work. Most were relatively short, though they could be fairly lengthy as well. The great Isaiah scroll that was discovered at Qumran (1QIsa), for example, is a large work consisting of 17 sheets of parchment, about 24 feet in length and nearly a foot wide, with 54 columns of text. (Would this have been comparable to the Isaiah scroll from which Jesus read according to Luke 4?)

In terms of how the scroll form of scripture affected its interpretation, it is significant that each scroll contained a separate "book." This physical separation of different books of the scriptures into different scrolls is reflected in the very terminology that the authors of the New Testament use to refer to the "scriptures" in the plural rather than with a collective singular, and the terminology "the books," in Greek τὰ βίβλια, that gives us the term *Bible*.[6] Although the "scriptures" clearly

---

6. The collective term for "scriptures" was the plural *hai graphai*, which is used in Matt 21:42; 22:29; 26:54, 56; Mark 12:24; 14:49; Luke 24:27, 32, 45; Acts 17:2, 11; 18:24, 28; Rom 1:2; 15:4; 16:26; and 1 Cor 15:3. The singular term "scripture" (*hē graphē*) was also used, but almost exclusively in reference to a particular scriptural text that was being cited. See Mark 12:10; Luke 4:21; John 2:22; 5:39; 7:38, 42; 10:35; 13:18; 17:12; 19:24, 28, 36; 20:9; Acts 1:16; 8:32, 35; Rom 4:3; 9:17; 10:11; 11:2; Gal 3:8, 22; 4:30; 1 Tim 5:18; and 2 Tim 3:16 (where we do find use of a collective singular – *pasē graphē* to refer to scripture as a whole).

referred to an authoritative collection of writings, the collective under-standing of "scripture" took place not in any physical scroll, which would have been completely unmanageable, but in the mind of the reader or hearer who studied or listened to the "scriptures." A virtual and metaphorical megascroll of scripture could be assembled in one's mind, but not in a physical form. As a result, it was difficult to engage in any real cross-referencing between different "books" of scrolls since the very process of rolling and unrolling scrolls did not lend itself to random access of texts. That would have to wait for the codex form. It was thus not very easy to find a place in a scroll quickly in the same way that we can place a marker in a book, and then turn quickly to another page. The "binding" of scrolls together only took place in the sense that they were housed together in the same location (as in the "Torah ark" or *Aron Kodesh* of most modern synagogues). The notion of a singular "book" of scripture was conceptual at best.

Further, scrolls of scripture functioned primarily within communal contexts, most often in liturgical settings where the reading of scrip-ture out loud to a gathered congregation was the norm. Experts in the interpretation of the scriptures, the proverbial "scribes and Pharisees" referred to in the New Testament, would discuss and debate the mean-ing and application of the scriptures. Significantly, a host of binding oral laws and interpretations of the scriptures had developed along-side the written texts. These "traditions of the fathers" (see, e.g., the *Pirke Avoth,* and Gal 1:14) provided frameworks for the interpretation and application of the scriptures; they were eventually written down as the *Mishnah* around the year 200 CE.[7]

From Scroll to Codex

In the process of tracing the changing technologies of producing the biblical text/s, perhaps the most important shift we will encounter before our current digital turn is the shift from scroll to codex.[8] The codex form is, in essence, the same as what we think of as a bound book. In antiquity, this would commonly mean pages made from

7. On the Mishnah, see Barry Holtz, ed., *Back to the Sources: Reading the Classic Jewish Texts* (New York: Simon & Schuster, 1992). While the scriptural writings were always reproduced in scroll form, the oldest manuscripts of the Mishnah survive in codex form. See Michael Krupp, "Manuscripts of the Mishna. The Three Complete Mishna Manuscripts," in *The Literature of the Sages I.* Editor: Shmuel Safrai (Philadelphia: Fortress Press, 1987); 253–54.

8. See C. H. Roberts & T. C. Skeat, *The Birth of the Codex* (London: Oxford University Press, 1983); H. Gamble, *Books and Readers in the Early Church,* 49–66; and W. V. Harris, *Ancient Literacy* (Cambridge: Harvard University Press, 1989) 294–96.

papyrus or parchment that were cut to a uniform size, folded in half, written on both sides of the page, and bound together—typically by stitching and/or gluing the closed edges of the folded sheets together. The term "codex" derives from the Latin *caudex*, which refers to a thin wood tablet that was most often lined with wax and hinged with a thin leather strap to a facing tablet similarly covered with a wax surface. One could write (or practice writing) in these wooden "booklets" with a stylus, and then, basically erase or smooth over the writing and reuse the wax surface. The early papyrus codex typically consisted of a few pages and functioned as a small notebook. Soon enough, additional pages would be added and the codex would prove to be ideal for longer literary works. The convenience and ease of use of the codex form proved very practical and relatively cost-effective when compared to the more traditional book roll. T. C. Skeat notes that writing the same amount of text in a codex in contrast to a roll would, on average, save slightly more than 25 percent of the cost of papyrus or parchment materials.[9] The cost savings resulted from the ability to write on both sides of sheets rather than on just one side of a roll.

The codex was also easier to use than the roll (or scroll), as it could be held in one hand. The codex was typically smaller in size than a book roll, so it was easier to carry around. In addition, one could fit more text into the pages of a codex than was possible on a book roll. The "convenience factor" was undoubtedly one reason why the codex eventually came to completely replace (or nearly so) the book scroll within a few hundred years. Part of the advantage to the codex was the ability to access different parts of a book, different pages, without having to scroll forward or backward; one could literally simply turn a page or cluster of pages and have random access to the whole book. This seems self-evident to us, of course; but the transition from scroll to book did require some getting used to.[10]

---

9. "The Length of the Standard Papyrus Roll and the Cost-Advantage of the Codex," *Zeitschrift für Papyrologie und Epigraphik* 45 (1982): 169–75.
10. See the humorous video of the medieval help desk showing a monk trying to figure out the technology of the newfangled book in contrast to the accustomed scroll: https://www.youtube.com/watch?v=pQHX–SjgQvQ. By the medieval era, the scroll was actually rarely used.

Fig. 2.5. Wood tablet covered with wax, used for writing in the Roman Empire (first century CE). Museo de Santa Cruz, Toledo, Spain.

As has often been noted, the earliest Christians uniformly adopted the codex for copying their scriptures, even at a time when the book roll was still far more common for non-Christian writings. All eleven of the second-century Christian scripture fragments that we know of come from codices. Exactly why Christians took to the codex so quickly is a matter of some debate, but Harry Gamble's argument that a collection of Paul's letters constituted the earliest Christian codices is persuasive. The author of 2 Peter 3:15–16 already refers to what appears to be a single collection of Paul's letters, calling them "scripture." The notion of Paul writing to seven churches (a complete number), and the pre-served order of the letters going from longest to shortest, both indicate an intentional "book," a single codex that contained all of Paul's letters as a unified whole.[11]

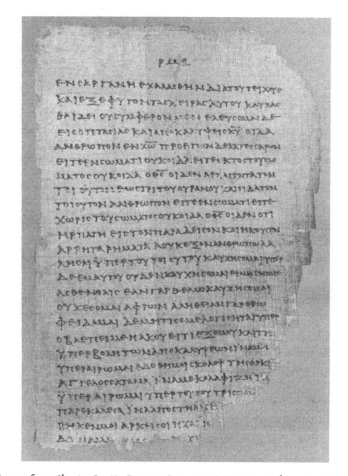

Fig. 2.6. A page from Chester Beatty Papyrus P46, containing 2 Corinthians 11:33-12:9. Ca. 200 CE.

The ability to read the Pauline corpus in a single bound volume no doubt led to grouping other similar Christian writings, for example, the Gospels, together in a single codex. And this is precisely what we have with the Chester Beatty Papyri, usually dated to around 200 CE. This group of papyri, all in codex form, were discovered in 1931[12] and consists of several codices from the Septuagint and the New Testament. The manuscript p45 is a single codex that contains all four canonical Gospels and the book of Acts, while the manuscript p46 is a sin-

---

11. See Gamble, *Books and Readers in the Early Church*, 58–66.
12. See F. G. Kenyon, *The Chester Beatty Biblical Papyri: Descriptions and Texts of Twelve Manuscripts on Papyrus of the Greek Bible* (London: Emery Walker Ltd., 1933–1937).

gle codex that contains the Pauline corpus. Thirty fragmentary pages remain of an original 110-page codex of the Gospels and Acts, while 85 pages remain of an original 104-page codex of Paul's letters.

The use of the codex had a significant impact on the interpretation of the Christian scriptures. Fundamentally, the authority of the writings of the New Testament shifted from individual books to the collection as a whole (τὰ βίβλια). Rather than separate disconnected writings having authority, it was now the singular and collective book that held authority. The writings were viewed as inspired, to be sure, but "the Book" was now a sacred book, the singular talisman of divine authority bound between two covers. The sacralizing of the Bible as a single book reached its early climax shortly after the Emperor Constantine issued the Edict of Milan in 313, making Christianity a legal religion, and soon thereafter, the preferred religion of the empire. The early church historian Eusebius reports in his *Life of Constantine* (iv.36) that the emperor sent him a letter asking him to arrange for fifty copies of the scriptures to be prepared, in light of the rapid expansion of Christian churches.[13]

> I have thought it expedient to instruct your Prudence to order fifty copies of the sacred Scriptures, the provision and use of which you know to be most needful for the instruction of the Church, to be written on prepared parchment in a legible manner, and in a convenient, portable form, by professional transcribers thoroughly practiced in their art.

The imperial imprimatur on the making of fifty high-quality copies of scripture as single books completes what amounts to the sanctification of the Bible as a singular bound volume, *the* singular book of scripture, between whose covers was the whole word of God.

The third and fourth centuries saw the continued spreading of Christian scriptures in codex form.[14] The concept of multiple booklets now contained in one larger book gave a sense of unity and authority to the collected works as a whole. The unity came simply by having multiple sacred texts bound together in one volume next to each other.

---

13. See D. L. Dungan, *Constantine's Bible: Politics and the Making of the New Testament* (Minneapolis: Fortress Press, 2007).

14. The two most important surviving manuscripts of the Christian Bible are Codex Sinaiticus and Codex Vaticanus, both from the fourth century. On Codex Sinaiticus, see D. C. Parker, *Codex Sinaiticus: The Story of the World's Oldest Bible* (Peabody, MA: Hendrickson, 2010). On Codex Vaticanus, see B. Metzger and B. Ehrman, *The Text of the New Testament: Its Transmission, Corruption, and Restoration*, 4th ed. (New York: Oxford University Press, 2005) 52–136. Both codices can now be viewed online: http://codexsinaiticus.org/en/ and http://digi.vatlib.it/view/MSS_Vat.gr.1209. See also W. H. Hatch, *The Principal Uncial Manuscripts of the New Testament* (Chicago: University of Chicago Press, 1939).

The Bible as book thus became holy and sacred as an object in which the whole is more than the sum of its parts. The sacred character of each writing in the Bible was enhanced by its association with each other writing. The sanctity of the whole further added a sense of the sacred to each individual writing. The codex facilitated the fixing of a particular set of writings as authoritative scripture. If one could point to a singular book as containing the whole of scripture, the practical advantages of only having to open one sacred book, albeit a large book, became obvious.

Fig. 2.7. A page from Codex Vaticanus, one of our earliest codex manuscripts, containing the end of 2 Thessalonians and the beginning of Hebrews. Fourth century.

The codex form thus hastened the closing of the biblical canon. There is a significant correlation, for example, between Codex Vaticanus and the well-known 39th Easter letter from Bishop Athanasius in the latter half of the fourth century. Athanasius's letter is justly famous, as it provides the first known list of canonical writings to match the New Testament canon that became standardized as 27 "books." As Athanasius wrote: "in these [27 writings] alone the teaching of godliness is proclaimed. No one may add to them, and nothing may be taken away from them."[15] The correlation of Athanasius's list with Codex Vaticanus is striking in that the relatively unusual order of the books of the New Testament is the same in both: Gospels, Acts, the Catholic Epistles (James, 1 and 2 Peter, 1, 2, and 3 John, and Jude), the Pauline Epistles (including Hebrews between 2 Thessalonians and 1 Timothy), and Revelation. As Christians were solidifying what belonged and what did not belong in the New Testament, the continued use of the codex spurred along the understanding of a singular book as containing a singular scripture.

The Jewish world continued to use the technology of the scroll for its sacred texts, and still does in the context of synagogue worship services. But the change from scroll to codex in the production of the sacred scriptures of Christianity brought a huge change in the very concept of scripture. Whereas the earliest Christians typically conceptualized "scripture" in plural terms (and a plural form—hai graphai, literally, the writings), Christian tradition developed a more unified understanding of scripture as a singular collection of writings, a single sacred book. The continued use of scrolls in Jewish worship settings may, in part, have been a response to distinguish Judaism from the nearly uniform Christian adoption of the codex.

From Handwritten Codex to Printed Book

The handwritten codex continued to be the norm for Christian scriptures for over a thousand years. Over time, the preferred writing material shifted from the papyrus codex to the even more durable parchment codex (using treated goat or sheep skin). The languages of the biblical codices expanded to include Latin, in the form of the Vulgate (which Jerome had translated from Hebrew and Greek in the late fourth century). The Bible was also translated into other languages that

15. Warning about adding to or taking away from a written text can already be seen in the closing verses of the book of Revelation (22:18–19).

were important in other parts of the church (e.g., Syriac in the East, Coptic in Egypt).[16] The handwritten Bible codex remained the standard form up through the invention of moveable type and the printing press with Johannes Gutenberg in the fifteenth century. As has often been noted, it is difficult to exaggerate the significance of the impact that the printing press had on the development of books and reading, and on Western culture overall. It is equally difficult to exaggerate the impact the printing press had on the development of The Book, The Bible. In 1455, Gutenberg printed the Latin version of the Bible (Vulgate) using his newly invented printing press.[17] The advent of moveable type allowed for multiple copies to be printed much more quickly than had ever been the case for handwritten manuscript codices. Thus, the cost of production decreased significantly, and the dissemination of the Bible increased greatly. It was now possible not only for a virtually infinite number of copies, but to make them all identical.

Fig. 2.8. The Lenox Copy of the Gutenberg Bible. New York Public Library.

16. See the richly illustrated *In the Beginning: Bibles Before the Year 1000*, ed., Michelle P. Brown (Washington, DC: Smithsonian Institution, 2006), originally an exhibition at the Freer Gallery of Art and the Arthur M. Sackler Gallery. See also C. de Hamel, *The Book: A History of the Bible* (London: Phaidon Press, 2001).
17. On the Gutenberg Bible, see R. Abel, *The Gutenberg Revolution: A History of Print Culture* (New Brunswick, NJ: Transaction Publishers, 2011); C. de Hamel, *The Book. A History of the Bible*, 190–215; and especially, the magisterial two-volume work by E. Eisenstein, *The Printing Revolution in Early Modern Europe* (Cambridge: Cambridge University Press, 1993). See the Morgan Library and Museum's dedicated website on the Gutenberg Bibles owned by the Library: http://www.themorgan.org/collection/Gutenberg-Bible.

Just to give a sense of how quickly things changed with the advent of the printing press, in 1424 (some thirty years before Gutenberg's press), the Cambridge University library owned a total of 122 books.[18] After Gutenberg, by 1500, there were some 15,000 books in print. Between 1517 and 1520, Martin Luther had published thirty works, from pamphlets to books. During this four-year period, these same publications sold over 300,000 copies, and Lutheranism exploded onto the scene.[19] "Going viral" in Luther's day meant getting the word out with printed leaflets—tens of thousands of them. Luther's famous 95 Theses went through 14 print runs of 1,000 copies each in 1518 alone.[20]

Just as the codex form had important implications for biblical interpretation, so also did the mass production of the Bible on a printing press have enormous significance for the interpretation of the Bible. First of all, the ability to have a standardized text of the Latin Vulgate that could be printed and reprinted was a vast improvement for the stability of the text, rather than painstakingly copying and recopying handwritten manuscripts. Even though the Latin Bible went through 80 further editions in the fifteenth century alone, they mostly represent corrections of the text and changes in print type. All but two of the printed editions of the Latin Bible in the fifteenth century trace their lineage to the Gutenberg Bibles.[21] Second, in addition to a more standardized text, the most significant advantage to the printing press was the ability to print mass quantities in a fraction of the time it took to hand-copy the Bible, and at a fraction of the cost. This allowed the Bible to be disseminated far more quickly, not only to monasteries and churches, but to anyone of means with an interest in reading the Bible for themselves, across Germany and the rest of Europe. A third significant feature took place with the rise of Lutheranism and the translation of the Bible into the vernacular from the Latin, and then, the quick printing and circulation of vernacular versions of the Bible, which filtered throughout the rise of Lutheran churches in short order, together with Luther's own writings.

Finally, more subtle, but perhaps even more important, the Gutenberg revolution resulted in a shift from a culture of images (statues, paintings, stained glass) to a culture of words on a printed page. If, at

18. J. Naughton, *From Gutenberg to Zuckerberg: Disruptive Innovation in the Age of the Internet* (New York: Quercus, 2012), 7.
19. Eisenstein, *The Printing Revolution in Early Modern Europe*, 148.
20. "How Luther Went Viral," *The Economist* 401 (2011): 93–96; http://www.economist.com/node/21541719.
21. de Hamel, *The Book: A History of the Bible*, 215.

the end of the sixth century, Pope Gregory the Great saw statues as "the books of the illiterate,"[22] the advent of Gutenberg's printing press in the fifteenth century "made it possible to dispense with the use of images for mnemonic purposes and thus reinforced iconoclastic tendencies already present among many Christians."[23] The illiterate, in this view, should not be given images but should be taught to read.

The ability to read had not been so important when hand-copied books were both scarce and expensive. It might have been important for the noble class to read—and, of course, the priests—but not so much for the average peasant. But Gutenberg's printing press changed all this. The growing availability of comparatively inexpensive books, especially Bibles, combined with the Protestant Reformation's newfound emphasis on the Bible as the very Word of God, resulted in greater authority and reverence for the *printed* Word of God. The increasing significance of the Word proclaimed from the sacred Bible made its physical presence all the more important as a symbol of God, a talisman of the divine. The book itself came to be viewed as being as sacred as the story it told. Furthermore, if Christ was God incarnate, then the very materiality of the printed Bible provided another way to experience the enfleshment of the divine Word. If, for Catholics, Eucharist and the sacrifice of the Mass had focused on the physicality of the bread and the cup as the body and blood of Christ, for some Protestants, the Bible—which held the very words of God, Christ, and the apostles, "enfleshed" on a printed page—was the substantial, tangible approximation to the physical incarnation of the Word, a very real presence indeed. It is no wonder that this led to a certain kind of excessive reverence and hyperauthorization of the Bible as book in the Protestant tradition, an idolatry that worshiped the Bible, rather than the God to whom the Bible bears witness. This fostered a movement "which was more compatible with Protestant bibliolatry and pamphleteering than with the Baroque statues and paintings sponsored by the post-Tridentine Catholic Church."[24] Thus the idolatry of the Bible as *the* Book, *the* Word of God, began to replace what Protestants saw as the idolatry of Roman Catholic statues and other religious art.[25] It also

---

22. See Celia M. Chazelle, "Pictures, Books, and the Illiterate: Pope Gregory I's Letters to Serenus of Marseilles," *Word & Image: A Journal of Verbal/Visual Enquiry* 6, no. 2 (1990): 138–53.

23. E. Eisenstein, "Defining the Initial Shift: Some Features of Print Culture," in D. Finkelstein & A. McCleery, eds., *The Book History Reader*, 2nd ed. (New York: Routledge, 2006), 232–54, 243.

24. E. Eisenstein, "Defining the Initial Shift: Some Features of Print Culture," 243. To be sure, printed images began to replace the images of statues and paintings, especially in illustrated Bibles. Religious art continued along with the growing influence of religious books, just as print books today have continued along with the growing influence of digital books.

resulted in a certain de-authorization of the Bible within the Roman Catholic tradition as any kind of standalone authoritative book that could be read and understood, apart from official church teaching by the Magisterium. Protestants increasingly embraced the printed Bible as the sacred Word of God, while the Roman Catholic tradition grew wary and suspicious of Protestant claims based exclusively on the Bible. Only in the aftermath of Vatican II in the 1960s would Roman Catholics and mainstream Protestants come to approach the Bible in more common terms, with an emphasis on historical and contextual reading of the Bible.

But this was just the beginning for the printed Bible. While the fifteenth century saw the invention and spread of printing using moveable type, the sixteenth century was a period in which mass dissemination of Bibles took place, accompanied by a sharp rise in rates of literacy. Between the 1520s and the 1550s, the Bible in the vernacular became a common possession of average households. For many, it was the first and only book that they owned, a prized possession that contained the Word of God in a language they could both read and understand. And so, the fault lines between the Roman Catholic Church and the Protestant Reformation were set, largely defined and framed by sharp disagreements over the mechanism by which divine authority was mediated—the Roman Catholic hierarchy or the Protestant printed Bible. That divide persisted from the sixteenth to the twentieth century, from the Council of Trent (1545–1563) to the Second Vatican Council (1962–1965), shortly after which computers and a new digital world came onto the scene with increasing prominence.

25. The prominent twentieth-century theologian Reinhold Niebuhr put it well: "The Reformation insistence upon the authority of Scripture, as against the authority of the church, bears within it the perils of a new idolatry. Its Biblicism became, in time, as dangerous to the freedom of the human mind in searching out causes and effects as the old religious authority." *The Nature and Destiny of Man*, vol II, 152 (New York: Charles Scribner's Sons, 1964). See also pp. 202, 229–31, on "bibliolatry."

3

A Brief History of Digital Bibles

Very little has been written about the history of digital Bibles. This comes as no great surprise, given that digital Bibles have only been around in any serious way for about a generation. But within one human generation we have become accustomed to seeing hundreds of digital generations. While it is not uncommon for books to go through one edition after another over a period of years, it is far more common to see digital programs go through one update after another in rapid succession. Just as an example, the computer program I currently use, a Mac using the OS X operating system (currently 10.12.4), has gone through seven versions already by October of 2016 alone (10.11.3–10.12.4). In 2015, it was updated eight times, including the major update from the Yosemite to El Capitan operating system (10.10 to 10.11, and now to 10.12, Sierra); six updates in 2014; six in 2013; eight in 2012, and so on. The 10.0 operating system (Cheetah) was introduced in March 2001, and since then, it has gone through 98 updates, averaging a little more than six updates each year.[1] Some of the updates have been more significant than others, but each one is the equivalent of a new edition of a book, some with minor tweaks, some with major revisions. By comparison, the web browser Firefox has gone through 47 versions (not counting many additional updates of each version)

1. See http://robservatory.com/a-useless-analysis-of-os-x-release-dates/.

since its introduction in 2004.[2] And since its introduction in 1984, the Microsoft Windows operating system has gone through dozens upon dozens of versions.[3] It is, of course, far easier to make changes in computer programs, essentially adding or changing code, and issue such updates through the miracle of wireless downloads, than it is to publish a new or revised edition of a physical book. The history of digital Bibles has a similar record of new programs and constant updates. We will be exploring many of these programs in their most recent versions below in chapter 7. At present, however, let us go back and trace the history and development of digital Bibles since the advent of computers in the twentieth century.

The first inkling that computers might be useful for analyzing classic Christian texts came about through the work of an Italian Jesuit by the name of Roberto Busa (1913–2011).[4] Busa was a scholar of Thomas Aquinas, and he held a position in Philosophy at the Jesuit Aloisianum College in Gallarate, Italy, near Milan. He was interested in how a computer might help to create a printed concordance of the writings of Aquinas. To that end, he met in 1949 with Thomas J. Watson, the founder of IBM, and persuaded him to sponsor the project, the *Index Thomisticus*. The project took about 30 years and eventually produced 56 printed volumes (in 65,000 pages!), all based on the computer tagging and indexing of Aquinas's works (11 million Latin words). This work led Busa to establish the Center for Literary Data Processing, an early venture into humanities computing.[5] Along the way, he worked with the changing methods of nascent computing, from computer punch cards (with electro-counting machines), to magnetic tapes,[6] finally to CD-ROMs (published in 1992), and to a web-based version of the Aquinas concordance in 2005.

---

2. See https://en.wikipedia.org/wiki/History_of_Firefox - Version_46.
3. See https://en.wikipedia.org/wiki/History_of_Microsoft_Windows.
4. See Steven E. Jones, *Roberto Busa, S.J., and the Emergence of Humanities Computing: The Priest and the Punched Cards* (New York: Routledge, 2016). Jones offers a thorough and critical analysis of the first ten years of Busa's project in historical perspective. His goal is to evaluate the mythic story of Busa in all of its "complicated history" (p. 3). See pp. 100–101 on Busa and the Bible.
5. The Center later changed its name to as CAAL, or Centro per L'Automazione dell'Analisi Letteraria. In 1992, Fr. Busa founded the School of Lexicography and Hermeneutics within the Faculty of Philosophy at the Pontifical Gregorian University.
6. See R. Busa, "The Annals of Humanities Computing: The *Index Thomisticus*," *Computers and the Humanities* 14 (1980): 83–90.

Fig. 3.1. Roberto Busa at the control console of the IBM 705 at IBM World Headquarters in New York in 1958.

It should not come as a surprise that Busa would seek to use the computer to assist in the study of Aquinas rather than the Bible. In the Roman Catholic world of the 1940s and 1950s, Aquinas was arguably a more important authoritative source than the Bible, and Busa was, after all, an Aquinas scholar. Busa's pioneering work using the computer to help with the study of classic Christian texts was later followed by efforts to use the computer to analyze biblical texts. One early work was the somewhat idiosyncratic and wide-ranging little book by A.Q. Morton and James McLeman, *Christianity in the Computer Age,* published in 1964.[7] Morton, the lead author, was a minister in the Church of Scotland, and also a trained mathematician. McLeman was a chaplain in Scotland. The basic thrust of the book was to encourage a mod-

---

7. New York: Harper & Row, 1964. The book was published in Great Britain under the title *Christianity and the Computer.* The dust jacket of the book states part of the authors' goals: "The book is also an indictment of the church's failure to keep pace with the demand of a secular, scientific age, of its failure to change its approach to society and evangelism, and its inability to meet modern man on his own ground."

ern, critical, and scientific approach to the Bible. Intellectual honesty demanded that the Bible be approached with scientific rigor. What is this scientific approach? For Morton, it meant entering the Greek text of the New Testament onto computer tape, and then running various programs to conduct statistical tabulations. In particular, Morton was interested in how such statistical analysis might help determine which letters attributed to Paul were, in fact, written by Paul. So Morton carried out what can best be described as stylistic word frequency studies using the computer. His contention was that by examining the frequency of the most common words, he could determine writing patterns for an author. One test involved measuring the frequency of the Greek word *kai* ("and") in the sentences of Paul's letters. Another test examined the number of sentences having the Greek word *de* ("but") at the beginning. Morton then assembled a table showing the frequency of the word *kai* in all fourteen epistles (including Hebrews). He concluded with great confidence:

> Table Four [Table 3.2 below] shows the use of *kai* in all fourteen epistles. The differences are very large indeed. In Romans, 1st and 2nd Corinthians and Galatians the writer uses about one half *kai* per sentence. The rest have more than one *kai* per sentence. To be written by the same author as the writer of Colossians, the four from Romans to Galatians would need to have had another eight hundred *kais* in them. . . . Differences of this size are only found between different authors, never in the works of one author.[8]

For Morton to draw such broad conclusions on such relatively slim grounds may strike us as going well beyond the evidence. But it shows the kind of early confidence that some scholars felt was justified by invoking the language of science and computers when applied to religious beliefs, and to the Bible in particular. The hype on the book's dust jacket made the same appeal in a dramatic overstatement: "Newspapers around the world headlined the report by two scholars that a computer had proved that only five of the fourteen Epistles of St. Paul could, in fact, have been written by him." (I have been unable to confirm this assertion.) Morton went on to publish a whole string of computer-based studies on the Bible that received relatively little attention.[9]

---

8. *Christianity in the Computer Age,* 94; also cf. p. 32. Kenneth J. Neumann concluded that Morton's methods did not result in statistically meaningful data; *The Authenticity of the Pauline Epistles in the Light of Stylostatistical Analysis.* SBLDS 120. Atlanta: Scholars Press, 1991.

TABLE FOUR

THE PAULINE CORPUS: The occurrence of *kai*

No. of sentences having:	Romans	1st Corinthians	2nd Corinthians	Galatians	Ephesians	Philippians	Colossians	1st Thessalonians	2nd Thessalonians	1st Timothy	2nd Timothy	Titus	Philemon	Hebrews
No *kai*	386	424	192	128	32	42	23	34	16	49	45	18	12	155
One *kai*	141	152	86	48	29	29	32	23	11	38	28	9	6	94
Two *kais*	34	35	28	5	19	19	17	8	9	9	11	6	3	37
More than two *kais*	17	16	13	6	17	12	9	16	5	10	4	4	1	24
No. of sentences	578	627	319	181	97	102	81	81	41	106	88	37	22	310
No. of *kais*	242	281	185	72	137	107	99	99	49	91	68	36	17	251

Fig. 3.2, from A. Q. Morton, *Christianity in the Computer Age* (1964).

As for the world of the Hebrew Bible, Yehuda Radday applied computer-assisted statistical linguistics to the Book of Isaiah, with the goal of seeing what light computer analysis might shed on the debate over the literary unity of Isaiah. In his article "Isaiah and the Computer: A Preliminary Report," Radday stated that his goal was "to objectivize the controversy between divisionists and unitarians [on the authorship of Isaiah] by strict quantification which does not allow any personal convictions, religious prejudice or literary taste to influence conclusions."[10] He analyzed the roughly 18,000 words in Isaiah with attention to various statistical data (number of syllables, semantic groups, prefixes, suffixes, grammatical particulars, etc.). The goal was to see if he

9. E.g., *It's Greek to the Computer* (Montreal: Harvest House, 1971); *A Critical Concordance to the Acts of the Apostles (The Computer Bible)* (Biblical Research Associates, 1976); *The Genesis of John* (Edinburgh: Saint Andrew Press, 1980); *The Gathering of the Gospels: From Papyrus to Printout* (Lampeter: Mellen Press, 1995). R. T. Fortna, a highly respected scholar of John's Gospel, put it well in his review of Morton's *Genesis of John*: "A most peculiar book, seemingly written by a committee who never met." *Computers and the Humanities* 17, no. 3 (1983): 154 See also Morton's rather quirky essay, "The Annals of Computing: The Greek New Testament," *Computers and the Humanities* 14, no. 3 (1980): 197–99.

10. Y. Radday, "Isaiah and the Computer: A Preliminary Report," *Computers and the Humanities* 5, no. 2 (1970): 65–73; 73. Radday is currently Emeritus Professor of Jewish Studies at the prestigious Technion-Israel Institute of Technology, Haifa.

could find discernible patterns that might show whether Isaiah was written by one person or more, all based on the habits of patterns of speech which computer analysis could display in stark relief. Drawing on twenty-nine criteria, he concluded that the chances that the author of Isaiah 1–39 also wrote Isaiah 40–66 were 1:100,000. More specifically, he concluded that Isaiah 1–23 was the work of the same author, that Isaiah 49–66 was the work of another author, and that Isaiah 40–48 was likely the work of still another author. Analysis of Isaiah 34–35 was inconclusive.[11]

Radday's application of the computer to the Bible garnered more public attention and controversy when he published results of his analysis of the book of Genesis. As the New York Times headline put it, "Computer Points to Single Author for Genesis."[12] In contrast to the widely accepted documentary hypothesis claiming multiple authorship of Genesis, Radday's five-year linguistic analysis of Genesis showed that there was an 82 percent probability that Genesis had been written by one author.[13] Since so much of computer analysis of literary texts depends on the ways in which the programmer inputs and generates data, not many biblical scholars were persuaded by Radday's conclusions. Applying computer analysis to digitized texts of the Bible can be a fairly mechanistic process that still requires human interpretation and argumentation. The process is not nearly as objective as the use of a computer might suggest.

The early use of computers in the research of such scholars as Busa, Morton, and Radday in relation to religious literary texts was paralleled in a variety of other fields within the humanities in the 1960s and 1970s. In 1966, the journal *Computers and the Humanities* began publication, various academic institutions established centers dedicated to the use of computers in the humanities, and a burgeoning number of conferences were regularly held on the topic.[14] Great emphasis was placed on coming up with standardized approaches to the digitization of literary texts. How should digitized versions of texts be "marked" or

---

11. Radday, "Isaiah and the Computer," 69.
12. *The New York Times,* November 8, 1981; A.7.
13. This study was eventually published as *Genesis: An Authorship Study in Computer-Assisted Statistical Linguistics* (Rome: Biblical Institute Press; 1985), by both Y. Radday and H. Shore.
14. This journal was published during 1966–2004, when it ceased publication and changed its name to *Language Resources and Evaluation,* focused on linguistic studies and language processing. On the general history of humanities computing, see the authoritative article by another pioneer in the field, Susan Hockey, "The History of Humanities Computing," *A Companion to Digital Humanities,* ed. S. Schreibman, R. Siemens, & J. Unsworth (Oxford: Blackwell, 2004), 3–19. Hockey (1946–present) is Emeritus Professor of Library and Information Studies at University College, London.

"tagged" so as to be available to various computer programs and computer analysis? It was not until 1986 that SGML (the Standard Generalized Markup Language) was published and soon became the widely adopted standard to be used for marking all digital texts. This was followed by TEI (the Text Encoding Initiative), which was published in 1994, and which became a universal standard for encoding text. The introduction of the World Wide Web in the 1990s, of course, changed everything once again, and XML (Extensible Markup Language) has increasingly become the default system for marking not only text, but also images and audio for distribution on the web. Along with the XML standard for describing and defining digital data, HTML became the standard for displaying data in visual form.

If all of this sounds rather technical and academic, that's because it is. The initial use of computers in relation to the Bible was fundamentally an academic undertaking. In part, this was due to early computers being both large and expensive, important to universities and research institutes, but out of reach for individuals, and not immediately helpful to churches. Thus, the Bible in a digital world was initially a primarily academic world, with concerns about encoding the biblical text in digitized form and conducting word frequency and stylistic analyses to contribute to the debates about the likely authorship of various books of the Bible, as well as other historical and literary aspects of the biblical text.

Although the use of computers for the study of the Bible started off in very academic quarters, it did not take long for the church to realize the significance of computers for Bible study, especially after the advent of personal computers, which, beginning in the 1980s, were smaller and more affordable. Thus, as it emerged in the 1980s and beyond, the use of computers to study the Bible can be seen as falling into two general categories, two parallel tracks, one more academic in scope and the other more oriented to the confessional faith of believers, of churches, and the education of seminarians preparing for ministry. While there is, to be sure, significant overlap between the two (which we will explore toward the end of this chapter), the academic and ecclesial approaches truly function in different ways with different purposes, with rather different operating principles. To put it sharply, the academic approach emphasizes the scholarly study of ancient texts in their ancient contexts, quite apart from canonical boundaries, and without any necessary attention to the potential religious significance of the texts for modern believers. By contrast, the more ecclesial approach is overtly evangelistic in scope, with the goal of spreading the Word of God so that more Christians can better know and use the Bible in their paths of discipleship. The religious claims of the biblical texts and their significance for the faithful today are front and center. In order to narrate the development of these two tracks after the initial phases of the 1960s and 1970s, in what follows I will present two different stories—one that traces a pioneer in the more academic history of digital Bibles, Professor Robert Kraft, and the other that traces a pioneering program in the more ecclesial history of digital Bibles that started its life at Dallas Theological Seminary. We begin with Professor Kraft.

Robert Kraft and the Academic History of Digital Bibles

Professor Robert Kraft (b. 1934), a longtime and prominent professor (now emeritus) of early Christianity and Judaism at the University of Pennsylvania (Philadelphia), has been one of the most significant pioneers in computer applications for the Bible.[15] In a 2004 article, "How I Met the Computer, and How it Changed my Life," Kraft reflects on his 35 years of engaging with the Bible via computers. A generation before the emergence of the field now called Digital Humanities (DH), Kraft and others were truly already employing many aspects that have come to be identified with DH.[16] In the 1970s, Kraft was working with other scholars who had formed the International Organization for Septuagint[17] and Cognate Studies (IOSCS). One goal was to produce a new lexicon of "Septuagint" Greek. Kraft suggested they employ emerging computer technology to take on the task. Three related goals came about: 1) developing a morphological analysis of the Jewish scripture

---

15. Robert Kraft, "How I Met the Computer, and How it Changed my Life," SBLForumArchive, 2004. http://www.sblsite.org/publications/article.aspx?articleId=246. For his extensive resume, see http://ccat.sas.upenn.edu/rak/cv.html.
16. On Digital Humanities, see, e.g., S. Schreibman, R. Siemens, and J. Unsworth, eds., *A Companion to Digital Humanities* (Oxford: Blackwell, 2004); and in particular, the essay in the same volume by Charles Ess, "'Revolution? What Revolution?' Successes and Limits of Computing Technologies in Philosophy and Religion" (pp. 132–42). See also the new edition, *A New Companion to Digital Humanities*, S. Schreibman, R. Siemens, and J. Unsworth, eds. (Oxford: Blackwell, 2015). Both are available online. For Digital Humanities and biblical studies, see C. Clivaz, A. Gregory, & D. Hamidović, eds., *Digital Humanities in Biblical, Early Jewish and Early Christian Studies* (Leiden: Brill, 2013). On the closely related topic of the Bible and new media studies, see C. M. Ess, ed., *Critical Thinking and the Bible in the Age of New Media* (Lanham, MD: University Press of America, 2004), especially M. Palmer's essay, "Scripture Study in the Age of the New Media" (pp. 237–66). Finally, the Dutch publisher E. J. Brill recently announced a new series in Digital Biblical Studies (https://eabs.net/site/wp-content/uploads/2012/11/cfp_DBS_cmyk_v7.pdf).
17. The "Septuagint" refers to the Greek version/s of the Jewish scriptures (the Christian Old Testament).

texts in Greek (the focus of the work at the University of Pennsylvania), 2) creating a digital version that would produce the Greek and available Hebrew texts in parallel form (the focus of the team at Hebrew University), and 3) digitizing all published variants of the Greek Septuagint texts for wide dissemination. The eventual result was published as *Computer Assisted Tools for Septuagint Studies (CATSS), Volume 1, Ruth,*[18] co-edited by Kraft and the prominent Israeli scholar Emanuel Tov (of Hebrew University).[19] This was a highly academic and technical project aimed at specialists in the field of biblical studies, specifically Septuagint studies.

Kraft was, of course, by no means alone in this work. There was an active group of collaborative researchers, primarily biblical scholars with deep interest in computer applications, who worked together to advance the field. But there were also computer experts interested in humanities computing who contributed to the work. Already in 1972, David W. Packard (the son of Hewlett-Packard founder David Packard) began to develop a dedicated mini-computer for the purpose of studying ancient Greek texts, the IBYCUS machine, the first computer to allow scholars to do computerized searches of classical Greek writings in digital form.[20] The IBYCUS machine would use the database known as the TLG (the Thesaurus Linguae Graecae).[21] This computer was a modified Hewlett-Packard 1000, available for use through the Princeton Institute for Advanced Studies. With funding from the National Endowment for the Humanities and from the Packard Humanities Institute, the Septuagint project accomplished its first two goals (morphology and a Greek/Hebrew parallel text), while the third goal of digitizing textual variants proved more elusive. Kraft's home institution, the University of Pennsylvania, developed its own Center for the

18. Atlanta: Scholars Press, 1986. This was volume 1 of CATSS, presenting the book of Ruth in Greek–Hebrew aligned parallel text (pp. 85–175). For a full statement of the accomplishments of CATSS, see the Final Performance Report to the NEH from 1995: http://ccat.sas.upenn.edu/ rs/rak/catssreport.html, as well as the bibliography of publications relating to CATSS: http:// ccat.sas.upenn.edu/rs/rak/catssbibliog.html.
19. A CD-ROM version was released in 1987 by the Packard Humanities Institute (PHI), with a subsequent corrected version released in 1994. For more on the CATSS project and machine-readable texts, see J. J. Hughes, *Bits, Bytes and Biblical Studies: A Resource Guide for the Use of Computers in Biblical and Classical Studies* (Grand Rapids: Zondervan, 1987), 549–56.
20. See J. J. Hughes, *Bits, Bytes and Biblical Studies,* 118–22.
21. https://www.tlg.uci.edu/about/ibycus.php. As the project site states: "Since its inception the project has collected and digitized most texts written in Greek from Homer (c. 8 BCE) to the fall of Byzantium in 1453 CE and beyond. Its goal is to create a comprehensive digital library of Greek literature from antiquity to the present era. TLG research activities combine the traditional methodologies of philological and literary study with the most advanced features of information technology." See also J. J. Hughes, *Bits, Bytes and Biblical Studies,* 577–79.

Computer Analysis of Texts (CCAT) in the mid-1980s, led by Kraft's colleague, Dr. John Abercrombie. The Septuagint project was one of CCAT's major undertakings. Beyond the Septuagint, CCAT also digitized and distributed various related biblical materials, including Greek texts, English Bible versions, the Latin Vulgate, and Aramaic Targums, among other early Jewish and Christian texts. CCAT also produced materials for the Packard Humanities Institute CD-ROM that included Latin texts and biblical materials. The IBYCUS machine was retired in 1999, and digital texts were migrated to CD-ROMS, and by 2001, to an online system.[22]

In addition to his work with CATSS and CCAT, from 1984–1994, Kraft wrote "Offline," a regular and important column for the *Council on the Study of Religion Bulletin,* and then for the *Religious Studies News.* The column was a service of the Society of Biblical Literature's Computer Assisted Research Group (CARG), which was active from the early 1980s through 2011 (and which Kraft chaired from 1984 to 1988). Each column addressed different aspects of how computer-assisted research could enhance the study of ancient Jewish and Christian texts, including biblical texts.

Kraft's initial April 1984 column was entitled "In Quest of Computer Literacy," and was a clarion call for scholars and graduate programs to get up to speed on the use of computers as the wave of the future. Kraft made sure that computer literacy was a requirement for graduate students at Penn from 1994 on. He wrote: "We want our graduate students to be able to use a computer system comfortably for scholarly purposes, the most obvious of which is in the preparation of research papers, reports, and other written work."[23] This also entailed having a basic understanding of how computer programs worked. Along the way, he wrote columns on such topics as "hypertext,"[24] news of conferences, and new computer hardware and software related to the study of biblical and related ancient texts. His goal was to encourage scholars in the humanities to become more familiar with technologies that could enhance the study of ancient texts. As Patrick Durusau wrote when Kraft stepped down from writing and overseeing "Offline" in 1994: "Robert Kraft, through the Offline column and other efforts, has brought the seamless integration of computers into religious studies closer to reality."[25]

22. https://www.tlg.uci.edu/about/history.php.
23. Thus began the "Offline" series. *Council on the Study of Religion Bulletin* 15, no. 2 (April 1984).
24. *Religious Studies News* 2, no. 5 (November, 1997).

Again, much of this work was rather technical and appropriate for academic contexts. Beyond the task of marking or tagging ancient texts so that they could be machine-readable, and even beyond the programs that were developed to conduct various analyses of the digitized texts, there was also a philosophy undergirding the kind of work that Kraft and his colleagues represent. This philosophy can be seen most clearly in Kraft's 2006 Presidential address to the Society of Biblical Literature, "Para-mania: Beside, Before and Beyond Bible Studies."[26] The main thrust of Kraft's presidential remarks address his concern for all of the nonbiblical texts that typically receive short shrift from biblical scholars in a rather anachronistic manner when it comes to historical study of early Christianity in particular.

Kraft makes the perhaps ironic point that he does not consider himself to be a "Bible scholar," with an exclusive or narrow focus on the canonical Bible. Rather, he considers himself to be a scholar of early Jewish and Christian literature, including many biblical texts. Hence, "Beyond Bible Studies" refers to a wide range of early texts that may or may not be in the Bible per se, but come from the time frame of the first few centuries in early Judaism and Christianity.[27] This framing leads him to address directly what he calls "The Tyranny of Canonical Assumptions: The *Para*scriptural Worlds."[28] Since the "Bible" as we know it did not exist as a physical book until the fourth century, the privileging of the canonical writings in the study of earliest Christianity is more anachronistic than it is historical. Before Constantine, there was no such physically unified singular book as our Bible today. As Kraft puts it rather succinctly, "The 'tyranny of canonical assumptions' is the temptation to impose on those ancients whom we study our modern ideas about what constituted 'scripture' and how it was viewed."[29] Even more serious "is the failure to recognize that those whom we study are not necessarily playing by our rules. When they say 'scripture' . . . they might refer to literature or traditions different from

25. "Offline 45" (16 May 1994). Kraft's final "Offline" column appeared in February of 1994, Offline 44. See Jay Curry Treat, "Computing and the Religious Studies Department at Penn." https://www.sas.upenn.edu/~jtreat/rs/rscpuhx.html#offline, 1996.

26. *Journal of Biblical Literature* 126, no. 1 (2007): 3–27.

27. Kraft, "Para-mania: Beside, Before and Beyond Bible Studies," 8. The term "early Judaism" is a technical term that scholars use to refer to post-exilic Judaism from about 200 BCE to 200 CE. Ironically, this period used to be called "late Judaism" in older Christian scholarship on Judaism at the time of Christian origins. See my article, "Jewish/Christian Relations at 25: Retrospect & Prospect," in *Ancient Jew Review* (http://www.ancientjewreview.com/articles/2014/12/9/jewishchristian-relations-at-25-retrospect-prospect).

28. Ibid., 10–18.

29. Ibid., 17.

those we recognize, or even to materials antecedent to or derived from what has survived for us."[30] Kraft develops this point further in the second section of his address, "The Problem of Textual Myopia: The Paratextual Worlds." His point is simply that to use the Bible as if it were the only or even the primary window onto the early Christian world is to place canonical blinders on the work of historical reconstruction and analysis.[31] For historians, the Bible must invoke all of those paratexts that were running around alongside these later canonical texts. All of these "extra-biblical" texts point to a world far richer and more complex than we typically imagine (especially when we wear Bible-blinders unaware). As Kraft states, "the actual pasts are much fuller than the texts on which we initially depend."[32]

Although he does not take the opportunity in his SBL Presidential address to discuss his important work in the use of computers in relation to early Jewish and Christian texts, his work on the Septuagint textual traditions and his "Offline" columns make it clear that one primary goal for engaging the digital world is to make all ancient texts readily available for study and debate. The digitizing of these early Jewish and Christian texts (including some biblical texts) provides a more level playing field for historical scholarship by making distribution of texts outside of the Bible accessible, whether we are talking about the so-called Apostolic Fathers or Christian writings before the Council of Nicaea (325 CE) or the Jewish writings from Qumran. Operating within a richer contextual world simply makes for better historical analysis.

I am reminded of a conversation I had several years ago with Prof. Bart Ehrman, a prolific and sometimes controversial scholar of early Christian literature who operates very much in the broad approach that Robert Kraft has championed. Along with his bestselling (and now into its 6th edition) *The New Testament: An Historical Introduction to the Early Christian Writings*,[33] he had produced an edited collection of texts intended to accompany his introduction. This volume, published by Oxford in 2003, is *The New Testament and Other Early Christian Writings: A Reader*. I have long used his introductory textbook for my Freshmen Intro NT courses, but I have not adopted his *Reader*, opting instead for an actual Bible. During one conversation, he asked me why I was

---

30. Ibid., 18.
31. It is no accident that one of Kraft's early books focuses on the second-century Christian writings, *Barnabas and the Didache*, The Apostolic Fathers: A Translation and Commentary, vol. 3, ed. R.M. Grant (New York: Thomas Nelson & Sons, 1965).
32. Kraft, "Para-mania: Beside, Before and Beyond Bible Studies," 22.
33. New York: Oxford University Press, 2015.

not using his *Reader* along with his *Introduction*. My response was that, while I was supplementing the Bible with other early Christian writings (the usual—Coptic Gospel of Thomas, Infancy Gospel of Thomas, Acts of Paul and Thecla, etc.), I was concerned that if I used his *Reader*, students wouldn't know what was in the New Testament and what wasn't. His response was telling in a wonderful way. "Precisely!" he said. His point, much like Kraft's, was that if we are doing serious historical work on Christian origins in the first few centuries, then the canonical status of any writing is quite irrelevant.[34] Digital access to the wide range of early Christian texts both within and outside of what later became the Christian canon of scripture is indeed an important corrective to the often anachronistic and tyrannical privileging of the Bible in historical study of the early Christian world.

The work of Prof. Kraft is thus representative of the more academic approach to the digital Bible, with its emphasis on exploding the boundaries of the canonical Bible by digitizing not only the Bible but also hundreds of noncanonical writings from the same general era for historical and literary analysis.[35] It is important to note that the rise of Departments of Computer Science within universities across the United States (and abroad) was accompanied by a mostly unrelated rise in the number of Departments of Religious Studies at state and secular universities in the 1960s and 1970s. The emphasis in religious studies departments was on descriptive historical and literary analysis, with a fairly sharp commitment to the separation of church and state. Prominent religious studies programs developed at the University of Pennsylvania, the University of Virginia, the University of California at Santa Barbara, and Indiana University (my alma mater), among many others. That there would be a natural fit between the humanistic and historical emphases in the study of religion and the use of computer technology to aid in such study makes good sense, given the kinds of cross-fertilization that often happen in academic institutions. The introduction of computer-driven analysis to the field of religious stud-

34. Although I agreed, and still agree, with this objection to the privileging of a Christian canon of scripture in historical study, my response to Ehrman was that I was also engaged with my students in the history of interpretation of biblical texts up through the modern era, for which the canonical status of these Christian writings was and is an important aspect.
35. As Prof. Mark George (Iliff School of Theology) comments in private correspondence, it is worth pointing out that these efforts have been led by scholars of early Christianity, in part because so much textual material is available for this time period. Although similar work has been underway for the Hebrew Bible/Old Testament, it lags behind and is not as coordinated as projects for early Christianity. He notes, for example, that there is nothing like a database for Hebrew Bible/Old Testament studies that is comparable to the TLG for scholars of early Christianity.

ies lent a more scientific atmosphere to the endeavor of religion schol-ars, and showed the potential value of computers for the humanities in the work of computer scientists.

As we prepare to shift to the story of the more faith-based approach to digital Bibles, it is helpful to consider two books that were published six years apart: *Bits, Bytes and Biblical Studies,* by John Hughes (Zon-dervan, 1987), and *Computer Bible Study: Up-to-Date Information on the Best Software and Techniques,* by Jeffrey Hsu (Word, 1993). The book by Hughes is subtitled "A Resource Guide for the Use of Computers in Bib-lical and Classical Studies." And what a resource guide it is! Weighing in at 642 pages, this book is nothing short of a comprehensive tome on everything related to the Bible and computers as things stood in 1987. This is a book for geeks, in the best sense of that word. Hughes leaves no stone unturned in the world of hardware, software, and everything in between and beyond. He discusses the technical details of computer architecture, goes well beyond the forest into the depth of the trees in analyzing word processing and related programs,[36] addresses the state of online services at the time, machine-readable ancient texts and text archives, Bible concordance programs, and archaeological programs, to name but a very few topics he covers. Beyond this book, Hughes also wrote and edited the newsletter *Bits and Bytes Review* from 1986 to 1991, which regularly updated and expanded upon his book.

By contrast, Jeffrey Hsu's *Computer Bible Study* shows how things had developed in only six short years, so that by 1993 an ecclesial and confessional approach to the use of computers in studying the Bible, including sermon preparation, now began to rival more acad-emic approaches. Hsu, an expert in computer information systems, wrote the book to enable studying the Bible as the Word of God.[37] As the book's back cover states, "Whether your goal is personal Bible study, preparing Sunday school lessons, sermon preparation or advanced bib-lical research, there are new computerized study tools that will save

---

36. Just as an example of the highly detailed discussions, section 2.7 of the book addresses "Font-and-Printer Utilities," with subsections on "Print Processors" (2.7.1), "Font Editors" (2.7.2), "Font Sets" (2.7.3), pp. 177–92. Or consider the section from Chapter 4 on "Computer-Assisted Language Learning," in which he discusses 14 different Hebrew programs and 19 different Latin programs (pp. 398–420).

37. This is to imply nothing about the faith commitments of those engaged in more academic study of the Bible using computers. Far from it. In addition to his very academic book on biblical studies and computers, John Hughes also edited *God's Word Complete Concordance* (with W. D. Mounce as co-editor) in the God's Word series (World Publishing, 1996); as well as editing and contributing to *Speaking the Truth in Love: The Theology of John M. Frame* (Phillipsburg, NJ: P & R, 2009). Frame (1936–) is a conservative theologian in the Calvinist tradition who taught at Westminster Theo-logical Seminary, and now teaches at Reformed Theological Seminary in Orlando, FL.

you precious time." At just over 200 pages in length, Hsu's guide is directed at Christians who want to make use of what was then the still relatively new world of personal computing as it related to study of the Bible. Although he covers in much less detail much of the same kind of territory as Hughes, the tone is rather different. Each chapter opens with a quote from scripture and then proceeds to discuss such topics as electronic Bibles, educational software for children, methods for doing word study or topical study of the Bible, or how to get a sense of geography as it relates to the Bible by using various software programs. The emphasis throughout is on how to make use of computer tools with digital Bibles to encourage deeper understanding and appreciation of the Bible as the Word of God.

Digital Bibles in Service to the Church and Christian Faith

This takes us, then, to the second part of the story of digital Bibles, which began in the early 1980s. Bible Research Systems engineered a way to transfer the biblical text from computer tapes to compressed storage on eight disks. Their program, Verse Search, was the first commercial digital Bible (1980), allowing a word search of the entire Bible in one hour, which was quite fast in 1980.[38] Other early programs from the mid-1980s included Online Bible (which was not actually online, but was available as shareware for PCs), Bible Reader, WORD Search, and The Perfect Word. But arguably the most significant and sophisticated early digital Bible for use in church-related work was Dallas Theological Seminary's CD Word Library.

Dallas Theological Seminary (DTS) is an evangelical school in the dispensationalist tradition for the training of men and women in ministry. Their mission is clearly stated: "to glorify God by equipping godly servant-leaders for the proclamation of His Word and the building up of the body of Christ worldwide." And their high view of scripture is equally clear: "God's direction for DTS is simply to equip students with the truth of the Bible, trusting it to change lives."[39] Given this

38. See "25th Anniversary for Bible Software is Celebrated with New Release" (2005, October 11). *The Free Library* (2005). https://www.thefreelibrary.com/25th Anniversary for Bible Software is Celebrated with New Release.-a0137395881. See also John Dyer's very useful infographic, "The History of Bible Software" (http://donteatthefruit.com/2016/09/the-history-of-bible-software-infographic/), from September 2016. My thanks to Tim Bulkeley for calling my attention to these references.

39. http://www.dts.edu/about/. For those unfamiliar with the language of "high" and "low" views of scripture, a "high" view of Scripture tends to divinize the Bible as the inerrant and infallible revealed Word of God that transcends the contexts in which it was written, whereas a "low" view of scripture tends to emphasize the Bible as a highly contextual human book, expressing chang-

focus on the Bible, it comes as no real surprise that one goal was to make the Bible available in digital form for the purpose of study and research. Toward that end, in the mid 1980s, Dallas Theological Seminary decided to create a Bible software program for use on a personal computer, which was still in its infancy.

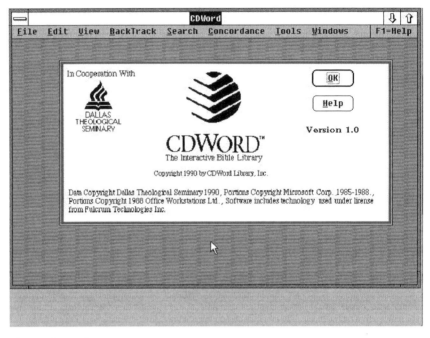

Fig. 3.3. CD Word.

In 1989, DTS released the first version of the *CDWord: The Interactive Bible Library*.[40] It boasted significant use of hypertext to interlink the Greek New Testament (Nestle-Aland 26), the Rahlfs Septuagint, two Greek lexicons (BAGD and the Intermediate Liddell/Scott), four English translations (KJV, NIV, NASV, RSV), three one-volume commentaries (*Harper's Bible Commentary*, the *Bible Knowledge Commentary*, and the

ing human understandings of God and what it means to be faithful to God. Note the presumption in the DTS statement about "the truth of the Bible," and that the Bible changes lives. I presume this is an instrumental understanding of the Bible as the tool that God uses to change lives.
40. See W.H. Harris, III, "Bible Software History 101," *Bible.org Blogs* (http://blogs.bible.org/netbible/w._hall_harris_iii/bible_software_history_101), Feb 6, 2008; and Emma Finley, "25 Years of Digital Bible Initiatives at DTS From CDWord to Logos Bible Software" (http://www.dts.edu/read/logos-bible-software-cd-word-project/), December 16, 2013. The narrative that follows draws from these sources, as well as from a helpful 2015 Wikipedia article: https://en.wikipedia.org/wiki/Logos_Bible_Software.

Jerome Biblical Commentary), and two Bible dictionaries (*New Bible Dictionary* and *Harper's Bible Dictionary*). The newspaper *USA Today* published a story on it with the headline "Computers Join the Congregation."[41] The short article noted the use of CD-ROM storage that allowed the CD Word Library to hold almost 21,000 pages of text. The $595 price tag was not inexpensive, nor was the Hitachi laser optical disc reader, but for anyone seeking an advanced Bible study program, this was state-of-the-art. There were other digital versions of the Bible available through Parsons Technology (Quick Verse, offering the KJV), the hand-held Franklin Pocket King James Version Electronic Holy Bible, a device featuring the KJV, though the RSV was also available, and a Zondervan hand-held electronic device with a version of the NIV. But these were much simpler programs that basically gave only the biblical text on a simple screen, without the ability to hyperlink to the kinds of tools that the CD Word Interactive Library made available. (See Fig. 3.4G.)

Although the CD Word program was widely praised as a helpful Bible study tool, the combination of its cost, the cost of copyrights and development, and relatively modest sales all led to a decision by the DTS Board to sell the technology in 1991 to Logos Research Systems, the forerunner of Logos Bible Software. Logos released its first version for Microsoft Windows in December 1991, followed by version 2.0 in 1995 with the development of a library system not unlike the earlier CD Word program, but much more robust. In 2001, Logos released a completely redesigned program, the Libronix Digital Library System with Series X software. Logos remained an exclusively PC system until 2008, when it released Logos 1.0 for Macintosh computers, followed by the 2009 release of Logos 4, which was now designed to run on Windows, Macintosh, iPhone, and iPod Touch. In 2011, Logos released Vyrso, a Christian e-book store and e-reader app that was integrated with Logos software. 2012 saw the development of cloud-based software that added the Proclaim church presentation software for collaborative Sunday morning use. In 2014, Logos Bible Software rebranded itself as Faithlife Corporation, a nod to the increasing diversity of products and services that was now being offered in addition to digital Bible study. Logos Bible Software 6 was released toward the end of 2014, and incorporated multimedia, Ancient Literature cross-references, an integrated Factbook, and original manuscript images.[42] Logos 7 was introduced in 2016; we will explore it in chapter 7 below.

41. *USA Today*, August 16, 1990, 4.D, Life Section.
42. Bob Pritchett was the individual most instrumental in the development of Logos Bible Software.

Beginning in 2013, all students at Dallas Theological Seminary started receiving nearly $14,000 worth of Logos Bible Software for free.[43] DTS underwrites the cost of the software through donor support and a small part of student technology fees. Students who graduate from DTS with a Masters or Doctoral degree get to keep the software for life. The software list includes nearly 300 titles of programs related to the study of the Bible and beyond.[44] The historic connection between DTS and Logos Bible Software surely figures into this collaboration; it is a remarkable collection that DTS students receive for free. Some of the resources are of much greater value for Bible study than others. For example, the standard Greek–English lexicon for studying the New Testament (typically referred to as "BDAG" in reference to its four editors)[45] is of much more practical use than Stephen's Textus Receptus from 1550!). No doubt some of the titles are included simply because they are in public domain, and hence free to anyone (the KJV of the Bible and Pilgrim's Progress, to name but two).

The same kind of purpose for studying the Bible evident in DTS and Logos Bible Software can readily be found in other Bible software programs. Olive Tree Bible Software boasts that it helps "over 4 million people connect with God."[46] E-Sword is a downloadable Windows Bible study program that is the "Sword of the Lord with an electronic edge." Founder Rick Meyers states that "GOD combined my passion for His Word and my pleasure of programming, and e-Sword was birthed!"[47] The Sword Project (unrelated to e-Sword) is an open-source Mac-based program "for research and study of God and His Word."[48] Accordance Bible Software, the widely used Bible-study program for Macs in particular, is unusual among Bible programs, as its opening screen makes no implicit or explicit faith claim; rather, it says "simply brilliant," in reference to the quality of the program itself. The most widely downloaded Bible app for smartphones is YouVersion, with over 250 million downloads. YouVersion presents itself as "a simple, ad-free Bible that brings God's Word into your daily life."[49] It comes replete with various

He serves as the President and CEO of Faithlife.Corp. Interviews with him may be accessed through blog.logos.com.
43. http://www.dts.edu/logos/.
44. http://www.dts.edu/download/student/DTS-Logos-Student-Resources.pdf.
45. W. Bauer, W. Arndt, F. Gingrich, F. Danker, eds., *A Greek-English Lexicon of the New Testament and Other Early Christian Literature*, 3rd edition (Chicago: University of Chicago Press, 2001).
46. https://www.olivetree.com.
47. e-Sword was started in 2000 and to date has been downloaded over 30 million times in its various versions across over 230 countries.
48. http://crosswire.org/sword/about/index.jsp.
49. https://www.youversion.com.

Bible study plans, videos, and sophisticated social media applications. We will explore various features of these and other Bible study programs in chapter 7 below, but for now, my point is to call attention to the openly evangelistic tone of most Bible study programs. This is one aspect of the software culture associated with study of the Bible that we will develop more fully in chapter 7.[50]

Thus far, we have explored both more academic and more faith-based approaches to the digitization of biblical literature. But there are also efforts by academics and clergy alike (often in the same persons) to have a more integrated approach to the biblical text that pays attention both to the historical contexts of the original authors and readers as well as to the situations of modern readers (and readers of the biblical texts throughout history). This is not necessarily an aspect of digital Bibles per se, but it is a reflection of a trend in biblical studies that has also gone digital. One good example of this attempt at integration can be seen in the difference between the two editions of the Interpreter's Bible Commentary (IBC), separated by a generation. The first edition of the IBC was a twelve-volume set published in 1957 by Abingdon Press, the main press of the United Methodist Church, though very ecumenical in scope.[51] The goal of the IBC was to reflect the best of what was then modern biblical scholarship, on the one hand, and the best in homiletics and preaching, on the other hand, at least from a generally Protestant outlook. This was *the* Bible commentary set that all newly minted clergy desired from the end of the 1950s through the early 1970s. The layout of the volumes was telling. At the top of each page was the biblical text, divided into two columns. The column on the left was the King James Version of the text, while the column on the right was the Revised Standard Version of the biblical passage. Beneath the biblical text was a line across the page, and under this line was a commentary written by a biblical scholar discussing the original context and meaning of the passage—what it had meant when it was written and first read. Then, below this commentary was another black line across the page, and under this was a second commentary written by someone skilled in preaching. Their task was to discuss what this bib-

---

50. For the notion of "software culture" I am drawing especially on the work of Lev Manovich, *Software Takes Command* (New York: Bloomsbury Academic, 2013).
51. The general editor was George Buttrick (1892–1980), a highly respected preacher and theologian, often ranked in terms of influence at the same level as Billy Graham and Martin Luther King Jr. He served as pastor of Madison Avenue Presbyterian Church in New York from 1927–1955. After retiring he became a professor of preaching at Harvard Divinity School (1955–1965), and then lectured frequently on preaching at the most prominent Protestant seminaries in the country (e.g., Union, Garrett, Vanderbilt, Southern Baptist).

lical text might mean in a modern context, all as a help to preachers everywhere seeking ideas and inspiration for their sermons. The black line between what the text *meant* and what it *means* was central to the entire conception of *The Interpreter's Bible* commentary. The goal was to attend both to the historical meaning of the text and to the contemporary application of the passage, though the very layout of the commentary communicated that these two worlds were literally worlds apart. There was little, if any, integration between the two. (See Fig. 3.5G.)

By contrast, a generation later, Abingdon Press published a completely new version of the Interpreter's Bible. Its name, appropriately enough, is *The New Interpreter's Bible* commentary, again a twelve-volume set, published in 2003.[52] Rather than having the King James Version and Revised Standard Version of the biblical text at the top of each section, the versions have been updated to the New International Version and the New Revised Standard Version (again in parallel columns). This time, rather than highlighting the distance of the original biblical text from the modern reader, the goal was to have a more integrated approach. To that end, each book of the Bible was assigned to one scholar, whose task was to provide both a lengthier "Commentary" and briefer "Reflections" that followed and built directly upon the more exegetical "Commentary" section. This approach provides a much more integrated interpretation of the biblical text than the older version of *The Interpreter's Bible*. In both the *Interpreter's Bible* and the *New Interpreter's Bible*, most of the authors were/are respected scholars connected to seminaries and schools of theology. But in the case of the *New Interpreter's Bible*, the goal was not to separate "then" and "now," but to show the connections, attending to both the historic and modern contexts at the same time. Significantly, *The New Interpreter's Bible* is available not only in print form, but also in digital form—on CD-ROM. More importantly, it is also available for purchase (as a downloadable text) as an additional module within various Bible study software programs (e.g., Logos, Accordance).[53]

---

52. The general editor of the *New Interpreter's Bible* commentary was Leander Keck (1928–), a prominent New Testament scholar with close ties to the church (he is an ordained member of the Christian Church (Disciples of Christ). He taught at Vanderbilt University and Emory University before becoming Dean of Yale Divinity School (1979–1989).

53. Other more recent Bible commentary series seek a similar kind of integration of historical study with contemporary reflection. See, e.g., *The IVP New Testament Commentary, Word Biblical Commentary, Tyndale New Testament Commentary, Pulpit Commentary, The Bible Speaks Today, NIV Application Commentary, The 21st Century Biblical Commentary,* and *Sacra Pagina,* most of them available as downloads.

This brief overview of the history of Bibles and biblical literature in digital form leads to several conclusions. First, we have seen that some more academic interests and developments in the digitization of biblical literature have sought to be agnostic in regard to the Christian biblical canon that arose well after the literature in question. The concern regarding anachronistic and privileged treatments of early Christian writings that eventually came to be part of the New Testament is a valid concern. One function of the "digital turn" has been a kind of democratization of ancient texts, resulting in more ready access to and dissemination of other early Christian literature not in the Bible, literature that often gets ignored by scholars and nonacademics alike, to the detriment of a richer historical portrait of early Christianity.

Second, we have seen how more faith-based approaches to the Bible as Holy Scripture result in digital Bibles that are brimming with study aids of all kinds. If, once, it was thought that the Bible was written in a sacred tongue rather than in the vernacular,[54] one could understandably wonder if the hundreds upon hundreds of digital aids accompanying any number of Bible study programs, in fact, has resurrected the notion of the Bible as sacred language, needing exposition upon exposition in order to be understood by mere mortals. This is partly fueled in many digital programs by an extremely high view of the Bible as the very Word of God. It is almost as if one could never say enough about the Bible. As we will see below in chapter 7, the sheer volume of information that comes along with digital Bibles raises concerns about whether the amassing of information is mistaken for knowledge and understanding. As a biblical scholar who also self-identifies as a Christian, I sometimes wonder if digital Bibles might be so awash in digital commentaries, dictionaries, lexicons, and other helps (all well-intended) that the biblical text itself gets utterly drowned out. Does the mass of digital aids actually result in the over-interpretation and suffocation of the biblical text by heaping so much upon it, and ironically, from those who wish to approach the Bible as a conversation about faith? Has the conversation turned to cacophony? Are we back to a Babel of Bibles, now in digital form?

Third, and finally, the "digital turn" has not only allowed for greater attention to paratextual worlds surrounding the biblical writings, it has also helped to mediate a more dynamic navigation or negotiation

54. The Hebrew Bible in particular was thought to reflect the sacred language of God. See, e.g., S.L. Goldman, *God's Sacred Tongue: Hebrew and the American Imagination* (Chapel Hill, NC: University of North Carolina Press, 2004).

between historical analysis and modern faith claims grounded in the biblical texts themselves. If, on the one hand, there is a surplus of information that might actually make a better understanding of early Christian worlds more difficult, on the other hand, as Robert Kraft points out, "the actual pasts are much fuller than the texts on which we initially depend."[55] The challenge of navigating these worlds with sufficient knowledge and humility will no doubt persist, if increasingly in digital form.

55. Kraft, "Para-mania: Beside, Before and Beyond Bible Studies," 22.

4

———

This is Your Brain on Screens

In *The Nature of the Book,* Adrian Johns observes that "it is becoming increasingly clear that people in the past and of other cultures do not read in anything that might unproblematically be called the same way as us."[1] The history of reading in different times and cultures shows remarkable development and change. In antiquity, not everyone who could read could also write. Prior to Gutenberg's invention of moveable type in the 1450s, only a relatively small percentage of people could read at all. Writing, reading, and books were matters left mostly to the few who were well-educated and to government and religious institutions in more urban areas—namely, those with some power. As we saw in chapter 1, changing technologies of writing led also to significant developments in the reading and interpretation of texts, from cuneiform to scroll to codex to print.

From Gutenberg through the twentieth century, print culture was the dominant form of spreading information and knowledge. Pamphlets, flyers, newspapers, posters, declarations, magazines, periodicals, encyclopedias, and books of all kinds conveyed information to

---

1. Adrian Johns, *The Nature of the Book: Print and Knowledge in the Making* (Chicago: University of Chicago Press, 1998), 384. In contrast, A. K. Gavrilov argued that "the phenomenon of reading itself is fundamentally the same in modern and in ancient culture. Cultural diversity does not exclude an underlying unity." "Reading Techniques in Classical Antiquity," *Classical Quarterly* 47, no. 1 (1997): 69. In my view, Johns has the weightier argument. The form and function of reading has changed dramatically across time and culture.

an increasingly reading public. The advent of audio recording, radio, and television led some to fear that the book was in its final days. The explosion of all things digital has more recently led some scholars to refer to "the late age of print,"[2] as though print culture were on its way out. Although most observers agree that the printed book, in fact, is here to stay, print culture has certainly been dramatically affected by the new digital mediums. One way in which print culture has both developed and been transformed is by the "screen culture" of digital books, e-books. To be sure, books have a long history of different kinds of writing material (papyrus, parchment, paper),[3] different scripts and styles of writing, and a plethora of sizes and shapes. The one constant in a physical book, however, is the format of words or images on a page that one physically turns to get to the next page, whether from right to left (as in English and other romance languages) or from left to right (as in Hebrew and Arabic).[4] This constant in the physicality of books disappears in the realm of virtual books, digital books on screens. The shift from real ink on a page to pixels on a screen has brought with it a more ephemeral and transitory experience in reading.

Changing images on screens, of course, predates the rise of digital technology. The advent of the television in the mid-twentieth century introduced people to the broadcasting of images on screens, initially in black and white, and then in color, beginning in the 1960s. TV sets also brought with them the notion that one could change channels and view successively different images on the same screen. It took a while before computer screens offered anything like comparable images on screens. Prior to the invention of computer displays on screens, one only saw flashing indicator lights (as on the Univac), or punch cards (as with the ENIAC), or paper tape whose punched holes could be translated by an electronic typewriter, or teletypes that would print out on paper the results of computer program applications.[5] In the early 1970s, cathode-ray tubes—so common in televisions—started to be used with computers as display screens. Eventually, plasma and LCD

2. See, e.g., Jay David Bolter, *Writing Space: Computers, Hypertext, and the Remediation of Print*, 2nd ed. (New York: Routledge, 2001). Chapter 1 is entitled "Writing in the Late Age of Print" (pp. 1–13); Theodore Striphas picks up on this image in his *The Late Age of Print: Everyday Book Culture from Consumerism to Control* (New York: Columbia University Press, 2009).

3. On the history of paper, see Mark Kurlansky, *Paper: Paging Through History* (New York: W. W. Norton & Co., 2016).

4. Of course, one *reads* in the opposite direction of the page turn: from left to right in Romance languages, and from right to left in Semitic languages.

5. See http://www.pcworld.com/article/209224/displays/historic-monitors-slideshow.html#slide 20.

(liquid crystal display) screens were introduced as computer monitors, culminating in the LED (light emitting diode) and OLED (organic light emitting device) screens of today. But as we shall see, there is more to screens than meets the eye.

The fundamental question that researchers have now been exploring for a number of years is how reading on a digital screen might or might not differ from reading a printed page, a physical book. For our purposes, how does this discussion relate to reading the Bible on a digital screen? Does reading the Bible on paper or on screens have any different impact on how one perceives or understands the biblical text? In order to answer this fundamental question, we will need to address some related questions about the act of reading in general. To that end, in what follows, we will be addressing various issues that have some bearing on the larger question about reading the Bible on screens. We will begin, first, with a simple discussion of the complicated question of *how* the brain reads. This will lead to a consideration of different ways in which we read, followed by an exploration of how these different kinds of reading relate to differences of genre. Although reading on screens has been around on personal digital devices since the 1980s, the real digital revolution occurred in 2007 with the introduction of iPhones and Kindles in the same momentous year. After a discussion of this turning point, we will examine some reading issues that arose as a result of this revolution, especially the problem of how the brain deals with multitasking and how a hierarchy of screens might help to address this problem. All of this will lead us to the ongoing debate about reading on screens versus reading on paper, especially as it relates to the Bible. Is there something significantly different about reading the Bible in a physical book rather than on a screen? With this preview in mind, we turn to the brain and reading.

1) How the Brain Reads and Neural Plasticity

Over the last decade, several important studies have appeared that seek to solve the puzzle of how the brain actually goes about reading. Our eyes take in text (or our fingers take in braille) and our brains translate the images into letters, syllables, words, sentences, and meaning. But how? The development of new brain imaging techniques (especially fMRI)[6] allows scientists to study what parts of the brain are

---

6. fMRI stands for "functional magnetic resonance imaging." fMRI machines measure the blood oxygenation that occurs in the brain in relation to neural activity. It also maps a three-dimensional

activated before, during, and after reading occurs. Two books in particular have been influential in using such imaging techniques to answer the question of how the brain reads: Maryanne Wolf's *Proust and the Squid: The Story and Science of the Reading Brain* (New York: Harper, 2007), and the French neuroscientist Stanislas Dehaene's *Reading in the Brain: The Science and Evolution of a Human Invention* (New York: Viking, 2009). The subject has also been addressed in relation to reading words on a physical printed page versus words on a digital screen in Nicolas Carr's *The Shallows: What the Internet Is Doing to Our Brains* (New York: W.W. Norton, 2010) and Naomi Baron's *Words Onscreen: The Fate of Reading in a Digital World* (New York: Oxford, 2015), along with a host of articles in both academic and more popular journals.[7]

What both Wolf and Dehaene show is that the ability to read is not something that the brain does naturally; it is not a skill with which we are born. This comes as no great surprise, given that it takes years to learn how to read. Whereas spoken language is something that our brains adapt to relatively quickly in the coordination of hearing and speech, reading turns out to be a rather more complex adaptation in which the brain essentially recycles some neurons for the purpose of reading. Although humans have been around for nearly 50,000 years in something like our modern form, humans only started writing about 5,400 years ago, and the alphabet (in any language) only came into existence about 3,800 years ago. How did humans develop this capacity to read? Dehaene's hypothesis is that the human brain eventually gained the capacity to engage in "neuronal recycling." "According to this view, human brain architecture obeys strong genetic constraints, but

---

image of any region of the brain. See Dehaene, *Reading in the Brain*, 69–72; and, for a more general overview of fMRI, Patrick W. Stroman, *Essentials of Functional MRI* (Boca Raton, FL: CRC Press, 2011).

7. See especially E. de Groot, "Problematic Screen Reading: Is it Caused by Our Brain?," *TXT: Exploring the Boundaries of the Book* 1, no. 1 (2014), http://www.txtleiden.org/2014/problematic-screen-reading; F. Jabr, "The Reading Brain in the Digital Age: The Science of Paper versus Screens," *Scientific American* (April 11, 2013), http://www.scientificamerican.com/article/reading-paper-screens/; D. Zax, "This Is Your Brain on E-Books," *MIT Technology Review*, (April 12, 2013), https://www.technologyreview.com/s/513766/this-is-your-brain-on-e-books/; J. Stoop, "Reading and Learning from Screens Versus Print: A Study in Changing Habits," Part 1, *New Library World* 114, nos. 7/8 (2013): 284–300; and Part 2, *New Library World* 114, nos. 9/10 (2013): 371–83; E. Siegenthaler, "Comparing Reading Processes on e-Ink Displays and Print," *Displays* 32 (2011): 268–73; T. Hillesund, "Digital Reading Spaces: How Expert Readers Handle Books, the Web and Electronic Paper," *First Monday* 15, no. 4 (2010); A. Sneed, "Everything Science Knows About Reading on Screens," *Co.design*, http://www.fastcodesign.com/3048297/evidence/everything-science-knows-about-reading-on-screens; Z. Liu, "Reading Behavior in the Digital Environment: Changes in Reading Behavior Over the Past Ten Years," *Journal of Documentation* 61, no. 6 (2005): 700–712; and the older but still valuable survey by A. Dillon, "Reading From Paper Versus Screens: A Critical Review of the Empirical Literature," *Ergonomics* 35, no. 10 (1992): 1297–1326. These are but a few of the studies that have appeared over the last number of years.

some circuits have evolved to tolerate a fringe of variability."[8] Much has been made of "brain plasticity"[9] and the ability of the brain to reshape itself for varying purposes and to varying degrees. From Dehaene's perspective, what he calls "a fringe of variability" is rather limited, and yet, it accounts for the brain's ability to develop the capacity to read.[10] Perhaps more importantly, Dehaene argues that the brain was not designed for reading; rather, writing systems evolved in keeping with our brain's constraints.

Along the same lines of thought, Wolf explains that our brains can learn how to read because there is some degree of open architecture, some degree of plasticity that allows for the formation of new connections and structures between different neurons. Picking up on Dehaene's earlier studies, Wolf states:

> If one were to expand Dehaene's view somewhat, it would seem more than likely that the reading brain exploited older neuronal pathways originally designed not only for vision but for connecting vision to conceptual and linguistic functions ... our brain had at its disposal three ingenious design principles: the capacity to make new connections among older structures; the capacity to form areas of exquisitely precise specialization for recognizing patterns in information; and the ability to learn to recruit and connect information from these areas automatically. ... These three principles of brain organization are the foundation for all of reading's evolution, development, and failure.[11]

While the brain adapts to reading by creating new neuronal circuits, there are limits to the mechanics of reading. Our eyes are not particularly adept at reading, as Dehaene points out. Rather than moving smoothly across a sentence on a page (whether a printed page or a screen), our eyes jerk along in what are called saccades, the rapid movement of our eyes between fixed points. Along the way, our eyes

---

8. Dehaene, *Reading in the Brain*, 6.
9. See Gianfranco Denes, *Neural Plasticity Across the Lifespan: How the Brain Can Change* (Hove, UK: Psychology Press, 2015).
10. "Far from being a blank slate that absorbs everything in its surroundings, our brain adapts to a given culture by minimally turning its predispositions to a different use. It is not a *tabula rasa* within which cultural constructions are amassed, but a very carefully structured device that manages to convert some of its parts to a new use" (*Reading in the Brain*, 7).
11. *Proust and the Squid*, 12. Wolf is drawing on Dehaene's previous books *The Number Sense* (New York: Oxford University Press, 1997); and *From Monkey Brain to Human Brain* (with co-authors J. R. Duhamd, M. Aarber, and G. Rozzolatti; Cambridge, MA: MIT Press, 2003). The "failure" to which Wolf refers is the phenomenon of dyslexia, where the brain's neuronal pathways for reading get a bit confused. Both she and Dehaene devote significant chapters to dyslexia and brain function as a way to understand why the reading process works, but at times does not. (Wolf is the director of the Center for Reading and Language Research at Tufts University.)

actually only "read" two or three letters at a time, which our brains then combine to form words and sense units that are then processed for meaning.[12] The physiology of reading is one thing, but more is involved than just the eyes and the brain, which leads us to consider "haptic reading."

Haptic Reading

Haptics refers to nonverbal communication involving touch. It might come as a surprise, but the rest of our bodies, especially our hands, are also deeply involved in the reading process.[13] When our hands hold a physical book, they communicate information to the brain that supplements what our eyes see. Our hands can feel the thickness of a page. In the case of a print Bible, our hands adapt to turning pages that are often onion-skin thick. These are pages unlike other pages in other books. Our hands tell us that these are somehow special pages. And special they are. Publishers of Bibles often use a special grade of very thin yet opaque paper so that printing on both sides of a page will both be legible (without ink bleeding through from the other side of the page) and still manageable for the fingers to grab and turn a page.

Holding a book in our hands also conveys an awareness of the thickness of the book, including how far we have read with each page turn, and how far we have to go. The feeling of turning a page communicates progress in reading. Haptic sensibility also allows us to turn back a page or two, or to flip through a book with an awareness of where we are in contrast to e-readers with their one single flat screen. Scrolling through virtual pages does not communicate the same extent of information to the brain as does the haptic flipping of physical pages. The text stays put on printed pages, whereas the virtual text is rather ephemeral on the digital page. There is a haptic frame for printed pages that does not exist for virtual pages.

The combination of reading a stable printed page and the haptics

---

12. *Reading in the Brain*, 12–17. "In summary, our eyes impose a lot of constraints on the act of reading. The structure of our visual sensors forces us to scan the page by jerking our eyes around every two or three tenths of a second. Reading is nothing but the word-by-word mental restitution of a text through a series of snapshots" (17).

13. See Anne Mangen, "Hypertext Fiction Reading: Haptics and Immersion," *Journal of Research in Reading* 31, no. 4 (2008): 404–19; Anne Mangen and Jean-Luc Velay, "Digitizing Literacy: Reflections on the Haptics of Writing," *Advances in Haptics*, Mehrdad Hosseini Zadeh, ed., InTech Open Access Publisher (2010); Available from: http://www.intechopen.com/books/advances-in-haptics/digitizing-literacy-reflections-on-the-haptics-of-writing, and Ryo Kitada, "The Brain Network for Haptic Object Recognition," in H. Kajimoto, S. Saga, & M. Konyo, eds., *Pervasive Haptics: Science, Design, and Application* (Tokyo: Springer, 2016): 21–37.

of reading results in something called "haptic memory." As our eyes move across a printed page and as our hands hold a book, our brains perceive a frame of reference that associates printed words and sentences with spatial location. This is why we can often remember where something is on a printed page in a book, but not so much on a screen. One reason for this is the stability of the page in contrast to the variability of where words appear on a screen. But another reason involves the relationship between our short-term and long-term memories and how memories get formed. The more sensory input our brains receive over a longer period of time, the more readily such input gets stored in long-term memory. When we are reading a physical book, the input from both eyes and haptic sensing combine to make the transition from short-term to longer-term memory. As we continue to do more reading on screens, the question remains to what degree our brains will adapt to develop new neural pathways that might result in comparable longer-term memory when we read digital books rather than physical books.

Certainly, the manufacturers of dedicated e-readers are concerned precisely about mimicking the haptic physicality of books as much as possible. This is why so much attention has gone into the development of more readable e-ink, of displaying virtual page turns, of showing the virtual thickness of how much of a book has been read and how much further there is to go, of showing page numbers in addition to location numbers, and most recently, the Kindle's new "Page Flip" capability that shows the actual framed page, as well as adding the capacity to flip backwards and forwards through multiple pages on screen. It would be an understatement to say that e-readers have progressed immensely from Kindle's first release in 2007 to the most recent releases of Kindle's Paperwhite and Voyage e-readers. Still, the jury remains out on how the brain perceives such developments in digital reading when compared to printed physical books.

Location, Location, Location

Related to this haptic knowledge of the page is a kind of knowledge individuals using e-readers tend not to have of the Bible—namely, the location of different books of the Bible, or the order of different books. Students who use e-readers or smartphones for reading the Bible tend not to know that 1 Corinthians comes right after Romans, or that the Acts of the Apostles comes between the Gospel of John and Romans or that Philemon comes just before Hebrews. The canonical order of books in the Bible is typically lost on individuals using e-readers, since they can simply touch the table of contents and jump immediately to whatever book they want, rather than having to flip physically through the pages of a print Bible. I have found that many of my students can, ironically, find a biblical passage on their e-Bibles readily enough, but they have no idea where one biblical text is in relation to any other. When it comes to e-readers and the Bible, the Bible becomes simply one more book that has been downloaded.

Another concern involves the canonical divisions of the Bible and the relative importance of the sections of Torah, Prophets, Writings and Gospels, Pauline Letters, and Catholic Epistles (along with Acts and Revelation). With e-Bibles, such canonical contours get lost. The primacy of Torah and Gospels that emerges from the canonical shaping of the Bible by the faith communities that produced it fades from any sense of immediacy that the Bible as a printed book communicates. Here, the concern is that the e-Bible becomes a book without covers, without boundary markers, no beginning (Genesis), middle (Psalms), or end (Revelation).

In an article for *The Christian Post,* a conservative evangelical web publication, Michael Gryboski asks "Are Digital Bibles as Holy as Paper Bibles?"[14] He begins his essay by recounting a swearing-in ceremony that made a minor splash because the U.S. Ambassador to Switzerland was sworn in on a Kindle version of the Bible, since no physical Bible could be found at the time.[15] For some, the print version of the Bible has, and should have, an inherent respect "that doesn't attach itself to a Kindle or the iPad," a position expressed by Professor Donald Whitney of the Southern Baptist Theological Seminary. Why should such respect be conferred on the print Bible and not on a digital Bible? Whitney explains, "Because the Bible is nothing else. It is a holy book to Christians and it is the Word of God. If you have a digital device it may contain the Bible but it also contains other things."[16] Here, Whitney is invoking the notion of the singularity of the Bible as THE sacred book, which sets it apart from all other books. To be sure, this is a high view of scripture. But is it wrong? Is there a kind of "contamination factor"

---

14. *The Christian Post,* July 15, 2014, http://www.christianpost.com/news/are-digital-bibles-as-holy-as-paper-bibles-123342/.
15. See the story by Brian Fung in *The Washington Post* (June 2, 2014), https://www.washington-post.com/news/the-switch/wp/2014/06/02/a-u-s-ambassador-was-just-sworn-in-on-a-kindle/.
16. *The Christian Post,* July 15, 2014, http://www.christianpost.com/news/are-digital-bibles-as-holy-as-paper-bibles-123342/.

that occurs by lumping the e-Bible together with any number of other books and programs? Some clearly think so.

On the other hand, G. Brooke Lester, a professor of Hebrew Bible at Garrett-Evangelical Theological Seminary (a United Methodist seminary near Chicago), expresses the view that while perhaps unconventional, there is nothing inherently wrong with the idea of being sworn in on a digital Bible. He notes the increasing use of digital Bibles and predicts that their use will become less and less strange over time. Further, he concluded, "if electronic Bibles result in more people reading biblical texts, and not just letting themselves be told what's in the Bible, then digital Bibles will represent a big win for American Christians."[17] In this view, it is the substance of the text, its message and meaning that is most important, and the delivery system is secondary at best. Print Bible, audio Bible, e-Bible—what matters for Lester and others is that the content of the Bible becomes more familiar. For some, that goal would best be accomplished through the use of dedicated print Bibles, so that its special character as scripture would be maintained. For others, like Lester, the form that the Bible takes is quite literally immaterial. Indeed, from this latter perspective, the Bible is unleashed from the shackles of its binding as a print book, and is free to flow through whatever form allows people to encounter God. Here, the notion of "liquid scripture" in different forms might best be compared to how water can be found in solid, liquid, and gaseous forms. In a parallel manner, scripture can be found in solid form (the physical print Bible), liquid form (on screens of all kinds), and in a metaphorical gaseous state (spoken word). Different people will, no doubt, be responsive to the multiple forms that scripture takes as written word, preached word, embodied word, and beyond.

2) Different Kinds of Reading

An awareness of how the brain reads, and how it perceives a physical book in contrast to a virtual book, leads us now to a discussion of different reading strategies that we adopt, depending on what we are reading and what our reading goals might be.

17. Ibid.

Skimming and Expansive Reading

Sometimes, we *skim* or *scan* a text, letting our eyes glance at a table of contents, or fall on topic sentences in a paragraph or on major headings and division markers. In this way, we get the gist of a text without any of the substantive details. As Woody Allen once quipped, he took a speed-reading course and read all 1,200 pages of Tolstoy's *War and Peace* in twenty minutes! His conclusion? "It involves Russia." Perhaps we skim something to discern whether, in fact, we really want to *read* it, word by word, sentence by sentence. Even when we decide we really do want to slow down, sit down, and read, say, a long book or article, we still may decide at times to skim along a few pages that we find boring or too detailed or too technical. I know for a fact that not one student in my thirty years of teaching has actually read all of the genealogy in Matthew 1:1–16! (That's why I always start my Intro NT classes with this exact passage! It looks *so* unpromising, let alone unpronounceable, yet contains some remarkable surprises for the uninitiated.)

This kind of skimming or scanning of text has been described by Ziming Liu as "extensive" reading, where the goal is to work quickly through a large amount of material to get a sense of what it contains.[18] Some would call this "surface" reading, not in a pejorative sense, but in the sense of probing or sampling a text. Academic scholars are well known for doing precisely this kind of power browsing, and given the huge amount of material that comes across most scholars' desks, the ability to skim or scan is crucial. It serves as a kind of reading triage, where one tries to get a sense of what might be more important or less important to tackle in more depth at any given point in time. Such reading is often discontinuous or fragmented, as one leaps about a text.[19]

But what would it mean to read the Bible in this kind of skimming or surface manner? If the Bible is a sacred text that reveals something about God, then do we really want to be skimming or scanning it? Does skimming a text suggest that it is less important than another text that one reads carefully? If we skim through the finer points of sacrificial regulations in the book of Leviticus, does this imply it is less important than other parts of the Bible? It really all depends on one's pur-

18. "Reading Behavior in the Digital Environment: Changes in Reading Behavior over the Past Ten Years," *Journal of Documentation* 61, no. 6 (2005): 700–712.
19. See J. Guillory, "How Scholars Read," *Association of Departments of English Bulletin* 146 (Fall 2008): 8–17.

pose in reading or studying different portions of the Bible. To be sure, some parts of the Bible are typically viewed as more important, and hence authoritative, than other parts. This is partly a function of which faith community is reading the Bible in which particular context. We pay less attention to what we consider the less important parts. In this way, we are always in the process of authorizing and de-authorizing different parts of the Bible. Thus, we might encourage careful reading of Jesus's Sermon on the Mount in Matthew 5–7 as expressing the heart of the gospel, while at the same time giving short shrift to the Epistle of Jude. Thus, in the sixteenth century, Martin Luther saw the Epistle of James as an "epistle of straw" that did not belong in scripture, and he thought the Book of Revelation was a dangerous book that should not be read by Christians. In the twentieth and twenty-first centuries, liberal Protestants have dismissed 1 Timothy 2:8–15 as having any authority because of its view of women as second-class persons who are not fit to provide leadership. The very shape of the biblical canon suggests to many that the Torah portion of the Bible should be considered as more important than the later Writings, since it contains the law of Moses. Similarly, the Gospels should be considered as more important than the letters of Paul since they actually relate substantive information about Jesus rather than Paul's more applied theological interpretations of the significance of Jesus's death and resurrection. Within the Roman Catholic Church, for example, the Vatican II document *Dei Verbum* ("On Divine Revelation" V.18) explicitly states: "It is common knowledge that among all the Scriptures, even those of the New Testament, the Gospels have a special preeminence, and rightly so, for they are the principal witness for the life and teaching of the incarnate Word, our savior." This is why one stands up when the Gospel is read in the Roman Catholic liturgy, and why one sits down for the other readings from scripture.

But to bracket issues of canonical authority for a moment, what would it mean to skim or scan different parts of the Bible? It really depends on one's purpose for doing so. A student in a class on "The Bible as Literature" may well choose to skim various sections of the reading to get the gist of a passage or a genre within the Bible. A parishioner well acquainted with the Bible may decide to quickly review a passage simply to be reminded of a story or saying. A preacher may thumb through a Gospel or a letter of Paul's, glancing at the headings of different chapters, looking to be inspired for a sermon topic or sermon text. Or someone completely unfamiliar with the Bible may take it out of the hotel room drawer and flip through the pages of what remains to them a very strange book.

A theological issue related to skimming the biblical text on a screen versus reading a printed text of the Bible is the question of what has been called a "canonical reading" of the Bible. Various scholars and church leaders have emphasized the "canonical shape" of the biblical text, meaning that the final form of the Bible provides an authoritative interpretive framework for understanding the parts of the Bible in light of the Bible as a whole. In this view, the final form of the canonical text functions as a unified interpretive guide. The most well-known proponent of this approach was Brevard Childs (1923–2007), an influential Professor of Old Testament at Yale Divinity School. One of his goals was to seek a unified approach to the whole of the canonical Bible as Sacred Scripture, over against the fragmentation of the Bible that seemed to be the result of historical critical method and its breaking down the Bible into component parts. As he put it, the shape of the biblical canon "not only serves to establish the outer boundaries of authoritative Scripture, . . . but forms a prism through which light from the different aspects of the Christian life is refracted."[20] Thus, from this view, the order and sequence of the Bible's contents in its canonical form is of paramount importance for understanding the Bible as scripture. Although Childs does not make the claim, it follows that this canonical shaping can really only be fully appreciated in the very physicality of the printed and bound canonical biblical text. (Childs's main work was completed before personal computers and digital Bibles became commonplace.) The unbound Bible on a screen does not lend itself to an immediate awareness of any particular shape of the Bible, canonical or otherwise. From this perspective, skimming the Bible on screens would necessarily seem to undermine understanding the Bible in its canonical frame. Of course, this raises the question of to what degree the shape of the biblical canon (and whose canon?) is an artificial construct of the early church as opposed to part of divine revelation. But for the present, let us return to different kinds of reading without regard to the theological debates over the canonical shape of the Bible.

---

20. Brevard Childs, *Biblical Theology of the Old and New Testaments: Theological Reflection on the Christian Bible* (Minneapolis: Fortress Press, 1992), 672. See also his *Introduction to the Old Testament as Scripture* (Philadelphia: Fortress Press, 1979), and *The New Testament as Canon: An Introduction* (Philadelphia: Fortress Press, 1984). See further J. Siker, "Disciples and Discipleship in the Fourth Gospel: A Canonical Approach," *Studia Biblica et Theologica* 10 (1980): 199–225; and C. Bartholomew and S. Hahn, eds., *Canon and Biblical Interpretation* (Grand Rapids: Zondervan, 2006).

Intensive and Immersive Reading

Another kind of reading is often called "close" reading, "deep" reading, or as Z. Liu calls it, "intensive" reading, and T. Hillesund terms it "immersive reading."[21] Hillesund makes the helpful distinction between "immersive imaginary reading" and "immersive reflective reading." With *imaginary* reading, a reader is carried away into imagined worlds, with rich stories of characters and events. One gets "lost" or "caught up" in the story. In terms of the Bible, some of the parables of Jesus evoke this kind of imaginary reading, especially when done using various devotional techniques such as *lectio divina* or the prayerful imagining of oneself into a biblical story as developed by Ignatius of Loyola in his *Spiritual Exercises*. With *reflective* reading, a reader gets involved with the arguments of a text, with a more abstract and theoretical world of ideas and concepts. In terms of the Bible, the letters of Paul or the Epistle to the Hebrews would, in places, lend themselves to this more reflective approach. With both imaginary and reflective reading, indeed with all the ways one might describe close or deep reading, the reading experience is typically more continuous and connected than discontinuous or fragmented. This approach to reading also takes more dedicated time and a certain isolation so as not to be interrupted.

Finally, just as there are different ways of reading, there are also different types of readers. Maryanne Wolf identifies five types of readers: 1) emerging pre-readers, 2) novice readers, 3) decoding readers, 4) fluent comprehending readers, and 5) expert readers.[22] We typically associate these different kinds of reading with different developmental stages of reading as one grows older and moves from toddler to kindergarten through primary school to junior high and high school, to college and beyond. The more one reads, the better one gets at decoding complications that arise with multiple meanings of words, with various grammatical constructions, and the like. Eventually, we hope, our children will become fluent readers and expert readers.

Of course, there are many adults who never learned to read well,

---

21. Liu, "Reading Behavior in the Digital Environment: Changes in Reading Behavior over the Past Ten Years." T. Hillesund, "Digital Reading Spaces: How Expert Readers Handle Books, the Web and Electronic Paper," *First Monday* 15, no. 4 (2010), http://firstmonday.org/article/view/2762/2504. I still remember being quite surprised when as an undergraduate I sat in a professor's office marveling at all the books, and I asked him (as I have often been asked), "Have you read all of these?" The professor laughed and said "I don't think I've read a whole book in five years!"
22. *Proust and the Squid*, 114–33.

for a variety of reasons. Sometimes, it has to do with a learning disability. Sometimes, it has to do with teachers who promote students along from one grade to another without the students having demonstrated the requisite skills to advance to the next level. Sometimes, it has to do with other circumstances beyond both a teacher's and student's best efforts. Over the last few years, I have been conducting regular Bible studies with prisoners at Men's Central Jail in Los Angeles, typically in groups of 8–12 individuals. After greeting the men, opening with a word of prayer (most often from one of the prisoners), and passing out Bibles for those who did not have one, I would ask them to turn to whatever passage we were going to study. I always asked them to take turns reading out loud, so that they could hear their own voices reading the scriptures. Some did so eloquently. Others struggled to pronounce almost every word. My experience matched what the U.S. Department of Education's 2003 National Assessment of Adult Prison Literacy Survey showed—that a significant number of those imprisoned are either functionally illiterate or operate at a grade-school level of reading. My point is simply that what Wolf shows in regard to different types of reading can be found across different populations, regardless of age. (Reading the Bible in prison is, to be sure, a whole other subject than the topic of this book. Still, it is significant that prisoners have no access to the kinds of digital reading that we take for granted.)

3) Different Genres for Reading

In addition to different kinds of reading and readers, there are also many different genres for reading. As we learn to read, we also learn to adapt our reading to the kind of genre we are reading. Thus, we read a letter to the editor in a newspaper differently than we read a recipe for a cauliflower casserole, and we read a crossword puzzle differently than we read a cartoon, or a lengthy news story, or an obituary, or a box score from a baseball game, or a short story, or a novel, and so on. This is the case, regardless of whether we are reading something on paper or on some kind of screen. The brain still processes the letters and words or images of these different genres in the same way—recognizing patterns and processing them to produce meaning. But part of producing the meaning of what we read involves being attentive to the kind of genre we are reading. Such attention allows a poem to soar in our imagination, a cartoon to be funny, a political news report to motivate us to write or call our congressional representative, a box score to cheer or lament our hometown team.

The Bible, of course, also has different genres, and we adapt our reading strategies to the kind of genre we are reading, whether it be the laments from the Psalms, the wisdom sayings from Proverbs, the prophetic invective from Amos, the love poetry from the Song of Songs, the genealogy from Matthew 1:1–16, the parables of Jesus from Mark 4, the passion narrative from Luke 23, one of Paul's letters, the historical narrative of the Acts of the Apostles, or the wild apocalyptic images from the book of Revelation. And this is to name but a few of the genres we encounter in the biblical text. Whether we are reading the Bible in print form or on screens, the kind of material we are reading makes a difference for how we read. Being attuned to genre marks a central feature of appropriate reading and interpretation. Ignoring the kind of material we are reading will inevitably lead to misreadings of the Bible, whether in print or on screens. Further, if we ignore the fact that we are always engaged in the process of *interpreting* what we read, whether as individuals or as communities of faith, we do so at the peril of any kind of serious reading.

4) Not All Screens Are Created Equal

When personal computer screens first came flickering to life in the 1980s, there was no question that very few people would do any extensive reading on these monochrome screens with very limited options for how to display text. I have vivid memories of my first computer, a Kaypro II, which I purchased in 1983 for around $1,600, a small fortune for a graduate student. It had a 2.5 MHz microprocessor with a miniscule 64 KB of RAM, dual single-sided 5¼-inch floppy disks, and an 80-column green monochrome 9-inch CRT display. By contrast, a 2017 Apple MacBook Pro has a speed of 3.6 GHz, well over 1,000 times faster than the old Kaypro, with up to 16 Gigabytes of RAM, and up to 1 TB of internal memory, along with external drives that can hold even more Terabytes of data, and dazzling color on flat screens, both large and small, with incredible resolution and speed. Clearly, over the years, the computer revolution has continued unabated. IBM introduced CGA and EGA graphics in the 1980s to add color display. MacIntosh computers followed a parallel track, starting off with monochrome displays in the early 1980s, and introducing color displays on the Mac II in 1987. That same year, IBM brought out multisync VGA screens for their popular PS/2 (Personal System 2) line of computers, a video display that became the industry standard. Multisync VGA technology, which had been pioneered by NEC (formerly the Nippon Electric Company), allowed for different resolutions, scan frequencies, and refresh rates, all at the same time. All of these displays were the relatively bulky CRT screens (Cathode Ray Tubes) that had been familiar from televisions for decades. But in the late 1990s and early 2000s, Liquid Crystal Display screens became sufficiently advanced that these relatively flat-screen color LCDs grew increasingly popular. By 2007, LCD screens were out-selling the older style CRT displays, completely replacing them a few years later as LCD screens became thinner, more powerful, and less costly. But so far, we have really only been discussing desktop computer screens, which were, after all, the primary ways in which digital technology first came to individual consumers.[23] At this point, people had certainly become accustomed to reading web pages (remember Netscape?), e-mails, and pdfs (portable document files) on screens, but few people envisioned doing any serious reading of extended books such as the Bible on desktop or laptop computers.

Fig. 4.1. The Kaypro II (1983).

23. See   http://www.pcworld.com/article/209224/displays/historic-monitors-slideshow.html#slide 20.

5) The 2007 Revolution: iPhone and Kindle are Born

But then came 2007, and with it, a new revolution within the ongoing revolution of digital technology, digital communication, and digital screens. In January 2007, Steve Jobs introduced the world to Apple's revolutionary iPhone, combining phone, music, and internet in one hand-held device.[24] And thus was the first truly "smartphone" born. The touchscreen gave it quite literally a more tangible feel, and the use of Corning's "Gorilla Glass" gave the device a durability not seen in previous displays.[25] A quick succession of upgrades appeared over the following years. In 2008, the iPhone 3G, which now boasted third-party applications in the newly introduced "App Store" was introduced. This would be a crucial development, as now digital Bibles and Bible apps could be downloaded onto the phone. The single most popular Bible app, "YouVersion," was also launched in 2008 on the App Store, and quickly grew to be the most widely downloaded (and free) Bible app (more on YouVersion later). The iPhone 4 appeared in 2010, now with a sharp Retina display screen and the new social media program Face-Time (in addition to the juggernaut Facebook, which had been available on the app store since 2008). This was followed in 2012 with the iPhone 5, sporting yet another redesign that included a larger screen and vastly improved speed, memory, and battery life. Since then, the iPhone 6 has appeared in various iterations,[26] and most recently, the iPhone 7 has appeared with an updated operating system.[27] With the 10th anniversary of the iPhone (June 2017) at hand, most everyone anticipates the release of the iPhone 8 with still further major enhancements.[28] (See Fig. 4.2G.)

It is also important to call attention to Apple's release of the iPad in 2010, and its subsequent cousins, which hovered between phone and laptop, and which provided a portable user-friendly large screen for reading. And, of course, there are many other smartphones and tablets by other manufacturers that have been quite successful, especially the

---

24. Rene Ritchie, "History of the iPhone: Apple Reinvents the Phone," *iMore*, August 31, 2015, http://www.imore.com/history-iphone-original; Rene Ritchie, "History of iPhone 3G: Twice as Fast, Half the Price," *iMore*, September 1, 2015, http://www.imore.com/history-iphone-3g.
25. See https://en.wikipedia.org/wiki/Gorilla_Glass.
26. Rene Ritchie, "iPhone to iPhone 6: History in Specs," imore.com, September 23, 2014, http://www.imore.com/iphone-iphone-6-history-specs.
27. Apple's iPhones are not, of course, the only significant smartphones on the market, nor are they universally praised. Google's Android software has been a fierce competitor to Apple's iPhone, especially in the Galaxy series of smartphones manufactured by the Samsung Corporation. See https://en.wikipedia.org/wiki/Samsung_Galaxy#Release_history.
28. https://www.macrumors.com/roundup/iphone-8/.

Android phone and tablet, along with other Windows-based hardware/ software. I have focused here on the iPhone because it truly marked the dawn of a new kind of interface that would become so important for digital Bibles.

The other revolutionary development from 2007 was Amazon's introduction of the dedicated Kindle e-reader.[29] The first-generation Kindle reader had a six-inch display with four shades of gray, resizable fonts, and the capacity to hold hundreds of books that could be downloaded over a 3G network, or synced to a computer. The first Kindle created quite a buzz in the worlds of reading and publishing alike. It was now possible to carry a huge library of books that could be accessed at will, digitally. While the quality of the virtual printed page paled in comparison to the real thing, it was nonetheless quite readable. Even at nearly $400 apiece, the first Kindles sold out in less than six hours. Amazon had begun life as an online bookseller in 1995, eventually adding CDs and many other items to its inventory. Around the same time, Google announced its plan to digitize millions of books from dozens of prominent libraries. There had already been slightly more modest projects to digitize books, like Project Gutenberg (founded by Michael Hart in 1971) and the Perseus Digital Library Project, which began in 1985 at Tufts University, with a focus on digitizing texts from the Greco-Roman world.[30] But the plans announced by Google sent shock waves through book publishers, the offices of copyright lawyers, and libraries trying to decide how to anticipate navigating the future balance between physical and digital collections. Amazon was poised to take advantage of the growing trend toward digital books, and the introduction of the Kindle in 2007 solidified a shift toward both digital books and reading on digital devices.

Just as Apple came out with one generation of the iPhone after another, so did Amazon produce new versions of its dedicated e-reader. The Kindle 2 appeared in 2009 in a slimmer form with enough memory to hold some 1,500 e-books. It added a feature that allowed the text to be read out loud, as well as support to include the downloading and reading of pdf files. 2010 saw the release of the Kindle DX and the Kindle DX Graphite (with much-improved e-ink), a larger screen format (9.7-inches compared to the 6-inch regular Kindle) that was geared

29. David Nield, "A Brief History of the Amazon Kindle: The Gadget That Changed Reading," *The Gadget Website*, August 6, 2015, http://www.t3.com/features/a-brief-history-of-the-amazon-kindle.
30. See M. Lebert, *A Short History of EBooks* (1971–2008) (NEF, University of Toronto, 2009), available as a free e-book from Project Gutenberg, http://www.gutenberg.org/files/29801/29801-pdf.pdf. See also http://www.perseus.tufts.edu/hopper/.

toward the reading of newspapers and magazines. The DX did not sell well, even after the Kindle DX Graphite was released, with much-improved e-ink and even with increased contrast for easier reading. The DX was discontinued after only a few years on the market. Digital books outsold print books on Amazon for the first time in 2011. The Kindle 4, Kindle Touch-Screen (Kindle's first touch-screen), Kindle 5, and Kindle Paperwhite were released in quick succession in 2011 and 2012. The Paperwhite boasted a much improved screen for reading, so that whether reading in direct sunlight or in a dark room, the text on the screen could still be read quite easily. It also included dictionaries in multiple languages. The 2013 Kindle Paperwhite 2 added better pdf support, along with better translation and note-taking capabilities. It added a new font (Bookerly) to reduce eye strain, and packed more pixels per square inch than ever before (300 ppi). With adjustable light and a no-glare screen, it was a very lightweight and compelling e-reader. The 2014 Kindle Voyage added still greater screen resolution with automatic illumination depending on the ambient lighting. Beyond the different models of Kindle, the Kindle software has also been upgraded on a regular basis not only for hardware Kindles, but also for the Kindle app versions on smartphones, tablets, and computers. The most recent software improvement available on Kindles (summer 2016), and on Tablet readers with the Kindle app, is "Page Flip," which makes a serious move toward functioning more like a physical book by adding page borders and the ability to scan several whole pages at once to improve navigation. This development represents a clear effort to add a virtual sense of haptic perception to the reading experience. Just as there are many good smartphones in addition to Apple's flagship iPhone, so there are a few good e-readers in addition to Amazon's flagship Kindle. Barnes and Noble's Nook has made a small but significant dent in the market, as has the Kobo reader. But the various Kindles have cornered much of the market in dedicated e-readers.[31] The primary virtue of the Kindle, in addition to its constantly improving screen, has been its dedicated focus on reading, unlike the iPad or other tablets, which included myriad distractions to reading by virtue of having web access and streaming video. (See Fig. 4.3.)

31. For a comparison of e-book readers, see: https://en.wikipedia.org/wiki/Comparison_of_e-book_readers.

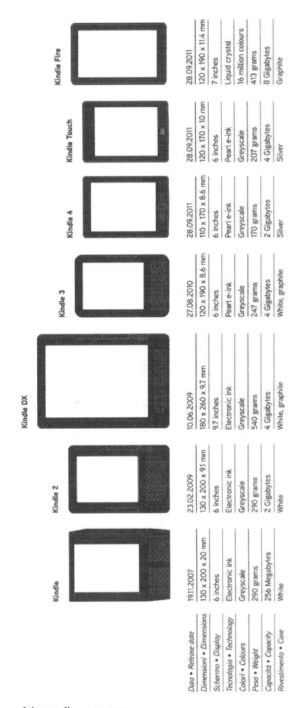

Fig. 4.3. History of the Kindle, 2007–2011.

The synergy between smartphones and e-readers has truly been nothing short of revolutionary for reading and publishing. The hardware and software platforms of both smartphones and e-readers have, to some degree, become blended, in large measure because of the apps that can run on smartphones and tablets alike. While I currently prefer to read e-books on my iPad using Kindle software, my wife prefers reading on her iPhone 6 or on her Kindle Paperwhite. She uses an older iPhone for listening to stories, while I rely on my iPhone for texting and talking, but not reading. I have a Kindle Paperwhite, but prefer the slightly larger screen size of the iPad (the regular one, not the mini!). Ironically, I also find it easier to highlight and mark text in the Kindle app on the iPad, rather than the hardware Kindle. My mother-in-law (Margie) loves her Kindle Paperwhite and reads everything on it. She has macular degeneration, which makes any reading difficult, but the ability to change both the font and especially the size of letters makes it ideal for her. She also prefers the smaller size of the Kindle in comparison to a tablet, and she is not particularly interested in having the kind of web access that a tablet provides. She reads novels and especially her Bible on her Kindle. Without the Kindle (or some kind of e-reader), she would no longer be able to read her Bible, which she would sorely miss. (At 88, she still goes to two or three Bible studies a week at her local Methodist church.) Each person's experience of the now ubiquitous smartphones, tablets, and e-readers will, of course, be somewhat different. We will have more to say about all this in the next chapter that looks at survey data regarding the use of such devices for reading the Bible.

6) The Reading Brain and the Print vs. Pixels Debate

When personal computers first came on the scene in the early 1980s, there was little thought that anyone would do serious reading on computer screens. Not only were screens bulky and stationary, they were extremely limited in their capabilities. Most often, they could only display monochrome text, with color monitors not becoming standard until the late 1980s for both IBM PCs and Apple computers. While the introduction of LCD screens and especially flat screens in the new millennium made reading screens easier, reading on a computer screen remained a relatively clunky experience, even on emerging portable laptop computers.

Fig. 4.4. The Reading Brain.

Already, by the early 1990s, important studies were being carried out comparing reading on screens with reading on paper. The most significant study was Andrew Dillon's 1992 "Reading From Paper versus Screens: A Critical Review of the Empirical Literature."[32] At the time, of course, he was looking at various studies dealing with what, from our perspective, were relatively primitive screens. His general conclusions certainly reflect the problems with image quality on screens and practical issues with portability of screens in the late 1980s and early 1990s. This was still very early on in the world of personal computing, with strong advocates on both sides regarding either the superiority of the printed book or the inevitable superiority of the screen as self-evident.

A 2005 study by Ziming Liu examined "Reading Behavior in the Digital Environment: Changes in Reading Behavior over the Past Ten Years."[33] He concluded that in an increasingly digital environment, younger readers (digital natives) would likely learn to use a variety of reading strategies on screens (browsing, keyword spotting) in an attempt to cope with the growing mountains of available digital information. But he also noted that readers would continue to use printed media, often printed from digital sources, and that print media was

32. *Ergonomics* 35, no. 10 (1992): 1297–1326.
33. *Journal of Documentation* 61, no. 6 (2005): 700–712.

better especially for in-depth reading as it usually involves annotating and highlighting. In 2005, making annotations on digital screens was awkward at best.

As we have seen, however, everything changed in 2007 with the introduction of the iPhone and the Kindle. As each generation of smartphones, tablets, and e-readers have improved, what had once been thought unlikely at best (reading on screens) is now ubiquitous. All of these developments lead to a natural comparison between reading print on a page versus reading pixels on a screen. In general, the current verdict remains fairly consistent that the brain comprehends and remembers content from reading printed pages better than from reading digital screens. After surveying over 100 studies from researchers in psychology, computer engineering, and information science, a recent *Scientific American* article (2013) concludes:

> evidence from laboratory experiments, polls and consumer reports indicates that modern screens and e-readers fail to adequately recreate certain tactile experiences of reading on paper that many people miss and, more importantly, prevent people from navigating long texts in an intuitive and satisfying way. In turn, such navigational difficulties may subtly inhibit reading comprehension. Compared with paper, screens may also drain more of our mental resources while we are reading and make it a little harder to remember what we read when we are done.[34]

To be fair, there are some studies that conclude a fairly level playing field exists between paper and screens, especially with the technological improvements in e-ink.[35] But such studies are very much in the minority.

A recent 2016 Dartmouth study compared screen reading versus paper reading with a focus on what kinds of learning comprehension took place in each format. Their findings added another dimension to the differences between learning from screens versus paper. In short, they found that screen reading helped to reinforce details of learning, but paper reading helped better with understanding abstract concepts.[36] As the researchers put it, using the analogy of seeing the forest

34. Ferris Jabr, "The Reading Brain in the Digital Age: The Science of Paper vs. Screens," *Scientific American,* April 11, 2013, http://www.scientificamerican.com/article/reading-paper-screens/.

35. E. Siegenthaler, P. Wurtz, P. Bergamin, & R. Groner, "Comparing Reading Processes on e-ink Displays and Print," *Displays* 32 (2011): 268–73. See also A. K. Taylor, "Students Learn Equally Well From Digital as From Paperbound Texts," *Teaching of Psychology* 38, no. 4 (2011): 278–81.

36. The study concluded: "individuals who completed the same information processing task on a digital mobile device (a tablet or laptop computer) versus a non-digital platform (a physical print-out) exhibited a lower level of construal, one prioritizing immediate, concrete details over abstract,

or the trees, reading on digital screens was good at helping readers see the trees, but reading on paper was better at helping readers see and conceptualize the forest.

So why do most studies conclude that reading comprehension is better when reading on paper versus reading on screens, and how might all of this apply to reading the Bible in a physical book rather than on a digital screen? Three factors in particular contribute to this general pattern of conclusions: distractions, multitasking, and how our eyes physically read screens in contrast to print.

Distractions

In his recent *New York Times* opinion piece, "Addicted to Distraction," Tony Schwartz recounts how he had come to realize that he was finding it increasingly difficult to marshal sufficient concentration to read anything more than a page or two in the many books that were stacking up on his bedside table. The cause? He was spending so much time online, reading bits and pieces of emails and data and simply clicking away at different sites that he was training his brain to have a very short attention span. "The brain's craving for novelty, constant stimulation and immediate gratification creates something called a 'compulsion loop,'" all leading to his growing awareness of his diminishing attention.[37] Nicholas Carr begins his book *The Shallows* with a similar account of his own experience. "I used to find it easy to immerse myself in a book or a lengthy article. . . . That's rarely the case anymore. Now my concentration starts to drift after a page or two. I get fidgety, lose the thread, begin looking for something else to do."[38]

As we all know, reading takes dedicated concentration. The more that distractions enter in to our reading, the less we comprehend of what we are reading. That is why if we find ourselves off in a daydream while reading, we have to go back and re-read the previous sentence or paragraph to get a renewed sense of the narrative flow. A book has only one dedicated function—to be read—and one interface, the printed page. There is nothing within the book itself to distract. Distractions may arise when something else enters our field of vision or

decontextualized interpretations." G. Kaufman & M. Flanagan, "High-Low Split: Divergent Cognitive Construal Levels Triggered by Digital and Non-digital Platforms," *Proceedings of the 2016 CHI Conference on Human Factors in Computing Systems* (2016), 2773.
37. T. Schwartz, "Addicted to Distraction," *New York Times*, Sunday Review, Opinion; November 28, 2015, http://www.nytimes.com/2015/11/29/opinion/sunday/addicted-to-distraction.html.
38. *The Shallows*, 5.

a sound startles us. Thus, seeing a person walk past or hearing a leaf blower outside can distract us. And so, we lift our eyes from the page, and then, have to re-engage our concentration on what we were reading, at least if we were reading anything that might be considered a longer form of reading (a book, a short story). But digital screens, especially on smartphones and tablets, have multiple functions and various apps that are frankly designed to interrupt and distract. If we are reading on a smartphone, there is every chance that our reading will be interrupted by a text message, a tweet, a calendar reminder, a phone call, an instagram, and so on. The situation is even worse if we are reading a website article or book (or Bible) on a laptop or desktop. Websites on computer screens are designed to interrupt with pop-ups, with ads, with one window nested inside another, with scrolling text, with one image after another, with the invitation to click on one thing that leads to another. The only linear reading on any website is the linear reading path that each user creates as they click merrily along.

Just as an example, take a look at a very popular Bible website, biblegateway.com. (See Figs. 4.5G and 4.6G.) As the webpage opens, we are shown a variety of choices on which to click. It is a relatively straightforward and uncluttered website. Still, a host of options awaits. What first catches our eye (and that's what it does) is the "Verse of the Day." The verse in the screenshot happens to be the NIV version of Luke 1:68–70—"Praise be to the Lord, the God of Israel, because he has come to his people and redeemed them. He has raised up a horn of salvation for us in the house of his servant David (as he said through his holy prophets of long ago)." Why this is the "verse of the day" is not at all clear. It does not appear to be the lectionary reading for today.[39] You can also choose to listen to an audio reading of the verse (as read by Max McLean, from The Listener's Audio Bible). The reader/viewer is also offered the opportunity to subscribe to the Verse of the Day, to have it e-mailed to your inbox each morning. Should you choose to subscribe to this free service, be advised (as the small print does) that

39. I had a very helpful email exchange with folks at biblegateway.com about the Verse of the Day. In response to my question about how the Verse of the Day was selected, I received a reply that stated "I asked a member of our content team, and he said the verse of the day list has been around so long, no one is really quite sure of its origins. The best we could find described it this way: 'Our Verse of the Day Scripture passages were initially selected based on popularity, importance, and other factors.'" I then sent a follow-up question asking if there was one person who decided on the verses and how far in advance they were scheduled. Again I received a very helpful response: "There isn't one person who makes the decision for the verse of the day. We have the whole year planned already and it's the same each year. You can actually access all the verses using this link: https://www.biblegateway.com/usage/votd/votdlist/." My thanks to the biblegateway.com staff.

By submitting your email address, you understand that you will receive email communications from Bible Gateway, a division of The Zondervan Corporation, 3900 Sparks Drive SE, Grand Rapids, MI 49546 USA, including commercial communications and messages from partners of Bible Gateway. You may unsubscribe from Bible Gateway's emails at any time. If you have any questions, please review our Privacy Policy or email us at privacy@biblegateway.com.

"Fair enough," I think. Beneath this, I am given the opportunity to click on an ad that will take me to an ATT website to shop for the "best data network." (On another occasion, there was an ad for an investment service for "investors who want to retire comfortably," if you happen to have a $500,000 portfolio.) The ads rotate when I refresh the screen, as now there is an ad for tracking my smartphone. *"Why was I on this page? Oh yeah, the Bible, the Bible,"* I think to myself. I can keep scrolling down the page to four rectangular boxes: Create Your Account; Our Blog; Scripture Engagement; Bible Gateway Plus. It's almost like the TV gameshow *Let's Make A Deal,* where you are enticed to choose what's behind Door #1, Door #2, or Door #3, though in this case, there is also Door #4 (and there are no zonks). Below these possibilities are links to the "Latest from Bible Gateway." Today's "Latest" includes *The Beyond Suffering Bible,* a new Bible from Zondervan, which operates Bible Gateway, as well as "Use Emoji to Search the Bible on Bible Gateway;" and "The Wired Soul: An Interview with Tricia McCary Rhodes," with the teaser "Technology has greatly improved much of our lives, but in the process our brains (and souls) are being daily rewired and disoriented. View this post." To the right of this are books that Bible Gateway recommends for discounted purchase. Today's offerings include *The Jesus Storybook Bible: Every Story Whispers His Name,* and *The Best Yes: Making Wise Decisions in the Midst of Endless Demands.* This last title would certainly be useful in navigating the website! (The book titles also rotate to various other books.) Having scrolled down the page, I now scroll to the very top, where I see a black banner with several clickable options: the Home icon, and then four headings to the immediate right—Bible—Study—App—Store. When I let the arrow hover over Bible, submenus appear beneath both Bible and Study. The submenus give me more options. The left-hand submenu offers: Passage Lookup, Keyword Search, Available Versions, Audio Bibles, and Bible Engagement. The right-hand submenu offers: Topical Index, Devotionals, Reading Plans, Newsletters, and More Resources. Hovering over "App" does nothing, and hovering over "Store" brings up four options: Bible

Gateway Plus, Bibles, Audio, and More. ("*I suppose I should have begun here at the top of the screen,*" I think.) When opening Bible Gateway, the cursor blinks in a blank box, inviting me to "Enter keyword, passage, or topic." Tough choice. Just for fun, I type "computer," but I get zero results. To be expected, I suppose, given that the word "computer" does not appear in the Bible.[40] So, I choose "love" instead and am rewarded with all 686 appearances of "love" in the Bible, in the NIV version. This turns out to be a "keyword search." I can, of course, choose any of 150 versions in 50 languages to search. But I will stick with English. I select the New Living Translation, and find 759 references to love in that version, which raises the interesting issue of translation: the NLT has translated some Hebrew or Greek words with "love" some 73 times more than the NIV. I imagine I will get a different number of references for "love" with each new translation I select, given the various ways the Hebrew and Greek words for "love" get translated in different versions.

In all, there are over 50 possible things to click on in this one web page. Such large quantities of embedded hypertexts have become the norm rather than the exception. Even on web pages such as Bible Gateway that are relatively well organized and easy to navigate, the potential to be led down any number of rabbit holes is huge. How many times have you clicked along on a website and then thought, "Um, what was I doing or looking for? How did I get here?" Repeated distractions are disorienting, and most computer screens are designed precisely to get you to click away with abandon. Even if all we wanted was to open the Bible and read the Gospel of Matthew online, the display would be rather cluttered, with a great variety of potential disruptions along the way. We do not typically think so painstakingly about websites and their designs, but just describing the available options on this relatively user-friendly Bible website gives us a clue about how navigating even a Bible website might lead less to a deepened understanding of the Bible than to what Nicholas Carr describes in relation to the Internet overall as "the shallows"[41] In a chapter entitled "The Juggler's Brain," Carr addresses the problem of all the distractions the Internet presents. "The Net seizes our attention only to scatter it."[42] As a result,

---

40. Here, I am reminded of a wonderful line from Woody Allen from his book *Without Feathers* (a play on an Emily Dickenson poem; New York: Ballantine Books, 1986). One section of the book is entitled "The Scrolls," about some suspect ancient scrolls that have been discovered. Their antiquity is suspect because the word "Oldsmobile" occurs several times in the text!
41. *The Shallows: What the Internet is Doing to Our Brains* (New York: Norton & Co., 2010).
42. Ibid., 118.

we find it difficult to settle on any one thing for the prolonged length of time it takes for our brains to engage in deep reading, or for longer-term memories to be formed. Rather, we click and skip from one thing to another, typically scanning and then moving on.

In truth, websites such as Bible Gateway (bible.org, ebibleteacher.com, biblestudytools.com; biblehub.com) with all of the clickable options are clearly aimed at deepening familiarity with the Bible, including practical reading exercises. And that can only be good. (*Honest.*) But it does raise a troubling question: can we be led into a deeper understanding of the Bible through a medium that encourages shallow engagement? Or is it possible to move beyond "the shallows" of the online world, even as we make use of the myriad tools for online bible study, and progress into genuinely deep reading, engagement, and reflection upon the Bible and its interpretation? This is a question to which we will return toward the end of the book.

What were we discussing? Oh yes, distractions. But now, a second issue arises that is related to the problem of distraction—namely, multitasking.

Multitasking

As we noted above, physical books are single-function objects. They are designed for only one purpose—to be read. One can certainly try to multitask while reading a book. For example, listening to music while reading is possible because the two activities activate different parts of the brain. But when song lyrics come into play, then reading is compromised because both reading and lyrics activate the language center of the brain, and the two compete. Many people think they are adept at multitasking. They think they can talk on the phone, browse the web, send text messages, post Facebook photos, listen to music, watch TV, and study or read all at the same time! Alas, almost all studies show that this is not the case. In fact, what the studies show is that multitaskers typically do each task poorly.[43]

43. See the following more popular summaries of the research: J. Taylor, "Technology: Myth of Multitasking," *Psychology Today*, March 30, 2011, https://www.psychologytoday.com/blog/the-power-prime/201103/technology-myth-multitasking; Evin O'Keefe, "How Multitasking is Killing Your Brain," *High Performance Blog*, July 8, 2015, https://www.teamwork.com/blog/the-myth-of-multitasking/; I. Lapowsky, "Don't Multitask: Your Brain Will Thank You," April 8, 2013, http://www.inc.com/magazine/201304/issie-lapowsky/get-more-done-dont-multitask.html; T. Bradberry, "Multitasking Damages Your Brain and Career," *Forbes.com*, October 8, 2014, http://www.forbes.com/sites/travisbradberry/2014/10/08/multitasking-damages-your-brain-and-career-new-studies-suggest/#2dc43d8d2c16; Kendra Cherry, "Multitasking: A Few Reasons Why Multitasking Reduces Productivity," VeryWell.com, May 22, 2015, https://www.very-

The *desire* to multitask and make efficient use of our time makes perfect sense. But the *reality* of multitasking is quite another matter. The problem with the idea of the multitasking brain is very fundamental. To put it simply: our brains are not designed for complex multitasking. Walking and chewing gum at the same time? Sure. Preparing a meal you've cooked 100 times before while listening to NPR or talking with a guest in the kitchen? Yes. But reading a textbook for a class while watching a Netflix movie you haven't seen before and carrying on a texting conversation with three friends? Not so much. Attempting to engage in multiple complex tasks at the same time is like overburdening a computer's CPU (Central Processing Unit) and overtaxing its RAM (Random Access Memory). The more tasks we assign, the slower it goes, until finally it crashes and we get the wheel of death on the screen. The same thing happens to our brains when we multitask complex and competing processes. The more things we ask our brain to control, the slower and less efficient it gets.

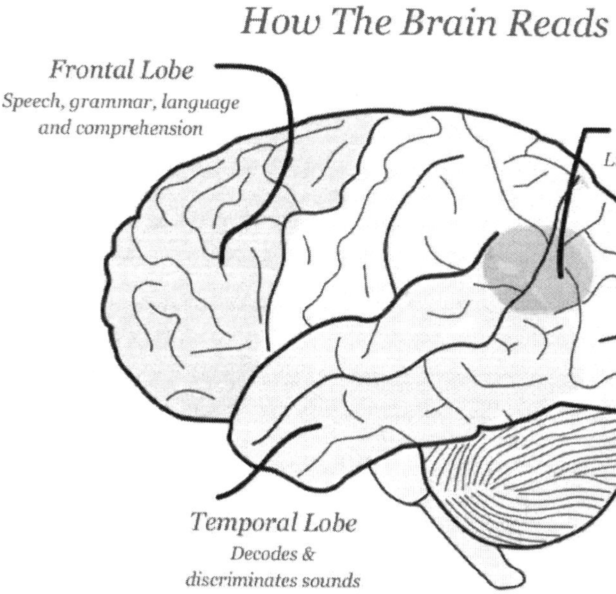

How The Brain Reads

Fig. 4.7. How the Brain Reads.

well.com/multitasking-2795003. The most comprehensive, if technical, research study is Dario D. Salvucci and Niels A. Taatgen, *The Multitasking Mind* (New York: Oxford University Press, 2011).

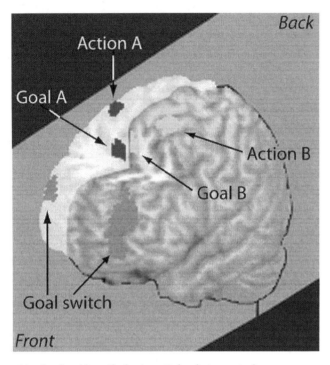

Fig. 4.8. Cognitive load and how the brain switches between tasks.

The problem with multitasking has to do with the *cognitive load* it places on our brains. Cognitive load refers to the total amount of working memory our brains use in any given task. Our brains are just not well equipped to carry out multiple demanding tasks at the same time. Brain scans show that when we introduce a new task, our brains engage in a switching process that takes both energy (oxygenated blood) and time. The more complicated the task, the more energy and time it takes. And if we try to take on too many mental tasks at the same time, our brains go into cognitive *overload*. "When the load exceeds our mind's ability to store and process the information — when the water overflows the thimble — we're unable to retain the information or to draw connections with the information already stored in our long-term memory."[44] Naomi Baron describes this as a "central processing bottleneck" in our brains.[45]

44. *The Shallows,* 125. See also Torkel Klingberg, *The Overflowing Brain: Information Overload and the Limits of Working Memory* (New York: Oxford University Press, 2009).
45. *Words Onscreen,* 179. Ironically, those who see themselves as accomplished multitaskers turn out to do worse on standard dual-task experiments than those who have less confidence about their

As Dario Salvucci and Niels Taatgen have shown, "multitasking in the head is often more intense, and more difficult to work around, than multitasking of the hands or eyes. One good example is trying to read while others are talking: the cognitive, and more specifically linguistic, workload of both tasks creates interference and makes the dual-task scenario difficult."[46] They argue that multitasking behavior can be expressed as cognitive threads—independent streams of thought that work to accomplish both simple and complex tasks. Not all tasks, of course, require the same level of cognitive attention. Tying a shoelace becomes a rote task after repeating it thousands of times. But I clearly recall my children concentrating hard on the task (with tongues poking out for added concentration) when they first were learning to tie their own shoes! Thus, there is a continuum of multitasking that ranges from concurrent multitasking (for things that have a very low cognitive load) to sequential multitasking (for things that have a high cognitive load). Concurrent multitasking is when our brains can handle multiple relatively simple cognitive threads at the same time, whereas sequential multitasking refers to how our brains function when we attempt to handle more complex sets of cognitive threads at the same time, like reading a book while also surfing the web, or driving a car and texting at the same time.[47] With sequential multitasking, our brains do things one at a time, with significant loss of concentrated understanding should we try to switch too quickly from one complex task to another.

What does this mean for the reading the Bible on screens? If we are reading the Bible on dedicated e-readers whose sole purpose is displaying the text of books, then such dedicated screens will significantly reduce the problems of comprehension associated with multitasking. If, however, we are reading the Bible on a web page (as we saw above), then chances are we will both be distracted by all the bells and whistles of a Bible website, and we will have decreased comprehension of what we are reading in the Bible due to the cognitive load that multiple screens place on our brains.

---

multitasking abilities. See Eyal Ophir, Clifford Nass, & Anthony Wagner, "Cognitive Control in Media Multitaskers," *Proceedings of the National Academy of Sciences* 106, no. 37 (2009): 15583–87.

46. *The Multitasking Mind*, 6. Salvucci and Taatgen have developed a general field theory of multitasking that they call "threaded cognition." Their goal is to explain why we are good at multitasking some things, but not very good at others.

47. Ibid., 8, 43.

Skimming Eyes

Beyond the issues of distractions and multitasking, studies of eye movement when reading show differences between how we read the physical pages of a book compared to how we read screens. The basic distinction is between what is called Z-Shaped Pattern reading and F-Shaped Pattern reading. When we read physical book pages, our eyes start on the left-hand margin and move horizontally to the end of one line, and then, return at a slight downward angle to the beginning of the next line, to the end of that line, and so on. Thus, the Z-Shaped Pattern. But when we read computer screens (in this case, web screens) the dominant reading pattern is F-Shaped. What this means is that we begin reading at the top left of a screen and go across the first line on the screen to the end, as with reading a physical book page. But then, when our eyes move down to the next line, we read across in a second horizontal movement that typically covers a shorter area. Our eyes start to scan down the left-hand side of the screen (if we are reading left to right) and glance to the right in a line of text to see if there are keywords that should command our attention. Reading in a Z-Shaped Pattern requires, quite naturally, more concentration and more time. Reading in an F-Shaped Pattern requires less concentration and is faster, because we are not so much reading screens as we are scanning and skimming them.

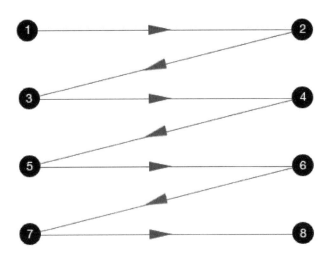

Fig. 4.9. Z-Pattern Reading of Print Text.

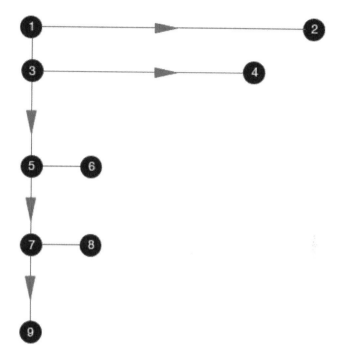

Fig. 4.10. F-Pattern skimming of screens.

See Fig. 4.11G for heat maps from user eye-tracking studies of three websites. The areas where users looked the most are colored red; the yellow areas indicate fewer views, followed by the least-viewed blue areas. Gray areas did not attract any fixations.

The basic research on the physiology of reading screens was conducted by Jakob Nielsen and published in 2006, and has subsequently been refined and confirmed.[48] The implications of this research are rather significant for web page design. First, users will not read online texts thoroughly in the typical word-by-word manner that is the case with Z-Pattern reading of physical pages. Exhaustive reading on web pages is rare; it is called web-*browsing* for a reason! Even when it comes

---

48. "F-Shaped Pattern for Reading Web Content," *Nielsen Norman Group,* April 17, 2006, https://www. nngroup.com/articles/f-shaped-pattern-reading-web-content/. The Nielsen Norman Group is a research and consulting firm. This initial study eventually grew into a book based on an analysis of 1.5 million instances where users looked at websites, with the goal of understanding how the human eyes interact with design: J. Nielsen & K. Pernice, *Eyetracking Web Usability* (Berkeley, CA: New Riders, 2010). Their confirmation of F-Shaped reading on the web has been enormously influential in web design. See, e.g., J. Bergstrom & A. Schall, eds., *Eye Tracking in User Experience Design* (Amsterdam: Elsevier, 2014); and S. Krugg, *Don't Make Me Think, revisited: A Common Sense Approach to Web Usability,* 3rd ed. (Berkeley, CA: New Riders, 2014).

to well-designed pages such as the Bible Gateway site we explored above, it remains the case that users will skim and scan rather than engage in any kind of deep reading experience. Second, users will pay most attention to the top left of the screen since from an early age we learn to start there with any "page." This is why web designers typically put the most important information at the top of the screen. Readers will read more of a first paragraph than a second or subsequent paragraphs. Third, the text that is most easily read are short bullet points down the left-hand side of a screen page. These patterns in reading computer screens are general, and there are important variables such as the mixture of text and image on a screen. Still, Nielsen's studies indicate that users typically only read about 20 percent of text on a given website.[49]

7) The Hierarchy of Screen Bibles

Even with all of the different choices for reading on screens, a clear hierarchy has emerged for reading e-books, regardless of what kind of digital book we might be reading. From best to worst, the general hierarchy of text display is as follows. At the top are dedicated e-readers such as the Kindle Paperwhite or Kindle Voyage, which excel at and aim for one thing—to duplicate as much as possible the experience of reading a physical book, with the added bonus of what e-readers can do in terms of storing thousands of books and having screens that can change lighting, font, and size of the text. Next are tablets such as the iPad, which have such apps as the Kindle software, and which operate much like dedicated e-readers, with the added bonus (or distraction) of the multifunctional ability to access a web browser, text messenger, e-mail, photos, music, and any manner of digital multimedia. Next come laptop computers, with larger screens and reading software, and which are still sufficiently lightweight and portable for personal use, if not for taking to a church service. And in last place are standard desktop computers. Even with their flat screens and high resolution, they are the least comfortable and most eye-straining for dedicated reading of much beyond an e-mail or a text message.

Yes, I know. We've left out smartphones. The personalization and miniaturization of computers into smartphones has clearly won the

49. J. Nielsen, "How Little Do Users Read?," *Nielsen Norman Group* (May 6, 2008) https://www.nngroup.com/articles/how-little-do-users-read/. See further N. Carr, *The Shallows*, 134–37; and N. Baron, *Words Onscreen*, 42–43, 164–65.

day for portability when it comes to multifunctionality. We increasingly use them for virtually (!) everything from banking to texting to gaming to talking to reading to taking photos and videos to . . . to . . . to. . . . The apps seem endless, as does the process of updating and auditioning new apps on a regular basis. The usability of smartphones is very much a moving target, as they have developed and matured at a rapid pace. In 2009, Jakob Nielsen described "mobile usability" as an oxymoron; that is, usability was very poor. But since then, in newer studies from 2015 by the Nielsen Norman Group, researchers found marked improvement in the usability of mobile devices.[50] In particular, the release of smartphones with larger screens (now called *phablets!*), such as the iPhone 6 and 6 Plus, has generated an increase in the number of books being downloaded and read on smartphones. The ergonomics of the larger screen sizes appeal to many users. (The average screen size has grown from 3.9 diagonal inches in 2011 to 5.1 diagonal inches in 2014.) In her *Wall Street Journal* article, "The Rise of Phone Reading," Jennifer Maloney writes "it's not the e-reader that will be driving future book sales, but the phone."[51] Since people always carry around their smartphones, but mostly leave e-readers and print books at home, if an opportunity for reading should arise, they will read on their smartphones, especially if they have a larger screen size to facilitate reading.

Screen size matters. This is one reason why smartphone screens keep getting bigger and bigger. The iPhone screen has almost doubled in size in its current 6 form when compared to its original 3-inch size. Screen size matters because the more limited the amount of text that the eye can take in, the smaller the context, with the consequence of reduced comprehension. The eye cannot simply glance at what comes before or after a section of text for orientation. This is readily done in a physical book, but one has to scroll up or down on a screen. It may not seem like a big deal, but the brain finds this all rather disorienting, as it has to re-establish physical parameters and physical frames. In a printed book, the physical parameters and frame of the page remain constant, even if the eye has to scan before or after a particular text. Yes, one does, at times, have to turn a page, but the brain remem-

---

50. R. Budiu, "The State of Mobile User Experience," *Nielsen Norman Group,* March 22, 2015, https:// www.nngroup.com/articles/mobile-usability-update/; R. Budiu, "Mobile User Experience: Limitation and Strengths," *Nielsen Norman Group,* April 19, 2015), https://www. nngroup.com/articles/ mobile-ux/.
51. J. Maloney, "The Rise of Phone Reading," *The Wall Street Journal,* August 14, 2015, http://www. wsj.com/articles/the-rise-of-phone-reading-1439398395.

bers the physical contours of the page one was just on, allowing for smoother transitions than occur when scrolling through digital text on screens.

Another factor that makes the Bible on smartphones not so smart has to do with the atomization of the text. This is related to the problem of screen size and decontextualization. When you have a print Bible and are looking for a passage, there is a linear awareness, even a tactile awareness, of the shape of the biblical canon as a whole. Torah, Prophets, Writings, Gospels, Letters. Want to find the Psalms? Just open the Bible in the middle. Want to find the book of Revelation? Just go to the end of the New Testament. Not so with digital Bibles. Yes, you can do a search and enter book, chapter, and verse, but that gives you no sense of the canonical shape of the Bible as a whole. This does not matter so much for historical studies of the origins of the biblical texts. But it does matter for the life of the church, past and present, and for the continuous stream of the history of biblical interpretation. Because the Bible as a book with covers has functioned throughout Christian history as the primary and common touchstone of the Christian narrative, it actually does matter to be familiar with the historic form of the Bible as a written text. Yes, the Bible has also been presented in passion plays and in images on stained glass windows. But even these dramas and images are grounded in the written text and a general sense of the linear narrative of the physical Bible. Knowing where something is in the Bible, knowing something of its topography, is part of knowing the story it tells. With digital Bibles, gone are the "sword drills," or speed drills of racing others to find particular passages in the (print) Bible. This has meant less familiarity with what is where in the Bible, and in general, less familiarity with the content of the Bible as a whole.

One inherent problem with reading on smartphones is directly related to their greatest strength—their portability and multitasking capacities. Because they are portable and we take them everywhere with us, the probability of being distracted and interrupted while trying to read is greatly increased. The other great feature of smart phones—multitasking—also makes it difficult to have much confidence that there will not be difficulties with reading comprehension, given the number of apps that we often have open at once on our phones. If we are toggling between e-mail, messages, web links, music, texting, and reading the Bible, should we really be surprised that depth of comprehension might suffer significantly in the process? As for studies that show our eyes scanning more than reading digital screens, it remains unclear if the relatively small screen size of smartphones means that reading suffers the same difficulties as on larger screens, with our eyes scanning more than actually reading.

When my daughter-in-law Meredith heads out of her house to attend a Bible study, she is typically loaded down with at least two children (a four-year old and a baby), which means she also has diaper bag, purse, stroller, and more. The convenience factor of simply relying on her iPhone Bible rather than adding a bulky study Bible to her already well-loaded arms means that she has gotten used to reading the Bible on her iPhone screen. She uses her regular print Bible at home, but the ability to shift back and forth from print to screen has everything to do with the practicalities of life. It's still the Bible, at least in content if not in traditional form. So there can clearly be a functional benefit to digital Bibles, whether for my mother-in-law in light of her macular degeneration, or for my daughter-in-law in light of being a mother of small children.

The fact that we typically always have our smartphones close at hand is precisely what has driven the popular YouVersion app of the Bible. Their motto is "The Bible Is Everywhere." With over 275 million downloads, that's not far from the truth! And if the Bible is with you, then you always have the opportunity to read it, even if episodically. The presumption here is that any exposure to the Bible is good, whether you have two minutes or two hours to read. The app is clearly evangelical in scope, and proudly so. By offering the app for free in over 1,500 versions and in over 1,000 languages, the clear goal is to promote Bible literacy for anyone with access to a smartphone and an internet connection. There are a number of other Bible apps for smartphones and tablets that offer similar features as YouVersion, all of which we will discuss in more detail below. I point to YouVersion in this context simply as the most widespread Bible app available for smartphones. The app is well known in evangelical circles, if not in academic ones.

Digital Bibles and Plastic Brains?

Before drawing this chapter to a close, it is important to call attention to one particular factor that is as yet unknown about the potential of the reading brain in relation to digital screens. In short, as a species, humans have to date really only lived with digital screens for a very limited period of time, hardly a generation—and much less than a generation if one takes 2007 as the starting point for a dramatic shift to digital screens for reading. What if we simply do not yet know whether the human brain will become better at retaining information presented in digital form on screens? While the studies of Dehaene and Wolf, on the physiology of the reading brain, mentioned early on in this chapter, are not particularly optimistic, who knows? Is it possible that we simply need to live for a longer period of time with these screens, especially as they continue to evolve, before we really know enough to say anything definitive? After all, as a digital immigrant, I can attest that while I did all right with early computer games (Pong, Mario Brothers, et al.), my digital native sons had what appeared to be a sixth sense for quickly navigating incredibly complicated and sophisticated video games that I could only watch them play with not much understanding, given how fast things moved (Final Fantasy, Minecraft, Call of Duty, and any number of sports games). Is it possible that our brains will continue to develop to become better at dealing with distractions, with multitasking, with the limitations of our physiology? Will future generations of readers become as adept at retaining information from digital books as current readers are with print books?[52] And yet, at the same time, it is noteworthy that even digital natives tend to prefer physical print when it comes to reading material that they really want to study and learn. Future studies will doubtless continue to probe these and related questions.

Summary and Conclusions

So where does this discussion of Bibles, brains, and screens leave us? Several trends stand out. First, it is abundantly clear that there is no turning back from all that books on screens have to offer. They are instantly accessible, typically much less expensive than physical books, can be downloaded by the truckload onto a small handheld device, can be read on various platforms that are all synced with each other, can be adjusted for different font size/style and lighting, and as a result, are increasingly more reader-friendly. This does not mean, of course, that print books are on the way out. But they are being challenged by reading on screens of all kinds. Second, it is equally clear that most studies show individuals have better comprehension when reading physical ink on paper than virtual pixels on screens. As we have seen, there are various reasons for this having to do with several problems inher-

52. My thanks to Prof. Mark George for pressing this question in private correspondence.

ent in screen reading: distraction, the myth of multitasking, and our tendency to scan and skim screens rather than really reading them. Third, when we apply the first two conclusions to reading Bibles on screens, we find ourselves attracted to the potential of digital screens, yet also somewhat cautious about the possibility of decreased understanding and shallower reading of the sacred scriptures. We have also seen, fourth, that not all screens are equal when it comes to reading. The closer the approximation to physical paper, the better the comprehension and the more likely we will remember what we read. Fifth, how do we address the concern that individuals reading the Bible on screens are reading an amorphous book without covers? Do people have any real sense of the geography of the biblical text itself, of what's where, when using digital Bibles on screens? There are both additional beneficial aspects to digital Bibles, and additional problems and concerns. This is to be expected in the first generation or two of the rapid transition to the digital age. The age of print remains, but we do wonder if, in fact, it is the late age of print, as well as how reading habits and comprehension will be affected as we move ever more fully into the digital realm.

I close this chapter with yet another question about reading the Bible, whether in print form or on screens. It is a question that could be raised at any point along the way in our discussion of digital Bibles on screens. Simply put: does one, in fact, read the Bible like any other book? On the one hand, there is no easy answer to this question. If we read a book with an awareness of its character and the contexts that led to its writing, then yes, we can and do read the Bible like any other book. But on the other hand, we do not typically view the Bible as "any other book." It is a sacred text. Scripture. While it is true that the different books in the Bible are far more varied than chapters of perhaps any other book, nonetheless, it remains a book, and has been one for most of Christian history in one form or another. It could be argued that the only real cohesion in the Bible is the glue in its physical binding, but that would be a gross exaggeration. The cohesion rests in the common sense that the Bible (at least the Christian Bible) is telling the story of God's relationship to Israel, the coming of Jesus, and the life of the earliest church. It's not far from the Gospel of Luke's sense of the narrative of God's salvation history.

Perhaps the irony inherent in our concern regarding discontinuous reading is that the unified text of the Bible has long been read episodically. This is the case whether we are talking about the lectionary cycle or one of many Bible reading plans. There may be continuous reading from one week to the next, or there may be a good deal of skipping around and editing of passages assigned for reading. In other words, do we really read the Bible in other than an interrupted manner? Interrupted by the events of a week between Sundays, or interrupted by discontinuous blocks of reading, or interrupted by constant cross-referencing between one passage and another, sometimes in the same book, but often between rather disparate texts. Does reading the Bible on an e-reader really create any more displacement for the reader than already exists? We shall return to this question toward the end of the book.

5

———

Survey Says . . .

So what are people actually doing with digital Bibles? What are the trends? Having explored some of the issues related to the history of digital Bibles and how our brains read screens—including Bibles on screens—what kind of data do we have about real-life use of digital Bibles? While Naomi Baron (*Words Onscreen*) and others have carried out surveys on digital reading in general, relatively few surveys have been conducted that examine the use of digital Bibles in particular. But let us begin by painting the larger picture of what surveys show about reading digital books in general. Within that context, we can then turn to the more specific question about what surveys indicate about the use of digital Bibles.

General Surveys on Digital Books

There are a number of surveys about digital book usage in general, from the reading public, to e-textbooks in school, to publisher and university surveys. They all point to a common trend. After the introduction of the Kindle in 2007 and the iPad in 2010, e-reading took off; people downloaded millions of e-books, and sales of paper books slumped. Prognosticators were ready to declare the death of paper books in anticipation that these trends would continue. As it happens, however, e-book sales have fallen off somewhat recently, and sales of paper books have stabilized. E-books still make up a larger share of the book market today than they did when Kindles and iPads were introduced, but the trends indicate that people are reading both digital screens and printed paper. Print does not appear to be going away, and digital does not appear to be swallowing print whole. At least in the American market, consumers are hybrid readers. Much the same can be said for international book markets in Europe and Asia. At the 2016 BookExpoAmerica (BEA), Rüdiger Wishenbart, the Director of International Affairs for the trade group, issued the annual Global Ebook Report:

> Altogether, what we currently see is most probably the 'end of the digital beginning,' and the beginning transition into the next, perhaps even more challenging phase, where writing, publishing and reading morph into fluid settings; where any content, in any format, is available for almost any user — yet without much stability both with regard to who is offering what, as well as how that offer is taken in by the many fickle audiences around the world.[1]

Similar fluctuations were reported by a Pew Research forum in October 2015. The report on reading books showed that overall, the percentage of individuals who have read at least one print book in a given year has declined from 71 percent in 2011 to 63 percent in 2015, a drop of 8 percent. During that same period, the percentage of individuals who had read a book in any format dropped from 79 percent to 72 percent, a drop of 7 percent. So the drop in those reading books in general and books in print were roughly equivalent. As for e-book readers, the survey showed an increase from 17 percent in 2011 to 27 percent in 2015, a significant 10 percent gain showing a clear acceptance and trend toward e-book reading. This should not be a great surprise, given that the iPad had just been introduced in 2010, and that newer versions of the Kindle were still selling strongly. Still, between 2014 and 2015, e-book reading fell by 1 percent. In terms of sales (a different measure than the percentage of individuals reading print or e-books), the Pew report concluded that "Digital sales, which comprise about 20% of the market, have slowed sharply, while print sales have stayed relatively strong, according to the Association of American Publishers."[2] This is a

---

1. https://tinyurl.com/lc2bpg8. The behemoth Amazon does not report on its e-book sales, which is but one recurring difficulty in analyzing e-book sales overall. Since 2015 Amazon has opened several brick and mortar bookstores.
2. https://tinyurl.com/nflnwwn.

slightly different story than what had been reported a year and a half earlier in a Pew study from January 2014. That report saw e-book reading at 28 percent (slightly higher than 2015), but even more significantly, it showed that half of Americans now own either a dedicated e-reader or a tablet on which they read.[3] The sharp increase in ownership of digital reading devices accounts for much of the increase in e-book reading overall. It is still important to note that print book versus e-book reading is not in any way a case of either/or; rather, it is both/and.

In her book *Words Onscreen,* published in early 2015 (with research completed in 2014), Naomi Baron draws on publisher and marketing research, on studies carried out by various universities conducting experiments with e-textbooks, and on her own studies of reading patterns among college students in the United States, Germany, and Japan. Her research shows a convergence of the different studies that points in a common direction. Overall, students prefer reading printed textbooks to e-textbooks. Roughly 60 percent of students preferred reading from printed materials rather than from digital displays. The longer the text to be read, the more students preferred reading print rather than screens. Even when students indicate a preference for reading on screens, often they will print out the material to be read so that they can mark up the text for studying. Students have a significant preference for printed text when it comes to making annotations and taking notes. A *Washington Post* story from February 2015 picked up on Baron's work and showed that college students, digital natives all, largely preferred reading in print rather than on digital screens.[4]

Textbook makers, bookstore owners, and college student surveys say millennials still strongly prefer print for pleasure and learning, a bias that surprises reading experts, given the same group's proclivity to consume most other content digitally. A University of Washington pilot study of digital textbooks found that a quarter of students still bought print versions of e-textbooks that they were given for free in digital form. Don Kilburn, the North American president for Pearson (the dominant presence in educational publishing), put it well: the move to digital "doesn't look like a revolution right now. It looks like an evolution, and it's lumpy at best."[5]

---

3. http://www.pewinternet.org/2014/01/16/e-reading-rises-as-device-ownership-jumps/.
4. Michael S. Rosenwald, "Why digital natives prefer reading in print. Yes, you read that right." *The Washington Post,* February 22, 2015.
5. Ibid.

The National Association of College Stores issued a 2015 "Student Watch" report on "Attitudes and Behaviors Towards Course Materials," which indicated that adoption of digital course materials was growing at a relatively slow rate of 3 percent per year.[6] In addition, a 2016 report from the Independent College Bookstore Association entitled "Going Digital: Faculty Perspectives on Digital and OER Course Materials"[7] included a survey question about when faculty thought course materials would primarily be in digital form. Almost a quarter of the respondents (24 percent) answered "Never." The report also indicated that faculty are somewhat skeptical about the added value and instructional benefit of digital content. In general, it appears that an initial surge in digital content has slowed, and that both paper and digital materials will continue to be used in teaching and learning.

Beyond college students and textbooks, the real question is whether readers of print texts are reading significantly different kinds of material than readers of digital texts. The surveys tend to show that e-readers have been popular for shorter texts and for consuming what Baron calls "gulps of information."[8] This is certainly one reason why such traditional publications as *The New York Times* has had relative success with the digital market, though for its smartphone users the subscription model has now been replaced by the free NYT Now app. (Digital subscriptions to the "paper" are still available on tablets and computers.) Digital screens appear more user-friendly for lighter reading than for more serious deeper reading. Baron refers to this phenomenon as "Brighton Beach Reading,"[9] namely, the kind of reading you might take to the beach during a vacation: a magazine, a short novel, one-off reading, something that does not require much commitment or concentration. And since, as we have seen, digital displays do not necessarily lend themselves to much concentration, it makes sense that digital readers are good for lighter fare (especially if they also come equipped with multitasking functions).

What do surveys show regarding why individuals might prefer e-readers to print books? Baron summarizes the main appeal of digital reading, condensing them to five basic factors: convenience, cost, possible environmental benefits, democratizing access, and addressing the high cost of textbooks for education.[10] By comparison, in September

6. http://www.nacsfoundation.org/research/studentwatch.aspx.
7. http://www.campuscomputing.net/sites/www.campuscomputing.net/files/GOINGDIGITAL-2016 ICBAFacultySurvey_2.pdf. OER stands for Open Educational Resource.
8. *Words Onscreen*, 19.
9. Ibid., 93–96.

2015, the *National Book Review* published a somewhat tongue-in-cheek list of "10 Reasons to Love E-Books" over print books:[11]

1. You can search them.
2. The environment.
3. They are cheaper.
4. Size. Ever go on a long vacation? (replete with reference to beach reading!)
5. No one gets to see the title and judge you for your terrible taste in literature.
6. Getting published is cheaper so there are more authors, and more books.
7. You can have your book anywhere, since you are already carrying your cell phone.
8. You can get almost any public domain book for free.
9. References and citations can be hyperlinked.
10. You can read in the dark!

This list was generated in response to a report that e-book sales had declined by 10 percent, while print book sales were fairly stable. A week later, to balance the scales, the *National Book Review* published another top ten list, this time singing the praises of print books, again somewhat tongue in cheek:[12]

1. Print books have pages that are nice and soft to the touch, making reading physically pleasurable.
2. Print books lead to greater comprehension and memory of what was read.
3. Print books are yours for life and are tangible.
4. Print books are physical reminders of your intellectual journeys.
5. Print books are great to share.

10. Ibid., 62–92. The possible environmental benefits include saving trees, reducing the polluting effects of manufacturing paper, and a lower need for landfills or recycling for paper trash. The potential environmental impact of increased production of digital devices and the spread of server farms has been less studied.
11. Noah Benjamin-Pollak, "Rant: 10 Reasons to Love E-Books," *National Book Review*, http://www.thenationalbookreview.com/features/2015/9/24/rant-10-reasons-to-love-e-books-despite-those-new-sales-numbers. See also Michael Angier's "Top Ten Reasons Why E-Books Are Better than Print Books," http://successnet.org/cms/sales-and-marketing/top-ten-reasons-why-ebooks-are-better-than-printed-books. Angier's reasons include, additionally: e-books are quicker to obtain (downloading), they are more easily updated and upgraded, and the technology will continue to be upgraded.
12. "Drop That Kindle! 10 Reasons Print Books are Better than E-Books." http://www.thenationalbookreview.com/features/2015/10/2/drop-that-kindle-10-reasons-print-books-are-better-than-e-books?rq=Drop That Kindle.

6. You can write in the margins of a print book, dog-ear the important pages, and underline the key sentences with a pencil.

7. Print books have jackets, so people know what other people are reading —which makes reading a community-building act.

8. Print books are fairer to writers, giving authors a higher percentage of royalties than for e-books.

9. Print books are better for your health, since light-emitting e-books can interfere with the ability to sleep.

10. Print books are theft-resistant (i.e., who wants to steal a physical book?).

The author also gives a bonus reason to prefer print books: if you drop a print book in the bathtub, you can dry it out with a hairdryer. (An e-reader would not likely be as forgiving.)

Humor aside, the reasons on both sides are given fairly often. And again, it's not an either/or so much as it is a both/and. But what about digital Bibles versus print Bibles? What do surveys have to say about that comparison?

Surveys on the Use of Digital versus Print Bibles

Beginning in 2011, the American Bible Society began commissioning an annual "State of the Bible" report from the Barna Group, an evangelical Christian research and polling firm based in Ventura, CA (*https://www.barna.org*).[13] The surveys are relatively general in scope, and are based on over 1,000 telephone interviews and another 1,000 online surveys using a nationally representative panel. The primary goals of the 2011 survey were to determine four things: perceptions of the Bible, Bible penetration,[14] Bible engagement, and Bible literacy. Within the different areas of the survey, questions were asked regarding: beliefs about the Bible, the Bible's role in US society, how many people owned a Bible, how often people read the Bible, what version of the Bible people read, motivations for reading the Bible, frustrations with reading the Bible, and different formats used—including digital

---

13. The Barna Group has conducted dozens of surveys ranging from American views on police brutality, to evangelical views of Hollywood, to what Americans believe about abortion, or cohabitation, or any number of other topics.

14. "Bible penetration" refers to the number of Bibles owned by households in America, what kinds of individuals/families own Bibles, and how many people purchase Bibles. From 1998 to 2013, the percentage of households owning a Bible has dipped slightly, from 92% to 88%. Elders and Boomers are more likely to own a Bible, while Millennials are less likely. The American Bible Society/Barna Group, *The State of the Bible 2014*, p. 9, http://www.americanbible.org/uploads/content/state-of-the-bible-data-analysis-american-bible-society-2014.pdf.

formats. Each successive year, additional components have been added to the survey, such as "Politics and the Bible" (2013), "Moral Decline and Social Impact" of the Bible (each year since 2012), and "Giving to Non-Profit Organizations" (each year since 2013). There are also occasional briefer updates from the Barna Group, such as the October 2013 report on "How Technology is Changing Millennial Faith," the April 2014 report on "The State of the Bible: 6 Trends for 2014"; and the October 2014 report on "Millennials and the Bible: 3 Surprising Insights." In addition to the regular 2015 State of the Bible report, the American Bible Society also issued a separate report on the State of the Bible in relation to Teens (February 2015), asking the same kinds of questions, but with a focus on teenagers.[15] The 2016 State of the Bible report focuses on "What Do Americans Believe about the Bible and Politics"—not overly surprising, given the political events of 2016 surrounding the U.S. presidential race.[16] The Barna Group has also now published *The Bible in America: 6-Year Trends*, a more comprehensive study that presents a cumulative analysis of their polling on the Bible in America from 2011 to 2016.

For our purposes, the most significant data that has been published by the American Bible Society and the Barna Group has to do with the use of digital or print Bibles. The 2011 report includes two tables related to digital use of the Bible. In their first table (Table 3.9; p. 53), respondents are asked to indicate all formats of the Bible that they have used in the preceding year. Beyond the general data gathered for different formats, the survey also breaks down respondents by generation and religious affiliation (see Fig. 5.1). As you can see from the table, nearly 90 percent of all respondents indicated that they read from a print version of the Bible on their own, while 37 percent stated that they used the internet or a computer to read Bible content. Only 18 percent stated that they searched for Bible verses or content on a smartphone, and even fewer (12 percent) stated that they read an electronic version of the Bible on an e-reader. A second table (3.10; p. 54) asked how many individuals had downloaded a Bible app onto their phone. Only 13 percent had done so in the 2011 survey.

15. http://www.americanbible.org/uploads/content/Teens_State_of_the_Bible_2015_Report.pdf.
16. http://news.americanbible.org/blog/entry/corporate-blog/state-of-the-bible-2016-what-do-americans-believe-about-the-bible-and-polit.

TABLE 3.9
BIBLE FORMATS USED
Question: These days, the Bible is available and used in different formats. For each format I read, please tell me whether or not you have used that format in the past year?

% among Bible readers	all adults	Mo-saic	Bust-er	Boom-er	Elder	prac-ticing Prot-estant	prac-ticing Cath-olic	non pract. Chris-tian	no faith/other faith
read from a print version of the Bible on your own	89%	80%↓	89%	92%	89%	93%↑	98%↑	84%↓	89%
attended a small group or Bible study, where you studies the Bible in a group, not including weekend worship services	53	50	56	48	60	71↑	40↓	36↓	39
used the Internet on a computer to read Bible content	37	50↑	43	39	10↓	42↑	26	30↓	57↑
listened to an audio version of the Bible	28	26	29	29	26	36↑	19	20↓	21
listened to a teaching about the Bible via podcast	24	29	23	23	23	26	23	18↓	36
searched for Bible verses or Bible content on a smart phone or cell phone	18	37↑	23↑	14↓	3↓	22	8↓	15	22
read an electronic version of the Bible on an e-reader such as Kindle or iPad	12	17	13	12	4↓	13	13	8	16
n=	633	85	200	242	97	269	46	209	52

Note: A (↑) or (↓) sign indicates that data for that segment is statistically significantly higher or lower than the total response for all adults. Differences are statistically significant at the 95% confidence level or higher.

Fig. 5.1. The State of the Bible 2011.

By 2015, the situation had changed significantly. Here, the "Use of Bible Formats" portion of the State of the Bible report had a couple of surprises. The first surprise was that the percentage of individuals who said they read a print Bible on their own was 93 percent (up from previous years). The second surprise was, I suppose, not really a surprise at all so much as it was a clear indication that digital Bibles had taken off. "Half of all Bible readers say they used the Internet on a computer to read Bible content (50%); 40% searched their smartphone or cell phone to find Bible content or Bible verses; and 35% downloaded or used a Bible app on their smartphone."[17] (See Fig. 5.2G.) The report also showed that the two youngest generations (Millennials and Gen-

17. "The State of the Bible 2015," 20.

Xers) led the way in using digital Bible formats (19 percent preferred a smartphone or tablet app). When asked to choose which Bible format they preferred to use, 76 percent of all respondents stated their preference for a print version of the Bible, while 11 percent preferred a smartphone/app, and 6 percent each preferred online and audio versions.

The years between 2011 and 2015 indicated a similar growth in the use of digital Bibles. "The data shows a continuing shift to digital formats. The number of readers who use their smart phone or cell phone to search for Bible content has increased each year, with a six percent increase from 2013 (18% in 2011, 23% in 2012, 29% in 2013, and 35% in 2014)." In 2014, about one-fourth of adults (24 percent) read the Bible on an e-reader (e.g., Kindle, iPad), compared to just 17 percent in 2013. The number of people who used tablets and smartphones to search the Bible almost doubled during 2011–2014 (from 18 percent to 35 percent), but in 2014, 84 percent still preferred to read the Bible in print, compared to only 10 percent who preferred digital screens. The 2015 State of the Bible for Teens showed, unsurprisingly, that teens make the greatest use of digital Bibles overall. Close to half (44 percent) of teens have used their cell phone or smartphone to search for Bible verses or Bible content. More than a third say they have downloaded or used a Bible app on a smartphone (38 percent) or used the Internet to read Bible content (36 percent). As more and more digital natives mature, so also will the use of digital Bibles.

As I was submitting the final copy-edited manuscript of this book to the publisher, I came across one final report from the Barna Group, the *State of the Bible 2017: Top Findings* (posted April 4, 2017).[18] In the section relevant to use of digital Bibles, the report indicates that Bible users still prefer print, but increasingly they also use other formats. The report states: "The way Americans engage with the Bible is changing. Though most Bible users (91%) still prefer to use a print version of the Bible when engaging with scripture, an equal number (92%) report using another Bible format than print in the past year. Use of technology-related formats are all on the rise. More than half of users now search for Bible content on the internet (55%) or smart phone (53%), and another 43 percent use a Bible app on their phones. Since 2011, the use of basically every other Bible format has increased."

Beyond these annual reports from the American Bible Society,

8. https://www.barna.com/research/state-bible-2017-top-findings/.

another national study on "The Bible in American Life" was released in 2014 by the Center for the Study of Religion and American Culture, housed at Indiana University/Purdue University in Indianapolis (IUPUI) and funded by the Lilly Endowment. Somewhat like the American Bible Society, the IUPUI study began collecting data on the Bible in American life in 2011. Their goal was to provide a "perspective on the Bible's role outside of worship, in the lived religion of a broad cross-section of Americans."[19] This study has a more academic focus than the more ecclesial focus of the "State of the Bible" reports from the American Bible Society. The IUPUI study made use of two flagship survey groups, the General Social Survey (GSS), conducted every other year by the University of Chicago's National Opinion Research Center, and the National Congregations Study (NCS). By surveying participants, they sought to garner information both on individual views of the Bible and congregational approaches to the Bible in America.

Section 8 of the study takes a look at "Reading the Bible on the Internet and E-Devices," tracking how technology has been changing the way people read. Overall, they found that 31 percent of Bible readers use the Internet to read the Bible, and 22 percent use e-devices for that purpose (p. 7, 31). Among these digital Bible-readers, the study found differences in terms of age, income, and educational level. Those under 60 years of age are more likely to use digital Bibles, whereas those over 60 are much less likely to do so. Lower income and less well-educated households tended to read the Bible in print rather than with digital devices. As the report explains, in part, this may be due to the simple fact that lower income households simply cannot afford computer ownership and broadband Internet at the same rate as wealthier and more highly educated households.[20] The educational level was a particularly noteworthy factor in use of digital Bibles (and digital resources in general). The general conclusion of the report is that "younger people, those with higher salaries, and most dramatically, those with more education among the respondents read the Bible on the Internet or an e-device at higher rates" (p. 32).

Neither the American Bible Society/Barna surveys nor the IUPUI survey draw any correlations concerning *how* individuals or congregations using digital Bibles interpret the Bible similarly or differently

19. "The Bible in American Life," 2.
20. See *Exploring the Digital Nation - America's Emerging Online Experience*, United States Department of Commerce, June 2013. http://www.esa.doc.gov/reports/exploring-digital-nation-americas-emerging-online-experience.

from those using print versions of the Bible. Both sets of surveys show that regardless of print or digital format, the King James Bible still remains the dominant version used, though it is losing significant ground to the NIV (New International Version) in particular.[21] The official Roman Catholic version of the Bible (the NAB, New American Bible) and the typically preferred Bible for academic study, the NRSV (New Revised Standard Version), both trail far behind.

In addition to the publication of the formal IUPUI survey, a 2014 conference was also held in Indianapolis on "The Bible in America." One session of the conference was devoted to "The Bible as Book: From Print to Digital."[22] Within that session, one paper included some survey information about the use of digital Bibles: John Weaver (Abilene Christian University), "Transforming Practice: American Bible Reading in Digital Culture." Weaver was interested in two questions related to digital Bibles: 1) whether people who read digital Bibles continued the practice of reading print Bibles as well; and 2) to what extent readers of digital Bibles engage in religious practices most often associated with print Bibles, for example, memorizing biblical passages. In order to gather some data that would help answer these questions, Weaver posted a survey on the public discussion boards of two very popular Bible software companies, BibleWorks and Accordance Bible. (Though both programs work on either PCs or Macs, BibleWorks has long been a go-to program for PCs, while Accordance Bible has long been associated with Macs.) He received 112 responses to the 20-question online survey. Part of his goal in getting responses from this participant pool was to get a sample from individuals of different religious backgrounds who were likely to have used digital tools for reading and studying the Bible.

It is understandable, given the sample pool, that 86 percent of those surveyed affirmed that they regularly read the Bible in a digital format. The most common formats used were an app on a smartphone or tablet (73 percent) or a Bible program on a desktop or laptop (53 percent). A

21. See Paul C. Gutjahr, "From Monarchy to Democracy: The Dethroning of the King James Bible in the United States," in H. Hamlin and N.W. Jones., eds., *The King James Bible after 400 Years: Literary Linguistic, and Cultural Influences* (Cambridge: Cambridge University Press, 2010), 164–80.
22. The other two papers were by: Daniel Vaca (Brown University), "Making Bibles into Books: The Evangelical Book Industry's Turn Toward the Bible, 1950-1980"; and Bryan Bibb (Furman University), "Readers and their E-Bibles: The Shape and Authority of the Hypertext Canon." The proceedings from the conference are published in *The Bible in American Life*, ed., P. Goff, A. Farnsley, & P. Thuesen (New York: Oxford University Press, 2017). This book was published just after I completed work on the present volume, though each of these contributors generously shared their essays with me before publication.

slight majority (57 percent) reported that they read the Bible in digital form more than in print form, in contrast to 23 percent who indicated that they read the Bible more in print form. Weaver called particular attention to a majority of respondents (69 percent) who said that they "regularly use printed Scripture for specific times or types of reading, when not primarily using the digital text."[23] What stood out here was the number of individuals who preferred print Bibles for devotional reading—namely, "intensive reading." Here, Weaver picks up on Ziming Liu's study that draws a helpful distinction between "intensive reading" (more closely associated with paper texts) and "extensive reading" (more closely associated with screens).[24] The connection between devotional reading and print Bibles makes sense, given the reflective, deep, and focused nature of devotional reading and prayer. Based on current Bible reading patterns, Weaver suggests that in the future, we will continue to see greater hybridization of media in Bible reading practices. By "hybridization of media" Weaver means that increasingly, digital reading technologies will "support the devotional reading of printed scriptures as a valued Christian practice."[25] Another set of surveys has been carried out by one of the leading scholars in religion and digital media, Tim Hutchings, a professor at Stockholm University.[26] Of special interest is Prof. Hutchings's article on "E-Reading and the Christian Bible."[27] After discussing various views on reading digital versus print Bibles, Hutchings describes a survey that he conducted in 2013 regarding the use of online Bibles. Although his sample size (257 responses) was significantly less than the some 2,000 individuals surveyed for each of the "State of the Bible" reports (or the 1,551 individuals surveyed for the IUPUI study), he posed one open qualitative question in particular that perhaps is more revealing than much of the quantitative data revealed in the other studies. His open question was simply this: "In what ways (if any) have digital media

23. Weaver, "Transforming Practice: American Bible Reading in Digital Culture," 253.
24. Ziming Liu, "Reading Behavior in the Digital Environment," in *Paper to Digital: Documents in the Information Age* (Westport, CT: Libraries Unlimited, 2008).
25. Weaver, "Transforming Practice: American Bible Reading in Digital Culture," 253.
26. See, e.g.: "Now the Bible Is an App: Digital Media and Changing Patterns of Religious Authority," in *Religion, Media, and Social Change*, ed., K. Granholm, M. Moberg, & S. Sjö (New York: Routledge, 2014), 143–61; "Christianity and Digital Media," in *The Changing Map of* World Religion, S. D. Brunn, ed.(Dordrecht: Springer, 2015), 3811–30; "Network Theology: Christian Understandings of New Media," *The Journal of Religion, Media, and Digital Culture* 1, no. 1 (2012), https://www.jrmdc.com/journal/article/view/8/5; "Studying Apps: Research Approaches to the Digital Bible," in *Digital Methodologies in the Sociology of Religion*, ed., S. Cheruvallil-Contractor & S. Shakkour (New York: Bloomsbury Academic, 2016), 87–108; and "Real Virtual Community," *Word and World* 35, no. 7 (2015): 151–61.
27. *Studies in Religion / Sciences Religieuses* 44, no. 4 (2015): 423–40.

changed your relationship with the Bible?" Of the 257 respondents to the survey, 201 answered this question. About 10 percent responded that using a digital Bible had not changed their relationship with the Bible.

About 40 percent indicated that they worried about some negative effects of using a digital Bible. Hutchings identifies three themes that emerged in this regard. First, some of those surveyed worried that reading the Bible on a screen in some ways secularized the Bible so that it was no different than anything else that might appear on the screen. One respondent wrote that "we must be deliberate and careful not to allow God's Holy Word to become just another app" (p. 435). This was related to a concern about the distractions that came with digital reading. Second, a common complaint was that using a digital Bible to access verses resulted in a noncontextualized and disjointed reading of scripture. Connected to this concern was the feeling of losing a sense of the physical location of a passage within the whole Bible. And third, several individuals expressed that they missed the Bible as a physical object, a sacred text in material form that can be touched and held. The notion of having a real personal connection with the Bible as a kind of physical symbol for God's presence was something that people missed when reading the Bible on an e-reader. There is a certain comfort in having "my" Bible as a familiar companion with tangible pages rather than a sterile screen with e-ink. In this way, many people feel like they have a more personal connection with a physical Bible.

But many respondents had very positive things to say about their experience of the Bible in digital form. There was added value to reading the Bible as a digital text. Most common (58 percent) was reference to the ease and convenience that came with digital Bibles. If the Bible is an app on your smartphone, it is always with you, and many found this to be an attractive feature of digital Bibles. Individuals with difficulties in reading because of poor eyesight also praised the ways in which the text of a digital Bible could be enlarged. A good number of respondents (34 percent) felt that a digital Bible was easier to study because they could readily access different translations along with other Bible study helps offered by various programs and apps. Only 13 percent of the individuals surveyed stated that they read the Bible more frequently because of its availability in digital form. There is one way in which Hutchings observed that e-reading of the Bible may well track differently than other kinds of e-reading. While 90 percent of e-book readers also read paper books,[28] when it comes to the Bible, those who use digital Bibles "frequently asserted that they had almost or even entirely stopped using and carrying their paper Bibles" (p. 437). How widespread this is, or why this is the case is not immediately apparent. Is it simply a habit that digital Bible readers have developed because of the convenience factor and other bonuses to digital Bibles (various translations, study aids, etc.)? As Hutchings notes, it certainly warrants further study.

Other surveys have been less formal, but still informative. In October 2012, Bobby Ross Jr., then the managing editor of *The Christian Chronicle*, and now the chief correspondent, wrote a short essay on "Digital vs. print: Readers weigh in on Bible choices." He relates a personal story in which he got up to preach at Roswell Church of Christ in Kansas City, KS, and realized that he had left his Bible on the front pew. He attributes this forgetful act to two things: he spends more time writing than preaching (and hence gets a little nervous in the pulpit), but more importantly, "I've converted in recent years to digital Bible reading and study, so I've become unaccustomed to carrying around a thick, printed version of the Scriptures."[29] In reflecting on this incident, he decided to conduct a brief survey of the readers of *The Christian Chronicle*, an international newspaper for Churches of Christ. He received 75 responses, with readers fairly evenly divided between use of print and digital Bibles, with a number saying they use both. The responses were mostly anecdotal, but they are nonetheless informative. Some said they loved using their leather-bound King James Version, which they had lovingly marked up over the years. Others preferred using a digital Bible because they could access a variety of study tools without having to lug around a library of print books. And some carried both a print Bible and a digital Bible—the first to use for reading, the second to use for checking other translations and tools, whether during a sermon or during a Bible study.

While digital Bibles still carry a stigma for some people, that stigma is fading. This can already be seen in another essay Ross had written three years before, in 2009, "Texting during worship? No, just reading the text."[30] The title of the essay reflects the kind of raised eyebrows

---

28. This is according to the Pew Internet and American Life Project; see L. Rainie, et al., *The rise of e-reading,*" Report of the Pew Internet and American Life Project (2012); http://libraries.pewinternet.org/files/legacy-pdf/The rise of e-reading 4.5.12.pdf.

29. *The Christian Chronicle*, October 2012; http://www.christianchronicle.org/article/digital-vs-print-readers-weigh-in-on-bible-choices.

30. *The Christian Chronicle*, September 2009; http://www.christianchronicle.org/article/texting-during-worship-no-just-reading-the-text.

people used to get if they had their smartphones out during a worship service. How rude to be texting or playing a game during worship! But increasingly, the stigma of using a smartphone on which to read scripture has faded, even when perfectly good print Bibles are available right there in the pew rack in front of you (at least in Protestant churches). A certain tension still remains between what people consider a "real" Bible bound in leather versus a digital version "bound" between iPad covers. Ross relates the story of one pastor who has been using an iPad in the pulpit for reading the Bible. After one service, a woman told him that she wished he would use the Bible when he preached. His response? "I showed her the app and asked which Bible she wanted me to use."[31]

Because smartphones and tablets have been so personalized to and by the individual user, perhaps some readers of digital Bibles have been able to transfer the feelings of attachment they had for their print Bible to the digital Bible. They still have full access to the biblical text, but now can do so in an enhanced manner. Part of the enhancement includes combining Bible study/reading with various social media platforms, whether it is by posting on Facebook, or a virtual reading group on Goodreads, or a chat room or blog on one of the popular Bible study apps (YouVersion, BibleWorks, Accordance, eSword, OliveTree, etc.). The digital Bible is very much an enhanced Bible. But, as we shall see in chapter 7 below, not all enhancements are helpful or necessarily good.

From Surveys to Knowledge

What is the net result of these various surveys? Several things clearly stand out. First, over the past several years, there has been a significant increase in the number of people using digital screens to read and/or study their Bibles. Given how many digital screens have been manufactured in the last few years, this observation is not a particular surprise. Apple Computers recently announced that in the summer of 2016, they sold their 1 *billionth* iPhone! The number of digital screens that have been manufactured is over 8 billion—enough for every man, woman, and child on the face of the planet. And most of those living in more affluent countries own several digital screens. (Not counting televisions, I count ten digital screens in my household between my wife and myself: each of us has a smartphone, tablet, Kindle, laptop, and desk-

1. *The Christian Chronicle,* October 2012; http://www.christianchronicle.org/article/digital-vs-print-readers-weigh-in-on-bible-choices.

top). Second, it is clear that print books and print Bibles are not going away. Far from it. With children's books and Bibles, in particular, people are very attached to their books with covers. Third, people tend to rely more on paper for deep reading, while they tend to rely more on screens for scanning and surfing. These two different mediums really service two different modes of reading. Fourth, while the use of surveys helps to amass quantitative data regarding reading trends for digital Bibles, and such data supports the general results just articulated, much of the qualitative evidence is perhaps, by necessity, relatively anecdotal in nature. Finding helpful objective (i.e., not self-reporting) qualitative measures for evaluating the use and impact of digital Bibles is difficult. In part, the difficulty comes from the knowledge that we are in the middle of whatever shift is currently going on between print culture and digital culture. It is difficult to have perspective on the transition we are currently experiencing. It is hard to see the forest when you are standing among the trees!

Surveys, Meaning, and the DIKW Pyramid

Where is the life we have lost in living?
Where is the wisdom we have lost in knowledge?
Where is the knowledge we have lost in information?[32]
—T.S. Eliot, *The Rock* (1934)

To these lines from a chorus in T.S. Eliot's pageant play, *The Rock,* we might also add the question "Where is the information we have lost in data?" Eliot's questions probe a confusion about the relationships between information, knowledge, and wisdom. How often do we mistake mere knowledge for genuine wisdom? Or mere information for true knowledge, or bits of data for useable information? Although, in his questions, Eliot was not addressing anything remotely related to digital technology, he was asking about fundamental relations between the building blocks of informed discourse—information that leads to knowledge, which in turn, can lead to practical wisdom.

In the 1980s, several prominent leaders in the worlds of information systems and knowledge management began using slightly different versions of what has come to be called the DIKW hierarchy or pyramid.[33] Within this hierarchy, raw data (D) is organized into useable

---

32. T. S. Eliot, *The Rock: A Pageant Play* (New York: Harcourt, Brace, & Co; 1934), The Chorus, part 1.
33. R. Ackoff, "From Data to Wisdom: Presidential Address to ISQGSR [International Society for General Systems Research]," *Journal of Applied Systems Analysis* 18 (1989): 3–9; M. Zeleny, "Manage-

information (I), about which people engage in knowledgeable reflection (K), and which ideally leads to some form of wisdom (W). Even with the difficulties of defining the different terms used, there is something about the DIKW hierarchy that makes intuitive sense. One can readily imagine the kind of connections that can be made when we understand something about the relationships between data, information, knowledge, and wisdom. Just as an example:

Data: wolves eat rabbits, rabbits eat grass, grass holds soil in place, rain causes soil to erode. (There is no explicit connection between any of these bits of data.)

Information: killing wolves will lead to more rabbits eating more grass. (Here, a connection is drawn between two bits of data.)

Knowledge: the more rabbits that eat grass (because there are fewer wolves), the more humans will have to deal with erosion of soil because the rabbits have eaten too much grass. (Here, different pieces of information have been put together to form a logical conclusion.)

Wisdom: we should not kill too many wolves, so that there will be a balance in the natural world between wolves and rabbits, and there will be less soil erosion. (Here, knowledge has moved to something actionable on the basis of processing data and information. Knowledge has shifted to wisdom about how humans should act in relation to wolves and rabbits.)

So how might this apply, if at all, to the survey data we have seen about digital Bibles? Let's try an example:

Data: more people are reading books on their smartphones and tablets, people tend to skim and scan when reading screens, resulting in less comprehension. (Again, there is no necessary connection between these bits of data.)

Information: more people are reading Bibles on screens with less comprehension, or—conversely—more people are reading Bibles on

ment Support Systems: Towards Integrated Knowledge Management," *Human Systems Management* 7 (1987): 59–70; and N. Sharma, "The Origin of the 'Data Information Knowledge Wisdom' Hierarchy," April, 2008, http://tinyurl.com/m8644d6. See also the very helpful review by J. Rowley, "The Wisdom Hierarchy: Representations of the DIKW Hierarchy," *Journal of Information Science* 33 (2007): 163–80; and D. Weinberger, *Too Big to Know: Rethinking Knowledge Now That the Facts Aren't the Facts, Experts Are Everywhere, and the Smartest Person in the Room Is the Room* (New York: Basic Books, 2014), 1–17.

screens with a different purpose than when reading print Bibles. (How would we know which is the case? Regardless, here, a connection is made between the bits of data.)

Knowledge: the more we can make screens replicate the experience of books, the more people will have a deeper understanding of the Bible, or—conversely—when people want to do word searches or skim the Bible, it is more helpful to use a digital Bible, but when people want to engage in devotional reading of the Bible, it is more helpful to use a print Bible. (Again, how would we know which knowledge is most appropriate to the linking of different pieces of information?)

Wisdom: We should not read the Bible exclusively on screens lest we end up with a more shallow and fragmented comprehension of the Bible, or—conversely—we should read the Bible in print form if we want a deeper understanding of the Bible, or . . . or . . . or. . . . (It is not exactly clear what wisdom we should garner from the data that the various surveys have revealed.)

Okay. Let's try it again with another example drawn from the surveys about the use of digital Bibles:

Data: Bible websites provide hundreds of translations and versions of the Bible, digital Bibles provide a variety of tools to help interpret the Bible

Information: the combination of many translations and many interpretive tools in digital Bibles can be very helpful in reading and understanding the Bible (or, conversely, the many translations and interpretive tools are so overwhelming in number that it is hard to know how to filter through them all so that they provide more help than confusion).

Knowledge: there may be many translations and tools available in digital form, but there is still one Bible held in common across the Christian faith (okay, except for the Apocrypha!).

Wisdom: Less can be more; while it is good to compare various translations and to make prudent use of digital exegetical tools (commentaries, concordances, word studies, etc.), it is important not to get so carried away by the many digital helps that one loses the biblical forest for the trees.

As a heuristic tool, the DIKW hierarchy can be useful in helping us see the connections and interrelatedness between the different levels of data, information, knowledge, and wisdom. Based on the connections we make in the survey data on digital Bibles, the DIKW model can be used to attain greater understanding of some of the important differences between print Bibles and digital Bibles. But this model still relies on the process of distilling the many grapes of data into a wine worthy of the name knowledge or wisdom. At the same time, as David Weinberger points out in his book *Too Big To Know*, the amount of information available in the digital realm simply defies management. Instead, the nature of the Internet itself, and the digital realm with it, changes how we manage knowledge.

> It's the connecting of knowledge—the networking—that is changing our oldest, most basic strategy of knowing. Rather than knowing-by-reducing to what fits in a library or a scientific journal, we are now knowing-by-including every draft of every idea in vast, loosely connected webs. And that means knowledge is not the same as it was. Not for science, not for business, not for education, not for government, not for any of us.[34]

And not for how we approach or know the Bible either.

Weinberger suggests that we are moving to a "new institution of knowledge"[35] that is rather different from the older model of constantly reducing data and information, squeezing it into usable knowledge and nuggets of wisdom. As humans, we are in the process of adapting to a new shape of knowing, based on various networks of meaning rather than a single hierarchy. The contours of this emerging shape, Weinberger argues, have the following characteristics:

- **It's wide.** The casting of the digital net may indeed only plumb "the shallows" (as Nicholas Carr argues), but in what is perhaps a truthful oxymoronic statement, "sufficient width can be its own type of depth."[36] When applied to digital Bibles and the gazillion digital resources that accompany them, it points to the reality that people are pursuing thousands of different paths in accessing and seeking to understand the Bible, empowered in new ways by new possibilities, courtesy of the digital realm that were never even conceivable before. The "lure of the click" (or "clickbait" for a more

34. D. Weinberger, *Too Big to Know,* 5.
35. Ibid., 13–18.
36. Ibid., 13.

negative spin!) opens up digital rabbit holes that may land you in a fourth-century commentary by Chrysostom, a sermon by Joel Osteen, or a debate about textual variants. You just never really know! This kind of breadth was never possible before the digital era.

- **It's boundary-free.** Just as the digital Bible is a book without covers, so is the digital realm one that in many respects defies and removes boundaries. Experts have traditionally served as gatekeepers for interpreting the Bible. One of the attractions of a popular academic site for New Testament studies, *ntgateway.com*, is that I can send students there in the confidence that they will find fairly mainstream and trustworthy scholarship on the New Testament. Students who navigate that site are unlikely to come upon some of the more wacky approaches to the New Testament. The site is hosted by Logos Bible Software (one of the primary Bible programs) and edited by Mark Goodacre, a respected Professor of New Testament and Early Christianity in the Department of Religious Studies at Duke University. But such moderated sites represent only one click-option, one path to travel, among millions of others. A random search for "Bible" on Google produced a staggering 388 million hits in half of a second (by contrast, "porn" generated over 2 billion hits). Increasingly people reading the Bible using digital resources are deciding for themselves what appropriate exegetical boundaries might be. This is closely related to the next shift in knowledge.

- **It's populist.** It has long been noted that the Internet is a highly democratizing presence. From Wiki-leaks to self-promoted blogs of all kinds, from bible studies (almost 40 million hits) to daily verses tweeted on Twitter, people are voting with their keyboards, mouse clicks, and swipes for the Bible and accompanying content that they want to consume. The surveying and analysis of this kind of digital consumption is still in its infancy. What will attention to the populist character of digital Bibles reveal? The populist movement propelled by the digital age also has, to some degree, dethroned "experts." What are experts? They are "full-time professional knowers," to quote David Weinberger's definition.[37] The cult of expertise is still alive and well, but increasingly, people are fairly confident that they can acquire much of this expertise if they simply browse enough web pages, whether it is webMD to engage in self-diagnosis, or an app

---

37. Ibid., 48.

on how to invest in the stock market. The difficulty, of course, is that information is not at all the same as knowledge or wisdom, a problem to which we will return below.

• **It's "other"-credentialed.** Because of the democratizing power of the Internet, credentialed interpretation of the Bible in books or in online materials is less compelling than it once was. "Credentialed" interpretation is what expert biblical scholars have to say (some with and some without PhDs). But increasingly, non-experts feel perfectly free to offer their interpretations of the Bible, and they often view professional biblical scholars as out of touch, or as preoccupied with deconstructing the Bible, rather than applying the Bible to the modern faith lives of believers. As a result, interpretations that are trending online have become, in some way, self-authorizing. If people are talking about it, if they are sharing it on Facebook or tweeting about it, if it goes viral, then it takes on its own kind of authority simply by repetition. If one is struck by a link on "Martians in the Bible" (with over 200,000 hits), it is easy enough to click on it and follow up. You can add a comment, repost it on Facebook, and then, generate a whole new stream of comments from people who are separated by much more than six degrees! The volume of non-expert repetition can drown out the voices of experts.

• **It's unsettled.** Patterns of knowing, Weinberger argues, have changed in unsettling ways in the digital age. In a time when people can decry as a hoax near unanimous scientific evidence pointing toward a planet with a fever (global warming), it becomes clear that the notion of data-driven "actionable" knowledge is in no small trouble. Is the digital Bible leading to the same kind of trouble, where if enough people click on an idea, it becomes truth? It is no accident that the *Oxford English Dictionary*'s choice for the 2016 word of the year was "post-truth"![38] Appeals to the Bible have long been suspect as "making the Bible say what you want it to say," and Lord knows there is plenty of evidence for that. But the exponential expansion of websites about the Bible has created a rather wide-open market of ideas about what it means to be a people of the book. Indeed, a year after the release of the first Kindle in 2007, Christine Rosen wrote a provocative essay on "People of the Screen,"[39] raising

38. https://en.oxforddictionaries.com/word-of-the-year/word-of-the-year-2016.

important questions about what in the world it means to be people of the book at the dawn of the digital screen era. She has several concerns about screen reading as opposed to print reading. In particular, she responds to advocates of screen interaction and digital literacy who claim that print literacy is passive, while screen literacy is active. James Paul Gee, a strong proponent of video games as learning tools, told the New York Times, "You can't screw up a Dostoevsky book, but you can screw up a game."[40] Rosen's critical response is telling:

> Gee's statements suffer from a profound misunderstanding of the reading experience and evince an astonishing level of hubris. The reason you can't "screw up" a Dostoevsky novel is that you must first submit yourself to the process of reading it—which means accepting, at some level, the author's authority to tell you the story. You enter the author's world on his terms, and in so doing get away from yourself. Yes, you are powerless to change the narrative or the characters, but you become more open to the experiences of others and, importantly, open to the notion that you are not always in control. In the process, you might even become more attuned to the complexities of family life, the vicissitudes of social institutions, and the lasting truths of human nature. The screen, by contrast, tends in the opposite direction. Instead of a reader, you become a user; instead of submitting to an author, you become the master. The screen promotes invulnerability. Whatever setbacks occur (as in a video game) are temporary, fixable, and ultimately overcome. We expect to master the game and move on to the next challenge. This is a lesson in trial and error, and often an entertaining one at that, but it is not a lesson in richer human understanding.[41]

The parallels to reading the Bible as "book" rather than as "screen" are instructive, and point to the transformative character of reading the Bible as scripture in the context of a confessional community. What might it mean to immerse oneself in a biblical narrative, to allow scripture to interrogate, confront, change, and shape our identity, and not just for us to interrogate scripture?[42] We not only read the Bible; the Bible also reads us. Reading the Bible as "book" allows us to see differ-

---

39. http://www.thenewatlantis.com/docLib/20081020_TNA22Rosen.pdf.
40. http://www.nytimes.com/learning/teachers/featured_articles/20081009thursday.html. See also J. P. Gee's influential *What Video Games Have to Teach Us about Learning and Literacy* (New York: Palgrave Macmillan, 2007).
41. http://www.thenewatlantis.com/publications/people-of-the-screen.
42. See S. Fowl and G. Jones, *Reading in Communion: Scripture and Ethics in Christian Life* (Grand Rapids: Eerdmans, 1991), 29–55.

ent individuals and communities of faith over time navigate the conversation both with God and about God. It also allows us to enter into that conversation with those who likewise wrestled with these sacred texts across the centuries. Is it possible to do this with screens as well? Of course it is. But there is something substantive, as Rosen suggests, about being people of the "book," and not just people of the screen, something about covers and the sequence of narratives along with the messy canonical shape with which the church has had to deal century on end.

Another aspect of the *unsettled* nature of the Bible in digital dress has to do with what might best be referred to as Bible "mash-ups." The notion of mash-ups is common in music, where a DJ or a songwriter might mix and remix snippets of various songs across a wide range of genres to create something both used and new at the same time. In 2006, Kevin Kelly, the former editor of the magazine *Wired,* imagined mash-ups and remixes of digital books. Just as songs are now juggled and reordered into new albums, so also Kelly imagined that the digital realm would foster "virtual 'bookshelves'—a collection of texts, some as short as a paragraph, others as long as entire books" that would be mashed-up "to be read as snippets or to be remixed as pages."[43] Here, the notion of digital technology as the ultimate creative deconstructive tool raises many questions about the very nature of writing or narrative or authorship. Now, truth be told, one could well argue that the Bible has been "mashed-up" and remixed for centuries on end.[44] What is a lectionary cycle but a kind of "mash-up," or many a sermon that remixes rather disparate parts of the Bible? Even the biblical books themselves are "mash-ups" of a sort, whether we're discussing the JEDP sources of the Pentateuch, or how the Gospels of Matthew and Luke make use of Mark's Gospel and a hypothetical source scholars call "Q," or how the Gospel of John remixes quotations and echoes of the Jewish scriptures and festivals to point to Jesus as the ultimate revelation of God.[45]

This is not unlike what I like to refer to as the "fifth gospel" that most Christians have assembled in their brains—namely, a unified

43. See Rosen, "People of the Screen," 31.

44. See M. Novelli, *Shaped By the Story* (Grand Rapids: Zondervan, 2008). "In technological terminology, a *mashup* is a Web application that combines data from more than one source into a single integrated tool. The Bible is like this—a mashup of different writings from different authors inspired to tell the unified Story of God and his love for people" (78).

45. See, e.g., Richard Hays's *Echoes of Scripture in the Letters of Paul* (New Haven, CT: Yale University Press, 1993), and his more recent *Echoes of Scripture in the Gospels* (Waco, TX: Baylor University Press, 2016).

mega-gospel that is the believer's or the community's own internal creation. Thus, for example, it is very common for us to combine the birth stories of Matthew and Luke into one "mega birth story," in which we mix elements from both Gospels together that actually do not belong together. We read and interpret the one in light of the other. The distinct parts of the Bible, especially parts with parallels elsewhere, blend together and become a new story. The still popular, but false, notion that Mary Magdalene was a prostitute is another good example of blending different Gospel accounts together. If you take the story of the unnamed woman who anointed Jesus in Mark 14:3–9 and Matthew 26:6–13, link it to the parallel account of the unnamed "sinful" "woman of the city" from Luke 7:36–50, and finally, add Mary of Bethany's anointing of Jesus from John 12:1–8, the mash-up result is that a sinful woman named Mary, "from the city" (i.e., a prostitute?), anointed Jesus. Mary of Bethany has been forgotten, and it couldn't be Mary the mother of Jesus, so it must be the other most well-known Mary, Mary Magdalene, now doomed to prostitution because people blend different stories together and create a new one. (And hadn't Luke 8 said that Jesus had cast out seven demons from Mary Magdalene?) Still, from Kelly's perspective, "Once text is digital, books seep out of their bindings and weave themselves together. The collective intelligence of a library allows us to see things we can't see in a single, isolated book."[46] In this view, it is not just the individual sections of the Bible morphing and blurring with other sections of the Bible; rather, the Bible now morphs with other books on the same digital device. So does the Bible, indeed, simply become one book among thousands of others?

Snippets and Mantra Texts

Beyond the new ways of knowing in the digital age to which Weinberger calls attention are some rather old ways of knowing that have taken advantage of the digital medium. In surveying the use of Bibles in digital media, one ubiquitous practice is the appeal to text snippets seen in the many "Verse of the Day" offerings on websites and digital Bible apps far and wide. Almost every Bible program I looked at has this feature, which often can be enhanced in any number of ways. My email inbox is filled daily with Verse of the Day texts and artwork.

The Verse of the Day in Fig. 5.3 comes from Logos Bible Software.

---

46. Kevin Kelly, "Scan This Book!" *New York Times Magazine* (May 14, 2006).

With its musical notes, purple sky, and mountain majesty, the image evokes not only the text of 1 Chronicles 16:23, but also of the song America the Beautiful!

Fig. 5.3.

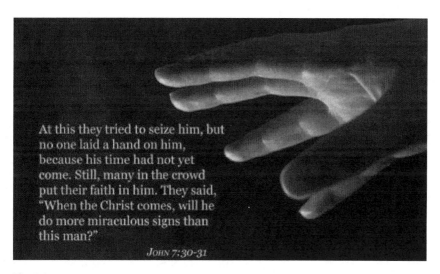

Fig. 5.4.

There's even a "Verse of the Day" website (*verseoftheday.com*). Today's verse (July 30, 2016) happens to be John 7:30–31, "At this they tried to seize him, but no one laid a hand on him, because his time had not yet come. Still, many in the crowd put their faith in him. They said, "When the Christ comes, will he do more miraculous signs than this man?" If you want an image to illustrate the verse, all you need to do is scroll down the page a bit (see Fig. 5.4).

There's also the "Light for the Day" website (*lightfortheday.com*), which today features Psalm 74:17, "You have made summer and winter," replete with an artful black and white photo of someone riding a bicycle with snow falling all around them. How ubiquitous is the Verse of the Day feature? A Google search brought up over 20 million hits. That's a lot of verses for a lot of days!

The snippet texts are certainly decontextualized, but frankly, there's nothing new about this practice. In fact, the earliest Christians did much the same in their use of what were their Biblical texts (what Christians today call the Old Testament) as they reflected on fundamental guides for faith that they adapted from the scriptures. In early Christianity, such passages as Isaiah 53 and Psalm 110 were commonly quoted to demonstrate connections between the death and resurrection of Jesus and the sacred scriptures of the earliest Christians.[47] Today, such "motto texts" include the ever-present John 3:16, Jeremiah 29:11, Psalm 23, 1 Corinthians 13, Philippians 4:13, and so on.[48] The Christian news magazine *Christianity Today* reports that the top five shared verses using the YouVersion Bible app in 2015 were: Proverbs 3:5–6, Philippians 4:6–7, Joshua 1:9, Romans 12:2, and Romans 15:13.[49] The combination of Twitter and the digital Bible is particularly well-suited for the tweeting of such mantra texts. (A Google search of "Bible and Twitter" generates over 63 million hits!)

The digital age, then, has introduced different ways of knowing, different ways of assembling data and sharing information, different ways of construing knowledge and discerning actionable wisdom. How does this rather different shape of knowing impact the way we read the Bible? How do surveys on digital Bibles and their use help us to understand better what changes are taking place in reading and interpreting the Bible? Part of the difficulty in using any survey data arises in our

---

47. See, e.g., W. Bellinger & W. Farmer, eds., *Jesus and the Suffering Servant: Isaiah 53 and Christian Origins* (Harrisburg: Trinity Press, 1998); and D. Hay, *Glory at the Right Hand: Psalm 110 in Early Christianity* (Nashville: Abingdon, 1973).

48. See various lists of most popular verses: http://www.biblestudytools.com/topical-verses/the-25-most-read-bible-verses/; http://www.biblegateway.com/blog/2009/05/the-100-most-read-bible-verses-at-biblegatewaycom/; http://www.christianitytoday.com/gleanings/2015/december/most-popular-bible-verses-200-million-youversion-app-2015.html.

49. http://www.christianitytoday.com/gleanings/2015/december/most-popular-bible-verses-200-million-youversion-app-2015.html.

efforts to assemble and interpret the data in meaningful ways.[50] Along the same lines, we have to ask "meaningful for whom?," and "meaningful to what end?" In the case of digital Bibles, one clear goal of the surveys is simply to accumulate raw data on distribution and use of digital Bibles relative to print Bibles. This raw data can then be organized into meaningful information—namely, information that provides us with greater understanding of what kinds of reading patterns are emerging in relation to digital and print Bibles. Such information, in turn, is used by publishers of both print and digital Bibles to provide knowledge and evidence that can guide reasoned discussion and debate about current and future directions for different forms and formats in which the Bible should be distributed.

The quest is always for "actionable data." Zondervan, for example, is the publisher of the very successful NIV (New International Version) Bible. Some years ago, their own market surveys led them to a decision that resulted in the publication of what might be called "boutique Bibles," or niche Bibles, print Bibles (and now, some in digital form) geared toward very targeted audiences. The list of these different "boutique Bibles" is rather astonishing.[51] The NIV Lifehacks Bible,[52] the NIV Celebrate Life Recovery Study Bible,[53] the NIV Life Connect Study Bible,[54] or the NIV Faithgirlz Bible, Revised,[55] are but a handful of the dozens of NIV Bibles one can purchase. (My personal favorite is the NIV *Thinline Bible: Stock Car Edition 1984*, with the following advertising blurb: "Gentlemen, start your—Bibles! Featuring exciting and inspiring full-color inserts with photos of and insights from stock car racing's finest personalities.") Yes, something for everyone!

0. See F. J. Fowler, *Survey Research Methods*, 5th ed. (Los Angeles: Sage, 2013), 1–13, 134–39; "How to Analyze Survey Data: Survey Best Practices" SurveyMonkey; https://www.surveymonkey.com/mp/how-to-analyze-survey-data/.

1. See http://www.zondervan.com/bibles/niv-bibles.

2. The blurb for the *NIV Lifehacks Bible* states: "From cooking to organizing, "Lifehacks" improve all aspects of your day, but did you know they can also enrich your spiritual life? The NIV Lifehacks Bible gives you practical and achievable techniques to build Godly habits and enhance your walk with God."

3. "Find freedom from life's hurts, hang-ups, and habits with the NIV Celebrate Recovery Study Bible. Featuring a foreword by Rick Warren, this real-life spiritual guide includes articles based on the eight recovery principles of the Celebrate Recovery program and the accompanying Christ-centered twelve steps."

4. "Grow deeper in your spiritual life with the NIV LifeConnect Study Bible. Dr. Wayne Cordeiro includes articles bringing the truths of the Scriptures to your life today, as well as Scripture, Observation, Application, Prayer (SOAP) articles that offer an interactive framework to apply the Word of God to your life. Free digital resources included."

5. "Packed with exciting features that help tween girls better understand themselves and Scripture, the Faithgirlz Bible teaches girls that the Bible is real, relevant, and, best of all, that the story of God and his people is also their story. With in-text features written by tween expert Nancy Rue."

What distinguishes one NIV Bible from another is not the translation—as all are the NIV translation[56]—but the format and accompanying paratext. Paratext refers to any additional features to the publication of the Bible that extend beyond the actual text of the translation. Thus, chapter headings are paratext, and not part of the original text that is being translated. Commentary provided at the bottom of a study Bible is another good example of paratext, especially since different kinds of commentary are responsive to different needs and desires of different readers. Sometimes, paratext is quite subtle (e.g., chapter and verse numbers were added long after the time of writing), and sometimes, rather more direct (the additional materials in any of the NIV boutique Bibles).

This is but one example of how data from surveys about the Bible get transformed into information which publishers can and do use to make knowledgeable decisions about marketing the Bible. Let me hasten to add that there is nothing inherently wrong or unethical with this process. Far from it. While some Bible publishers want to publish nothing but the basic biblical text without any explanatory notes or helps (the goal of the American Bible Society),[57] other Bible publishers seek to produce value-added Bibles that they think individuals, congregations, and niche markets will find useful. Yes, they may make some money along the way, but there is no book that is distributed more widely or more commonly for free than the Bible, in both print and digital form.

Now that we know a little more about what surveys tell us regarding the use of digital Bibles, another question arises: "Is There a Bible in This Church?"

---

56. The NIV translation has gone through various editions with some changes in translation. The first complete Bible was issued in 1978, with subsequent editions in 1984 and 2011.
57. As early as 1815, the General Association of Bible Societies in the United States (the forerunner of the American Bible Society) determined that it would "disseminate the Scriptures of the Old and New Testament, according to the present approved edition, without note or comment." J. Fea, *The Bible Cause: A History of the American Bible Society* (New York: Oxford University Press, 2016), 13. See also P. J. Wosh, *Spreading the Word: The Bible Business in Nineteenth-Century America* (Ithaca, NY: Cornell University Press, 1994).

6

Is There a Bible in This Church?

In 1982, the controversial literary theorist and cultural critic Stanley Fish, then a professor at the University of Chicago, published a book that caused quite a stir: *Is There a Text in This Class? The Authority of Interpretive Communities.*[1] In it, Fish argued that texts have no real meaning apart from communities that value and interpret texts, and that the notion of authorial intent is a fiction imposed on a text by a community of readers. Thus, according to Fish, a text means what interpretive communities say the text means. "It is interpretive communities, rather than either the text or reader, that produce meanings."[2]

Within the framework of the larger church community, this emphasis on the authority of interpretative communities has long been recognized, especially within the Roman Catholic Church. In the Vatican II document *Dei Verbum* (*The Dogmatic Constitution on Divine Revelation,* 1965), for example, the Catholic Church made it quite clear that scripture *means* what the Magisterium (the teaching authority of the church) *says* it means. "The task of authentically interpreting the word of God, whether written or handed on, has been entrusted exclusively to the living teaching office of the Church, whose authority is exercised in the name of Jesus Christ" (*Dei Verbum* 10.2). Similarly, the *Catechism of the Catholic Church* states explicitly:

1. Cambridge, MA: Harvard University Press, 1982.
2. Fish, *Is There a Text in This Class?,* 14.

The task of giving an authentic interpretation of the Word of God, whether in its written form or in the form of Tradition, has been entrusted to the living teaching office of the Church alone. Its authority in this matter is exercised in the name of Jesus Christ. This means that the task of interpretation has been entrusted to the bishops in communion with the successor of Peter, the Bishop of Rome.[3]

Otherwise, one would end up with thousands of competing interpretations and hundreds of independent church communities, all touting their particular interpretation as the correct one. A sense of unified authority would be lost. This is exactly what has happened, of course, in the Protestant tradition.[4]

Utilizing Stanley Fish's notion of interpretive communities as authorizing particular readings of texts, in the case of the Roman Catholic Church, it is the Magisterium which serves as the official body that authorizes the interpretation and meaning of the biblical text. In contrast to Fish, however, the Church also recognizes the importance of authorial intent and the contributions of scholars in reconstructing that intent as best they can. Authorial intent serves as one among several factors in determining the interpretation and meaning of the text. Again, to quote from *Dei Verbum*:

Since God speaks in Sacred Scripture through men in human fashion, the interpreter of Sacred Scripture, in order to see clearly what God wanted to communicate to us, should carefully investigate what meaning the sacred writers really intended, and what God wanted to manifest by means of their words. To search out the intention of the sacred writers, attention should be given, among other things, to "literary forms." For truth is set forth and expressed differently in texts which are variously historical, prophetic, poetic, or of other forms of discourse. The interpreter must investigate what meaning the sacred writer intended to express and actually expressed in particular circumstances by using contemporary literary forms in accordance with the situation of his own time and culture. For

---

3. *Catechism of the Catholic Church*, 2nd ed. (USCCB, 1994), p. 26; par. 85. It is notable that the editors of the online version of the *Catechism* (http://ccc.usccb.org/flipbooks/catechism/index.html#44) went out of their way to make the screen version appear and *sound* as much like a physical book as possible. The book appears open, with both left and right side pages showing, and a little bit of virtual shadow in the middle where the crease from the spine of the book would be. Clicking on the edge of a page turns the page either forward or backward, replete with the thick sound of a turning page, accompanied by a visual top corner of the page initiating a turn, followed by a very graphic turning of the whole page. One can also see the virtual thickness of the book and how many pages there are before and after the page you are viewing.

4. Of course, on the other hand, localizing interpretive authority in one group of the church makes it difficult for other groups to challenge this authority on the very basis of scripture, as the Protestant Reformers did.

the correct understanding of what the sacred author wanted to assert, due attention must be paid to the customary and characteristic styles of feeling, speaking and narrating which prevailed at the time of the sacred writer, and to the patterns men normally employed at that period in their everyday dealings with one another.[5]

This was a significant nod to the importance of historical critical analysis of the biblical texts, which represented a major shift in the position of the Roman Catholic Church toward biblical interpretation, one that opened up much more common ground with longstanding Protestant biblical scholarship.[6] It is certainly one reason why a Roman Catholic University would be willing to hire me, a Presbyterian minister, to teach scripture! (My colleague in Hebrew Bible, Dr. Daniel Smith-Christopher, is an active Quaker.)

Whereas, for Fish, there really is no "text in this class" independent of the interpretive community, for the Christian church the Bible is a unified multivocal foundational set of texts that was written by a variety of interpretive communities, with which the living church remains in active conversation. The contexts out of which the authors of the Bible wrote make a difference for the contexts in which the church interprets the Bible as scripture. So, in reframing Fish's question from "Is There a Text in This Class?" to "Is There a Bible in This Church?" my goal is to ask what kind of "text" the digital Bible is for the church in relation to the print Bible. How does the digital Bible function differently (if at all) from the print Bible in the context of the life of the church and its members?

In order to answer this question we will be exploring a variety of topics in this chapter related to how digital Bibles function in and for church communities. We will begin with the basics, namely, the biblical text itself. How do digital approaches to scripture impact our understandings of the biblical text? Here, the role of digital tools in analyzing the biblical text in its original languages will come into focus. Even more significant will be a consideration of the role of digital Bibles in the process of translation and dissemination. Related to issues of translation are paraphrases of the Bible, which in digital form are increasingly difficult to distinguish from actual translations. From

---

5. *Dei Verbum*, 12.

6. See the article by R. E. Brown and T. A. Collins, "Church Pronouncements," *New Jerome Biblical Commentary* (Englewood Cliffs, NJ: Prentice Hall, 1990), 1166–74. The article does a good job of tracing various official church teachings on biblical interpretation in the Roman Catholic tradition in the 19th and 20th centuries. See also the Pontifical Biblical Commission's *The Interpretation of the Bible in the Church*, released in 1994 (https://www.ewtn.com/library/CURIA/PBCINTER.HTM).

translations and paraphrases, we will move to look at paratexts in digital Bibles and print Bibles. As noted in the previous chapter, paratexts refer to all those little helps that editors have added to the basic text of the Bible over the centuries—things such as verse numbers, chapter headings, explanatory notes, and cross-references. Paratexts take on a whole new dimension in the age of hypertext. One important development in the digital age is the ability of individuals to pick and choose not only which translation/paraphrase of the Bible they find most appealing, but also the ability to craft their own personalized translation of the Bible by drawing upon the many available translations that have been published. This mash-up of Bibles has been termed the "Frankenbible"! We will look at some examples of the Frankenbible coming to life. The chapter also includes consideration of the function of digital Bibles in the liturgical life of the church, as well as the growing role of digital audio Bibles. Toward the end of the chapter, we will take a look at a very important development that has been brought about in the realm of Children's Bibles in the digital age. Related to this are the many Bible game apps that have been developed. So yes, this will be a long chapter. But, as we all well know, not everything can be reduced to 140 characters.

The Biblical Text: Stable Instability

The story of the formation of the Christian Bible has been often told. There is no need to reinvent the wheel on this topic.[7] What has received less attention, and is therefore less well-known, involves the many versions and translations the Bible has gone through over the centuries.[8] Although many people are aware of those little notes in small type at the bottom of a page of the Bible that say "other ancient authorities read . . . ," most people really do not care, if they notice such editorial notes at all. As far as they are concerned, they have the text. It's right there in front of them in English, in black and white. But, of course, this is not quite the case. Thus, it is important to take a step back from the biblical text and ask not so much about the formation of the Christian canon of scriptures, but about the actual writing and transmission of the books that make up the Bible. In order to under-

7. See, e.g., B. M. Metzger, *The Canon of the New Testament: Its Origin, Development, and Significance* (New York: Oxford University Press, 1987); and L. M. McDonald, *The Biblical Canon: Its Origin, Transmission, and Authority* (Grand Rapids: Baker, 2006).
8. See B. M. Metzger and B. D. Ehrman, *The Text of the New Testament: Its Transmission, Corruption, and Restoration*, 4th ed. (New York: Oxford University Press, 2005).

stand the significance of the role that digital tools can play in reconstructing this process of text transmission, it is helpful to contextualize this conversation within the larger realm of the discipline of textual criticism.

Textual criticism is the discipline in any field of study that seeks to reconstruct the earliest version of handwritten manuscripts from an author or authors before the advent of the printing press. Typically, the manuscripts are copies of copies of copies of copies of . . . you get the idea. When it comes to the Bible, we have no "autograph versions," no original manuscripts that served as the basis for later copies. All we have are the generations of copies of copies. The field of textual criticism within biblical studies is a highly technical discipline that involves comparing and evaluating many different manuscripts of the same biblical materials. The *goal* of textual critics in the field of biblical studies is really very simple: to establish the text. This is really no different from the task of any scholars working to establish the text of authors who wrote before the printing press. Scholars seeking to reconstruct the works of Plato face the same problems, but with far fewer manuscripts to go by. So what constitutes *"the* text"? It is the text that the majority of scholars working together on a committee of experts in textual criticism decides is representative of the earliest recoverable version of a biblical passage.[9] These scholars work through as many manuscripts of a given text as exist, comparing and contrasting the different readings in a process called "collation." They then weigh the relative value of the different manuscript readings on the basis of various criteria, and then, come to a consensus (or at least a majority decision) as to the earliest recoverable reading in the original language. In the case of the Bible, this means working with manuscripts in the original languages of Hebrew, Aramaic, and Greek, for the most part. Other languages enter in, but that leads to another discussion about translations (a discussion that is most pertinent in the realm of digital Bibles). Once scholars have established a working "critical text," namely, a composite version of the text that approximates as closely as possible what they think best represents the earliest reconstructed version, the critical text of the Hebrew Bible or the Greek New Testament is published and includes what is called a critical apparatus (see Fig. 6.1).

9. It should be noted that some text critics argue that there is no necessarily common "original" text that was later changed in the process of transmission. Different versions of the Bible emerged at different times in different places with different readings. Only later, when bishops had the power to do so, did the church seek to conform these different versions into one common version. We will address this further below.

273 ΚΑΤΑ ΙΩΑΝΝΗΝ 7,48–8,7

τοῖς οἱ Φαρισαῖοι· μὴ καὶ ὑμεῖς πεπλάνησθε; 48 μή τις ἐκ Mt 27,63!
τῶν ἀρχόντων ἐπίστευσεν εἰς αὐτὸν ἢ ἐκ τῶν Φαρισαίων; 12,42 Mt 21,32
49 ἀλλὰ ὁ ὄχλος οὗτος ὁ μὴ γινώσκων τὸν νόμον ἐπάρα- Dt 27,26
τοί εἰσιν. 50 ⸀λέγει Νικόδημος πρὸς αὐτούς, ⸂ὁ ἐλθὼν 3,1!s
πρὸς αὐτὸν [τὸ] πρότερον,⸃ εἷς ὢν ἐξ αὐτῶν· 51 μὴ ὁ νόμος
ἡμῶν κρίνει τὸν ἄνθρωπον ἐὰν μὴ ἀκούσῃ πρῶτον παρ' Dt 1,16s; 19,18
αὐτοῦ καὶ ⸂γνῷ τί ποιεῖ⸃; 52 ἀπεκρίθησαν καὶ εἶπαν αὐτῷ·
μὴ καὶ σὺ ἐκ τῆς Γαλιλαίας εἶ; ἐραύνησον καὶ ἴδε ⸆ ὅτι
⸉ἐκ τῆς Γαλιλαίας προφήτης⸊ οὐκ ἐγείρεται.⸆ 1,46! sed 2Rg 14,25

⟦53 □Καὶ ⸀ἐπορεύθησαν ἕκαστος εἰς τὸν ⸁οἶκον αὐτοῦ,⸌
8 Ἰησοῦς δὲ ἐπορεύθη εἰς τὸ ὄρος τῶν ἐλαιῶν. 2 ˙Ὄρ- L 21,37s
θρου δὲ πάλιν ⸀παρεγένετο εἰς τὸ ἱερὸν □καὶ πᾶς ὁ
λαὸς ἤρχετο πρὸς αὐτόν, καὶ καθίσας ἐδίδασκεν αὐ- Mc 2,13
τούς⸌. 3 ˙Ἄγουσιν δὲ οἱ γραμματεῖς καὶ οἱ Φαρισαῖοι
⸂γυναῖκα ἐπὶ μοιχείᾳ⸃ κατειλημμένην καὶ στήσαντες αὐ- Nu 5,12ss
τὴν ἐν μέσῳ 4 ⸀λέγουσιν αὐτῷ⸆· διδάσκαλε, ⸂αὕτη ἡ γυνὴ
κατείληπται ἐπ' αὐτοφώρῳ μοιχευομένη⸃· 5 ⸂ἐν δὲ τῷ
νόμῳ ⸀ἡμῖν Μωϋσῆς ἐνετείλατο⸃ τὰς τοιαύτας ⸁λιθάζειν. Lv 20,10 Dt 22,22-24
σὺ ⸀¹οὖν τί λέγεις⸆; 6 □τοῦτο δὲ ἔλεγον πειράζοντες αὐ- 6,6
τόν, ἵνα ⸀ἔχωσιν ⸂κατηγορεῖν αὐτοῦ⸃.⸌ ὁ δὲ Ἰησοῦς κάτω Mt 22,15 L 6,7
κύψας τῷ δακτύλῳ ⸁κατέγραφεν εἰς τὴν γῆν⸆. 7 ὡς δὲ

50 ⸀ειπεν δε 𝔓66 ℵ f | ⸂† *1–4 6* 𝔓75 ℵ2 B T ¦ ο ελθ. νυκτος πρ. αυ. (⸉K N Δ Ψ 0250 *al*) Ψ 0250 𝔐 lat sy ¦ ο ελθ. νυκ. πρ. αυ. το προτ. Θ *f*1.13 (33). 565. 892. (1241) *al* r1 syh** ¦ ο ελθ. πρ. αυ. νυκ. το πρωτον (*sed pon. p.* αυτων) D ¦ – ℵ* ¦ *txt* 𝔓66 L W • 51 ⸂επιγνωσθη τι εποιησεν D • 52 ⸆τας γραφας D (⸉W it vgcl) | ⸉*4 1–3* 𝔓66c ℵ D W Θ *f*1.13 𝔐 lat ¦ *txt* 𝔓(66*).75vid B L N T Ψ 892. 1424 *al* vgcl | ⸆⟦7,53–8,11⟧ *add. hic* D 𝔐 lat bopt; Hiermss (*cum obel.* S 1424mg *al, cum obel. ab* 8,2 *vl* 8,3 E Λ *al*) ¦ *add.* 7,53 *vl* 8,3sqq *p.* 7,36 225, *p.* 21,25 *f*1, *p.* L 21,38 *f*13, *p.* L 24,53 1333c ¦ *om.* 𝔓66.75 ℵ Avid B Cvid L N T W Δ Θ Ψ 0141. 0211. 33. 565. 1241. 1333*. 1424*. 2768 *al* a f l q sy sa ac2 pbo bopt; Tert Or Hiermss

Ad ⟦7,53–8,11⟧: 53 □ff2 | ⸀-θη K *pm* ¦ απηλθεν *f*13 *pm* ¦ απηλθον Λ 700 *al* ¦ *txt* D Γ 1. 28. 892. 1010 *pm* | ⸁τοπον 1. 892 *pc* • 8,2 ⸀παραγινεται D ¦ ηλθεν Λ *f*13 *pc* ¦ ηλ. ο Ιησους U 700 *al* r1 | □*f*13 *pc* ¦ *om.* και2 ... αυτους D *pc* • 3 ⸂επι αμαρτια γυν. D (⸉*pc*) ¦ προς αυτον γυν. εν μοιχ. K Π *pm* c ff2 • 4 ⸀ειπον U *al* e | ⸆(6) εκπειραζοντες αυτον οι ιερεις ινα εχωσιν κατηγοριαν αυτου D *pc* ¦ πειραζοντες K Π *pm* | ⸂... ειληπται ... Λ *f*13 28. 892 *pm* ¦ ... κατεληφθη ... K Π 1010 *pm* ¦ ταυτην ευρομεν επ αυτοφ. μοιχευομενην U 700 *al* ¦ *txt* D 1 *pc* lat • 5 ⸂M. δε (+ υμιν 1071) εν τ. ν. εκελευσεν (διακελευει 1071) D 1071 | ⸀ημων Γ 28. 1010 *pm* ¦ – (D) 118. 209 *pc* ¦ *txt* Λ *f*13 1 *al* (⸉K Π 892 *pm*, U 700 *al*) lat | ⸁λιθοβολεισθαι K Π *pm* | ⸀¹δε νυν D ¦ δε c ff2 r1 ¦ – 1071 | ⸆περι αυτης U Λ *f*13 28. 700. 1010 *pm* c ff2 • 6 □(*cf* 4. 11 *v. l.*) D M *pc* | ⸀σχωσιν Γ 28. 892. 1010 *al* ¦ ευρωσιν 1 *pc* | ⸂-ρησαι αυ. Γ 1010 *pc* ¦ κατηγοριαν κατ αυ. U Λ *f*13 28. 700 *pm* c ff2 | ⸁εγρ- K U Γ Λ *f*1 28. 700. 1010 *pm* ¦ εγραψεν *f*13 *pc* | ⸆(8 *v. l.*) ενος εκαστου αυτων τας αμαρτιας 264 ¦ μη προσποιουμενος K *pm*

Fig. 6.1. A page from the Nestlé-Aland Novum Testamentum Graece, 28th ed. by Barbara Aland and others (Stuttgart: Deutsche Bibelgesellschaft, 2012), showing John 7:48–8:7. Notice that the passage 7:53–8:11 is enclosed in double brackets in the text, indicating some doubt about its being a genuine component of the Gospel, and that the text-critical apparatus devotes an extended discussion to variations across the relatively few manuscripts that include it; see below.

The critical apparatus includes "variant readings," namely, other readings from various manuscripts that the scholars decided were not as close to the earliest versions as the readings they chose for the final composite text. The primary manuscripts containing the variant readings are listed, along with the primary manuscripts for the critical text. To say that this is the "final" text is always to say that this is the best approximation of the earliest text that we can reconstruct. As the New Testament textual critic David Parker has observed:

> The text is changing. Every time that I make an edition of the Greek New Testament, or anybody does, we change the wording. We are maybe trying to get back to the oldest possible form but, paradoxically, we are creating a new one. Every translation is different, every reading is different, and although there's been a tradition in parts of Protestant Christianity to say there is a definitive single form of the text, the fact is you can never find it.[10]

There is never, ultimately, a final form of the text. What we have are proximate or working final forms until the next discovery comes along, if it ever does (e.g., the nineteenth-century discovery of Codex Sinaiticus at St. Catherine's Monastery in the Sinai desert).[11] Things could change with new discoveries, as they did with important discoveries of older manuscripts in the nineteenth century or the Dead Sea Scrolls in the twentieth.[12]

Just to illustrate the kind of discussion that textual critics have about the best reading of a passage after collating the best available manuscripts, I give two cases from the Gospel of John. The first is a rather famous passage from John 7:53–8:11, the story of the woman caught in adultery, found only in John's Gospel. The impact of textual criticism can be seen quite clearly in how the editors of various editions and

0. As heard on the BBC program about "The Oldest Bible," broadcast October 6, 2008, http://www.bbc.co.uk/radio4/theoldestbible/. Parker is the Edward Cadbury Professor of Theology and the Director of the Institute for Textual Scholarship and Electronic Editing at the Department of Theology and Religion, University of Birmingham, United Kingdom.

1. See D. C. Parker, Codex Sinaiticus: The Story of the World's Oldest Bible (London/Peabody, MA: Hendrickson, 2010). See Fig. 6.2G. Codex Sinaiticus.

2. See, e.g., Kurt Aland and Barbara Aland, The Text of the New Testament: An Introduction to the Critical Editions and to the Theory and Practice of Modern Textual Criticism (Grand Rapids: Eerdmans, 1987); and D. C. Parker, An Introduction to the New Testament Manuscripts and Their Texts (Cambridge: Cambridge University Press, 2008). See also the somewhat controversial but engaging book by B. D. Ehrman, Misquoting Jesus: The Story Behind Who Changed the Bible and Why (San Francisco: HarperSanFrancisco, 2005). Ehrman, a noted textual critic, emphasizes the thousands of differences among the some 5,000 different surviving manuscripts of the New Testament manuscripts, stressing the instability of the New Testament text rather than its stable character. The book was on the New York Times bestseller's list for several weeks, and garnered wide discussion in public media.

translations of John have decided to deal with this passage in terms of what to relate to the readers. We can start with the bottom line: all textual critics agree that this story was not part of John's original Gospel text, because the oldest and best Greek manuscripts that we have of John's Gospel do not contain this story. It's really pretty simple. (To say this is to say nothing about the historicity of the story. That's another discussion entirely.) Different translations and editions of the Bible will usually have a brief explanatory note to let the reader know that the passage was a later addition to John. For example, the note in the NIV Bible, in brackets, states: "[The earliest manuscripts and many other ancient witnesses do not have John 7:53–8:11. A few manuscripts include these verses, wholly or in part, after John 7:36, John 21:25, Luke 21:38 or Luke 24:53.]" The text of John 7:53–8:11 is then given in a smaller italicized font to set it apart from the rest of the Gospel of John. The editors of the King James Version of the Bible (translated in 1611) used as the basis for their translation a different set of Greek manuscripts that are not as old as the best manuscripts we have today; the editors and translators of that time-honored version knew nothing about what only later scholars came to discover, and consequently, the passage appears in the KJV in the same font as the surrounding text, without any indication that it is not an original part of the Gospel.

As for the difference between the print and digital versions of this variant reading, it really all depends on the digital text being used. The NIV and NRSV print versions clearly mark the passage as a later addition to John's Gospel. The digital versions do as well, but it's not quite as easy to see the editorial note on the passage in the digital version. It all depends on whether one clicks or scrolls to the note, rather than simply glancing down to the bottom of a printed page to see that this passage has had a relatively transient life. The variant reading is somewhat clearer in the print version simply because of the layout of the printed page over against the digital screen version.

The second passage has a much more subtle, but still important, variation in text from John 20:30–31. This passage summarizes the purpose of John's Gospel: "Jesus performed many other signs in the presence of his disciples, which are not recorded in this book. But these are written *that you may believe* that Jesus is the Messiah, the Son of God, and that by believing you may have life in his name" (NIV). The text in question is the phrase I have italicized in verse 31, "*that you may believe* that Jesus is the Messiah." The NRSV version renders the passage with a little more clarity still: "these are written so that *you may come to believe."* The NIV has a note regarding this phrase indicating a variant reading, which would be translated as *"that you may continue to believe."*

So what's the difference? As it turns out, the difference is one Greek letter, a *sigma*. The text that scholars have chosen as the earliest version reads, in Greek, *pisteu[s]ēte,* with the *sigma* inserted by the editors in brackets. The question is whether the text should read *pisteusēte,* the aorist subjunctive form of the verb "to believe," or *pisteuēte,* the present subjunctive form of the same verb. The difference may be only one letter, one *sigma,* but the difference in meaning is significant. The aorist subjunctive form *(pisteusēte)* indicates the aspect of *coming to faith, coming to believe.* With this reading, the purpose of the signs in John's Gospel is to initiate faith, something for which we see evidence in John 2:1–11, where Jesus changed water into wine, and his disciples believed in him when they saw the sign. Similarly, in John 4:52–54, the Capernaum official came to believe in Jesus on the basis of the sign that Jesus performed in healing his son from a distance. One might say that this understanding of faith based on signs is a kind of seeing=believing theology. By contrast, the present subjunctive verb form, *pistuēte* connotes continuous or ongoing faith, hence the NIV's "that you *may continue to believe."* (Both the aorist subjunctive and the present subjunctive readings are, grammatically, purpose clauses.)

Why would an editor in the early transmission of John's Gospel make the subtle change from the one verb form to the other? Most likely, the change in the verb form, from the aorist to the present subjunctive, reflects a change in the theological vision of the Gospel of John, very possibly based in the experience of the community that produced this Gospel. In other words, even though Jesus did so many signs, the people still did not come to believe in him overall (John 12:37). In fact, they rejected Jesus. The experience of John's community, then, was that signs do not necessarily lead to belief. Thus, rather than John's Gospel (or an earlier "signs gospel") serving as a missionary document within the Christian-Jewish evangelizing of non-Christian Jews in the synagogue, the experience of rejection and being expelled from the synagogue (John 9:22; 12:42; 16:2–4) resulted in a revision of the Gospel now addressed to those who *already* believed. Hence, these signs are written "that you *might continue to believe,"* even though so many others have rejected this Gospel message. Rather than seeing-as-believing (a position criticized in the doubting Thomas story from John 20), for John, the new theological vision, represented in the textual variation in 20:31, is that believing leads to new ways of seeing (as evident in the figure of the Beloved Disciple in John). Yes, all that in one little sigma and the debate about which is the more original version of the text.[13]

Many of these debates over how to weigh the relative value of the different variant readings can be followed in the revealing book edited by Bruce Metzger on behalf of the Greek New Testament editorial committee, on which he served; he also chaired the translation committee for the New Revised Standard Version of the New Testament. The book is *A Textual Commentary on the Greek New Testament*.[14] As is the case of all of Metzger's books, this one is judicious and clear. It helps to know Greek to make sense of it all (!), but you can get a pretty good idea of some of the discussions about the Greek text that the editorial board held. After compiling and collating all of the manuscript evidence, they give various gradings to different readings: an "A" reading is if they're certain that they have the earliest reading; "B" if they're almost certain; "C" if the committee has had difficulty deciding about the best reading; and "D," that they really aren't sure at all.[15] They give the *omission* of the story about the woman caught in adultery an "A" reading—that is, they are certain it was *not* part of John's original Gospel. In summary, Metzger writes:

> Although the Committee was unanimous that the pericope was originally not part of the Fourth Gospel, in deference to the evident antiquity of the passage a majority decided to print it, enclosed within double square brackets, at its traditional place following Jn 7.52. Inasmuch as the passage is absent from the earlier and better manuscripts that normally serve to identify types of text, it is not always easy to make a decision among alternative readings. In any case it will be understood that the level of certainty ({A}) is within the framework of the initial decision relating to the passage as a whole.[16]

13. On the history of John's community and the development of the Gospel of John, the book by Raymond Brown remains seminal: *The Community of the Beloved Disciple* (Mahwah, NJ: Paulist, 1979).

14. 2nd ed., Stuttgart: Deutsche Bibelgesellschaft, 1994. The book is also available in digital form.

15. "In order to indicate the relative degree of certainty in the mind of the Committee for the reading adopted as the text, an identifying letter is included within braces at the beginning of each set of textual variants. The letter {A} signifies that the text is certain, while {B} indicates that the text is almost certain. The letter {C}, however, indicates that the Committee had difficulty in deciding which variant to place in the text. The letter {D}, which occurs only rarely, indicates that the Committee had great difficulty in arriving at a decision. In fact, among the {D} decisions sometimes none of the variant readings commended itself as original, and therefore the only recourse was to print the least unsatisfactory reading" (14).

16. *Commentary on the Greek New Testament*, 189.

As for the committee's evaluation of the passage in John 20:30–31, they gave it a "C" reading on the basis of the following rationale:

πιστεύ[σ]ητε {C}

Both πιστεύητε and πιστεύσητε have notable early support. The aorist tense, strictly interpreted, suggests that the Fourth Gospel was addressed to non-Christians so that they might come to believe that Jesus is the Messiah; the present tense suggests that the aim of the writer was to strengthen the faith of those who already believe ("that you may continue to believe"). In view of the difficulty of choosing between the readings by assessing the supposed purpose of the evangelist (assuming that he used the tenses of the subjunctive strictly), the Committee considered it preferable to represent both readings by enclosing ς within square brackets.[17]

As one can see, there is quite a lot that goes on behind the establishment of the Greek text that serves as the basis for all modern translations.

So, why rehearse all of this in a book on digital Bibles? There are two primary reasons to review such debates about textual criticism.[18] First, the "digital turn" in scholarship about the Bible has led to significant new developments in the practice of the discipline of textual criticism. This was already observed by the prominent textual critic David Parker in his 2003 article "Through a Screen Darkly: Digital Texts and the New Testament."[19] In this article, Parker states that the "use of computers in textual study of the New Testament is revolutionizing textual scholarship, and is about to lead to major changes in other branches of New Testament study."[20] How so? Parker notes three areas of "revolution": 1) the concept of the text within the computer (using computers to help collate manuscripts), 2) the study of manuscripts, and 3) the task of producing a critical edition of the New Testament. In sum, he calls attention to a significant change in how text critics can approach manuscripts, since manuscripts themselves can now be rendered, searched, and studied in digital form. This moves well beyond merely noting important variant readings between different manuscripts. It allows textual critics working with electronic transcription

---

7. Ibid., 219–20.
8. Robert A. Kraft was among the first scholars to comment on "The Use of Computers in New Testament Textual Criticism," in B. D. Ehrman and M. W. Holmes, eds., *The Text of the New Testament in Contemporary Research: Essays on the Status Quaestionis. A Volume in Honor of Bruce M. Metzger* (Studies and Documents, 46; Grand Rapids: Eerdmans, 1995), 268–82.
9. *Journal for the Study of the New Testament* 25, no. 4 (2003): 395–411.
0. "Through a Screen Darkly: Digital Texts and the New Testament," 395.

basically to explode the printed page of a critical edition of the New Testament and to provide a much thicker and richer description and analysis of all the relevant textual data related to any biblical passage. In particular, Parker reflects on the "strange ambiguity of textual scholarship. For textual critics, under the guise of reconstructing original texts, are really creating new ones."[21] The days of providing a printed reconstructed text with a limited critical apparatus are over in the digital age. The emphasis will shift from a reconstructed original (or closest approximation of the original) text to the many forms in which the biblical text has existed across the ages, and continues to exist. The traditional printed form of the Nestle-Aland Greek New Testament (now in its 28th edition) will take on significant new features in digital form. The digital edition of the critical text is now available through various publishers of Bible programs (Olive Tree, Accordance, Logos), and provides transcriptions of the oldest and most important Greek manuscripts[22] along with a hyperlinked interactive critical apparatus. How, one might ask, is any of this related to considering what kind of "text" the digital Bible is in the church? At its most fundamental level, the decisions made by scholars working on the critical text of the Greek New Testament will directly affect the foundational Greek text that is used as the basis for all future translations of the New Testament into any language. This may involve minor tweaks from one edition to another, or it could bring greater attention to previously neglected versions of the Bible that had relatively distinctive leanings in contrast to the homogenized composite text. This latter possibility could highlight theological tendencies of particular textual traditions or of influential church leaders in the history of the church. As one prominent New Testament scholar puts it, this would be a shift "away from a fixed, determined text to a 3D universe of texts-through-history."[23] Although it is unlikely to result in the unraveling of a composite approach to a unified text, the use of digital scholarship will enhance the ability of text critics to construct a much more three-dimensional world of how different versions of the Bible functioned throughout the history of the church.[24] Second, while most parish-

---

21. Ibid., 401.
22. See, for example, the Codex Sinaiticus Project and Webpage, which provides access to a digitized version of Codex Sinaiticus: http://www.codexsinaiticus.org/en/; see also D. C. Parker, *Codex Sinaiticus: The Story of the World's Oldest Bible* (Peabody, MA: Hendrickson, 2010). See also the new series, *Digital Biblical Studies*, announced by the Brill publishing house: http://www.brill.com/products/series/digital-biblical-studies.
23. In private correspondence from Dr. Neil Elliott.
24. To give but one example of a well-known manuscript with a particular theological bent, E. J. Epp

ioners will not be aware of the various stages that their personal, pew, or digital Bible went through, nonetheless, the work of scholars on the basic Greek text of the New Testament, for example, does, in fact, have a direct impact on every translation. Just think of what we saw in relation to the two passages discussed above from the Gospel of John. It is important for readers of the Bible to understand something of the process that the Bible has gone through from the writing of the manuscripts, to their being manually copied generation after generation, to the comparison of the many manuscripts, resulting in a critical edition of the Bible in original languages, to the many translations of the Bible into modern languages. In short, how did we get the biblical text that we have? It is incumbent on those who value the biblical witness to have a mature understanding of how the Bibles we use came to be. To adapt a well-stated bit of wisdom from the 2007 documentary *For the Bible Tells Me So,* "There's nothing wrong with having a fifth-grade understanding of the Bible, as long as you're in the fifth grade!"[25] One can both revere the Bible as a profound witness to God's presence in the world and have a deep understanding of the very human process by which the Bible came to be formed and handed down from one generation to another.

In comparing how print Bibles versus digital Bibles deal with questions about textual variants, print Bibles typically do a better job of communicating what has gone into the current edition and translation of the Bible that a person is reading. Print Bibles tend to be more transparent on this score, whereas digital Bibles usually require the reader to take an additional step or two (a click or two) to find out such information. It's not that the information is unavailable in digital forms of the Bible in translation; rather, it is that the information is not obvious in digital Bibles. Where digital Bibles excel is in the arena of being able to compare many different translations of the same passages, something that is both a strength and a weakness when trying to answer the question: Is there a Bible in this church?

showed how the late fifth-century Codex Bezae Cantabrigiensis, the "Western" Text of the Gospels and Acts, had overtly anti-Jewish readings at variance with other manuscript traditions. See E. J. Epp, *The Theological Tendency of Codex Bezae Cantabrigiensis in Acts* (Cambridge: Cambridge University Press, 1966). See also Bart Ehrman's *The Orthodox Corruption of Scripture: The Effect of Early Christological Controversies on the Text of the New Testament* (New York: Oxford University Press, 1997).

5. In the documentary, this statement is made by the Rev. Dr. Laurence Keene, from the Disciples of Christ Church.

From Critical Text to Translation in the Digital Age

The first digital Bibles were merely digital approximations of print Bibles, trying to replicate the pages of the Bible on the pages of a screen. Initially, there was a simple emphasis on reproducing the text, without much attention to format. But format and readability became increasingly important concerns for digital publishers of Bibles. At the same time, publishers of digital Bibles have increasingly sought to take advantage of the benefits of a digital platform: the ease of searching text, having multiple translations open in different windows at the same time, and allowing for hyperlinked resources to amplify the biblical text, among other features.

Perhaps the greatest irony when shifting from a discussion of textual criticism to translation of the biblical text is the simple observation that whereas the critical editions of the Hebrew and Greek texts of the Bible have been very stable for more than two generations, the number of different translations, paraphrases, and editions of the Bible in translation has soared nearly beyond measure, largely spurred on by the digital revolution and the widespread availability of digital versions of the Bible. Whereas both the Hebrew text of the "Old Testament" (to use a familiar Christian term) and the Greek text of the "New Testament" have gone largely unchanged from one edition to the next over the past fifty years, the proliferation of digital Bibles of all kinds has actually created a less stable text than their print cousins.

The variant readings in the critical apparatus of the Greek New Testament have changed slightly, but the consensus text has remained consistent for over half a century, long before computers came on the scene. Many scholars are convinced that we have arrived as close to an approximation of the so-called original text of the New Testament as we can reasonably hope to get, short of significant new manuscript discoveries.[26] The standard critical edition of the Greek New Testament designed for scholarly research has long been the *Novum Testamentum Graece* (*NTG*), edited initially by Eberhart Nestle (1851–1913), then his son Erwin Nestle (1883–1972), followed by Kurt Aland (1915–1984),

---

26. As a result, there has been increased interest in the versions of the New Testament that various church fathers used. To this end, the Society of Biblical Literature launched a series to address the versions used by different writers in the early church, *The New Testament in the Greek Fathers*. The volumes "make available the New Testament text as it is recoverable from the writings of the Greek Fathers. Each volume presents a critically reconstructed text of the New Testament of a given Father and evaluates the data in terms of its reliability and of the relationship of the Father's text to known textual groups." See https://www.sbl-site.org/publications/Books _NTGrF.aspx.

hence generically the Nestle-Aland Greek New Testament, though various other scholars were also closely involved in the editing process.[27] In addition to the *Novum Testamentum Graece* (published in Stuttgart by the Deutsche Bibelgesellschaft, and featuring the critical apparatus that includes textual variants), another edition of *The Greek New Testament (GNT)* was published by the United Bible Societies, starting in 1966, primarily for use by translators, with very limited reference to textual variants. By 1975, the *NTG* and the *GNT* (3rd edition) had the same text along with overlapping editorial committees.[28] The text of the 26th edition of the Nestle-Aland Greek New Testament (1979) was adopted as the text of the 27th edition (1993, with significant updating of the notes in the critical apparatus). In turn, the text of the 27th edition of the Nestle-Aland Greek New Testament was adopted as the text of the 28th edition (2012),[29] with one important change. The 28th edition took advantage of the completion of a major critical edition of the Catholic Epistles (1 and 2 Peter, 1, 2, and 3 John, James, and Jude), which resulted in 34 changes in the Greek text, most of them relatively minor.[30]

As for the text of the Hebrew Bible, it has been even more stable than the Greek New Testament. In part, this is due to the dominance of what is the oldest surviving complete manuscript of the Hebrew Bible, the Leningrad Codex (c. 1009 CE), the text of which was widely adopted by rabbinic scholars and Masoretes (Jewish scribes/scholars) shortly after the year 1000 CE. Toward the end of the 19th century, about 730 Hebrew Bible manuscripts had been catalogued. This number exploded to over 10,000 with the discovery of the Cairo Geniza in the 1890s, and was later further supplemented by hundreds more Hebrew Bible manuscripts with the discovery of the Dead Sea Scrolls, starting in 1947.[31]

The closest thing we have to a critical edition of the Hebrew Bible is the *Biblia Hebraica Stuttgartensia,* which is intended to be an exact print version of the Leningrad Codex.[32] New critical editions of the Hebrew Bible are in preparation that will take into account significant manu-

7. On the history of the Nestle-Aland editions of the *Novum Testamentum Graece,* see http://www.nestle-aland.com/en/history/.

8. The United Bible Societies *Greek New Testament* is now in its 5th edition (2014).

9. The 28th edition also introduced significant changes to the critical apparatus.

0. *Novum Testamentum Graecum: Editio Critico Maior* (German Bible Society 2013). Some of the changes in the text of the Catholic Epistles are orthographic, some have to do with word order, but none of them are of much significance for the interpretation and meaning of the Catholic Epistles. See J. K. Elliott, "A New Edition of Nestle-Aland, Greek New Testament," *The Journal of Theological Studies* 64, no. 1 (2013): 47–65.

1. See, e.g., M. Glickman, *Sacred Treasure, The Cairo Geniza* (Woodstock, VT: Jewish Lights, 2011); and G. Vermes, *An Introduction to the Complete Dead Sea Scrolls,* rev. ed. (Minneapolis: Fortress Press, 1999).

script traditions beyond the Leningrad Codex.[33] *The Hebrew Bible: A Critical Edition* (the *HBCE*, formerly called the Oxford Hebrew Bible) will be an eclectic text drawing on multiple manuscript traditions in a way parallel to the critical edition of the Greek New Testament. The Hebrew University Bible Project (*HUBP*) will, like the *Biblia Hebraica*, rely on one manuscript tradition, but unlike the *Biblia Hebraica*, it will reproduce in print and digital form the Hebrew text from the Aleppo Codex, a medieval manuscript that lacks much of the Torah. An important feature of all of these editions of the Hebrew is that they will be published as digital texts as well as in print. Further, the manuscripts themselves will increasingly be available in digital form, often with digital images, not unlike the Codex Sinaiticus manuscript in Greek.[34]

Digital versions of critical editions of the biblical text are becoming increasingly important, as are computer-based studies of both biblical manuscripts and the biblical text itself. Though often rather technical in nature because of what scholars who are working at the intersection of biblical studies and computer data analysis presume on the part of their readers, the interpretation of the Bible will both continue along fairly traditional lines and also see the growing application of the new field of Digital Humanities to the process. Already, in 2013, the Swiss scholar Claire Clivaz edited a volume on *Digital Humanities in Biblical, Early Jewish and Early Christian Studies*.[35] Along the same lines, the publisher of this volume, E. J. Brill, also recently announced a new series, *Digital Biblical Studies*. The description of the series from Brill points to serious scholarship that will be very academic and technical in character:

> The series aims to publish the latest research at the intersection of Digital Humanities and Biblical Studies, Ancient Judaism, and Early Christianity in order to demonstrate the transformation of research, teaching, cognition and the economy of knowledge in digital culture. In particular, DBS investigates and evaluates the practices and methodologies of Digital Humanities as applied to texts, inscriptions, archaeological data, and scholarship related to these fields.

32. It was published in fascicles during 1968–1976, with the first complete publication in 1976 by the German Bible Society in Stuttgart (hence the name).
33. On the critical text of the Hebrew Bible, see E. Tov, *Textual Criticism of the Hebrew Bible*, 3rd revised & expanded edition (Minneapolis: Fortress Press, 2012); and E. Würthwein, *The Text of the Old Testament: An Introduction to the Biblia Hebraica*, 3rd ed., revised & expanded, A. A. Fischer (Grand Rapids: Eerdmans, 2014).
34. For the digital text of the Leningrad Codex, see http://tanach.us/Tanach.xml. For the digital version of Codex Sinaiticus, see http://www.codex-sinaiticus.net/en/.
35. Leiden: Brill, 2013.

The primary areas of focus are the digital edition of ancient manuscripts, the evolution of research between big data and close reading, the visualization of data, and the epistemological transformation of ancient studies through digital culture. DBS will encompass collected essays as well as monographs, with a particular emphasis on cutting-edge research. Several ancient languages are in the scope of the series, including ancient Greek, Hebrew, Latin, Arabic, Coptic, and Syriac.[36]

These are very much the kinds of things that David Parker anticipated back in his 2003 essay on "Through a Screen Darkly." The goal of the studies in this series will seek to use digital tools to bring deeper understanding of the biblical text, which in turn will eventually also impact less academic and more ecclesial understandings of the Bible, including issues of translation.

Digital Dissemination and the Hydra of Translations

As noted earlier, digital Bibles really shine when it comes to comparing different translations of the Bible. With so many different translations, it becomes rather difficult to compare them even in digital format, especially across languages and editions. The most widely used digital app for accessing the Bible is YouVersion, with its slogans that "Now the Bible is an App" and "The Bible is Everywhere." And because the Bible is an app, you can take it with you anywhere your smartphone goes, which—of course—is everywhere. As of this writing (May 2017),[37] YouVersion has been downloaded over 275 million times. It offers over 1,500 versions of the Bible in over 1,000 languages, all for free. In English alone, at present, the app offers 48 different versions. Just for fun, here they are:

- Amplified Bible
- American Standard Version
- The Books of the Bible (NT)
- Common English Bible
- Contemporary English Version
- Contemporary English Version (Anglicized Version)

36. See http://www.brill.com/products/series/digital-biblical-studies.
37. I completed the manuscript for this book in January of 2017, but have updated some of the data as late as May of 2017. It seems to be in the nature of all things digital to change and develop rapidly.

- Complete Jewish Bible
- Catholic Public Domain Version
- Darby Translation (1890)
- Douay-Rheims Challoner Revision (1752)
- Easy-to-Read Version of the Holy Bible
- English Standard Version
- Good News Bible
- Good News Bible (Anglicized)
- Good News Bible (Catholic edition in Septuagint order)
- Good News Translation
- Good News Translation (U.S. Version)
- God's Word Translation
- St. Paul from the Trenches (1916)
- Holman Christian Standard Bible
- International Children's Bible
- The Scriptures (1998)
- Jubilee Bible
- King James Version
- King James Version, American Edition
- King James Version with Apocrypha, American Edition
- Hexham English Bible
- Modern English Version
- Metrical Psalms (1650)
- The Message
- New American Bible, revised edition
- New American Standard Bible
- New Century Version
- New English Translation

- New International Reader's Version
- New International Version
- New International Version Anglicized
- New King James Version
- New Living Translation
- Orthodox Jewish Bible
- Revised Version (1885)
- Tree of Life Version
- World English Bible
- World English Bible British Edition
- World Messianic Bible
- World Messianic Bible British Edition
- Young's Literal Translation of the Holy Bible

Noticeably absent from the list are the Revised Standard Version of the Bible, and its updated form, the New Revised Standard Version of the Bible. Also absent are the New Jerusalem Bible, the New English Bible, the Revised English Bible, the Inclusive Bible, the International Standard Version, and An American Translation. Most of these translations are not included because of copyright issues. But still, that is a huge number of available English versions![38]

The sheer multitude of translations cuts against the grain of what one or another individual translation appears to claim. The plethora of versions pushes against any particular authoritative version. There is no longer anything "standard" about the Revised "Standard" Version of the Bible, let alone the New Revised "Standard" Version. Similarly, there is nothing International about the New International Version of the Bible, nor anything distinctly "American" about the New American Bible. The Common English Bible may or may not be particularly Common. And so on. The claim to universality is belied by the sheer multitude of translations.

---

8. Well before the leap into the digital era, S. Kubo & W. F. Specht published *So Many Versions? 20th Century English Versions of the Bible* (1975, revised and enlarged 1983; Grand Rapids: Zondervan). They provide in-depth analysis of some 20 English versions, both translations and paraphrases, published before 1983.

The most popular version of the English Bible remains the King James Version, an English translation that has held sway since it was first published in 1611, over 400 years ago. The 2015 Barna Group survey of *The State of the Bible 2015,* conducted on behalf of the American Bible Society, reported that 39 percent of respondents listed the King James Version as the overall preferred version (though this differed somewhat for various groups), with the New International Version coming in second at 13 percent, followed by the New King James Version at 10 percent. And truth be told, there's nothing really very "new" about the New King James Version, as it relies upon the same manuscript traditions as the original King James Version. The New Revised Standard Version (a staple of courses on the Bible in colleges and universities), intended to be the successor Bible to the King James Version, came in at a paltry 3 percent.[39] See Fig. 6.3G.

Although the King James Version remains the most popular English version of the Bible, it is certainly not based on the oldest and best manuscripts. Despite the anonymous claim that "If the King James Version is good enough for God, it's good enough for me!," it is an outdated translation, notwithstanding its eloquence, its incredible influence on the subsequent English language (along with Shakespeare), and the clear scholarship it represented in 1611.[40] But it should be retired now that we know more about earlier manuscript traditions, let alone the importance of keeping translations current as languages change and develop. The New King James Version makes improvements by modernizing the English, but the editors chose to use the same underlying Greek and Hebrew manuscript tradition as had been used in 1611. Thus, when the New Testament of the NKJV was first published in 1979, it was already outdated by the newly discovered and superior Greek manuscript traditions that formed the basis of the Nestle-Aland *Novum Testamentum Graece.*[41]

What are we to make of the continued overwhelming popularity of the King James Bible? One thing we need to bear in mind is that as a translation, it had a nearly 300-year head start on any widespread competing English translation.[42] It had gained enough authority and

---

39. *The State of the Bible 2015* (New York: American Bible Society, 2015), 16. The copyright owner of the RSV, the National Council of Churches, also holds copyright to the NRSV.

40. See, e.g., *A Dictionary of Biblical Tradition in English Literature,* ed. D. L. Jeffrey (Grand Rapids: Eerdmans, 1992).

41. See Kubo & Specht, *So Many Versions?,* 273–307. The Old Testament of the NKJV was first published in 1982.

42. See A. Nicolson, *God's Secretaries: The Making of the King James Bible* (New York: HarperCollins, 2005); D. L. Jeffrey, ed., *The King James Bible and the World It Made* (Waco, TX: Baylor University Press, 2011);

acquired such a revered status that even new manuscript finds with more ancient texts were not enough to dethrone its version of the Bible. Its wording of the biblical text had become so ingrained that anything else simply sounded strange to the ear. The Bible was the sacred book, and the King James Version was the sacred translation. Even in digital format, the King James Version remains the most popular version used.

Still, the multiplication of English translations of the Bible over the last 100 years surely indicates the desire of different Christian faith communities to have a translation that reflects something of their religious convictions in the language chosen for translation, often in subtle ways, even while seeking to provide accurate renderings of the underlying Hebrew and Greek texts. Thus, it makes perfect sense that the Revised Standard Version (RSV) sought to provide a version rooted in the King James Version, but attentive to modern English usage and modern scholarship on ancient manuscript traditions for mainline Protestants (the RSV NT was first published in 1946, and the OT in 1952).[43] The New American Bible (1970) produced by a Roman Catholic translation committee, coheres with a broadly Roman Catholic vision of the continuity of tradition and slightly more formal language for liturgical usage. The New International Version was produced by an evangelical Protestant translation committee (1978) and published by a traditionally evangelical publishing house, Zondervan, based in the historically Dutch-Reformed city of Grand Rapids, MI. The translation committee was "motivated by our conviction that the Bible is God's Word in written form. We believe that the Bible contains the divine answer to the deepest needs of humanity, sheds unique light on our path in a dark world and sets forth the way to our eternal well-being."[44]

Each translation is, of course, also already the first step of interpretation. Whenever we read anything in translation, we are already involved in interpretation. This is simply because the semantic range of a word in one language often does not match the semantic range of a word in another language.[45] This is the case in going from any lan-

---

and L. Ryken, *The Legacy of the King James Bible: Celebrating 400 Years of the Most Influential English Translation* (Wheaton, IL: Crossway, 2011).

43. The New Revised Standard Version was first published in 1989, and sought to improve upon the RSV by updating English language usage, including adopting inclusive language for male and female when the original language appeared to infer all people, and not just "men."

44. From the Preface of the NIV Bible.

45. When someone greets me in Spanish with "buen dia" (have a good day), I used to respond by saying "tu también," thinking it meant "you too" (which technically it does). When I learned the proper response—"igualmente"—to my English speaking ears, it sounded like I was saying

guage to another, and it is also the case when translating the Bible from Hebrew or Greek to any language. Every semester, I tell my students that to read anything in its original language is to read it in color, while reading a translation is like reading it in black and white. The same content is communicated, but there are subtle overtones and nuances that do not translate well. Language is a living, moving target, which is why dictionaries must be updated on a regular basis, and which is also why we will never be done with the process of translating and retranslating the Bible into modern languages.

Digital resources can be a great help in coming to a deeper appreciation of the issues involved in translating the Bible. There are powerful computer programs that provide a veritable endless number of resources that can aid in the process of translation. But it is also the case that the ease of disseminating any number of English versions of the Bible in digital form can create the impression that the translation does not matter so much after all. People might be apt to think that because there are so many translations of the Bible in English, one translation is as good as another. But that is not actually true. All translations have certain orientations, as we have seen.[46] The real problem is that while some versions excel at effectively translating various portions of the Bible, other versions falter somewhat in providing the best translation of particular passages. Bibles both excel and fall short in different ways. But now that I have stated this, it begs the question of "according to whom?" Who gets to decide which translation of which passage is better or worse? And how is the average layperson who does not read Hebrew or Greek supposed to make decisions about translations? Does it really make that much of a difference? Is it really a problem that so many English versions are available and so readily disseminated in digital form?

Well, in a word, yes. Why is it a problem? The title of this chapter suggests why. If we are relying on the Bible as the sacred scripture of the church, then doesn't it matter whether or not we have a common text? It is not as if this is only a modern problem. Already, in antiquity, there were enough versions of the Greek Bible running around

"equally," which sounded like an odd thing to say. Of course, the "tu también" is the odd thing for a fluent Spanish-speaker to hear, since they hear "igualmente" as "you too"! Similarly, when I first heard the Dutch expression "Loop naar de maan" (literally, "walk to the moon"), I thought "what a strange expression," until I realized that its best English translation was "Go to hell!" Idiomatic expressions are particularly difficult to translate.

46. For good surveys of English translations of the Bible, see B. M. Metzger, *The Bible in Translation: Ancient and English Versions* (Grand Rapids: Baker, 2001), and M. J. Gorman, *Elements of Biblical Exegesis,* revised & expanded ed. (Grand Rapids: Baker Academic, 2010) 40–61.

that there was a concerted effort to arrive at a "correct" text. Similarly, there were so many Old Latin translations of the biblical text that in the fourth century the Pope sought to arrange for a unified version. The composite and eclectic text of the Nestle-Aland Greek New Testament (now in its 28th edition) shows how vigilant scholars have been in trying to come up with a common original language version that can serve as the basis of all translations. There is no manuscript that reads as the critical edition of the Greek New Testament reads, but such is the character of a critical edition that relies not only on one manuscript tradition, but seeks to take the whole of the evidence into account.

All of this brings us back to the irony that the critical edition of the Greek New Testament has been relatively stable, whereas the proliferation of widely varying translations and paraphrases has only become more widespread because of the radical ease of dissemination in the digital age. That there will be some latitude in different translations goes without saying, but if the dozens of versions are not in some kind of agreement, then questions about the stability of the text arise. And such questions do arise for the church, whether the faithful recognize the problem or not.

It has always been so. When the Hebrew Bible was translated into Greek around 250 BCE, the Septuagint became the dominant Greek version of the Hebrew Bible for Diaspora Judaism, as Greek was the dominant language for Jews living outside of Palestine. The story behind the Septuagint reflects how important it was to legitimize the translation of scripture so that it could be trusted as the word of God just as much as the original Hebrew.[47] The *Letter of Aristeas,* an early Jewish apologetic work from the second century BCE, relates the story of the Septuagint in order to provide assurance that the translation had divine guidance. In brief, the term Septuagint comes from the Latin word for "seventy" (often abbreviated simply as the LXX), referring to the tradition that King Ptolemy II commissioned the translation of the Torah for the great library at Alexandria in Egypt. (Alexandria was an important center for Jews in North Africa.) For the translation, the High Priest in Jerusalem was asked to assign 72 individuals for the task, though later Jewish tradition put the number at 70, perhaps to coincide with the story of the 70 elders who accompanied Moses to Mount Sinai (Exod 24:1–2, 9–11). The story goes that this group of 72 or 70 scholars travelled to Alexandria where, after 72 days (no coincidence there!), they

---

47. See K. Jobes & M. Silva, *Invitation to the Septuagint,* 2nd ed. (Grand Rapids: Baker Academic, 2015).

completed the translation of the Torah into Greek. Later on, the Jewish philosopher Philo of Alexandria (c. 25 BCE–50 CE) expanded on the legend, saying that the scholars were placed in separate rooms, yet produced exactly the same translation, proving that the Septuagint was divinely inspired (Philo, *Life of Moses*, 2.25–41).

But the Septuagint was not the only translation of the Hebrew Bible into Greek. The brilliant and controversial Christian scholar Origen put together the *Hexapla*,[48] a massive comparative version of the Old Testament with six columns: 1) Hebrew; 2) Hebrew transliterated into Greek characters; 3) the version by Aquila of Sinope; 4) the version of Symmachus the Ebionite; 5) a version of the Septuagint with indications of where the Hebrew is not represented in the Greek translation, along with signs of where there is no Hebrew text underlying the Greek text; and 6) the version of Theodotion. Origen would have absolutely loved the ability to compare these different Greek versions using computer analysis! The Septuagint, of course, was the Bible for the earliest Christians, since the New Testament as a sacred collection of writings did not take shape until between the end of the second century CE and the beginning of the fifth century CE.

The next major translation that would have a profound effect on the life of the church was Jerome's translation of the Hebrew and Greek Bible into Latin, the *Vulgate,* produced toward the end of the fourth century and the beginning of the fifth century CE. In 383 CE, Pope Damasus commissioned Jerome (c. 342–420) to produce a dependable text of the Bible in Latin. So many different versions of the Old Latin Bible were in circulation, that there was no standard text for Latin-speaking Christianity. Jerome was not anxious to take on this task:

> You urge me to revise the Old Latin version, and, as it were, to sit in judgment on the copies of the Scriptures that are now scattered throughout the world; and, inasmuch as they differ from one another, you would have me decide which of them agree with the original. . . . Is there anyone learned or unlearned who, when he takes the volume in his hands and perceives that what he reads does not suit his settled tastes, will not break out immediately into violent language and call me a forger and profane person for having the audacity to add anything to the ancient books or to make any changes or corrections in them?[49]

---

48. See A. Grafton, "Origen's Hexapla: Scholarship, Culture, and Power" in his *Christianity and the Transformation of the Book: Origen, Eusebius, and the Library of Caesarea* (Cambridge, MA: Harvard University Press, 2008), 86–132.

49. Jerome, *Letter to Damasus.* P. Schaff & H. Wace, eds., *Nicene and Post-Nicene Fathers of the Christian Church,* 2nd series (Grand Rapids: Eerdmans, 1890), 6:487–88.

But Jerome finally relented and agreed to the thankless task of producing one unified text from the many different versions of the Old Latin manuscripts, "almost as many forms of text as there are manuscripts"![50] Jerome's concerns about being criticized were well founded. He came under sharp attack from various quarters for daring to alter the various Old Latin versions, even though the Pope had made the request. Jerome fought back with sharp words of his own against people who "think that ignorance is identical with holiness."[51]

The Septuagint and the Vulgate were the two most important translations of the Bible before the Reformation translations of the Bible into the vernacular German, French, and English versions (among many others) in the sixteenth century. With each translation, errors both large and small were introduced. Such translation problems continue even in our sophisticated digital age, to which we will turn in a moment. But we can, first, consider but two translation errors in the classic Septuagint and Vulgate texts, errors that had a significant impact on later interpretation and belief.

In the Septuagint, one striking error had a direct and somewhat humorous impact on the story of Jesus's triumphal entry riding into Jerusalem on Palm Sunday, at least for the Gospel of Matthew. The passage in question is Zechariah 9:9, which the NRSV correctly translated from the Hebrew original:

> Rejoice greatly, O daughter Zion!
>   Shout aloud, O daughter Jerusalem!
> Lo, your king comes to you;
>   triumphant and victorious is he,
> humble and riding on a donkey,
>   on a colt, the foal of a donkey.

One feature of this particular passage is the occurrence of Hebrew parallelism, which is common in prophetic and poetic passages from the Hebrew Bible. This kind of parallelism involves repetition of an idea from one line to another. Thus, the passage in Zechariah 9:9 refers to a king who comes "triumphant and victorious," "humble and riding on a donkey, on a colt, the foal of a donkey." In the Hebrew original, the king is clearly riding on one animal—a donkey, or more precisely, a

---

50. Jerome, *Letter to Damasus.*
51. See B. M. Metzger, *The Bible in Translation: Ancient and English Versions,* 35. The criticism that Jerome received for revising the Old Latin into the Vulgate is reminiscent of those who were sharply critical of the Revised Standard Version of the Bible, which was intended to replace the King James Version of the Bible.

colt, the foal of a donkey. But the Septuagint translation gets tripped up by the Hebrew connective particle *vav*, which is best translated as the NRSV does, a connective comma ("on a donkey, on a colt, the foal of a donkey"). But the Hebrew particle can also be translated into Greek by the word "and" (*kai*), a much stronger connective particle, which is what the Septuagint does in a rather wooden manner in this passage. Thus, the Septuagint renders the prophetic statement about the king quite literally: he will be "riding on a donkey, *and* on a colt, the foal of a donkey." Thus, whereas the Hebrew original refers to *one* animal, the Septuagint can be read as referring to *two* animals. As Matthew 21 tells the story of Jesus's triumphal entry into Jerusalem, the author follows the story from Mark 11, but adds a significant reference to Zechariah 9:9, stating that Jesus has fulfilled this scripture. But in the process, Matthew changes Mark's story from Jesus riding *one* animal to riding *two* animals into Jerusalem, in both the Greek and in English translation. Matthew is following the overly literal translation of the Septuagint at this point, and so, he changes the story to have the fulfillment of prophecy be quite literal, no matter how foolish it may appear to have Jesus riding *two* animals at once![52]

In his translation from the Hebrew and Greek into the Latin Vulgate, one famous error that Jerome made was in his rendering of Exodus 34:29. The NRSV translates this passage from the Hebrew correctly as:

> Moses came down from Mount Sinai. As he came down from the mountain with the two tablets of the covenant in his hand, Moses did not know that the skin of his face shone because he had been talking with God.

The Septuagint also gets the passage right, translating the Hebrew word *karan* ("shining") into Greek as *dedoxastai* ("glorified"). In both the Hebrew and Greek versions of this passage, the meaning is relatively clear, that the skin of Moses's face was shining because he had been in the presence of God when he received the commandments. But when Jerome translated this passage, he rendered the Hebrew *karan* into Latin as *cornuta*—"horned," apparently because the Hebrew root for *karan* is *keren,* which can mean "horn" (cf. Ps 75:4). The Douay-Rheims Bible, the English translation of the Vulgate, translates the passage from Latin to English as follows:

---

52. John 12:15 also refers to Zech 9:9, but clearly reads the text as one animal, not two.

And when Moses came down from the Mount Sinai, he held the two tables of the testimony, and he knew not that his face was horned from the conversation of the Lord.

This translation would have significant implications for artistic representations of Moses, especially in the Renaissance era. Most famously, Michelangelo's statue of Moses depicts him with two literal horns (see Fig. 6.4). And in the twentieth century, Marc Chagall would famously depict Moses as having two hornlike rays of light emanating from his head (see Fig 6.5G). Some Christian interpreters, especially in the Middle Ages, linked Moses's horns to the horns of the devil in an anti-Semitic reading of the Vulgate.[53]

Fig. 6.4. Moses (1513–1515), by Michelangelo Buonarroti; marble. Notice the horns! Church of St. Peter, Rome.

53. See Joshua Trachtenburg, *The Devil and the Jews: The Medieval Conception of the Jew and Its Relation to Modern Anti-Semitism* (New York: Jewish Publication Society, 1993); and R. Mellinkoff, *The Horned Moses in Medieval Art and Thought* (Berkeley: University of California Press, 1970).

One final passage can serve to drive home the importance of accurate translation of the Bible for the vast majority of Christians who read neither Hebrew nor Greek. And in this particular case, the problems in translation, even in this digital age, have led to deep fissures in the life of the church. The passage is from 1 Corinthians 6:9–10, and it has been a much debated text especially in modern discussions about same-sex relationships. The NRSV translates the passage as follows:

> Do you not know that wrongdoers will not inherit the kingdom of God? Do not be deceived! Fornicators, idolaters, adulterers, male prostitutes, sodomites, thieves, the greedy, drunkards, revilers, robbers—none of these will inherit the kingdom of God.

In this vice-list from Paul there are two Greek words over which translators have struggled mightily: *malakoi* and *arsenokoitai*. The word *malakoi* literally means "soft ones" or "soft people," a way that ancient Mediterranean culture could refer to "'effeminate' males, and sometimes specifically to the receptive partner in same-sex intercourse, including male prostitutes."[54] The word *arsenokoitai* is a composite of two Greek words, "male" (*arsen*) and "bed" (*koitai*), suggesting the active role in a sexual encounter between two men. For the Greeks and Romans, it mattered a great deal who "played" the man and who "played" the woman in homoerotic sex. So how best to translate these two words? To give you a sense of the difficulty translators have had, here are a few of the English translations:

KJV (1611)	"nor effeminate nor abusers of themselves with mankind"
NKJV (1979)	"nor homosexuals, nor sodomites"
RSV (1946)	"nor sexual perverts"
NRSV (1989)	"male prostitutes, sodomites"
NAB (2002)	"nor boy prostitutes, nor practicing homosexuals"
NABRE (2011)	"nor boy prostitutes, nor sodomites"
NIV (1984)	"nor male prostitutes, nor homosexual offenders"
NIV (2011)	"nor men who have sex with men"
ESV (2001)	"nor men who practice homosexuality"
CEB (2011)	"both participants in same-sex intercourse"

---

54. V. P. Furnish, *The Moral Teaching of Paul: Selected Issues*, 3rd ed. (Nashville: Abingdon, 2009), 80.

Message (2002)	"those who abuse sex"
REB (1989)	"sexual pervert"
NLT (1996)	"or are male prostitutes, or who practice homosexuality"
GNT (1966)	"homosexual perverts"

Two problems, indeed errors from my perspective, are typical of several attempts at translation of this passage into modern English. First, the translation of *arsenokoitai* as "sodomites" in some Bibles is problematic because it presumes and invokes an interpretation of the story of Sodom and Gomorrah from Genesis 19 as a condemnation of same-sex relations between men, when in fact, at best, Genesis 19 provides God's condemnation of sexual violence—namely, rape.[55] Second, the use of the term "homosexual" in other translations is problematic because it provides an anachronistic rendering for a concept that the ancients did not have—namely, consensual same-sex adult relationships, or sexual orientation.[56] The term "homosexuality" itself was not coined until the late nineteenth century. While in 1 Corinthians 6:9, Paul apparently opposes the sexual practice of the *malakoi* and the *arsenokoitai,* I would suggest that the best translation that takes into account what Paul would have known in his first-century context is the following: "neither male prostitutes, nor the men who hire their services." What *malakoi* suggests, which many of the modern translations recognize, is that this partner in a sexual relationship is playing the "soft" role, the passive role, namely, the person on the receiving end (if you will) of penetration. The other person (the *arsenokoitai*) suggests the active role, namely, the person who has hired the services of a passive sexual partner to "play" the receptive role. The modern notion of sexual orientation was unknown in late antiquity, and when we anachronistically translate these terms to suggest that they had the same or similar concept of homosexuality that we do today, we are simply being wrong-headed. There was no such thing in antiquity as the LGBT movement, let alone a feminist movement, a Black Lives Matter movement, airplanes, or even a word in Greek for the color we call blue![57] There were slave revolts. There were various forms of sexual

---

55. See Mark Jordan, *The Invention of Sodomy in Christian Theology* (Chicago: University of Chicago Press, 1998).

56. See V. Furnish, "Homosexuality?" in *The Moral Teaching of Paul,* 3rd ed. (Nashville: Abingdon, 2009), 55–93; and Martti Nissenen, *Homoeroticism in the Biblical World: A Historical Perspective* (Minneapolis: Fortress Press, 1998).

57. See, or rather listen to, http://www.radiolab.org/story/211213-sky-isnt-blue/; see also http://

immorality. But all Paul knew—and that most likely indirectly—was of Gentile vices where some individuals rented themselves out as male prostitutes, others were rented out by their masters as slave prostitutes, and some pre-pubescent boys were courted as partners by adult men (not only as sexual partners, but as young men to be tutored in the ways of the world).[58] Thus Paul condemned pederasty and prostitution.

The reason various translations of the Bible go through repeated editions and updates is precisely because of the living character of language, even old languages. Our understandings of how best to translate ancient Hebrew and Greek words into modern languages involve not just word studies and comparisons, but understandings of entire cultures and modes of thinking. We want to avoid anachronisms in our translations, for anachronisms import our modern ways of thinking into an ancient text that had a rather different worldview. We are ever seeking to reconstruct those worlds so that we might find better approximations for language, better metaphors, better translations that will ever need to be updated and corrected. This is even more the case in the speedy world of digital texts that can be disseminated in a single moment, an upload, a download, a tweet, an email, a blog.

Is there a Bible in this church? Yes, but. . . . Which Bible? Which edition? Which church? How do we find any sense of unity when the foundational scriptures come to us and at us in so many different forms? Just as there is one Jesus but four Gospels, so is there one Bible but 1,500 versions! This is both true and hyperbolic at the same time. For just as there are clear patterns of similarity about Jesus across the Gospels, so are there vast similarities across the dozens of English translations and paraphrases. This is the case whether we are talking about print Bibles or digital Bibles. It's just that the differences are far easier to see and compare in the digital realm.

The multiplicity of translations combined with the utter democratizing impact of all things digital means that in most churches various translations are being used. On the one hand, this is problematic because it raises the concern that "the text" is not nearly as stable as one may have thought. On the other hand, however, this very multiplicity of versions is actually also an opportunity to realize that we are,

---

www.sciencealert.com/humans-couldn-t-even-see-the-colour-blue-until-modern-times-research-suggests.

58. See, e.g., Kenneth J. Dover, *Greek Homosexuality* (Cambridge, MA: Harvard University Press, 1978); Thomas K. Hubbard, *Homosexuality in Greece and Rome: A Sourcebook of Basic Documents* (Berkeley, CA: University of California Press, 1989); and Jeffrey S. Siker, ed., *Homosexuality in the Church: Both Sides of the Debate* (Louisville: Westminster John Knox, 1994).

in fact, reading both the same and yet different texts. It is an opportunity to understand that translation serves as one important step in the process of interpretation. A pastor or a congregation may have a preferred translation, but individuals in the congregation are just as likely to vote with their touchscreens and choose any of dozens of translations, to say nothing of paraphrases. This reality also increases the probability that digital readers will in fact check multiple translations, and that can only help to give a thicker texture to the biblical text.

The FrankenBible

In light of the many translations and versions of the Bible in circulation, it comes as no particular surprise that the digital age has brought us a new creature that has emerged onto the scene and into the fog of Bibles. Meet the FrankenBible. The FrankenBible was introduced in 2013 by Steve Smith at BibleTech, a quasi-annual event on Bible technology sponsored by Logos Bible Software. BibleTech is devoted to exploring the intersections of the Bible and technology. Smith's presentation was entitled "How to Train your Franken-Bible" (a nice play on the then popular animated feature, *How to Train Your Dragon*, from 2010). As *Christianity Today* reported, Smith told the gathered Bible-techies, "There are about 30 modern, high-quality translations of the Bible in English. . . . Can we combine these translations algorithmically into something that charts the possibility space of the original text?"[59] Algorithms are central to how computers work. An algorithm is "a set of steps that are followed in order to solve a mathematical problem or to complete a computer process."[60] Smith's approach to the biblical text is an approach to a digital text, or multiple digital texts that can be coded and analyzed to arrive at a translation according to the logic of a particular computer program. The 2013 BibleTech blurb had the following description of Smith's talk:

> This talk explores the viability of using machine learning and other math-filled buzzwords to computationally derive an English translation of the Bible. While automated processes often produce nonsensical or uncanny-valley-style translations that are just wrong enough to be unnerving, do we have enough linguistic and semantic Bible data to produce a reason-

9. T. Olsen, "Hacking the Bible: Inside the World of the New Bible Coders - and How They Will Change the Way You Think about Scripture," *Christianity Today*, March 6, 2014, http://www.christianity-today.com/ct/2014/march/bible-in-original-geek.html.
0. Merriam-Webster Dictionary.

able-quality automated translation of the Bible? And if so, what could such a translation and process look like?[61]

Toward this end, Smith created the Adaptive Bible website,[62] which allows any user to select words from different versions of the same biblical passage to create their own version, a kind of Bible mash-up. For example, let us say we wanted to create our own version of John 1:14 in Franken-Bible mode. Just click on the book of the Bible, and the chapter. Find the verse, and voilà! You get to choose how you want your version to read (see Fig. 6.6). "The Word became flesh/human/man [your choice] and lived/dwelt/took up residence/made his dwelling [your choice] among us." This is only a simple example, but it illustrates well how relatively subtle differences in translation can have a major impact on how we understand and interpret the biblical text. This has ever been the case, but now individuals can craft their own personalized Bibles, rather than relying on the work of a translation committee with all of the compromises they must work through together. The Franken-Bible allows the individual to create their very own iBible. This is simply a function of the digital age, where everything can be personalized and becomes a function of iThis and iThat. Not only do we have iPhones, and iBooks, and iMacs, we now also have the equivalent of iBibles.

Fig. 6.6. A screenshot of the Frankenbible of John 1:14, from the Adaptive Bible online (http://www.adaptivebible.com).

61. See http://bibleandtech.blogspot.com/2013/03/how-to-train-your-franken-bible-by.html.
62. http://www.adaptivebible.com/.

Boutique Bibles

The Franken-Bible is really just an expansion of the boutique Bible market that has driven Bible publishing, especially the NIV, for years. Rather than having a ubiquitous common text without additional notes and designed for the faith community as a whole (the goal of the American Bible Society),[63] Bible publishing—especially in the case of the NIV—has become a boutique business, where Bibles are targeted to ever more discrete micromarkets of consumers. Bibles are personalized "for you." The combination of American individualism and the personalization of all things digital has resulted in an explosion of Bibles tailored to virtually every imaginable consumer. The publisher of the NIV translation, Zondervan, is quite straightforward in their advertising: "The NIV is available in hundreds of styles and formats including print, Bible apps and eBibles." Bottom line? "There's an NIV for you."[64] It's all about matching individual consumers to a brand type. The website exclaims: "Whatever your current need, there's an NIV Bible that's just right for you!" It reminds one of shopping for a pair of jeans—pre-washed, denim, black, buttoned fly, flared bottoms, somewhat distressed. There actually is, of course, a denim NIV Bible.[65]

There are no fewer than 16 categories of NIV Bibles, and here they are: Study, Devotional, For Women, For Men, For Teens/College Aged, For Kids, Life Events, Text and Reference, Outreach, For New Believers, Travel, Larger-Print/Note-Taking, Leadership, Pastoral and Ministry, Unique Interest Bibles, and Study Resources. Under each of these categories, there are dozens of individual Bibles from which to choose. Hundreds and hundreds of *different* Bibles with *the same* translation. So, one Jesus, four Gospels? The NIV offers one translation, with hundreds of different personalized editions. Are you a cowboy? There's "The Way for Cowboys" NIV Bible. Into the outdoors? Try "The Heart of the Outdoors" NIV Bible, or "The Outdoorsman" NIV Bible, especially for hunters and fishermen. Care for something a little more traditionally feminine? There's the "Homeschool Mom's" NIV Bible in an imitation leather pink binding, or the "Real-Life Devotional Bible for Women," among many other choices. Among my personal favorites is

63. See J. Fea, *The Bible Cause: A History of the American Bible Society* (New York: Oxford University Press, 2016); and P. J. Wosh, *Spreading the Word: The Bible Business in Nineteenth-Century America* (Ithaca, NY: Cornell University Press, 1994).

64. http://www.thenivbible.com/products/?utm_source=Zondervan.com&utm_medium=banner&utm_campaign=NIV_Brand.

65. http://www.media.cru.org.sg/2015/03/02/niv-bible-dark-blue-denim/.

the NIV Beautiful Word Coloring Bible. Then, there's the "FaithGirlz" NIV Bible. The product description for this Bible states:

> Draw closer to God with a Bible that's made uniquely for you! This Bible connects you more closely not only to God, but also yourself and your friends—all with that special *Faithgirlz!* sparkle!

The FaithGirlz Bible includes various added features, such as "Dream Girl," where teen girls are encouraged to imagine themselves into a biblical story. Or "Bring It On," which offers quizzes to help the teen girl to get to know herself better. "Between You and Me" encourages teen girls to share what they are learning with friends. "Between God and Me" suggests guided journaling to "get brutally honest with God." The focus is on the individual. After all, it's all about me! Well, and you and me, and God and me, the Bible and me.

Many of these various editions are available in both print and digital form (currently the Faithgirlz Bible is only available in digital form). What distinguishes one version from another has to do with additional materials added in margins and special page features alongside the actual biblical text. The Outdoorsman's Bible calls attention to biblical passages that celebrate the natural world. The Stock Car Bible features pictures of race cars and "photos of and insights from stock car racing's finest personalities."[66] The Coloring Bible only needs colored pencils.

While it is easy to poke mild fun at the myriad editions of the Bible that have been crafted and marketed to so many on a personalized level, it is also the case that market research has, in fact, shown that many individuals do find particular editions of the Bible meaningful on a personal level. Otherwise, they would not sell. These many Bibles appeal to individuals by making a connection to their personal lives and showing how the Bible may relate to their particular interests. If there were a Jazz Bible (and not a Bible about jazz), I might well find it of interest, given my personal longstanding love of playing jazz piano. Although these different Bibles might separate one person from another because of the distinctive themes, I suppose that the common biblical text might provide a way for individuals from disparate backgrounds to connect with each other as a faith community. But it does appear that communal interests are subordinated to a more individualized faith when it comes to adopting a Bible, at least for the NIV

---

66. One can only hope that Ricky Bobby's "baby Jesus prayer" is not featured from *Talladega Nights!*

Bible, which makes perfect sense in a country (the United States) that so stresses individualism.

Digital Packaging and Paratext

The various editions of the NIV Bible are designed to communicate with readers in physically graphic ways through different bindings, cover art, and physical layouts. While these markers can be approximated virtually in the digital realm, the physical and graphic character of print Bibles is difficult to replicate with the same effectiveness in digital form. Digital packaging works differently than physical packaging, in Bibles no less than with other books. With print books, the focus is on tangibility, literally "touchability." But touchability in regard to the medium of print extends beyond the mere physical sensation of touch. It is enhanced by sight, smell, sound, and even taste. One sees a print book and takes in the book cover, the thickness and heft of the book, the spine of the book, the title and author, the font style, the graphics of the page design. As anyone who has been in a used bookstore knows, there is a distinct smell to old books, just as there is such a thing as a new book smell. The sound of a turning page, or the sound of leafing through a book communicates still more. Beyond sight and sound, today in my office I opened a hundred-year-old volume of Rahlfs's Septuagint (the Greek translation of the Old Testament); I could not only see the thick book and the bold printing embossed on the cover, as well as smell the age of the book, but I could also taste its musty molecules on my tongue, working together with the sense of smell to communicate its age. And then the touch. The weight of a volume, or its lightness, adds to the impression a book makes. Bibles are typically of significant heft, especially older family Bibles and pulpit Bibles. The weight of such Bibles signifies something about the weight of its words. The feel of the paper to the hand communicates still more, especially as print Bibles have evolved to have very thin strong pages to reduce the bulk of the book.[67] These are special pages in a special book.

Digital Bibles can also have a certain kind of tangibility, especially with touchscreens. One can "turn" a virtual page in a digital Bible, even see the virtual thickness of the book. But in essence, digital books offer a functional hybridity that is foreign to print Bibles. This hybrid-

7. See the interview with Don Kraus, the Oxford University Press Bible editor since 1984. http://blog.oup.com/2013/11/national-bible-week-learning-with-don-krauss-oup-bible-editor/.

ity is an aspect of the capacity to manipulate digital media in a great variety of ways. From e-ink text to audio links to electronic images to radical searchability of electronic text, digital "texts" are ultimately liquid, changing form and shape at the desire of the "user." And note I say "user" and not "reader." For while a reader reads a book, a digital "book" can be used in any number of ways—hence its hybridity. It can morph from one form to another. It transcends the mere physicality of a print book, a print Bible. What sets a digital Bible apart from a print Bible is its very capacity to shift across senses, from a digital text one reads, to a digital sound that one hears, to a digital image that one sees—from e-ink to audio to video—all embedded in the same device, whether a smartphone, a tablet, or a desktop computer. It is the capacity of one device to transition relatively seamlessly from one function to another that makes them so remarkable. Before these devices were invented you could read a physical book, listen to a physical analog record, and watch a movie on TV or in a theater. These were separate activities. But now, with the click of a mouse or the swipe of a finger, you can access all three "versions" nearly simultaneously in an integrated manner. Digital Bibles have the capacity to allow a person to read a text (in multiple versions), to hear the text read (again in multiple versions), to listen to any musical setting of the passage, to engage in serious scholarly analysis of the text (in original languages if desired), to see a movie clip of the text acted out, to watch a Bible study video of the passage, and to hear a sermon delivered on the passage.

The digital Bible is truly a book without covers.[68] What this means in practice is that the boundaries of the Bible are literally not "bound." The lack of physicality, apart from the virtual representation on a physical or projected screen, blurs the content of the Bible. It becomes one virtual book among hundreds or thousands on a digital reader. In its digital form, the Bible can have one hypertext after another that has the potential to lead down any number of rabbit holes, each one unique to the user who is clicking on or touching the onscreen links. While physical Bibles often do have notes at the bottom of the page, there is a major difference between a glance from the text to the note on the same physical page and clicking on a hyperlink that will take the user/reader to a completely different virtual "page," perhaps to a map, a dictionary definition, a parallel verse, an online article, a video clip, and on and on and on. A click can lead one hither and yon through

---

68. See W. van Peursen, "Is the Bible Losing Its Covers? Conceptualization and Use of the Bible on the Threshold of the Digital Order," *HIPHIL Novum* 1, no. 1 (2014): 44–58.

a panoply of further clicks, or one could click right back to the biblical text. The potential exists in a digital Bible to read a passage with dozens of paratexts that serve to modify or provide some form of commentary on the particular biblical text in question.

Traditional paratexts in print Bibles consist of such things as tables of contents, book and chapter headings, versification, maps, notes, cross-references, introductions to each book of the Bible, and sometimes, additional articles about the history or literature of the Bible. It all depends on the particular physical edition of the Bible. We have already seen how the NIV Bible has been marketed in dozens upon dozens of different physical (and digital) editions with paratexts tailored to particular niche markets as a way of personalizing and individualizing the Bible. In print Bibles the paratexts are provided by the publisher in a particular edition of the Bible. In digital Bibles the paratexts may originate with the publisher, but the user/reader is really in control of the additional content that may accompany the biblical text, as it all depends on what the user/reader chooses to click—100 hyperlinks or none at all.

Just as an example, let us take a hypertext ride through a churchgoer's YouVersion app as she or he is following along the reading of a biblical text for this week's sermon. Let's presume that this particular church uses the Revised Common Lectionary, so that this week (Labor Day weekend, 2016), we happen to have Luke 14:25–33 as the Gospel text, Jesus's difficult teaching about the cost of discipleship. I'm struck by the last verse of this passage (NIV): "In the same way, those of you who do not give up everything you have cannot be my disciples." A challenging message. The preacher begins her/his sermon. But now I'm curious about other translations of this passage, so I change the version to any of 47 other English versions. And now, I have clicked on Luke 14:33 and find a series of icons that appear on the right-hand side of my iPhone screen. I can send this verse as an iMessage, or e-mail it, tweet it, post it on Facebook, and add it to a reading list, among other options. I can click on an icon that takes me to what other community members in the YouVersion community of 275 million people are saying about this passage. Bishop Marvin Allison, whoever he might be, comments: "Those who deny self to do others good, and who devote themselves and all they have to Christ's service, will realize the happiness which the selfish man seeks for in vain." A woman named Cassandra comments, "God's grace is free but it's not cheap. It's a gift." Claudiomar comments in Spanish, "Preciso renunciar a todo . . . para poder, para Deus." I go back to the text screen, where I see I can also choose an image to accompany this text, including any photo on my iPhone! I can also elect to write a note about this verse. I can bookmark it and label it. I can highlight it in any number of colors. I can go to the publisher's website to learn more about the translation. I can tap the "Home" button and then tap "Chase the Lion," a 7-day reading plan that has preselected biblical passages that will challenge and encourage me to discover my "God-sized dream" and help me find "the courage to chase it." There are, of course, dozens of other reading plans I can select. I can also tap the "more" button at the bottom of the screen and select videos from "The Bible Project," or see what events are going on in my local area. (Apparently, I am missing a worship service at University Christian Church, in Los Angeles, where I could have gone to hear a sermon on "James Part 1: Mature in Christ.") I can also read the sermon outline about "turning trials into triumphs." Then, there's the "verse of the day." Or I can get "help" with an issue I'm having with the app. YouVersion has a brief blurb about the Bible app itself, and I am invited to rate the app, or volunteer, or donate, or view their privacy policy. I can go into my settings and make adjustments, or share the app with other people.

What was the biblical text for the day? What has the preacher been saying the last ten minutes? I've been lost in the cocoon of the app, weaving my own personal Bible cocoon (or echo chamber?) replete with more social media options than I know what to do with, more videos, more comments from other users, more links to other links, more, more, more. I have been sitting in a communal church service lost in an individualized Bible-world of my own making, with significant help from YouVersion! The irony is not lost on me that here I sit surrounded by fellow congregants (very real people all) in this very physical church in this very physical space, and yet, I have been absent—on a virtual exploration of various links and sites, some related, some unrelated. I zone in and out of the worship service and people around me. I'm interrupted by a hymn. Oh, sermon must be over. I shake the cobwebs from my mind and notice a few glares from fellow parishioners, and I'm not sure if these are scolding looks for being on my smartphone during church, or if they are jealous that I found a way to escape what I later hear was a less than thrilling sermon. How would I know?

Now, truth be told, the goal of YouVersion is not to distract by means of the Bible. Their goal is to make the Bible available and present, no matter where you are. In fact, YouVersion encourages you to connect with local congregations, to join a Bible study group, to commit yourself to a Bible reading plan, to focus and develop your faith. All they are doing is providing various ways to be engaged more with the Bible. Of course, more is not always more. Often, less is more, especially in the digital realm where we are tempted to click and click and click. This is why the Internet has been described as "the shallows" by technology critic Nicholas Carr. This is also why parents worry about how much "screen time" they should allow their children. YouVersion is providing a service, and a free one at that, which does make the Bible far more accessible in digital form than it could ever be in print form. The goal of YouVersion, and other Bible apps, is to provide various ways of interacting with the Bible. They cannot, however, provide the discipline it takes to actually do a Bible reading plan. Nor can they necessarily aid me in (or prevent me from) paying attention in a worship service. My worship experience may be enhanced by the capacities of the Bible app on my phone, or these same capacities may distract and take away from the worship experience because I'm off in the Bible spaces they have constructed.

I am reminded of something I'm sure we have all experienced—namely, clusters of people facing each other and all of them looking down to their smartphones texting, e-mailing, facebooking, surfing away with abandon, oblivious to all around them. As I ride the elevator from the parking lot to the third floor where my office is, I am often struck by everyone staring down at their screens, rather than looking at anybody else in the elevator. I regularly marvel at so many of my students who are more deeply engaged with the screen on their phone than with the friend next to whom they are standing. What does it mean when the Bible on a screen becomes a distraction to the communal character of Christian faith to which the Bible itself gives testimony?[69]

---

69. There has been an increase in the number of pedestrians injured by cars because the person crossing the street has been distracted by looking down at their smartphones, rather than paying attention to the traffic. This is to say nothing of the increase of car accidents due to people texting while driving. A few years ago, a YouTube video went viral that showed a bear wandering through a suburban neighborhood and a man accidentally walking into the bear (yes a bear) because he (the man, not the bear!) was looking down at his smartphone screen! (https://www.youtube.com/watch?v=bazVcSv8nnk).

Digital Bibles and Liturgy

What role do digital Bibles have in liturgical contexts of communal worship? On the one hand, the argument can be made that it really makes no difference whether one is reading a biblical passage from the lectern using a print Bible or a digital Bible. After all, typically, a lectern or pulpit mostly hides the book from which the scriptures are read. Increasingly, one finds the biblical passage projected on a large screen for all to read. You can certainly also follow along in your pew Bible, or in your missal, or—as we have seen—on your smartphone Bible app. There is something about not just hearing the text read aloud, but also reading along that helps to reinforce the reading.

But, on the other hand, the argument can also be made that using a print Bible in a liturgical setting communicates something rather different than a digital Bible. As Matthew Barrett has argued in his essay "Dear Pastor, Bring Your Bible to Church,"[70] the use of a digital Bible in the pulpit sends a very different message to the congregation than a physical print Bible. The print Bible is one book, *the Book,* and it has but one function—to serve as the sacred scriptures that bear witness to the God we worship. But a tablet reader, an iPad, or a Galaxy, or a Kindle Fire sends a rather different message. Visually, the tablet "is an icon of social media and a buffet of endless entertainment." It invokes all of the tempting interruptions that can point us away from the worship of God. By contrast, argues Barrett (himself an avid user of all things digital), "a print copy of the Scriptures in the pulpit represents something far more focused and narrow: a visible symbol of God speaking to his people."

Barrett also worries that a digital version of the Bible will lead to greater biblical illiteracy. I know I have found this to be the case with students and parishioners alike. "Turning" to a biblical text in a print Bible, whether in a classroom or a worship context, means flipping through the pages of the Bible and familiarizing oneself with the physical geography of the Bible as a book. By contrast, with digital Bibles, one simply enters a search for the passage in question, no muss, no fuss. One no longer needs to know where things are in the Bible, that the books of Joshua and Philippians are in different sections of the Bible, that there is a pattern of Torah, Prophets, Writings, and Gospels, Paul's letters, and more. The machine "knows" for you. Barrett also

---

70. *The Gospel Coalition,* August 18, 2013, https://www.thegospelcoalition.org/article/dear-pastor-bring-your-bible-to-church.

Fig. 3.4. The Franklin Pocket King James Version Electronic Holy Bible.

4 When therefore the Lord knew how the Pharisees had heard that Jesus made and baptized more disciples than John, 2 (Though Jesus himself baptized not, but his disciples,) 3 He left Judea, and departed again into Galilee.

4 Now when the Lord knew that the Pharisees had heard that Jesus was making and baptizing more disciples than John 2 (although Jesus himself did not baptize, but only his disciples), 3 he left Judea and

---

G. Jesus and the Samaritan Woman (4:1-26)

4:1-6. The introductory verses explain the reason for our Lord's journey from Judea to Galilee, and for his contact with the people of Samaria. The Pharisees were jealous of the popularity of the new movement, which exceeded even that of the Baptist in the Judean territory. The Synoptic Gospels are silent about baptism as an accompaniment of the ministry of Jesus, and an editorial note here limits this function to his disciples (see on 3:22). The direct route from Judea to Galilee lay through the region of Samaria, which, though forming part of the subprovince of Judea under the rule of the Roman procurator, was inhabited by the mixed population separated sharply from the Jews since the time of Ezra and Nehemiah. The bitter rivalry between Jews and Samaritans led to violent attacks upon stragglers in the trains of pilgrims journeying from Galilee to the temple feasts at Jerusalem. Luke 9:51-56 illustrates the inhospitality shown to Jesus and his disciples on one of these journeys. For this reason the alternate route by way of Perea was more popular. The Samaritan religion was based upon the Pentateuch, and its cultus had been centered in the temple on Mount Gerizim. Indeed, where the Hebrew text of Deut. 27:4 records the divine command that after crossing the Jordan into the Promised Land, the Israelites were to build a stone altar on Mount Ebal for burnt

---

Or Percy Gardner:

The ordinary Christian teaching about God needs infinite stiffening. . . . The sterner side of God is quite as prominent, even in the New Testament, as the more humane side; it is only that preachers have fallen into the way of dwelling on the latter to the exclusion of the former, whence the sickly onesidedness of our current religion. . . . Men have come to think of God as a weak and indulgent parent, who will not be hard on them in any case, who will think more of their happiness than of their perfection, and give them the things which they want, or think they want, . . . and veneration is drowned in a sickly flood of talk about divine love.[1]

Have not we ourselves proved many a time that Christ is never kinder than when his eyes, as he looks at us, are as a flame of fire, and he speaks to us terrible words; when he will make no compromise with us, but demands instant obedience, here and now, on pain of parting with him. If he had not loved us enough to be severe with us, he would have lost our souls. With awe and humility we need to give God thanks no less really for his wrath than for his mercy.

4:1-3. *The Necessity of Controversy.*—Now when the Lord knew that the Pharisees had

[1] *The Practical Basis of Christian Belief* (London: Williams & Norgate, 1923), pp. 136, 135. Used by permission.

heard that Jesus was making and baptizing more disciples than John . . . he left Judea and departed again to Galilee. Why? Probably to avoid the storm of controversy he saw blowing up. For since the authorities had become aware of the extent of this new and to them disquieting menace, they would shift their main suspicion from the Baptist to Christ as plainly now the more dangerous of the two. And he felt that in a noisy clamor around him the people might be distracted from the true ends of his mission and might be only too likely to lose their way in a mist of angry disputation, and never reach religion at all. So he went north. Would that his church had always been as wise as he! For if the Scriptures are final and conclusive witnesses that there is a real and necessary place for controversy (of which in this particular Gospel there is not a little), if often enough one must ring out the truth and stand to it unflinchingly, nevertheless, would not much more have been accomplished for Christ and his kingdom down the ages if all the time and energy and passion and enthusiasm expended in disputes around and about the gospel had been thrown into and spent upon the proclamation of that gospel? To which there comes the immediate question, "But what is the gospel? How can we know it, and be sure of its authenticity, and differ-

---

Fig. 3.5. A page from The Interpreter's Bible (1951). Photo by author.

Figure 4.2. Evolution of the Apple iPhone Family, 2007–2014.

Fig. 4.5. Home Page of Biblegateway.com, top half of page.

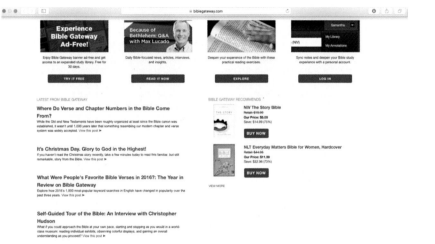

Fig. 4.6. Home Page of BibleGateway.com, bottom half of page.

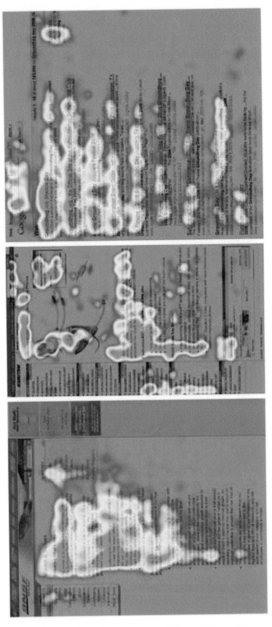

Fig. 4.11. The above heatmaps show how users read three different types of Web pages: an article in the "about us" section of a corporate website (bottom), a product page on an e-commerce site (center), and a search engine results page (top). There are differences, but all three heatmaps show a general F pattern.

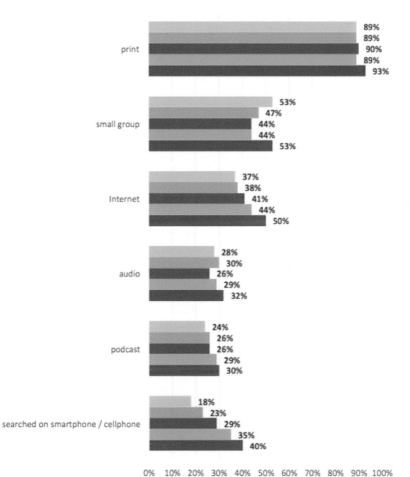

Bible Format Use, 2011-2015
% among Bible readers

■ 2011 ■ 2012 ■ 2013 ■ 2014 ■ 2015

print	
	89%
	89%
	90%
	89%
	93%

small group	
	53%
	47%
	44%
	44%
	53%

Internet	
	37%
	38%
	41%
	44%
	50%

audio	
	28%
	30%
	26%
	29%
	32%

podcast	
	24%
	26%
	26%
	29%
	30%

searched on smartphone / cellphone	
	18%
	23%
	29%
	35%
	40%

0% 10% 20% 30% 40% 50% 60% 70% 80% 90% 100%

Fig. 5.2. The State of the Bible 2015.

Fig. 6.2. Codex Sinaiticus.

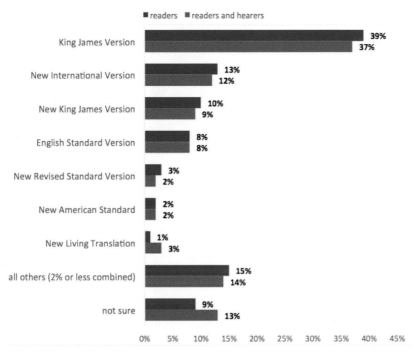

Fig. 6.3. The Bible Version Read Most Often

Fig. 6.4. *Moïse recevant les Tables de la Loi* (1963), by Marc Chagall.

Fig. 8.1. A screenshot of Logos Bible Software showing Luke 1.

Fig. 8.2. Another screenshot of Logos Bible Software, showing options (at left) for the Passage Guide and the Exegetical Guide.

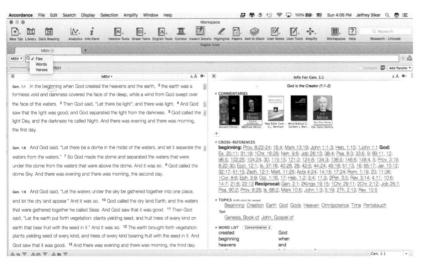

Fig. 8.3. Accordance Screen Shot.

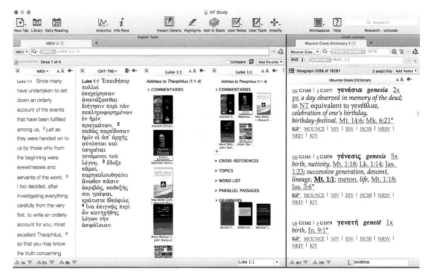

Fig. 8.4. A screenshot of the Workspace in Accordance displaying Luke 1.

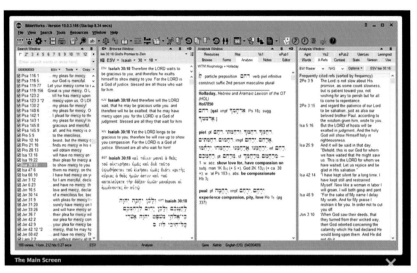

Fig. 8.5. A screenshot of BibleWorks on Isaiah 30:18.

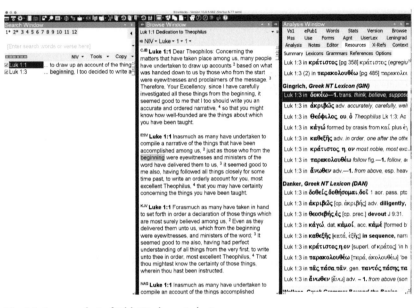

Fig. 8.6. A screenshot of BibleWorks on Luke 1.

worries that whereas baptism and eucharist are rather physical expressions of a corporate faith, a digital Bible is out of step with this physicality, and that only a print Bible functions in a manner parallel to the very real sacraments. A similar concern has been raised by John Bombero, a Lutheran pastor in San Diego, who has argued that "Digital texts are ephemeral; they are ontologically diminished."[71]

Bombero mourns what he sees as the disappearing Bible, the scriptures that get absorbed into a digital device and have no "real presence," to borrow a notion from sacramental theology. Where the Bible is not physically present, he argues, there is no "Bible *presence*." Instead, Bibles in digital media come with competition from a host of other virtual realities that distract and call for immediate attention—alerts, jingles, tones, vibrations, emails, texts, and apps upon apps. Most of all, Bombero worries about a connection between virtual Bibles and Docetism (the belief that Jesus only *appeared* to be human, but in fact, was only a Spirit). Whereas Docetism saw the material world as an evil realm to be escaped, "God the good Creator of the material world has always spoken and acted through creaturely means."[72] While the danger of bibliolatry ever persists—namely, the idolatrous worship of the physical Bible as the incarnate Word rather than of the God to whom the Bible bears witness—such idolatry is not remedied by rendering the Bible as a disembodied, somewhat gnostic, text. As Bombero argues, "When Theology takes the incarnation seriously, it steers disciples to the Bible and to sacraments that have real 'existence' in the here and now. . . . The Word is incarnate; the Word was also inscripturated." In this physical form, the Bible functions as God intended, according to Bombero, "iconic, instigating, familiar, and troubling—just like the incarnation itself."[73] I would imagine that Bombero would readily acknowledge the function of the preached oral/aural form of the Gospel message as well as its written form. But at the same time, there is something about the Bible as a common physical touchstone that is important for the believing community, especially in liturgical contexts.

I am reminded of a common practice in the context of Jewish worship services that highlights the importance of the tangibility of Scripture. When it is time to read the Torah portion of Scripture, the appro-

1. "The Book That Isn't Really There," *Modern Reformation* 22, no. 3 (May/June 2013): 30–35 (30), http://www.modernreformation.org/default.php?page=articledisplay&var1=ArtRead&var2=1444 &var3=issuedisplay&var4=IssRead&var5=130.
2. "The Book That Isn't Really There," 33.
3. Ibid., 35.

priate scroll is taken from the *Aron Kodesh* (Holy Ark) that houses the various scrolls, and the scroll is paraded up and around the aisles of the synagogue. As it passes by, people reach out to touch it with their *Tallit* (prayer shawls) or with their prayer book. The physicality of the connection to the word of God is palpable. It is difficult to imagine a digital device functioning in anything like the same manner.

Katja Rakow, a Professor of Religious Studies at Utrecht University, the Netherlands, has written a compelling essay that explores the notion of "Bibleness" in the digital age addressing, in part, the liturgical function of physical Bibles.[74] In particular, she appeals to Timothy K. Beal's notion of the "cultural iconicity" of the Bible, in which the Bible "projects a solid, bookish singularity, unity, oneness, and authority."[75] Can digital Bibles deliver the same kind of iconicity? Like Bombero, Rakow addresses the "problem of presence" associated with digital Bibles. But unlike Bombero, Rakow has a more subtle approach that recognizes different modes of Bible usage that seem to pair well with different kinds of Bibles, both physical and digital. In short, in some instances, the materiality of the Bible matters a great deal, and in others, it hardly matters at all.

Rakow posits three modes or types of usage for the Bible as a material object: 1) the commemorative mode, in which the Bible is a repository for memories; 2) what she labels the "semantic-hermeneutical" mode, in which reading and studying the Bible for meaning is in the foreground; and 3) the performative mode, which encompasses devotional, liturgical, and ritual practices that involve the Bible as a material object.[76] These types of usage can overlap, and there is a certain fluidity between them. The classic commemorative use of the Bible is the traditional big family Bible, into which families might insert pictures, press flowers, keep important papers, record births, baptisms, and marriages. Digital Bibles cannot serve as comparable repositories of memories. The digital device itself has little to no value apart from its immaterial apps and programs. The screen is merely a conduit and not a container.[77] Print Bibles can develop a certain patina that adds

74. "The Bible in the Digital Age: Negotiating the Limits of 'Bibleness' of Different Bible Media," in *Christianity and the Limits of Materiality*, ed., Minna Opas and Anna Haapalainen (London: Bloomsbury, 2017; forthcoming).

75. See Timothy K. Beal, "The End of the Word as We Know It: The Cultural Iconicity of the Bible in the Twilight of Print Culture," in J. W. Watts, ed., *Iconic Books and Texts* (Sheffield: Equinox, 2015), 207–24 (222).

76. Rakow draws these ideal types from her study of practices among contemporary Evangelical and neo-Pentecostal Christians.

77. As David Neff has argued, digital Bibles are "Bibles with no physical properties of their own. They

to their iconicity. They can show the wear and care of previous generations, connecting one generation to the next. My wife has vivid memories of her grandmother's well-worn Bible with paper markers throughout its heavily thumbed pages. In this way, physical Bibles carry a "Bibleness" that includes the biblical text, but also extends beyond it. By contrast, digital Bibles get updated to the next version, never looking back.

The "semantic-hermeneutical" mode of usage stresses the content and meaning of the biblical text, without much appeal to its material form. This is where the YouVersion app has succeeded so brilliantly by offering the content in maximum forms—over 1,500 versions in over 1,000 languages. Given the emphasis on reading and ease of reading, digital Bibles function very well in this mode, since one can take advantage of hyper-textuality, portability, convenience, and adjustable font sizes, along with other resources, to engage in serious study of the text. This mode of accessing the Bible also allows for a nonlinear approach to the Bible, as opposed to the closed-in and finalized form of rigid columns of text. The nonlinear functionality of digital Bibles and Bible study apps allows one to pursue hyperlinked rabbit holes ad infinitum.

The performative mode is where liturgy and devotional reading come into play. As with the commemorative mode of using the Bible, so with the performative mode, what comes to the fore is the Bible's cultural iconicity. This can be seen in very simple processions, for example, where the Bible has an honored place in the initiation of ritual worship. Its role as a sacred book, beyond mere sacred words, is significant. A procession with an iPad would be more than strange. The Bible evokes an aura of authoritative age and wisdom, whereas the iPad and similar digital devices evoke the most modern of technologies devoid of religious meaning. As Rakow notes, the "powerful relationship between words, the Word and the book becomes evident in Pentecostal and Charismatic contexts, where religious actors use the Bible in healing services or other religious practices."[78] This is another example of a different mode of "Bibleness," where the physical material object matters.

Liturgical forms of worship differ widely, of course, across the Christian tradition, from very informal and unscripted services to very for-

borrow their frame from computers, iPads, and smartphones." How the Physical Form of a Bible Shapes Us." *Christianity Today* 56, no. 1 (January 17, 2012): 60. http://www.christianitytoday.com/ct/2012/january/almostlooks.html.
8. "The Bible in the Digital Age."

mal and highly scripted services. The liturgical role that the Bible plays in the drama of worship largely depends on which church and what kind of liturgy is in view. To facilitate this discussion further, let us presume that we are talking about three different kinds of liturgical approaches to worship and the place of the Bible in each.

We can start with what might be termed "low –liturgical, high-tech" churches, where there is fairly little developed or complex worship. In such low-church settings, the worship service is primarily devoted to singing, prayer, Bible-reading, and sermon. There may be occasional communion and baptisms worked into the regular service, but by and large, the services are relatively informal. As a general rule, the less formal the setting, the more likely that digital Bibles will be used. In more casual worship settings, people often wear everyday clothes, and part of the point of such a style is to make it clear that God is an everyday kind of God, who uses the things of everyday life to work God's will. Yes, scripture is sacred, but its form is not. The Bible is the preached word, the word proclaimed. It is not, first and foremost, a physical object; rather, it is a mere vessel that holds the Word of God. In such church settings, it is not uncommon to see the preacher holding an iPad or even a smartphone, and reading the biblical text from a digital device, hence modeling this practice for the congregants. The biblical passage is likely also projected onto a large screen for all to follow along. The pastor may even encourage congregants to take out their smartphones and read along, perhaps even to tweet him/her during the sermon with comments and questions that can be worked into the sermon in real time. The boundary between sacred and secular, between sacred space/time and regular space/time, is not so hard and fast. It matters not whether the church meets in a high-school auditorium or uses a physical print Bible. Such churches are often independent churches, typically Protestant churches with a strong emphasis on the preached word and a casual setting. Perhaps most ironically, such churches have the highest view of the authority of scripture.

A second liturgical approach might be called "traditional mainstream" worship, which is typically denominationally affiliated (United Methodists, the Presbyterian Church USA, the United Church of Christ, the Evangelical Lutheran Church of America, some Episcopal Churches, among others). Here also, the emphasis falls on traditional Protestant notions of the centrality of the preached word, though Eucharist is more regular. Pulpit Bibles are most common in these settings, and these Bibles have a longstanding tradition within the liturgical framework of a worship service. Their usually large physical size serves as a symbol for the weight of the sacred words contained therein. There may also be pew Bibles--multiple copies of the same translation--and people will be encouraged to follow along. These worship services are typically somewhat more formal and congregants are more reluctant to break out such mundane devices as smartphones. Still, it is often the practice for these churches to have a variety of more formal (traditional hymns) and less formal (praise music with quasi rock bands) worship services, and the use of technology to project bible passages is increasingly common.

A bigger difference can be seen in the third kind of liturgical setting, especially in Roman Catholic worship services. Here, the eucharist is the central feature, though the Bible plays a significant role in the formalized liturgy. The Bible typically has a formal place in processionals at the beginning of the liturgy; for the reading of the Gospel lesson the congregation stands up, and the Bible is presented and venerated as a physical object that functions symbolically as that which mediates the transcendent Word of God. It would be very difficult to imagine a procession with an iPad being lifted up! The whole idea of the liturgy seeks to sacralize time and space, to move beyond the mundane and to lift the faithful to experience the presence of God. The liturgical trappings of the Roman Catholic worship service are intended to help mediate such a transcendent experience. And part of this includes the veneration of the physical book, the Bible, which in turn, points to God and God's story with humanity.

In somewhat more general terms, James Caccamo has offered some helpful insights on digital media and the future of the liturgy.[79] He compares the first wave of media change (the sixteenth-century development of movable type), and the second wave (the nineteenth through twentieth-century electronic age of telegraph, phonograph, radio, film, telephone, television) with what has emerged in our time as the third wave of media change—the digital era in its many forms. He notes how a primary element of each wave of media change has depended on *curation*, namely, "the use of human or machine intelligence to filter information, symbols, and experiences in order to focus attention on items that are most relevant for a particular audience."[80] During the first two waves of media change (moveable type and the

---

[79]. "Let Me Put It Another Way: Digital Media and the Future of the Liturgy," *Liturgy* 28, no. 3 (2013): 7–16.

[80]. Ibid., 9.

electronic age), a high level of curation by gatekeepers was the norm. "Publishers had catalog limitations, newspapers had page limits, television shows had limited time slots, and all were beholden to advertisers."[81] But in the emerging digital era curation has shifted in significant ways from those who used to control media access to a radical new democracy of media information, where anyone can create a blog, upload new music, create a website, a news stream, a YouTube video, a podcast, all in a relatively limitless manner. Rather than publishers and editors controlling limited outlets of information, the digital era now sees virtually unlimited dissemination of information to such a degree that the phrase "information overload" does not begin to do justice to the meaning of nearly five billion pages of online information in myriad forms. We cope with such overwhelming volume by instituting a wide range of filters, and so, crafting our own methods of curating e-mail, Twitter, Facebook, web links, podcasts, and the like.

What does this have to do with liturgy and digital Bibles? As Caccamo points out, lectionaries have long functioned as a way to curate the vastness of the Bible and mete it out one week at a time over a three-year cycle. This aspect of the Bible's role in liturgy is an expression of a church community's acceptance of church leaders as curators of the Bible for the worship life of the church. This is especially the case in traditions that have most often been identified with more formal and hierarchical structures of administration and leadership, for example, the Roman Catholic Church, the Episcopal Church, the Lutheran Church, and the Eastern Orthodox Churches. However, just as personal curation has emerged as a central feature in how we negotiate lives saturated by digital media of all kinds, so also in liturgical contexts, individuals are engaging increasingly in this kind of personal curation, focusing on how the liturgy does or does not meet their individual needs. Perhaps the most obvious ways in which our digital devices illustrate the hegemony of the individual can be seen in the very names of the devices themselves: the *i*Phone, the *i*Pad, the *i*Mac. Individuals create personal playlists, follow other individuals on Twitter, express themselves on Facebook and other social media. The Bible app *YouVersion* makes it clear that they have a version for *you*. Our digital devices can connect us to others in meaningful ways, but they can also isolate us from someone standing right next to us. Digital Bibles are inherently personal Bibles mostly on small individualized screens. They are not

81. Ibid.

really for sharing, like we might share a hymnal. But even hymnals have gone to large digital screens as individuals stare up in isolation at the words going by on the screen, even as they sing together.[82]

In a world that is "always on,"[83] and where we are plugged in to multiple digital screens, it becomes increasingly difficult to focus simply because we are always connected. Thus, rather than giving our full attention to our role in the worship life of our faith communities, we increasingly suffer from "continuous partial attention," a kind of peripheral attention wherein we have one eye and one ear on the so-called real world around us, and another eye/ear on the virtual world mediated via smartphones. It is no wonder that, often, a blurring occurs between the two. We are there and not there, attentive and nonattentive (or other-attentive, screen-attentive). We read/hear the scripture lesson, and yet at the same time, we are often quite literally not on the same page as the community of believers gathered for worship.

AudioBibles

We have been discussing differences between reading print Bibles versus reading screen Bibles. But what about AudioBibles? Is that reading? Is being read to the same as reading? Many people would say yes. Audio book sales overall have jumped significantly over the last few years.[84] Both my wife and one of our sons are committed audio book listeners. My wife tends to listen to novels (mostly mysteries) at night before falling asleep, as does our son. She sets the audio book timer for 30 minutes so that if she falls asleep, it won't take her long to find where she was! But what about the Bible as an audio book? The Barna Group's six-year study of *The Bible in America,* published in 2016, found that 28 percent of respondents listened to an audio version of the Bible, not far behind the 31 percent who stated that they downloaded or used a Bible app on a smartphone.[85]

2. See Sherry Turkle, *Alone Together: Why We Expect More from Technology and Less from Each Other* (New York: Basic Books, 2012).

3. See Naomi Baron, *Always On: Language in an Online and Mobile World* (New York: Oxford University Press, 2010).

4. In 2015 alone, sales of adult audio books jumped 38%, according to the Association of American Publishers. See Martha Ross, "Audio Books: Is Listening as Good as Reading?," *The Mercury News;* June 20, 2016, http://www.mercurynews.com/bay-area-living/ci_30054295/audiobooks-is-listening-good-reading.

5. *The Bible in America: The Changing Landscape of Bible Perceptions and Engagement* (Barna Group, 2016), 148. The 2011 *State of the Bible* report indicated that 28% of those surveyed used audio Bibles, while the 2013 report indicated a slightly lower 26%, which in 2015 was back up again to 28%. Thus,

When you think about it (and even when you don't!), for the vast majority of Christian history, the primary way that people "read" scripture was by *hearing* it read in worship contexts. Even after the advent of printed Bibles, which allowed people to start actively reading the Bible more on their own, the reading of scripture from a lectern or pulpit has been the most enduring form of Bible reading in the history of the church. Today, it is common for three forms of Bible reading to take place at the same time in a worship service. Someone will read from a print Bible for the day's lessons (or lections), while many in the pew will read along in a pew Bible, a missal insert, or on an e-reader, and the biblical passage will appear on a large screen for people to read along. Hearing and reading. Having multiple ways of experiencing the biblical text adds to memory and comprehension.

But what about dedicated AudioBibles? A glance at the app store for iTunes or at the Amazon website reveals various options for Audio-Bibles. Amazon lists *The Complete Audio King James Bible,* as read by James Earl Jones, as one of its bestsellers (on CDs). A number of apps available through iTunes also provide access to audio Bibles. On my iPhone, I have downloaded Zondervan's TNIV complete audio Bible. I admit, if an admission it be, that I have found the audio Bible rather helpful, especially when driving or out for a walk. This past year, I taught a course for a cohort of MA students that Loyola Marymount University has in the Diocese of Orange, a 40-mile drive from our location in Los Angeles. Every Tuesday, I would get in the car and make the 1 to 2 hour commute (always depending on the traffic in Southern California!), and I would set up my iPhone to play the biblical book we would be discussing in that day's class. This would allow me to listen to a large portion or complete text of a Gospel, or a letter of Paul's, or whatever we were going to go over in class. I would quite literally often hear things I hadn't noticed before, or I would hear them in a different way. One other thing I would regularly do is to put the Bible in "shuffle" mode, so that I never knew what chapter from what book of the Bible I was going to get. This was kind of fun and resulted in a form of mixed lectionary readings, a mash-up, where a passage from 1 Kings might be followed by something from the Gospel of Luke, and then, by a Psalm. The random character of texts combined in my mind to create unaccustomed links and connections. I would "see" and hear things I hadn't heard or seen before simply by virtue of the serial reading of unrelated texts.

the use of audio Bibles appears to have been relatively constant over the duration of the six-year study.

Of course, one can flip through the pages of a print Bible and do much the same. There's the old joke of someone seeking divine guidance who decided to open the Bible at random and put their finger down to a random passage. The person opened to Matthew 27:5, "And Judas went and hanged himself." "No, no," the person thought, let me try that again. He then opened to Luke 10:37, "Go and do likewise." "No," he thought, "Let's try one more time," at which point he opened to John 13:27, "Do quickly what you are going to do!" So as a guidance system, this kind of random reading is not necessarily helpful! But with an AudioBible, the shuffling of texts can be illuminating, especially since you get a whole chapter and not just a verse.

Another aspect of AudioBibles concerns the role that the "voice" of the reader plays in our understanding and perception of the text that is being read. Audio books in general rely on professional readers, or the authors themselves, to provide an engaging reading of the book in question. But when it comes to the Bible, the voice of the reader can often be overly formal. And as Dr. Neil Elliott quipped in personal correspondence, what happens when James Earl Jones is not only the voice of Darth Vader in the initial *Star Wars* trilogy, but is also the voice of God when reading the Bible? Not surprisingly, his AudioBible (James Earl Jones's, not Darth Vader's) of the entire King James Bible is among the most popular. It is not uncommon for individual listeners to like or dislike the reading voice of an audio book, and the same may well apply to AudioBibles. Of course, the same was the case with books on tape before the digital era, but audio books and AudioBibles alike have grown immensely as a result of digital media and are much more widely available. When we read the Bible to ourselves, either aloud or silently, there is a small inner voice that we hear, and we make automatic adjustments in our reading and imaginations to allow for the voices of different characters. But with AudioBibles we are rather stuck, for better and worse, with the voices and production values (sometimes dramatic music) of those producing the digital media.

Even though the percentage of those who use AudioBibles trails those using print Bibles by a large margin, and falls slightly behind e-Bibles, we need to remember that every worship service every week always has an aural/oral reading of scripture. One could argue, I suppose, that far more people hear scripture being read aloud in such services than ever read it for themselves in print or digital form. There are also many advocates for the advantages of audio reading in comparison to print reading in particular. Ian Small, the CEO of audiobooks.com, has written a short essay on "Why Audio is Better than Print."[86] It is certainly no surprise that the CEO of a company marketing audio books would take this position. According to Small, reading is better in audio for three reasons. First, when you read a book with your ears, the narrative performance of the book opens up a rich world that takes advantage of the auditory experience. Second, Small claims that several studies show reading retention to be good or better with audio than with print books. And because one can change the pace of narration, "audiobooks lend themselves to more focused and efficient consumption of books."[87] In regard to reading the Bible, efficient consumption is not really the goal, so much as spending time marinating in the text. One could replay a chapter or book of the Bible over and over again so that one would begin to know it by heart. Digital technology certainly makes this an easy possibility. Third, Small argues that audiobooks allow one to multitask, so that you could be working out and listening, or doing chores and listening, or driving and listening. This is again an argument based on the efficiency of reading and maximizing time usage. Here, the same question arises for reading the Bible as with Small's second claim—namely, is reading the Bible while multitasking really the goal? If anything, I would think the purpose of listening to the Bible being read is so that one could concentrate on the words, even in a multitasking context such as driving or exercising. Thus, while Small's arguments may apply to a paperback novel, the Bible as a "quick read" or a "quick listen" does not mesh particularly well with what many individuals are seeking when they listen to an audio version of the Bible. Multitasking is difficult enough in any context, but multitasking the Bible defeats the purpose of truly listening to or hearing the Bible in all of its richness. Still, I can attest to the benefit of quite literally hearing the biblical text read aloud while driving long stretches. It is also the case that those who cannot read because of eye troubles have a wonderful recourse in AudioBibles.

Children's Bibles and the Digital Realm

Beyond the Bibles that adults use in and out of church, whether print or digital, another important group of Bible users are children. Children's Bibles have long occupied a very significant place in the publish-

---

86. This is an "expert publishing blog opinion" released on August 11, 2016, and made available through http://www.digitalbookworld.com/2016/why-audio-better-print/.
87. Ibid.

ing and marketing of Bibles. Typically, a Children's Bible is a storybook Bible that retells classic Bible stories in simplified language that children can comprehend. Children's Bibles come in a wide range of editions with lots of pictures and relatively brief stories. When our daughter Ursula was young (she was born in 1991), we used to read one story each night from a children's Bible, stories that she still remembers. She still has the book, *The Children's Illustrated Bible,* Stories Retold by Selina Hastings (London: DK Limited, 1994).

In this digital era, there has been a significant shift in Children's Bibles, especially in light of children becoming more sophisticated users of digital devices, from smartphones to tablets at an early age. I still remember our grandson Charlie when he was four-years-old patiently waiting for a new children's app to load onto an iPhone. He turned to my wife and me and reassured us, "Don't worry, it's downloading!" Since the mid-1990s, children have been growing up as digital natives, in contrast to us older folks, who are digital immigrants. Digital natives text with abandon; digital immigrants tend to be more comfortable with e-mail. Digital natives tweet and Snapchat; digital immigrants wander with some trepidation into Facebook and other social media sites. What could be more natural than for children to use Bibles—in this case, children's Bibles—in digital form on screens that utilize a combination of text, image, and sound?

YouVersion has published the most widely downloaded children's Bible, *The Bible App for Kids Storybook Bible.* The YouVersion website touts its Bible app for kids as "Everything kids need to fall in love with God's Word." It includes the app, videos, a two-year companion curriculum, the storybook Bible in 26 languages, reading plans for kids, and various activities for kids (coloring sheets, adventure books, et al). The app also includes downloadable parent guides. It can be downloaded for free at bible.com/kids. This is one rare case in publishing where a Bible that started life as a digital app was only later published in print form.[88] This storybook Bible contains 41 Bible stories, evenly divided between Old and New Testament stories. The Old Testament includes stories about creation, the sin of Adam and Eve, Noah's Ark, Abraham, Moses, the Exodus, and so on. The New Testament stories include Gospel stories about Jesus, as well as stories about Paul from the Acts of the Apostles. The whole app concludes with "God's Good News," discussing how kids can be part of the story themselves. There

---

88. *The Bible App for Kids Storybook Bible* (Pompano Beach, FL: OneHope, Inc, 2015), developed by Life.Church.

are lots of vivid images along with animal and human characters that have simple animation. The stories are all paraphrased in simple English (or any of a number of other languages), and the app includes games to reinforce the content of the Bible, but also YouVersion's particular evangelical interpretation.

The final story ("God's Good News: Be Part of the Story") provides a summary of the entire Bible story. God created everything, including us. "God loves us and wants to have a relationship with us. . . . but sin and death came into the world through the disobedience of Adam and Eve, and so our relationship with God was broken." From there, the final story summary skips past the rest of the Old Testament and the story of Israel to go straight to the story of Jesus as God's saving response to human sinfulness.

> Because of His love for us, God sent His Son, Jesus, into the world. Sin broke our relationship with God, but Jesus came to fix it! . . . Jesus taught people about God's love. His perfect life shows us what love looks like. Even though Jesus never sinned, He died on a cross for our sins because He loves us. By doing this, He was carrying out God's plan to fix our relationship with Him.

This strong emphasis on the sinless perfection of Jesus and his death for human sin is one aspect of YouVersion's implicit traditional atonement theology.[89]

> Jesus rose from the dead, breaking the power of sin and death! . . . He returned to Heaven. Now Jesus lives forever! . . . He sent His Holy Spirit to live inside everyone who trusts Him. . . . when Jesus returns, God will make everything perfect again. He will make a New Heaven and a New Earth. Everyone who trusts in Jesus will live with Him, forever! . . . Trusting and following Jesus fixes our broken relationship with God! Are you ready to be a part of God's story?

As with most forms of evangelical Christianity, the theological emphasis invites individuals into personal relationships with Jesus. What this might look like for children is left somewhat ambiguous, and here, YouVersion appears to rely on both parents and the faith community to provide such answers, an indication that the process of discipleship is as much a matter of belonging to a faith community as it is about the individual's relationship with Jesus.

89. For how Jesus came to be seen as sinless and perfect in early Christian theology, see J. S. Siker, *Jesus, Sin, and Perfection in Early Christianity* (New York: Cambridge University Press, 2015).

Another widely downloaded children's Bible app is the *Superbook Kid's Bible, Videos and Games,* developed and published by the Christian Broadcasting Network (CBN).[90] The app, designed for both iPhone and iPad, is made for children aged 9–11, but clearly, younger children are also in view. Tapping "About Superbook" leads to the following explanation: "With instant access to entertainment, social networks and a host of mobile apps, today's tech-savvy youth learn and relate differently from any previous generation. In today's digital world, sharing the Bible with children is more challenging than ever." The *Superbook Kid's Bible* includes the biblical text (in any of dozens of translations), but a text that is interspersed throughout with hyperlinks to questions and answers, to profiles of biblical figures, to videos and pictures, and to games. There are also "Daily Bible Quests" hosted by a virtual robot named "Gizmo" that take the user to various games. The games include puzzles with biblical names, quizzes on the biblical text, and word scrambles of Bible verses.

The app comes with "Info for Parents," which states,

> We are working hard to create an engaging Bible app where your child will want to come and interact with God's Word. Whether playing our games, watching our video clips, or exploring our interactive questions about God, we want kids to have fun on our app while simultaneously learning about the Bible and growing in their relationship with Jesus.

The app has a clear commitment to the conservative evangelical approach to the Bible in line with CBN, which was founded in 1961 by televangelist Pat Robertson (of 700 Club fame). With its expertise and experience in television production, CBN first developed and launched *Superbook* in 1981 in Japan as an evangelical cartoon. It grew over time to be a fairly sophisticated animation Bible series with 52 episodes that was watched by over 500 million people in 43 languages and broadcast in more than 100 countries. It was not a big leap to take the success of *Superbook* and use its contents as an anchor for the rest of the digital app by the same name. The name of the app certainly has overtones that would appeal to children more than "the Bible." It implies superheroes and turns the Bible into a kind of animated superhero.

While the *Superbook Kid's Bible* includes games for kids, there are a host of other Bible games in the app stores for iPhones, Androids, and

---

. The app was released in 2015. I am using version 1.5.4, released June 30, 2016. The Bible app is available at: https://itunes.apple.com/us/app/superbook-kids-bible-videos/id606378030?mt=8.

tablets of all kinds. The more that the Bible can be approached as part of a fun game, the more kids (and adults) are likely to engage with it. I remember a Bible Trivia board game from years ago that proved to be great fun as it asked those playing to identify obscure people and places in the Bible. (Where was the Apostle Paul when he was let down in a basket over a wall? What were the names of Job's friends? What is the shortest verse in the Bible?) Since the advent of digital screens, the number of gaming apps has, of course, grown exponentially. Overall, by the year 2020 there will be an estimated 5 million apps available through the Apple App Store alone. Most of these are games. In May of 2016, for example, a total of 20,958 new games were added to the App Store. The next closest category was education apps with 2,472.[91] Just as there are nearly endless Bible apps available for smartphones and tablets, so are there hundreds of Bible game apps. A search of Amazon for "Bible Games" in the "apps and games" section lists over 300 games, including "Bible Hangman," "Bible Scrabble," "Park the Ark," "Bible Trivia," "Bible Bingo," and various Bible trivia games. Much the same can be found on Apple's app store, or on the Android app site ("Bible Crossword," et al.). The games are for children and adults alike. "Scripture Shaker," for example, is an app that allows you to access utterly random biblical passages simply by shaking your phone. You then have the option of seeing the particular passage in context (the app takes you to the biblegateway.com site.). The goal of most Bible game apps is to help in memorizing (or remembering) various Bible verses.

Zondervan's *The Beginner's Bible*[92] provides a website designed for children and includes videos, games, downloadable coloring sheets, mazes, drawings, and the like. The beginner's Bible was first released in 1989 as a colorful series of books for children under the age of 6. It became a very popular children's Bible, selling over six million copies, and was developed into a series of animated stories available on DVDs, and then, later as an online presence. The most recent version also includes apps for the iPad.

A somewhat different resource for kids comes in online form, kids4truth.com. This site is replete with daily devotionals for kids, clubs ("helping children become God-focused believers through essential Christian truth"), stuff to do ("ask a question," "download coloring pages," "meet a missionary," et al.), and multimedia "dynamations."

91. See https://techcrunch.com/2016/08/10/app-store-to-reach-5-million-apps-by-2020-with-games-leading-the-way/.
92. http://thebeginnersbible.com/kids.php.

The dynamations are Bible-based animations that include animated text and images intended to help children to experience various Bible stories and more. They include animations of creation, the birth of Jesus, the story of Israel, the life of Christ, but also a challenge to evolution, a memorial to the victims of 9/11, and a dynamation entitled "Before" based on Jeremiah 1:5 ("Before I formed you in the womb I knew you, and before you were born I consecrated you; I appointed you a prophet to the nations"). This dynamation is an openly "pro-life," anti-abortion animated dramatic reading and representation of Psalm 139 and Jeremiah 1:5, which is then paraphrased and interpreted as a strong anti-abortion message, ending with an image of a glorified Jesus holding a newborn in his arms (http://kids4truth.com/Dyna/Before.aspx).

Kids4Truth also sponsors an iTunes app for the iPad, "Memorize It!"—an app using the NKJV translation and designed to help children memorize "120 Biblical truths and verses." According to the blurb for the app,

> These truths lay the foundation and provide the building blocks for learning who God is and how He wants us to live. Utilizing visual, audio, record and reward features, this app offers a comprehensive approach to learning these important truths. Designed for grades Pre K through 6th, this app can stand alone or be used alongside the Kids 4 Truth curriculum in a church club or homeschool setting.

This adaptation of the Bible to the comic book genre has clearly been a successful strategy for marketing the Bible to children. Along with YouVersion's Bible app for children, *Superbook Kid's Bible* demonstrates what Ruth Bottigheimer concluded in her masterful survey of Children's Bibles from the dawn of movable type to the present (or at least as far as 1996).

> Children's Bibles express values and standards that are not universal and eternal but particular and ephemeral. Bound by place and time, they adapt an ancient and inspired text to changing manners, morals, ideas, and concerns. For authors, buyers, and readers in nearly every age children's Bibles have seemed to be texts faithful to the Bible itself. But their authors' common effort to use the Bible to shape a meaningful present has produced Bible stories that mingle sacred text with secular values.[93]

3. Ruth B. Bottigheimer, *The Bible for Children: From the Age of Gutenberg to the Present* (New Haven: Yale University Press, 1996), 218. For a more focused study of children's Bibles in 20th-century American Jewish culture (during 1915–1936), see Penny Schine Gold, *Making the Bible Modern: Children's*

Finally, in this age of texting with both adapted shorthand (LOL, IMHO, BRB) and emojis (☺), it was only a matter of time before someone came up with a new translation idea for the Bible that would appeal to much older kids, Millennials, digital natives all. And so was born the *Bible Emoji: Scripture 4 Millenials (http://www.bibleemoji.com)*.[94] Thus, the KJV of Matthew 5:44 ("But I say unto you, Love your enemies, bless them that curse you, do good to them that hate you, and pray for them which despitefully use you, and persecute you") becomes:

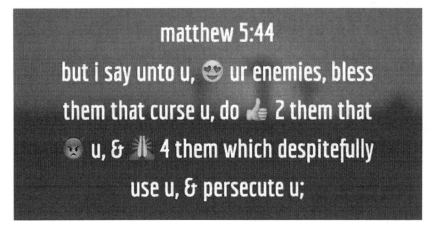

Fig. 6.7. The Emoji Bible rendition of Matthew 5:44.

It is also possible to create one's own Bible emojis for Twitter.[95] While the Emoji Bible is certainly cute, and perhaps even cool, I do wonder how well it meshes with what the apostle Paul emphasized about the message of the cross, not a particularly lighthearted or easily tweetable event or conception. (Fig. 6.8 shows the Emoji Bible rendition of Mark 15:36–39, describing Jesus's crucifixion.) It's not exactly clear to me what theological perspective the Bible Emoji communicates, aside from the general message that the Bible can be hip.

Bibles and Jewish Education in Twentieth-Century America (Ithaca, NY: Cornell University Press, 2004). For analysis of images in children's Bibles, see the essays in C. vander Stichele & H. Pyper, eds., *Text, Image, and Otherness in Children's Bibles: What Is in the Picture?* (Atlanta: Society of Biblical Literature, 2012).
94. http://tinyurl.com/l7rl2ju.
95. https://twitter.com/BibleEmoji?ref_src=twsrc^tfw.

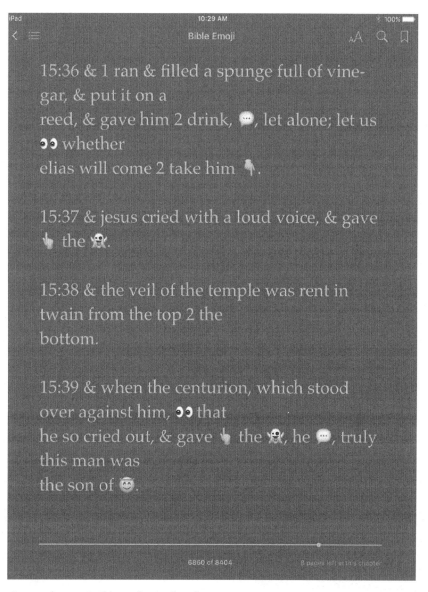

Fig. 6.7. The Emoji Bible rendition of Mark 15:36–39.

By virtue of the images chosen and the way in which Bible stories are retold, children's Bibles reflect the particular theological and social views of their publishers more than traditional print Bibles or their digital cousins, in which the textual translation and its accompanying paratexts dominate the paper or virtual page. There is more room for a kind of editorializing in children's Bibles, and in the digital realm the combination of image, sound, games, and text have launched a new and potentially influential form of a truly interactive Bible for kids. The challenge, of course, is that children do not yet have the critical skills to realize or understand the ways in which the Bible that is being read to them, or with which they are interacting, has been heavily edited and adapted from a particular theological viewpoint. Most often, children's Bibles presume a naïve literalism, which may be fine for the "Santa Claus years," but in fact, render a disservice when children gain sufficient critical analytical skills to begin to realize the problems with this kind of literalism. Unfortunately, many adults have never outgrown this approach to the Bible, resulting in an impoverished understanding of just how rich the Bible truly is as a reflection of people of faith deeply engaged in discerning God's presence in the whole of life.

7

Digital Bibles and Social Media

One of the most significant developments in our digital age is the radical shift that has occurred on a wide range of social media platforms.[1] In this chapter, we will look at some of the most important aspects of the Bible on digital social media, from tweets to blogs, from YouTube to Facebook, and the presence of the Bible on the web in general. The Bible in digital social media is where we can best see what I am calling the liquid character of the Bible, the way in which the Bible gets transformed from solid text to image and sound. The ability to change shapes and mediums across digital platforms has been one of the most important ways in which the Bible has been adapted to the digital age, especially in the form of mobile social apps. The printed text has been rendered into liquid 1s and 0s, the language of all things digital, whether as text on a digital screen, as narration on a digital audio player, or as both static and moving images on a digital video player.

The shift from print to digital is akin to the shift from analog to digital in music. Rather than recording the actual sound waves, digital music translates the sound waves into 1s and 0s that are then processed into audible signals. While there are self-described music purists who prefer the "warmth" of analog sound (including the pops and scratches

1. Facebook has over 750 million users. Twitter hosts more than 350 billion tweets each day. Every day, more than two billion videos are viewed on YouTube. And in 2015 alone, Americans sent 1.8 trillion text messages.

of an analog record), most people are quite happy to have digital access to their music libraries on iTunes or Spotify. They do not really hear the difference in the tonal character of the music. Digital is infinitely more portable. Still, in the world of music production, there has been a very clear shift from original analog instruments in the 1970s and 1980s to digitally "sampled" sounds in electronic instruments in the 1990s and early 2000s, and now, there is a resurgence back again to "real" analog sound creation (e.g., Moog synthesizers, among many others). Plastic vinyl records are also popular again even as digital music continues to thrive. Those who crave the warmth and feel of a traditional record album are, in many ways, parallel to those who prefer the gilt edges of their leather-bound Bible and the feel of a printed page between their fingers. It seems clear that material culture and digital culture will continue to walk side by side into the future, whether we're talking about music or Bibles on screens versus pages. This is not an either/or situation, it is a both-and. While some people prefer print Bibles because they are quite literally more tangible in a physical sense, others prefer digital Bibles because they are more convenient and adaptable. This is not so much a battle between two very different forms as it is a matter of a massive cultural and societal change that is taking place, sometimes in fits and starts, and sometimes seemingly overnight.

In many ways a parallel change occurred shortly after the invention of moveable type in the fifteenth century and with the subsequent mass media developments of the sixteenth-century Reformation era. The change was from a traditional form of the Bible in Latin to a new form of the Bible in the vernacular languages. When William Tyndale translated the New Testament from Greek into English (1525), and Martin Luther translated the complete Bible into German (1534), this launched a whole movement of translating the Bible into vernacular languages that people actually spoke, so that the Bible could be read and understood apart from its standard form in Latin. The translation from either the Latin Vulgate or from the Hebrew and Greek "original" into various vernacular languages of the people (English, German, French, et al.) was criticized by the official church as a domestication of God's word, a diminishing of the authority of the word of God as recorded in scripture, a de-sacralizing of the text now translated and read in the vulgar tongues of the people, rather than in the universal language of the church, Latin.[2] It also involved the de-clericalizing and democratization of the Bible, so that not only the priestly class, but also lay people could increasingly read and hear the Bible in their native tongue, especially since literacy was on the rise after the invention of the printing press with movable type.

In parallel ways I would suggest that the shift from print to digital Bibles reflects a shift to a new kind of vernacular. Despite what some decry as the domestication of the Bible into 1s and 0s on screens, the de-sacralization of the Bible on digital devices of all kinds, the shift from print Bibles to digital Bibles is simply a new vernacular of Christian faith for reading, hearing, and watching the Bible. This new vernacular language in the digital age is the language of texts and tweets and blogs and Facebook and YouTube videos. These digital media have become the new common language "spoken" as the native tongue of a whole new generation, and "spoken" as well by digital immigrants who have learned the new language and have come to appreciate and value it. Just as the printing of Bibles in the vernacular in the sixteenth century led to a de-clericalization and democratization of the Bible, so also in the twenty-first century, the digitizing of the Bible and its dissemination across all sorts of social media has led to a new kind of de-clericalizing and democratizing of the Bible, where just about anybody can post or upload or tweet just about anything they want about the Bible. And so they do!

At the same time, there is a certain irony with the proliferation of the vernacular, whether in print or digital form. In the sixteenth century, Luther became alarmed at some of the interpretations of the Bible that people reading the vernacular came up with, and so he actually sought to discourage regular lay people from reading the Bible lest they get confused. Instead, he wanted them to read his catechism and to leave the preaching and teaching about the Bible to reliable Lutheran pastors.

Today's digital age has generated televangelists who produce YouTube video Bible studies, whether we're talking about Joyce Meyers or Benny Hinn (each with over 300,000 views on YouTube) or Joel Osteen (with well over a million views on YouTube). They also produce brand-name Bibles, Joyce Meyer's *The Everyday Life Bible* (an amplified

2. During the fourth session of the Council of Trent (1546), the Council affirmed a decree on scripture that forbade the use of any version of the Bible other than the official Vulgate edition approved by the Church. The Council "ordains and declares, that the said old and vulgate edition, which, by the lengthened usage of so many ages, has been approved of in the Church, be, in public lectures, disputations, sermons and expositions, held as authentic; and that no one is to dare, or presume to reject it under any pretext whatever." (http://www.bible-researcher.com/trent1.html).

version), available via Kindle as an e-book, or in print form. Joel Osteen's *Hope for Today Bible* also comes in either digital or print form, and features the New Living Translation. It includes "Hope Notes" throughout as well as comments on why people should be hopeful. *The Master's Healing Presence Bible* by Benny Hinn Ministries only comes in a leather-bound KJV edition (for only $185!), but it includes 1,600 color-coded pages. The text of the Bible may be relatively stable, but the paratexts that frame the biblical witness reflect the diverse faith convictions of those who produce particular versions of the Bible, whether Joyce Meyer, Benny Hinn, or any of the hundreds of niche versions of the New International Version published by Zondervan, the dozens of specialized versions of the New Living Translation published by Tyndale House, or many other editions and translations.

While Luther celebrated the distribution of printed Bibles in the vernacular that allowed his movement to flourish, he also witnessed how rival views could be published just as readily. Even his own followers, at times, were moving in directions against which he fought in sermon and in print (e.g., the Peasants' Revolt in 1525 Germany). Similarly, the digital revolution has facilitated the development of churches and faith communities quite beyond the traditional boundaries of denominationalism. But even as leaders of these new church movements seek to shepherd their virtual flocks in particular directions and in particular interpretations of the Bible, individuals have been empowered by all forms of digital media to be distracted by and attracted anew to other movements, other leaders, other communities of faith. As they walk with their fingers across a digital touchscreen, and tap on this and then that, all things digital has become the new vernacular, the new normal. Digital Bibles on social media are but one aspect of this much larger set of movements.

In deciding which components of digital social media to cover in relation to the Bible, I have chosen to focus on four kinds of current social media: Blogs, Twitter, YouTube, and Facebook. In her book *The Social Media Gospel: Sharing the Good News in New Ways*,[3] Meredith Gould addresses four additional forms of popular social media and their role in the life of the modern church: LinkedIn, Pinterest, Instagram, and Snapchat. I have found that the Bible is not quite the large presence on these forms of social media, largely because they are driven more by images than by text. And let's face it, when you are dealing with the

---

3. Collegeville, MN: Liturgical, 2015; 2nd ed.

Bible, you are dealing with a whole lot of text! This does not mean that images are an unimportant component of the Bible in a digital era. Far from it. When various online Bible programs send out their respective "Verse of the Day," they are often accompanied by images and artwork that seeks to reflect the words. Still, as commentary on the biblical text they tend to be less concrete and more indirect. In what follows, then, we will consider digital Bibles in relation to blogging, Twitter, YouTube, and Facebook, along with some more general observations about the Bible on the web.

Bible Blogging and Vlogging

In the relative early years of the internet and digital social media (the late 1990s), "web logs" became "blogs." In 2004, Merriam-Webster declared "blog" the word of the year. Between 1999 and 2006, the number of blogs grew from a total of 23 to a total of over 50 million, and by 2010, to over 150 million.[4] Blogs tend to be text-heavy, and so, they have proven to be an appropriate match for discussions about the text-heavy Bible. A routine search of "Bible Blogs" on Google results in over 16 million hits, though these blogs are by no means limited to discussions of the Bible. One blog, at Bible.org, is an evangelical Christian site advocating an inerrant view of scripture, and has a header at the top of its webpage saying, "Where the world comes to study the Bible." While there are a number of links to Bible study, and a general promotion of the New English Translation, Bible.org serves as the umbrella site for a host of other sites, including a Bible.blog.

It comes as no surprise that the 16 million hits for Bible Blogs run across the theological and popular gamut. For example, the Bible Gateway Blogger Grid (BG²)

> is an international network of independent bloggers who meaningfully blog—and who are serious—about matters relating to the Bible. . . . With the hashtag #bgbg2, BG² reflects a broad array of blogs: from mommy bloggers to authors to speakers to pastors to seminaries to Bible professors and others, writing from North America, Europe, Africa, Asia, and Australia.[5]

Hundreds of blogs are listed in this bloggergrid, many of them relating

4. http://www.webdesignerdepot.com/2011/03/a-brief-history-of-blogging/.
5. https://www.biblegateway.com/blog/bloggergrid/.

to the Bible, but many of them with random postings about any number of things related to Christianity in general.[6]

Lines between blogs and other digital media on the internet are increasingly blurry. The website "patheos.com" advertises itself as "hosting the conversation on faith."[7] Its web page opens to a very busy amalgam of all kinds of clickables, including various channels. One of the channels, listed under "Topical Channels," is the "Preacher's Channel," which in turn, leads one to a blog entitled "On Scripture – the Bible."[8] Here, one finds such posts as "Ah, Jesus, I Get It Now! (Luke 17:5–10)" by Jacqui Lewis (posted September 27, 2016), or from September 17, 2016, "Hope: The Call to Action (Jeremiah 32:1–3, 6–15)" by Valerie Bridgeman, or Keith Anderson's "Uber and Amos: Economic Justice in the Gig Economy (Luke 16:1–13)," posted September 12, 2016, as well as "Lost and Found: Depression and Isolation (Luke 15.1–10)," posted by Karyn Wiseman on September 9, 2016. Patheos.com also hosts blogs aimed at Roman Catholics,[9] Eastern Orthodox, Evangelical Christians, Progressive Christians, Mormons, Jews, Muslims, Buddhists, Hindu, Pagan, Atheist, Spirituality, Politics Blue, Politics Red, Entertainment, and many more audiences. So while it does contain blogs on the Bible, it embeds them in a much wider array of other blogs and topics.

It appears that blogs are somewhat on the decline, as they are text-heavy and require a fair amount of work to keep updated. In part, this is a consequence of users shifting increasingly to mobile devices rather than desktop computers. Social media such as YouTube, Twitter, and Facebook are more readily used in the much more abbreviated forms of

---

6. The moderators of the site state: "This Blog features news about the Bible, interviews with authors about their Bible-focused books, and the latest announcements from Bible Gateway. It's the best place to stay current with Bible-related developments. We interview a variety of authors who write about Bible topics from many different angles; mostly, but not exclusively, from within the evangelical tradition. Our interviewing of an author does not signify that we agree with or condone everything the author writes; merely that we think Bible readers would find it thought-provoking. We hope what you find here will add to your understanding of and appreciation for the Bible as we publish periodic reflections about Scripture, Bible study, and associated subjects. We want you to engage with God's Word, online or off, and we hope what you read here helps you to do that."

7. The Patheos website notes that "according to the Pew Internet Project, more than 82 million Americans (and 64 percent of all Internet users) utilize the Web for faith-related matters. The importance of religion and spirituality, coupled with the growing use of the Internet for religious matters, point to the ongoing need for an online resource for religious and spiritual engagement and dialogue. Patheos fills this need." (http://www.patheos.com).

8. http://www.patheos.com/blogs/onscripture/.

9. There are also various blogs about Roman Catholic blogs. See "The Catholic Blog Directory" (http://catholicblogs.blogspot.com). See also Brandon Vogt, ed., *The Church and New Media: Blogging Converts, Online Activists, and Bishops Who Tweet* (Huntington, IN: Our Sunday Visitor, 2011).

screens accessed on smartphones. Both Bible blogs and "vlogs" (video blogs) continue to be a significant presence in digital social media, with blogs remaining longer form and primarily text-based discussions of the Bible. But, as noted by social media critic Dylan Kissane, writing for DOZ Marketing Software, blogging continues to morph, becoming blurred with other forms of social media. He argues that in 2016, for example, blogs will increasingly tend to "draw together text, images, online video, knowledge of pop culture and trends, business savvy, powerful and extensive social networks, and the skills to bring all of this to bear in a dynamic zeitgeist."[10] To what degree such trends will be reflected in blogs about the Bible, only time will tell. But as goes social media, so will forms of discussion about the Bible follow.

Some of these trends can be seen, as an example, in the "Blue Letter Bible Blog" (http://blogs.blueletterbible.org/blb/). The Blue Letter Bible (BLB)[11] started off in 1996 as a website that offered an online version of the King James Version of the Bible, a concordance, a lexicon, and commentary from various evangelical writers. It was named the Blue Letter Bible because it sought to provide a large number of hyperlinks (in blue) that would provide an expansive set of cross-references for the study of the Bible. The site currently has over 3.5 million hyperlinks, with links to more than 1,200 different websites. Over the last twenty years, the BLB has expanded greatly to include mobile apps, Twitter, and a host of online tools including a searchable Bible in 20 different versions, various study features (with audio, video, and text-based commentaries), devotionals, and links to the BLB ministries, including the BLB Blog. The Blog contains videos on how the New Testament was copied, sermon outlines for preaching on Romans, and a study on the book of Esther, among other features. As it the case with most, but by no means all, blogs about the Bible, the BLB Blog is resourced by a conservative evangelical group of Christians.

Blogs about the Bible often contain (out)dated posts rather than current discussions. For example, "essentialbibleblog.com" (http://www.essentialbibleblog.com) presents a whole series of blog topics and posts about the Bible, including "Top Ten Reasons the Bible Is True," which elicited 439 comments.[12] But as I click on "newer posts" in the Fall of

---

10. "5 Most Important Trends for Blogging in 2016" (http://www.doz.com/content/trends-in-blogging-2016).

11. The Blue Letter Bible is not to be confused with the *Jesus Centered Bible*, in the New Living Translation (Tyndale House Publishers, 2015), which highlights in blue more than 600 passages in the Old Testament (with comments) that the editors think point to the coming of Jesus.

12. http://www.essentialbibleblog.com/2013/03/top-10-reasons-bible-is-true.html - comments.

2016, the 439 comments that appear come from 2013 and 2014. Blogs often contain dated and outdated conversations. Blogs can get stale. Perhaps such dated discussions are really not an issue, since, inasmuch as they are reflections on the Bible, the discussions revolve around a rather old text itself. Is it really so much different from dipping into conversations about the Bible from another time and place? What remains very different about many blog posts about the Bible is that there is really no filtering of the posts of commenters, no gatekeeper or editor to weigh in on the quality of a post. On the one hand, this situation is utterly democratic, but on the other hand, the result can often be tremendously uninformed conversations. But "uninformed" comes in many flavors. Thus, one person's insightful blog post is another person's wrongheaded interpretation.

There are a number of recognized scholars who have dedicated blogs that are more popular in nature, in keeping with the social medium that is blogging. The question arises, of course, "scholars" recognized by whom? While most everyone will recognize the academic qualifications of these scholars, different confessional communities will inevitably align with whichever scholar is more in keeping with a particular theological viewpoint. Among the more conservative evangelical scholars, Darrell Bock, a professor of New Testament at Dallas Theological Seminary has a blog that addresses "Christ and culture from a theological perspective." Bock posted several things in 2015 on a *Newsweek* article and its approach to the Bible, but he did not post anything in 2016. This is the nature of blogs, as they can often be active for a while, and then, become dormant for a period of time. More middle-of-the road theologically is the blog by Prof. Mark Goodacre, a New Testament scholar in the Department of Religion at Duke University. He oversees the NTGateway.com website, but also has his own blog (http://ntweblog.blogspot.com). Here, one can follow conversations and post comments in response to a wide variety of topics, mostly related to the New Testament. In 2016, Goodacre had blog posts on such subjects as "The Gospel of Jesus' Wife," "David Bowie as Pilate in the Last Temptation of Christ" (shortly following the iconic singer/actor's death), and a reposting of an interview with Prof. John Barclay, a New Testament scholar who had recently published a tome entitled *Paul and the Gift* (Eerdmans, 2015), a book on the apostle Paul's understanding of God's grace.

More controversial is the New Testament scholar Bart Ehrman, a professor in the Department of Religious Studies at the University of

North Carolina, Chapel Hill. For several years, he has hosted a blog on the study of early Christianity. To participate in Ehrman's blog, one must join and pay a membership fee of $25 per year. This gives one access to over twenty different member categories, essentially different subject areas about which Ehrman has written. The categories range across Greco-Roman religion, the historical Jesus, the NT text and manuscripts, apocryphal gospels, films about Jesus, and many more. Significantly, Ehrman charges a fee to join his blog in order to raise funds to aid the hungry and homeless in the Raleigh-Durham-Chapel Hill triangle of North Carolina and beyond (https://ehrman-blog.org/philanthropy/).[13] Ehrman's writing has garnered particular criticism from evangelical conservative Christians (among whom Ehrman once counted himself),[14] especially as he has openly identified himself as a post-Christian, who nonetheless has strong humanist interests that link ancient and modern worlds.

Most Bible blogs, however, are less academic in scope and far more oriented to particular ministries that seek to engage their followers, and anyone else who cares to join in. The "Women's Bible Café," for example (http://www.womensbiblecafe.com/100-top-faith-blogs), has served since 2009 as a kind of clearing house, recommending a wide range of blogs for women interested in following particular women faith leaders, as well as women seeking to be part of online Bible studies (both inductive and topical) or other more general Christian-related book studies. Over 6,000 individuals belong to the Women's Bible Café small Bible-study groups. One of the most popular Bible study leaders is Beth Moore, who in Fall of 2016 led an online Bible study of 2 Timothy entitled "Entrusted." The Women's Bible Café invited individuals to join in:

> Every Sunday night I post our small group discussion questions here on the Womens Bible Cafe™ website. You'll get an email with the discussion questions on Monday morning. Join us in online small groups: **you choose a day and time** that is most convenient for you. We meet in one central location – the **Womens Bible Cafe Small Group via Facebook.**

The Women's Bible Café book club was offering two books for online

---

13. Specifically, the recipients of funds raised through the blog include The Urban Ministries of Durham (with a focus on aiding the homeless), The Food Bank of Central and Eastern North Carolina, and Doctors Without Borders, among others.
14. His blog now includes a "Bart Responds to Critics" section (https://ehrmanblog.org/membership/).

small group discussion using the same kind of format as for the Bible study. One of the books for Fall 2016 was a nonfiction book, *The Well: Why Are So Many So Thirsty?*, by Mark Hall, a pastor and lead singer for the Christian music group "Casting Crowns." The second book was fiction, *Lizzy and Jane,* a Jane Austen-inspired novel about faith and hope, by Katherine Reay.

A somewhat different set of blogs on the Bible is called *The Naked Bible,* hosted by Dr. Michael Heiser (http://drmsh.com/the-naked-bible/). I found this Bible blog by perusing a site that ranks the "top-100-christian-blogs" (https://redeeminggod.com/100-top-christian-blogs/). Dr. Heiser has a PhD in Hebrew and Semitic Studies from the University of Wisconsin-Madison, and works with Logos Bible Software, one of the most widely used Bible software programs on the market (to which we will turn our attention in the next chapter). His blogs include various Bible podcast episodes, especially on topics related to the Old Testament. It is not exactly clear why he named his blog *The Naked Bible*, but when one clicks on "About" the blog, he does indicate that his goal is to provide "serious academic content for understanding the Bible in its own context, unfiltered by creeds and traditions – but made decipherable to those who don't live in the ivory tower."[15] He is also concerned to offer "serious academic critique of the cyber-twaddle you find on the internet about the Bible and the ancient world." Thus, his "naked Bible" blog seeks to provide content without clothing it with any overt theological overlay.

Blogs about the Bible, then, can be an effective means of connecting with others to engage in online small group Bible study, as well as to view presentations of Bible studies on a great variety of topics. Not all blogs are created equal, of course, and so the quality and caliber of the blog is mostly in the mind of the person reading or participating in the blog. As we have seen, some blogs are primarily academic in scope, while others (most) may well draw on academic resources, but do so with a focus on pastoral and practical ministry.

Paul the Proto-Blogger?

In her book *Tweet If You ♥ Jesus,*[16] Elizabeth Drescher suggests that the Apostle Paul can be understood as a "proto-blogger." She focuses on the *how* of Paul's letter-writing ministry to the various churches he

15. http://drmsh.com/about.
16. *Tweet If You ♥ Jesus: Practicing Church in the Digital Reformation* (New York: Morehouse, 2011), 78–87.

established. In particular, Drescher notes that (not unlike modern blogs), Paul often provides a mash-up of different conventions in his letters, drawing on scripture, on the occasional saying of Jesus, on early creeds and hymns, on Stoic sources, and other material. More important, she calls attention to the fundamental function of both blogs and Paul's letters as forms of communication that invoke a community of faith, a "plural who," hence his constant appeal to "you" in the plural. He writes from an itinerant community of faith (see the co-senders of his letters) to a specific geographic community of faith. In the process of addressing local communities of faith, Paul invokes a collaborative model of ministry that can function in much the same way as a blog might lead to concrete collaborative action. Paul's letters "suggest forms of collaborative ministry that have not yet moved from face-to-face practice to digital practice in particularly intentional ways. Sharing news and opinions, offering compassion and encouragement, celebrating life transitions, and gathering for brainstorming or problem-solving are all things that everyone in a community of faith can do online—not just clergy or formally commissioned lay leaders."[17] In the digital realm, of course, the whole point of blogging is to engage a much larger audience than is possible through letter-writing. But even here, Paul is instructive, as he directs the Thessalonians to have his letter read in all the churches (1 Thess 5:27), and in Colossians 4:16 (whether from Paul or not), the Colossians are encouraged to swap letters with the church in Laodicea. Thus, Paul's letters have both a public and interactive aspect like a kind of primitive blogging.

Drescher's work evokes the creative idea that blogging about the Bible is a form of digital social media that runs in multiple directions. Yes, blogs can offer reflections on the Bible; they can draw on Paul's letters as pastoral and theological resources for addressing broad ecclesial issues. But blogs can also use the model of corporate communication that Paul offers in his letters by addressing specific and pressing issues of faith in the modern era, just as he did in his day and age. Our issues are certainly different than Paul's, as ours is a radically different culture than Paul's. Still, Paul's letters can be touchstones that authorize more mutual reflection and fewer electronic pulpits. "My hunch is that Paul would be just fine if your next blog post were less about his letter to the Philippians and more about what you've heard

. Ibid., 83.

lately on Facebook and Twitter about how people are understanding their faith."[18]

The Twittering of Scripture

"Pastors tell me, Twitter is just made for the Bible." This observation was made by Ms. Claire Diaz-Ortiz, a Senior Executive in charge of Twitter for Nonprofits (*New York Times*, June 2, 2012).[19] It is easy to understand why the Bible lends itself so readily to Twitter and its 140 character limit. This is just the right amount of space to tweet a favorite scripture verse, or to follow a Twitter account that will send daily scripture tweets. Such tweets are really just digital versions of the random and stray biblical texts that are scattered near and far, from greeting cards with religious messages, to billboards, to bus stop benches, to knick-knacks of all kinds. At a vacation beach house we had rented for a family reunion this past summer, I found a bowl full of seashells with different verses inscribed on them—each one its own kind of "tweet" on a shell. The Bible is ubiquitous, often in little pieces at a time.

I would argue that the Bible has actually always been "tweeted" in various ways without any particular concern for the integrity of the original passage's overarching context. This can already be seen in how authors of the New Testament writings long ago made use of various passages from what was their Bible, what Christians have come to call the Old Testament. For example, the Apostle Paul essentially appealed to Genesis 15:6 ("Abraham believed God, and God reckoned it to him as righteousness") in Twitter style as a divine slogan that was central to his understanding of faith in light of Christ. Paul had found a verse that linked faith and righteousness, the connection that is so crucial to his fight with those who insisted on Gentile law-observance (Romans 4, Galatians 3). We also find Paul basically tweeting and retweeting (correcting) slogans that were bouncing around the congregations he had established. For example, in 1 Corinthians 6:12, we find Paul quoting the Corinthian tweet/slogan "All things are lawful for me," and then, responding by retweeting/correcting this tweet: "'All things are lawful for me,' but not all things are beneficial. 'All things are lawful for me,'

---

18. *Tweet If You ♥ Jesus*, 85.
19. See P. Cheong, "Tweet the Message? Religious Authority and Social Media Innovation," *Journal of Religion, Media and Digital Culture* 3, no. 3 (2014): 1–19. Available online at: https://www.jrmdc.com/journal/article/view/27.

but I will not be dominated by anything."[20] While modern electronic tweets can serve as kinds of slogans that anchor a particular approach to the substance of faith, a similar approach can be found in the biblical text itself.

In Matthew's Sermon on the Mount, Jesus could be said to have "tweeted" well-known commandments from the Mosaic law, and then retweeted them with a kind of corrective or reinterpreted meaning attached: "You have heard that it was said, 'You shall not commit adultery.' But I say to you that everyone who looks at a woman with lust has already committed adultery with her in his heart" (Matt 5:27–28). Tweet and retweet. A general moral rule with a more specific, if still generalized, application. "You have heard that it was said, 'An eye for an eye and a tooth for a tooth.' But I say to you, Do not resist an evildoer. But if anyone strikes you on the right cheek, turn the other also" (Matt 5:38–39). Tweet. Retweet. Or take the tweeting of passages such as Psalm 110:1 ("The Lord said to my Lord, 'Sit at my right hand until I make your enemies your footstool.") as a proof text for the resurrection of Jesus (Acts 2:34). Or the ubiquitous tweeting of the suffering servant songs from Isaiah 53 as a foreshadowing of Jesus's death (Matt 8:17; Mark 15:28; John 12:38; Acts 8:32; 1 Pet 2:22–24, etc.). These functional "tweets" do appear in larger narrative frameworks, but nonetheless, they work in much the same way as the tweeting of various slogans.

While modern biblical scholars (like me) may fuss about context, context, context (literary, historical, social, etc.), religious practitioners (an academic term for "believers") have long engaged in what ultimately comes down to tweeting and responding to tweets. The one major difference between the "tweets" we find in the Bible compared to the actual tweets in the digital age has to do with the larger literary frameworks within which "tweets" in the Bible have functioned. Modern digital tweets of the Bible rarely reveal anything of the literary context of the biblical passage that is being tweeted. For example, the website faithandhealthconnection.org has a link to thirty daily positive affirmations that one can tweet.[21] These tweets function as short encouraging messages that serve to motivate and to reinforce faith commitments. Here are but two of such tweets from the website:

20. See, e.g., D. Burk, "Discerning Corinthian Slogans through Paul's Use of the Diatribe in 1 Corinthians 6:12-20," *Bulletin for Biblical Research* 18, no. 1 (2008): 99–121.

21. http://www.faithandhealthconnection.org/daily-positive-affirmations-using-bible-verses-on-twitter/. Other Bible twitter sites include: https://twitter.com/bible_time; https://twitter.com/nivbible?lang=en; and https://twitter.com/guidetothebible, among many others.

"God's principles are perfect. They are entirely worthy of my trust."
(Psalm 119:138)

"With God in my life, all things are possible." (Matthew 19:26)

The tweets work as individual messages from the Bible to the believer, from God to you, with a message of encouragement. Many of them are in the vein of "when the going gets tough, the tough get going" (no, *not* a verse from the Bible!). But some, such as the tweet from Romans 8:35–39, seek to focus more on a principle of faith, and summarize the thrust of a passage that is longer than 140 characters: "I can never be separated from the love of God." The slogan/tweet stands by itself, or it can imply a narrative frame. For those well-acquainted with the Bible, the echo of the larger narrative framework will also sound. While tweets by definition contain no narrative frame, neither are they utterly noncontextual. There is typically a social context that is invoked, even if not overtly.[22] And one tweet can build on another to create a conversation of tweets. Tweets can also invoke a larger narrative by including web links that amplify and contextualize the tweet. Even though the whole idea of Twitter is to work as a social media app that anywhere from 10 to 10 million people can "follow," it is fundamentally a form of personalized individual expression. In the case of the Bible, a communal book is used as the basis for generic reminders or statements of faith, all in 140 characters or less.

Another way in which the Bible can function as a series of tweets can be seen in the technical term used to describe discrete Gospel stories—*pericopes*, a Greek term that means "snippets." The Gospel of Mark consists famously of a relatively loose collection of such snippets, with such connectives as "and immediately this happened" or "and then this happened." This is not to say that on a macro level, the Gospel of Mark is not a sophisticated composition in its own right, but it is to recognize the oral stage of tradition in which relatively brief stories were told and retold. The larger narrative of collected and connected stories moves beyond the mere snippet to a much deeper story. But the snippets of disjointed miracle stories and parables can be understood in many respects as early Christian tweets that were written down and organized into a larger narrative whole. The larger patterns of con-

---

22. The (in)famous tweets of Donald Trump during the 2016 presidential race and beyond only made sense (if they did) against a larger narrative in the news cycle.

nections between independent stories provide a narrative shape that is greater than the sum of its parts.

Still, the twittering of the Bible can have some unfortunate effects. While it can highlight favorite biblical passages that individuals and communities might find inspiring, it can also lead to the fragmenting of the larger complex of biblical narratives into a reductionistic slogan that may be truthful in one regard, but is not even close to being the whole story. It is not that tweets are intended to replace the whole story, but often they do serve as a shorthand that stands in for the larger story, which is problematic. Tweets are not complicated, but the larger story certainly is. If stories and narratives are "thick," then tweets are "thin." As Stanley Hauerwas, among others, has long reminded us, the story is the story is the story.[23] It is precisely the different details and parts of a larger narrative that make the story as a whole meaningful. To take one snippet, one tweet, of the story as representative of the whole story is to miss the story as a whole. To reduce the Bible to John 3:16 or Psalm 119:138, or to any one verse, the sloganeering of the Bible, is to miss the nuances of the larger narrative, the thickness and messiness of the story, which is so much more a realistic expression of life as we know it than any tweet could ever represent.

Tweets are inherently reductionistic. Reducing the Bible to popular tweets not only takes the thickness out of the biblical narrative, it does so by removing the difficult texts from the conversation. It can render the Bible into a pollyannish feel-good book that never really goes below the surface of things. Such a twitterverse of mostly happy and pious biblical sentiments may be well-intentioned and may, in fact, provide encouragement or consolation, but in the process, the complex and competing visions of the biblical witness can get lost. Thus, I would argue, the crucifixion narrative is not really tweetable, Mel Gibson's ad for his movie *The Passion* notwithstanding: "He was born to die"; or as one student "tweeted" by means of his t-shirt, "His pain, your gain."

The difficulty with the twittering of the Bible is that a tweet is a minimalist text. It is not an embedded text in which one can see the context. Context can be inferred or invoked, but it is rarely explicit. But that can also be one of the beauties of tweets. They can be both specific and yet open to interpretation and application to each individual. The same tweeted message ("with God all things are possible," Matt

---

23. See, e.g., S. Hauerwas, *The Peaceable Kingdom: A Primer in Christian Ethics* (Notre Dame: University of Notre Dame Press, 1991). See also my discussion of Hauerwas's narrative approach in J. S. Siker, *Scripture and Ethics: Twentieth-Century Portraits* (New York: Oxford University Press, 1997), 97–125.

19:26) has a vast plurality of meanings, depending on how an individual interprets the message. There are certainly communities of individuals who follow the same twitter account, and who encounter the same Bible tweet. Such communities are bound together by a set of common beliefs and practices that provide the larger framework for understanding something like a "verse of the day," which can be tweeted, retweeted, instant messaged, or e-mailed.

But one cannot exactly read or tweet the WHOLE Bible at one time! Although it is bound as one book, it is not a book that can be read like a short story. It requires days, weeks, months, years to work through the Bible. Even those who aspire to read the entire Bible in a calendar year are relatively few, since it takes so much time. But that's what lectionaries are for—namely, the recognition that the unfolding of the entire biblical narrative plays out week after week, with one part of the Bible nuancing another part, with one reading reflecting upon another. One is never done with reading/hearing the story over and over again as it interacts with changing communities of faith over time. There are apps and programs that will text/tweet/email a given lectionary reading for the day or week, so that over a three-year cycle, you will, in fact, read the whole text of the Bible, one snippet at a time. In this regard, the twittering/tweeting/ emailing of snippets of biblical text can function very much like the reading of any print Bible according to a lectionary cycle. There are, of course, different kinds of both Bibles and lectionaries in this regard. One can purchase any of a number of "The Bible in One Year" readers that provide each day's set of snippets (either in print form or digital). The Roman Catholic Church also provides weekly missals containing the print or digital readings for any given week. Or one can grab one's old reliable leather-bound Bible and simply look up the passages, in which case, the larger contexts will be visible, but the reader may or may not take note of such interpretive contexts embedded in the textual frame. The most immediate frame is likely always to be the particular individual's context, which provides its own very personalized frame for the interpretation and appropriation of a passage, tweeted or not.

In *Tweet if You ♥ Jesus,* Drescher has a chapter entitled "Toward the Tweethood of All Believers," which addresses the need for pastoral leaders to be digitally conversant and competent if they want to communicate with people of faith in the modern age. This "Tweethood" of believers serves as a useful metaphor for the digital twitterverse that increasingly democratizes, and thereby, de-clericalizes much of religious leadership. "If leadership is an expression of conferred, inherent, or assumed authority that enables one person to engage, motivate, or inspire another to belief or action, there is often scant evidence of it in the digital domain from formally recognized lay and ordained leaders in ministry."[24] The world of Twitter is much less top-down than it is bottom-up, as the collective of individuals and relatively anonymous "followers" make or break the degree to which any person can corner a piece of the market on Twitter. As a social media platform Twitter excels in providing real-time shorthand conversation about a wide range of topics, depending on what people are following. Drescher concludes that "As a practice, then, digital leadership is fluid, distributed, and more often than not, collective rather than individual."[25]

While there are many twitter feeds that appeal directly to Christians, aside from "verse of the day" tweets, there are not a great number of Bible studies via twitter.[26] Meredith Gould suggests that one possible use of Twitter in relation to the Bible would be to create virtual communities of biblical readers and interpreters engaged in study of and conversation about the Bible.[27] Scheduled "tweet chats" already regularly occur on a wide range of topics, and perhaps those who find twitter a fruitful venue for social networking could do so in a more substantive way by making discussion of the Bible the central focus of the tweet chat. The church has not traditionally made significant use of tweeting for Bible study, but it would not be surprising if social media became so pervasive that such virtual tweet chats became more commonplace.

YouTube

If Twitter has become a dominant expression of digital media in terms of text and web links, so has YouTube become the most widely used digital app for posting and viewing videos, both short and long. YouTube began in April 2006, when its first video was uploaded (a trip to the zoo). While the "twitterverse" of the Bible has functioned primarily as a mechanism for tweeting "verses of the day," the YouTube juggernaut has proved to be a much more important form of digital

---

24. *Tweet If You ♥ Jesus*, 126–27.
25. Ibid., 127.
26. See one individual's take on the best Christian twitterverse at http://nwbingham.com/blog/the-best-of-the-christian-twittersphere/. Most of these twitter feeds are hosted by conservative evangelical Christians with a high view of scripture.
27. *The Social Media Gospel*, 81–83, 97–99.

social media for the study of the Bible. A simple search for "Bible" on YouTube garners over nine million hits, including over half a million YouTube channels dedicated to the Bible. YouTube provides an ideal venue for televangelists of all stripes to connect with their virtual flocks. For example, Beth Moore, the founder of Living Proof Ministries (http://www.lproof.org), is "dedicated to encourage people to come to know and love Jesus Christ through the study of Scripture." To this end, one can find more than 3,600 videos featuring Beth Moore teaching about the Bible.[28] A search for Joyce Meyer videos on YouTube results in nearly 100,000 subscribers and more than 40,000 results for sermons. This pales in comparison to the nearly 150,000 subscribers and 250,000 results for the popular televangelist Joel Osteen, featuring a mixture of his brand of positive encouragement, Bible study, and preaching on a wide variety of topics.[29]

The YouTube video universe offers parents many channels for children regarding the Bible. For example, ABCKidsInc.com offers a guide to "11 Awesome Bible Channels for Kids on YouTube."[30] It includes links to "The Beginner's Bible," a series of 25-minute animated Bible stories directed at children. Noah's Ark is the favorite (as is often the case with children's animated Bibles). It has been viewed nearly a million times on YouTube, and it offers a simplified version of the Noah story that emphasizes how God is angry that people are not caring for each other. Thus, God is going to flood the world and make a fresh start of things with Noah and his family (and all the animals on the ark, of course). It is presented as a relatively happy story with a loveable Noah, and with God's resonant echoing voice appearing in the twinkling of the stars. Happy cartoon music accompanies the story and images. The YouTube video version from ABCKidsInc.com is really not all that different from standard children's Bible versions in print form. But children will certainly be more engaged with the animated version, especially younger children who cannot read.

Other kids' channels include "What's In the Bible?,"[31] a successor series to the very popular Veggie Tales cartoons. Veggie Tales was created by Phil Vischer, and starting in 1993 forty-seven episodes were produced, featuring general Christian themes and also some Bible stories (including Noah's Ark). In his introduction to the "What's In the

28. https://www.youtube.com/results?search_query=beth moore.
29. https://www.youtube.com/results?sp=SCjqAwA%3D&q=Joel Osteen.
30. http://abckidsinc.com/awesome-bible-channels-for-kids-on-youtube/.
31. It features the animated newscaster Buck Denver, and friends. https://www.youtube.com/watch?v=G-Mnq_sqMus.

Bible" series, Vischer shows a copy of a large Bible to some animated characters, saying "This is a Bible." He then shows a slightly smaller version of the Bible, saying "and this is a Bible," then a still smaller version of the Bible, saying "and this is a Bible," and finally—and significantly—he shows his cell phone and says "and this is a Bible." But the animated characters protest, "That looks like a phone." Vischer concedes the point, but says that he has two different versions of the Bible on his phone.[32] Thus, already in the introductory moments of the video series, Vischer both includes the phone as a device that can contain the biblical text and concedes that the phone is a multimedia device that is also different from the print versions of the Bible. He does not make much of this distinction; rather, he is simply acknowledging how digital Bibles have developed in current usage and how many people now read their Bibles on such devices as cell phones. This will surely resonate with digital natives who understand at a very early age the importance of digital phones and their multimedia capacities.

Some digital Bible videos aimed at children come only with moving images and music, without text or spoken words. For example, one clever 3-minute video features the famous parable of the sower, with no words but only a mixture of African-themed music and other styles matched to the story narrative (ominous music for seeds being choked out by other plants; happier music for the end).[33] This video was posted by a Rev. Rufus Butner, a pastor of St. Luke's United Methodist Church in Goldsboro, NC, whose over 1,800 subscribers have viewed some 50 videos on the Bible over one million times. In the video, what appear to be green peas (with expressive faces) are sown by a farmer on the ground. But the ground is not very forgiving, and so, the animation shows the seeds getting stepped on, being eaten by birds, withering from the sun, and getting choked out by big bad weeds. The end of the story is, of course, much happier; the seeds that have fallen on fertile ground grow up into a great harvest. The digital video was produced by Max7, an evangelical organization committed to developing "a variety of Bible resources including curriculum, videos, music, and training materials for use through children's or young people's ministry."[34] The organization is called Max7 because they seek to help children live life "to the max" 7 days a week. The conservative evangelical and international roots of this ministry are evident from their statement of faith,

. https://www.youtube.com/watch?v=w4RowvUFziM.
. https://www.youtube.com/watch?v=fa3y8pH0ymw.
. http://www.max7.org/en/about.

the Lausanne Covenant,[35] tracing its heritage back to evangelist Billy Graham's outreach and heavily influenced by the British cleric John Stott.[36]

A rather different YouTube Bible series is "The Bible Reloaded: The Atheist Bible Study" (https://www.youtube.com/watch?v=3TDr-tuGIHrs). The goal of this Bible Study is to read through and comment on the entire Bible (in the NIV) from the perspective of two self-avowed atheists, Hugo and Jake. The irreverent tone of this YouTube Bible study can be readily seen at the very beginning of the first episode, which contains what amounts to a trigger warning to viewers: "This video may contain one or more references to the following: Rape, Incest, Misogyny, Murder, Genocide, Ghosts, Talking Animals, Prostitutes, Slavery, Impalement, Bear Mauling, or Tree Cursing." The tongue-in-cheek warning is clearly a reference to subject matter that will come up in the reading of the Bible. Their goal is to be knowledgeable about the Bible as the best way for atheists to engage in educated conversation with Christians, especially against literalist readings of the Bible. The channel has nearly 150,000 subscribers. In the first episode, on Genesis 1, they read the biblical text aloud, and offer secular and scientific commentary along the way. (How can light be created apart from the Sun?)

For the sake of comparison to all of the channels discussed above, the most popular YouTube channel is PewDiePie, a guy with over 48 million subscribers and over 13 billion (yes, billion) views. PewDiePie's real name is Felix Arvid Ulf Kjellberg, a Swedish web-based comedian and video producer who has become a viral social phenomenon. He reviews video games and provides social commentary on all manner of things. His fan base is known as the "Bro Army," and he has supported fundraising for various charities. This fits with the most popular YouTube stations, most of which feature music, comedy, and entertainment. Of the over half a billion YouTube channels, at least 2,000 have over a million subscribers. None of these channels are devoted to the study of the Bible—no great surprise, given the entertainment focus of YouTube. The Bible does not even break into the top 1,000 channels.

Still, the YouTube channels that do focus on the Bible have generated considerable attention. Almost all of the channels that deal with

---

35. http://www.lausanne.org/content/covenant/lausanne-covenant. The purpose of Max7 is "Serving you with free biblically faithful resources, for gospel ministry everywhere."

36. For another digital Bible video from Max7, again without words or text, see their story of the prodigal son, an updated version where the father and two brothers are all weight-lifters! http://www.max7.org/en/resource/prodigalsonweightlifter.

the Bible are relatively conservative and evangelical in tone. "I'll Be Honest" is a channel with over 115,000 subscribers and over 28 million views, and serves as a ministry of Grace Community Church of San Antonio, TX. "We are seeking to publish Biblical Christian Videos on the Gospel of Jesus Christ."[37] "Desiring God" has over 120,000 subscribers with nearly 20 million views.[38] "Grace to You" has over 80,000 subscribers with nearly 13 million views of videos featuring expository preaching from the Bible by John MacArthur, the pastor and teacher of Grace Community Church in Sun Valley, California.[39] He also has a radio program along the same lines (gty.org). "The Bible Project," with more than 150,000 subscribers and 8 million views is a nonprofit web-based organization that creates videos that walk through the biblical narrative book-by-book and theme-by-theme.[40] And on and on they go.

The Bible on Facebook

The data for YouTube usage is staggering—over a billion people with almost 5 billion videos watched every day. Even more incredible, though, is the digital footprint that Facebook has left worldwide. As of mid-2016, Facebook had over 1.7 billion monthly active users (the number had surpassed 1 billion in 2012). There has never been a more pervasive digital presence connecting more people in more ways than Facebook. A simple Google search of "the Bible on Facebook" yields 126 million results. There is a link, of course, between almost everything on the web related to social media and Facebook. Thus, one can go to "https://www.facebook.com/The-Bible" and see posts about everything, from "What Happens to Young Children at the Rapture?" to a post about a modern-day Boaz, to hundreds upon hundreds of Bible quotes (most often with images), to "Ten Ways to Love" (complete with scriptural warrants). There is an utter potpourri of posts, though throughout, one recognizes a conservative evangelical tone. Similar is the King James Bible Facebook page (https://www.facebook.com/King-JamesBibleOnline), or the MyBibleVerses Facebook page. The "open-bible.info" website has a series of scripture passages that people have suggested reveal what the Bible has to say about Facebook![41] The biblical passages get "votes" for whether or not people find them helpful.

37. https://www.youtube.com/watch?v=7FhAo2zN5SM.
38. https://www.youtube.com/user/desiringGod/featured.
39. https://www.youtube.com/user/JohnMacArthurGTY/videos.
40. https://www.youtube.com/user/jointhebibleproject/about.
41. https://www.openbible.info/topics/facebook.

Thus, Proverbs 18:24 ("A man of many companions may come to ruin, but there is a friend who sticks closer than a brother") gets 103 "helpful votes" (whatever that really means). Or a quote from 1 Corinthians 15:33 ("Do not be deceived: 'Bad Company ruins good morals'") receives 50 "helpful votes" as a useful way for thinking about Facebook (to say nothing of Paul quoting the poet Menander here). BibleGateway, the YouVersion app, Bible Screensavers, Bible Games, Bible Studies, among thousands of other links give only a small sample of the breadth (and shallowness) of most Facebook posts about the Bible.

The Globalization of Superficiality—of Biblical Proportions

Fr. Adolfo Nicolás, the Superior General of the Society of Jesus, coined a memorable way of thinking about the kind of impact that much social media has had upon society and culture at large that is plugged in to the digital universe. In an address on "Challenges to Jesuit Higher Education Today," given at a 2010 conference in Mexico City, Fr. Nicolás spoke about the danger of "the globalization of superficiality."[42] If the goal of universities is to promote depth of thought and imagination, Fr. Nicolás warned, the modern era of digital screens that absorb our attention can lead to a shallowness in thought and imagination.

> When one can access so much information so quickly and so painlessly; when one can express and publish to the world one's reactions so immediately and so unthinkingly in one's blogs or micro-blogs; when the latest opinion column from the *New York Times* or *El Pais*, or the newest viral video can be spread so quickly to people half a world away, shaping their perceptions and feelings, then the laborious painstaking work of serious, critical thinking often gets short-circuited.

The result is that superficiality can beget superficiality. Superficial understanding can lead to superficial relationships. Can one really have 1,200 Facebook "friends" and have such "friendships" mean very much? "When one is overwhelmed with such a dizzying pluralism of choices and values and beliefs and visions of life, then one can so easily slip into the lazy superficiality of relativism or mere tolerance of others and their views, rather than engaging in the hard work of forming communities of dialogue in the search of truth and understanding."

---

42. This address was published in 2011: "Challenges to Jesuit Higher Education Today," Conversations on Jesuit Higher Education: Vol. 40, Article 5. Available at: http://epublications.marquette.edu/conversations/vol40/iss1/5. Fr. Nicolás was Superior General from 2008–16.

This notion of forming "communities of dialogue" is extremely important when it comes to the Bible and biblical interpretation. Ideally, at least in my view, disparate voices can and should join together in engaged and respectful conversations about the meaning of the Bible and concrete biblical texts for the living out of faith. Never before, thanks to digital media, has it been so possible to be in such conversations with people of very different perspectives across all kinds of boundaries. And while such conversations are surely taking place, more often than not, modern forms of social media have resulted in silos and echo chambers, where people are not conversing within differences, but across similar lines of thought and reflection. People subscribe to channels of biblical interpretation that reinforce their own long held views and patterns of interpretation. This is not just the case for more conservative evangelical Christian voices; it is also the case for more liberal and progressive Christians. The search for "truth and understanding" to which Fr. Nicolás calls people of faith is best had in face-to-face conversations between groups of individuals seeking an empathetic understanding of other views, rather than caricatures of positions with which they disagree. While digital screens can certainly mediate some of these conversations, especially when people are physically separated, there is really nothing that replaces the thick texture of engaged conversation and respectful debate where the goal is mutual understanding and discerning together the leading of God's Spirit, even in highly conflicted situations. In such contexts, the Bible may truly become the faith community's Book, its scripture, its common trove of sacred, and at times, troublesome stories bearing witness to God's interaction with humanity.

As we surveyed the "technology of the Bible" in the opening chapter, we saw that the Bible went through various stages of technology in its textual transmission—from scroll to codex to printed book, and now, to digital screens. But we also noted that the Bible has not only taken textual form in written words on a page; for centuries, it took oral and aural form as it was read and recited aloud for the vast majority of the faithful who could not read. It took the form of stained glass and endless paintings and sculptures, communicating the stories in paint and stone that adorned sacred spaces in churches and that decorated the homes of wealthy patrons. It took the form of passion plays and countless dramatic works. It also took musical form in sung liturgies, in hymns, and in large choral works (e.g., Bach's *St. John's Passion*). And beginning in the twentieth century, it took form on film, from silent movies with subtitles to full feature films with sound and color, including the advent of digital film editing. In other words, the Bible is no stranger to changing genres, to shape-shifting from page to canvas to glass to sound to script to screen, and then, to tweet to blog to post to a tube about you. The Bible has proven to be resilient beyond belief because its stories are precisely the stories of belief. The Word of God becomes incarnate in so many, many forms. And perhaps it is this realization that has been brought home with a new awareness in this digital age. The age of print has been shattered and surpassed, or rather subsumed, as the world goes digital. The Bible remains a book, a volume, of bound pages; and yet, it has also ceased to have covers that mark beginning and end, for if there is one thing we know about the digital realm, it is that is has no real end in its billions and billions of links and sites and 1s and 0s. We may attempt to master the Bible as a text, but the internet, never. The most we can do there is to apply filters to render it manageable in one way or another.

Conclusions

And so are we doomed to the shallows of the internet, as Nicholas Carr has warned?[43] Do these shallows take the Bible with it? In the realm of digital social media, with what are we left in relation to the Bible? At the risk of drawing some conclusions about targets moving quite literally at the speed of electricity (akin to the speed of light), I offer the following closing reflections on the Bible in digital social media, at least the forms I have discussed here.

At the shallow end of the spectrum, we find Twitter and Facebook. I call this the shallow end because in the form of tweets and Facebook posts, the Bible is chopped up into discrete and limited texts that have no immediate context apart from the tweet or post itself. Tweets are simply out there as disembodied maxims, not unlike what you find inside a fortune cookie.

At the same time it is possible for tweets to convey texts that summarize a much larger body of thought, at least for those who already recognize the tweet as a springboard for a far larger conversation. For example, were I to tweet 1 Corinthians 2:2 ("For I decided to know nothing among you except Jesus Christ, and him crucified."), those with knowledge of Paul's letters and his theology would immediately recognize this tweet as a foundational statement of a much more elab-

43. *The Shallows: What the Internet is Doing to Our Brains* (New York: W. Norton & Co., 2011).

orate exposition of Paul's understanding of the identity and significance of Jesus and the cross. And so, it is not that the tweet itself as a catchphrase or slogan is ineffectual; rather, the tweet presupposes that the person or people reading the tweet already understand the larger context and framework of the passage and its significance. It can thus function as a statement with extraordinary echoes and ripples that requires extensive unpacking. But to the uninitiated, to those who do not live *inside* this world of Paul's letters, it can generate simply a puzzled shrug. There are also a host of biblical texts that function as "dog whistles" for different interpretations and different communities of faith. Tweets of biblical passages may presuppose a community of discourse, as well as particular interpretations of discrete sub-groups of believers. If a tweet is setting the topic for a discussion or Bible study, then it can indeed anticipate a much deeper conversation. But as a tweet out there on its own, it has very shallow roots and can be quickly dismissed, not unlike seed that is cast upon rocky ground.

Facebook posts generally fall into the same category of shallow expositions of the biblical text. As noted above, Facebook posts of and about the Bible most often function in the same way as tweets of or about the Bible. The primary difference has to do with the way each form of social media works, as one can "follow" anyone who has a Twitter account, but with Facebook, one must request and accept a "friend" request in order to share posts and have access to posts. Thus, Twitter is inherently anonymous, at least from the follower's side of the screen, while with Facebook each user can see who is posting what. With Twitter, one simply tweets out a brief message to whoever may be tuning in. With Facebook, one skims through the myriad posts of one's "friends" and stops to read whatever one decides to click on, knowing that the same scanning and filtering is taking place on the other side of the screen as well. The net result, however, does not amount to much of a difference between appeals to the Bible on Twitter and on Facebook. Short quotations of discrete biblical texts tends to be very typical. These snippets of the Bible are intended to be inspirational, perhaps reminders, reflecting the thoughts and feelings of whoever has posted whatever biblical text.

The digital social media with the greatest potential for depth and substance regarding the Bible are blogs and YouTube. The reason for this potential is not difficult to understand. Both blogs and YouTube can be discursive at some length, unlike Twitter and most Facebook posts. Blogs, indeed, are designed to host more extended conversations on more focused topics, and the study of the Bible lends itself to such a model, whether one is studying a particular book of the Bible or a particular theme. Similarly, YouTube videos can be packaged as self-contained discrete Bible studies, whether in the form of expositional preaching or in the form of a classroom lecture. There is quite literally something for everyone when it comes to the smorgasbord of YouTube videos available on the Bible. People click through to what they want to see and then watch away. What they see and take away regarding the Bible via social media is very much in accord with the broad scope of options both in and outside of churches across the religious landscape.

8

The Bible and Computer Programs

In turning from the place of the Bible in digital social media to the Bible and computer programs we are shifting gears from the role of the Bible in the more popular sphere of social media to several sophisticated computer-based programs that provide advanced capacities for analysis of the Bible as a whole, and the biblical text in all its parts. We have already explored some of the seeds of such computer programs for studying the Bible in chapter 2 (A Brief History of Digital Bibles). In this chapter, I want to take a closer look at what are currently four state-of-the-art computer programs that have been the most significant and most widely used for detailed study of the Bible and its interpretation. There are other programs, but these four have arguably cornered most of the market for students of the Bible seeking to take advantage of the advances in computer programming as it has been applied to study of the Bible. You could say that, in varying degrees, these programs have Bible geeks in view, individuals who drill down deep and want to go still further in their study of such topics as: original languages, the history of biblical interpretation, commentaries, translations, and pastoral applications. In short, these programs are geared to those who want to engage in all manner of critical analysis of the Bible in the many contexts of its interpretation. This chapter is for you!

The four programs I present in this chapter are: Logos Bible Software, Accordance Bible Software, BibleWorks, and Olive Tree Bible

Software. My goal here is to be both descriptive and evaluative. Let me state at the outset that each of these programs is excellent in its own way. Each has a slightly different target audience, though these overlap. In the course of preparing this chapter, I have had occasion to be in conversation with product specialists and salespeople for each of these programs, and I have generally found them all very helpful and understandably quite proud of their products. Each of these programs seeks to engage people in serious study of the Bible, whether in terms of academic study or with an eye toward practical pastoral ministry. The order of presentation I have adopted for these programs is based on when each program was initially developed and published. All of them have gone through numerous versions and updates. Thus, the reader should be aware that this chapter is being written toward the end of 2016, and that by the time of its publication, there will surely be still newer versions and updates. In the world of computer programs, it is ever so. This is perhaps one of the greatest ironies about digital versions of the Bible. The digital versions are ever changing, though the text they present is ever stable! None of the four programs presented here is particularly inexpensive. All of them require a serious commitment of time and energy to master the considerable capabilities of each program. And all of them come in downloadable form as dedicated computer programs. I will proceed by presenting and discussing each of the programs on its own terms without reference to the others. Only after presenting the four programs will I provide direct comparisons between them. I should also note that the discussion of Logos Bible Software is somewhat longer than the other three, primarily because I also consider its "Courses Tool," which is a unique (not to say, unproblematic) feature of the program in its attempt to provide an all-encompassing set of resources.

One final caveat before turning to each of the programs. Just as people have favorite translations of the Bible, so many students of the Bible have favorite Bible study programs. Sometimes, one's favorite is simply what one is used to and comfortable with. There's nothing wrong with this. People can be passionate and defensive about their Bible or Bible program of choice. It reminds me of the divide between people who prefer Windows PC computer platforms and people who prefer Apple's Mac computer platforms. My goal is not to persuade people that one translation or Bible program is objectively better than another. Personal taste and style of use make that a false goal. Rather, my purpose is to highlight significant features of the respective programs and to give my own opinion where it seems warranted. I have used and still use all four of these programs. So off we go.

Logos Bible Software

Logos Bible Software had its start as an independent program released initially in 1991–92 under the corporate name, Logos Research Systems. In 1995, the company acquired *CD Word: The Interactive Bible Library* that had been developed by Dallas Theological Seminary initially in 1989. *CD Word* was the earliest effort to provide a comprehensive Bible study program in digital form. (For the technical history of Logos Bible Software, the Wikipedia article gives good information.)[1] Logos has specialized in computer-based Bible study for 25 years, releasing ever more sophisticated versions of "Logos Bible Software" on a regular basis. Their latest offering (as of Fall 2016) is Logos 7, which adds still more layers to a program already thick with content.

In 2014, Logos rebranded itself as "Faithlife," an umbrella for the various initiatives that include the Logos Bible Software. The home-screen for Faithlife states their mission: "Grow in the Light. We use technology to equip the church to grow in the light of the Bible. Our team is committed to increasing biblical literacy and accessibility for every Christian around the world." One can then click on a nearly eight-minute high-energy video that touts the virtues of Faithlife and its primary product, Logos Bible Software. "Be better equipped to: study, learn, mentor, serve." Along with the techno music the mash-up of images features a quick succession of people using the computer software, a list of publishers and brands associated with Faithlife, quick images of some of the more prominent authors featured in Faithlife resources, a look at the Faithlife buildings and office spaces, followed by a glance at different Faithlife groups, people studying the Bible on tablets and computers, and then, a procession of one Faithlife product after another, forty-two programs in all. When the video finished, I felt overwhelmed, which I think is the general idea behind the presentation. So many resources are presented for so many different applications (a worship program, an e-book app, the Logos Bible Software program, the Faithlife Study Bible, Faithlife Women, and on and on) that one is left with the impression that Faithlife can provide one-stop browsing and shopping for anything the believing Christian might need or want by way of technology in their walk with God.

1. https://en.wikipedia.org/wiki/Logos_Bible_Software#Windows_and_Macintosh_versions.

The central Bible program is but one component part. Endless resources, all at the click of a mouse, along with the investment of significant time and money. The resources truly are staggering in scope, and the 42 programs comprise only a partial list. It is easy to get lost in all of the bells and whistles that Faithlife has to offer. But it is also easy to see that some resources will appeal to certain audiences and not so much to others. The idea of Faithlife is to offer a truly comprehensive set of resources for individual Christians, their congregations, and their leadership.

Just as overwhelming is the Logos Bible Software package itself, now in its latest iteration, Version 7 (released in August of 2016). The Logos 7 homepage features a video introduction that begins with the following words superimposed on the seven-minute video one is about to watch: "Fine-tuned to take you all the way from that initial spark of insight to sharing biblical truth with clarity." Here is a claim that will appeal to pastoral leaders, preachers, and frankly anyone who desires to share "biblical truth with clarity." The promise is that Logos 7 is the tool of choice, the video continues, since it now includes a Sermon editor, the ability to create slides and sermon outlines, all integrated with the Proclaim presentation worship software, ready to project images and sounds on a screen to enhance any sermon or presentation. The focus is on the interactive content of the program as a whole, so that one can go from biblical text to an article, a resource for the NT use of the OT, video lectures, archaeological tours, devotional ideas, and more. The emphasis is on a wide range of "interactives," such as the "speaking to God" interactive that highlights every place in the Bible where people are, as one might think, speaking to God. This gets further broken down into subsets of data (location, content, etc.). Or if you wanted to look at Bible manuscripts, there's an "interactive" for that. Logos 7 also organizes systematic theology around particular biblical passages, so that Christian theologians across history are linked to biblical texts on which they commented.

There are many purchase options for Logos Bible Software. One option is to purchase the "Logos Now" membership ($99 per year), which gives individuals all of the features of Logos, formally named the Logos Cloud Feature Set. (This does not include any of the library resources included in the base packages, which are required for the software to work as designed.) Beyond the Logos Now membership are various Logos packages, from the basic Starter package up through the Collector's Edition package. Each package comes with a respective digital library of discrete titles and data sets. The more advanced the package, the larger the library. The Starter package is advertised as "great for devotional study." It comes with some commentaries on the Psalms (hence, devotional study) and a total of 97 "books" in the library. For Bible study, it is called "basic." The packages progress from Starter to Bronze, Silver, Gold, Platinum, Diamond, Portfolio, and the ultimate Collector's Edition. While Starter comes with 97 digital books, the Collector's Edition comes with an astonishing 4,823 digital books. The price for the Collector's Edition is $10,799, a significant discount for buying these resources in a bundle, rather than separately. If one already owns a basic package, the discounts vary "dynamically," depending on which components one has already purchased. When one purchases a Logos library, or any single resource, one owns it for life, which means that one never pays twice for the same resource. There is also often sale pricing for special promotional offers. For a brand new Logos user, the total *value* of the resources in the Collector's Edition is a whopping $87,270 (library resources of $84,033 plus the Feature Set of $3,237). The current sale price is 10 percent off at $9,719. Again, if one already owns a library package, prices are adjusted accordingly.

The Collector's Edition contains more texts than one could read in a lifetime. The middle-of-the-road package, Gold, comes with 725 digital books and is termed "advanced" for Bible study and sermon preparation, but "intermediate" for original language exegesis and academic research. The cost? List price is $1,549. Moving to Platinum will put one in the "advanced" category for original language exegesis and academic research (for $2,149).

Another component of Logos software is the way in which it can be tailored to particular confessional traditions in multiple languages (English, Spanish, German, Portuguese, Korean, and Chinese). Logos has assembled different packages that integrate the biblical study materials with various faith traditions, including Anglican, Baptist, Lutheran, Methodist/Wesleyan, Pentecostal/Charismatic, Orthodox, Reformed, Roman Catholic, and Seventh Day Adventist. There's also a blog that accompanies each group. This feature recognizes that biblical interpretation often takes place in a specific confessional setting with received traditions that guide and shape the various perspectives on the Bible that these different traditions represent. Finally, by way of general comment, Logos also has a web app (https://www.logos.com/browser), smartphone and tablet apps. Also featured is Logos Mobile Ed (https://www.logos.com/mobile-ed/about), where one can watch lectures and take courses taught by nearly one hundred different Logos-affiliated faculty members (https://www.logos.com/mobile-ed/faculty), almost all of whom come from more conservative evangelical Protestant contexts. These courses represent the usual topics of an evangelical seminary curriculum (scripture, biblical languages, theology, history, pastoral studies, preaching, apologetics). The faculty page that lists the individuals and areas of expertise also states where each individual earned their PhD or DMin degree. The most prominent schools are those most commonly associated with the evangelical Protestant tradition (Wheaton, Gordon Conwell, Dallas Theological Seminary, Ashland Theological Seminary, Asbury Theological Seminary, Fuller Theological Seminary, Trinity Evangelical Divinity School, Denver Seminary, Southern Baptist Theological Seminary, Westminster Seminary, Biola University, et al.), along with a few institutions such as Yale University, the University of Pennsylvania, Cambridge University, and Princeton Theological Seminary, among others. The pedigree of the whole Logos program, then, is clearly oriented to more conservative evangelical Christians as the target market, though Logos has also made clear efforts to expand in more ecumenical directions as well (hence the specialized packages for different denominational affiliations).

Upon opening, the Logos Software program reveals a relatively busy screen, full of options. The opening screen, in fact, is jam-packed with features such as an online newspaper with dozens of stories and links from which to choose (I counted over 50!). These can, of course, all be tailored in any number of ways to make the screen simpler or even more complex. Any number of layouts can be chosen. When I opened a generic page, the program offered various lectionaries, reading plans, a Faithlife Today feature on "Origen: The Founder of Textual Criticism," another feature on "The Historical Context of the Apostle Paul," including a lecture by Prof. Lynn Cohick (a significant NT scholar at Wheaton College), various images (Capernaum, the ruins of ancient Tyre, the Garden of Gethsemane, the Roman Aqueduct at Caesarea), and many ads marketing the various Faithlife products (including Secrets to Saving Hundreds on Logos 7). Again, the page can be streamlined, but the busyness of the opening page serves to further indicate that Faithlife is seeking to be as comprehensive as possible, offering all things to all people in the realm of the study of the Bible, and beyond. The amount of material from which to choose is virtually endless, depending in part on which package one has purchased. One reason for all of the program's self-promotion, amidst all of the content, is to encourage users to purchase more advanced modules and packages. Indeed, as we will see, the marketing strategy permeates the product by showing resources that *could* be available if one purchased them. One is made aware of what parts of the program one is missing by not having purchased a more advanced version. Of all the computer-based Bible study software companies, Logos (Faithlife) is certainly the most aggressive in its marketing and self-promotion.

So let us take Logos Bible Software 7 for a spin through Luke 1:1–4, the very important prologue to the Gospel of Luke (see Fig. 8.1G). It all starts, of course, with the biblical text itself, which is available in a wide variety of translations (NRSV, ESV, NASB, KJV, NIV, etc.), along with the original language—in this case, Greek. One can click on Documents, Guides, and Tools on the menu bar. The Documents tab allows the user to collect various sorts of information related to the biblical text (bibliography, clippings, notes, visual filter, among others). Then, Logos offers several "guides" that the user can access in conjunction with the biblical text. The two primary guides for analyzing the biblical text are the "passage guide" and the "exegetical guide" (see Fig. 8.2G). The "passage guide" opens up to various commentaries, journal results (available in the more advanced academic packages), cross-references (according to the *Treasury of Scripture Knowledge*), parallels in Ancient Literature (Apostolic Father, Church Fathers, et al.), Parallel Passages in the Gospel and the Old Testament, Literary Typing, Cultural Concepts (for Luke 1:1–4 references to written records), various outlines of the passage, Biblical People related to the passage, and other categories (Biblical Places, Biblical Things, Biblical Events, Media Resources, Media Collections, Atlas, Music, Topics, Interesting Words, and then a host of additional resources one can purchase). Many of these other categories have little to no content in relation to Luke 1:1–4.

The "exegetical guide" in my platinum version opens to Bruce Metzger's *Textual Commentary on the Greek New Testament* (2nd ed.), along with the text-critical apparatus from the Nestle-Aland 28th edition of the *Novum Testamentum Graece*, as well as the Society of Biblical Literature (SBL) critical apparatus to the Greek New Testament. This is followed by various Greek texts of the passage (primarily the Nestle-Aland 28th edition and the SBL edition, which are really not at variance with each other). In addition to these standard editions of the Greek

New Testament, one can also open the *Elzevir Textus Receptus* from 1624, *Stephanus's Textus Receptus* from 1550, or the editions by Tischendorf, Scrivener, and the Byzantine text, among others. For the study of all modern translations of the Bible, which are based on the eclectic critical Nestle-Aland Greek New Testament, it might be interesting to know the history of the Greek text, but it really has little to no bearing on how one might go about interpreting the text for today. One can then look at various digital images of several ancient manuscripts available online that show Luke 1:1–4, though mostly in transcription. Prominent among these are Codex Sinaiticus, Codex Alexandrinus, Codex Vaticanus, and Codex Bezae. (Again, these are available primarily in advanced academic packages.) The Institute for New Testament Textual Research (in Münster, Germany) provides this dataset. This is followed by various grammars of New Testament Greek with reference to Luke 1:1–4, visualizations of the Greek syntax to make analysis a bit easier, and then, word-by-word definitions of the Greek terms in Luke 1:1–4, drawing on standard Greek–English lexicons (e.g., *BDAG* and Louw-Nida). As with the "passage guide," the "exegetical guide" also includes references and allusions to the passage in Ancient Parallels (church fathers, et al), and a wide variety of commentaries. Beyond the "passage guide" and "exegetical guide," Logos offers a Sermon Starter Guide, a Bible Word Study Guide, and a Topic Guide. They draw on the same set of resources, but organize them somewhat differently.

One can select from a number of different display layouts, including various Quickstart layouts, such as Bible and Commentary, Bible Journaling, Devotional, Greek Word Study, Lectionary Reading, Passage Study, and Study Bible, among others. When one clicks on the Tools menu at the top of the page, headings pop up for Library, Reference, Utilities, Passage, Lookup, and Interactive Media, all of which have a number of options. A few of the things included in the mix of options is a pronunciation guide, a handy "Weights and Measures Converter," a timeline for any period of the Bible and beyond (including alternate dates for such events as the death of Jesus or the "conversion" of Paul), and a "Groups" tool that allows one to interact with other members of one's Faithlife community group (which Faithlife encourages you to join).

The Tools menu in Logos 7 includes a new feature, the Courses Tool, which takes the user to a wide variety of courses, ranging from an "Introduction to 1 Corinthians" to "The Confessions of St. Augustine," and well beyond. Over 285 plans are included, each one consisting of discrete chapters with a variety of suggested times for sessions (five minutes to two hours). Each "course" lists required readings that accompany the various lessons within the course, indicating along the way which of the required readings you can access with your particular package of software and which you would need to purchase in order to do all of the "required reading" for the course. As an example, I clicked on the course for "Introduction to the Early Heresies of the Church." This is a course in 12 sessions, covering such topics as Montanism, Sabellianism, Arianism, Pelagianism, Gnosticism, and more. The description of the course reflects the conservative doctrinal approach that can be found throughout the Logos program:

> The Church is old and heresies are numerous. This study is not meant to present a complete list of ancient heresies, or defense against them—although we'll look at Tertullian against the Modalists. In fact, our entire system of doctrine can be said to be a defense against those who would abuse the Gospel by creating new things. That's why theologians write—to preserve sound, right doctrine (i.e., orthodoxy). What follows is a brief introduction to some of the heresies found in the early Church. The list is a beginning list, so while we cover Pelagianism, we do not cover semi-Pelagianism. Further, there is a list that is commonly recognized so that while some consider Arminianism a heresy and others consider Calvinism one, orthodox Christians the world over know that Pelagianism is actually a heresy. Trace these heresies to their current destinations—because heresies never die, they only lay dormant until the orthodox wane.

The references to "our entire system of doctrine" and the reason "why theologians write - to preserve sound, right doctrine"—presumes a very particular understanding of the task of theology that coheres with conservative evangelical notions of "right doctrine."[2] The course proceeds first with definitions of "Orthodoxy" and "Heresy," with two brief readings from the *Oxford Dictionary of the Christian Church* (*ODCC*). It is followed by a session on "Montanism," with required readings from the *Anchor Bible Dictionary* (*ABD*). This resource is only available to those

---

. The author of this particular course is listed as Joel L. Watts, who has written a number of things for Logos. His bio indicates that he "holds a Masters of Arts from United Theological Seminary with a focus in literary and rhetorical criticism of the New Testament. His interests include exploring the role of mimesis in human civilization, specifically in the study of religion and media, as well as science fiction and the way in which it has allowed mythology to be explored in light of scientific discoveries of the past century. He is the author of *Mimetic Criticism of the Gospel of Mark: Introduction and Commentary* (Wipf & Stock, 2013) and a co-editor and contributor to *From Fear to Faith: Stories of Hitting Spiritual Walls* (Energion, 2013)." His religious affiliation is the United Methodist Church.

who have purchased the "Gold" or above packages. Those who have the Starter, Bronze, or Silver packages would either need to upgrade or purchase this resource separately for an additional $159. The rest of the required readings for the course include some primary sources (e.g., Tertullian against Sabellianism, from volume 3 of the *Ante-Nicene Fathers of the Church* collection), and some additional readings from the *ODCC* and the *ABD*, but draw mostly on *The Baker Encyclopedia of Christian Apologetics,* by Norman Geisler, and then, a couple of sections from the *Systematic Theology* of Charles Hodge (1873), the *Systematic Theology* of A.H. Strong (1886), and the *Dictionary of Christian Biography* (1911).

As can be seen from the date of these last three resources, they all come from the late nineteenth and early twentieth centuries. Logos makes use of them because their copyright has expired and they are in public domain. The problem with this is that anyone taking this "course" is getting some rather dated and doctrinaire treatments dressed up in modern digital garb. It's not that the information contained in Strong or Hodge is necessarily incorrect, but—as is always the case—their writings reflect their times. In this regard, Logos Bible Software operates in much the same way as other Bible software companies by seeking to maximize the number of resources in the most cost-effective manner. Utilizing resources that may be old and out of copyright is one way to do this. Although descriptions of ancient heresies may not be much different today than a century ago in some respects, the context for understanding them and appreciating the wide diversity of early Christianity has indeed changed a great deal over the last century. The courses on the Bible (Intro to 1 Corinthians, Intro to Isaiah, etc.) draw on more modern resources, but the commentaries that are used for the "required readings" reflect a conservative evangelical Protestant approach (e.g., *Evangelical Commentary on the Bible, Baker Encyclopedia of the Bible, Evangelical Dictionary of Biblical Theology, Tyndale Biblical Commentaries*).

Most recently, Logos Bible Software has been offering "Topical Library Expansion" packages for those who want to add particular features to their Logos 7 program set without necessarily upgrading to a higher overall platform. At present, there are twenty-one such topical expansion packages, each coming in one of four sizes: small, medium, large, and extra-large, with each priced accordingly. Topics include: ancient texts and translations, apologetics, Bible backgrounds, biblical interpretation, Church Fathers, Church history, and so on. The "New Testament Studies" library expansion ranges from "small" (a library of seven additional volumes) to "extra-large" (a library of sixty-one additional volumes). By offering these sets of topical expansions, Logos seeks to tailor the larger sets of resources to narrower sets of personal interests. Indeed, the subject line of the email ad is "Logos Personalized Offers."

By way of general evaluation, the number of resources provided by Logos Bible Software is truly astonishing. But it can also be blinding. While one person may experience the hundreds and hundreds of resources to be a blessing, another person may well experience it as an avalanche of material that renders the user paralyzed by too many choices. For a program with such a vast array of resources, it is important to remember that information is not the same as knowledge or wisdom, nor does Logos claim it to be. This is not intended as a criticism of the Logos Bible Software, but it is an important reminder when using a program that has the number of resources available in Logos, a point of pride for the Faithlife company. The program has a steep learning curve, and mastery of its many features will lie beyond the scope of many. This is not a program designed for those merely interested in reading the Bible and perhaps a commentary or two. It is a program for deeply engaging the Bible in its original languages and historical contexts, beyond which Logos also provides a vast library of theological resources that covers the breadth of the Christian tradition. There are also many resources for pastors seeking help with sermon preparation and for those leading Bible studies. The trick is to choose a path through the myriad resources so that one is not overwhelmed by them. Fortunately, there are dozens of very helpful instructional videos to guide users through the various features of the program. Every Logos 7 base package includes LT271, a series of 30 videos that guide the user through a practical study of the Bible using the tools in Logos.

Published reviews of Logos Bible Software have, by and large, been extremely positive over its multiple iterations, precisely because of the sheer number of resources that are available, making this an all-in-one theological and pastoral resource, not just a Bible study program. But several concerns have also been raised, mostly by comparison with other Bible programs. So while I will save most of the comparisons for the end of the chapter, a few comparisons are necessary at this point to put some aspects of Logos into perspective. The user interface of Logos has been critiqued by some precisely because it overwhelms the user with so many choices.[3] Another issue has to do with the relative slowness of the Logos program in comparison to others, as well as the amount of memory (RAM) it takes to run the program. French scholar Timothée Minard conducted comparative speed tests on Logos 6, Accordance 11, BibleWorks 10, and BibleParser (a French program) and posted the results via a YouTube video that actually shows the comparative speeds of the programs performing different tasks.[4] The following chart shows the relative speeds of Logos, BibleWorks, and Accordance while performing various tasks:[5]

Task	Logos	BibleWorks	Accordance
Opening program after starting computer	29 seconds	20 seconds	9 seconds
Reopening software in the same session	15 seconds	3.5 seconds	1.7 seconds
Conducting a simple search	5.4 seconds	.4 seconds	.3 seconds
Conducting a complex search	4 seconds	4 seconds	.2 seconds
Conducting a syntax search	3.7 seconds	———	3.4 seconds

In addition to comparatively slow speed, Logos also tends to be a RAM hog in terms of system resources. In a comparison of Logos 6 with Accordance 11, Dustin Battles reports that with eight tabs of similar content open in both programs, Logos was using 540MB, while Accordance was using only 83MB. As Battles puts it "If you're not into computers, we'll say Accordance would be like a car going 6 times as far on the same tank of gas."[6] Still, Logos does offer the most resources among all of the programs, but access to the somewhat larger number of resources costs not only money, but also a trade-off in terms of time/speed and system resources.

---

3. See Dustin Battles, "Making Sense of Bible Software – Logos vs. Accordance," *Rooted Thinking* (December 15, 2014). It should be noted that Battles compares Logos 6 with Accordance 11, which were the current versions at the time of his review. http://rootedthinking.com/2014/12/15/logos-accordance/.

4. https://www.youtube.com/watch?v=-zQkG72utr4.

5. Minard reports that he conducted these speed tests using a PC Lenovo G580 Windows 8.1 intel i.3 (2.5 Ghz) 6 go RAM, on July 12, 2015.

6. http://rootedthinking.com/2014/12/15/logos-accordance/.

Accordance Bible Software

Accordance Bible Software began life in 1988 as *ThePerfectWord*, developed by Roy Brown. *ThePerfectWord* was one of the first Bible programs created for use on the Macintosh computer. This program was later sold to another company and renamed *MacBible*. In the early 1990s, Brown started a new company, OakTree Software, and together with the Gramcord Institute (and the lessons learned from developing *ThePerfectWord*), *Accordance* was launched as a program that would allow for the study of the Bible in a more scholarly mode, especially in making use of original languages. Accordance 1.0 was initially released in February 1994. The program has grown and become both more sophisticated and easier to use. Accordance 11 was released in 2014, and in November 2016, Accordance 12 (XII) was released. A Lite version of Accordance was also released for free use, so that people could try the program out without having to commit to purchasing a collection of resources they may not want or need. The idea of offering more tailored options for purchasing Bible software has been a growing feature for most of the programs. The goal of Accordance Bible Software is to focus in on the biblical text and to provide tools that go deep and that take advantage of a more intuitive approach to studying the Bible. The philosophy of Accordance is to approach the study of the Bible with the idea that "Bible study software shouldn't be cumbersome or complicated."[7]

The emphasis of Accordance falls on getting into the biblical text quickly and with many resources at hand. Although its resources are focused primarily on the Bible, it also includes much of the broader theological spectrum of various Christian traditions. Accordance offers important Jewish and Catholic resources in addition to a broad range of Protestant denominations, liberal and conservative alike. There are also many resources more related to Middle Eastern Studies than to biblical studies per se, including the Elephantine papyri, Ugaritic, and various rabbinic works. In its homepage "Why Accordance?" statement, the target audiences are spelled out clearly: "For the Rabbi/ Minister/Pastor," "For the Professor/Teacher," "For the Student," "For Personal Bible Study," and "For Wherever Your Studies Lead You." The listing of "Rabbi" before "Minister/Pastor" may seem to be a small thing, but it is a straightforward nod to the commitment of Accordance

---

7. "Why Accordance?" (https://www.accordancebible.com/Why-Accordance).

to provide resources for both non-Christian (especially Jewish) and Christian audiences. There are significant materials for the study of Hebrew and Rabbinics as well as an expansive array of materials for scholars and students of Christian origins and traditions. While Accordance seeks to provide helpful materials for faith leaders (including preaching aids), it also seeks to provide resources for serious academic work, and everything in between.

Going online to Accordance (https://www.accordancebible.com) allows one to see a brief two-minute promotional video that introduces the most recent version, Accordance XII. There are also additional more extended podcast videos that provide deeper introductions to the specific new features of Accordance XII. (Podcasts 148 & 149 give a combined thirty minutes of details about the collections and features.)[8] Accordance offers a host of podcasts that provide in-depth demos of the many features of the program, including sample Bible studies and closer looks at the various resources available.

The heart of the Accordance program revolves around its English, Greek, and Hebrew resources, each available at five levels: Learner, Discoverer, Pro, Expert, and Master. The higher the level, the more resources provided. The price points adjust accordingly. Thus, if one desired the entry level "English Learner" collection (just beyond the "Starter" collection), the current cost would be $199. This includes some 120 modules that range across English translations of the Bible (15 are included, but neither the NIV nor the NRSV),[9] commentaries, dictionaries, biblical studies, preaching helps, devotionals, history, theology, "writings" (almost all in public domain), Bible parallels, several public domain foreign-language translations (e.g., German, French, Spanish, Italian), and a surprising inclusion of some Greek and Hebrew resources.[10] Moving beyond English Discoverer ($399) and English Pro ($999) up to the English Expert level (for $3,999.00) would garner 39 different translations of the Bible in English, an astonishing 81 commentaries and major commentary sets (compared to 11 in the English

8. http://www.accordancebible.com/resources/multimedia/details/?id=156629, and http://www.accordancebible.com/resources/multimedia/details/?id=156788.

9. The NIV is not included because of the high fees for royalties, and the NRSV comes in the original language packages that most scholars prefer.

10. Among the included resources is the six-volume "Edersheim bundle." Alfred Edersheim (1825–1889) was a Jewish convert to Christianity who published several works on the Old Testament and on Judaism in the time of Jesus. Although it still contains important information, it is a very dated resource. Presumably, this bundle is included because the volumes are out of copyright, and hence free to distribute. As for the dictionaries, some are more helpful (e.g., the *Eerdmans Dictionary of the Bible*) and some less so (e.g., the 1913 edition of *Webster's Unabridged English Dictionary*), the latter included because it is in public domain.

Learner Collection), along with hundreds of additional titles in history, theology, writings, devotionals, and more. It also includes access to over 30 academic and pastoral journals. In all, it provides a comprehensive set of resources for serious study of the Bible in English translation.

The Greek and Hebrew Learner ($199) and Discoverer ($399) collections come with appropriate beginning Greek and Hebrew resources. They only divide into separate Greek and Hebrew tracks at the Pro/Expert/Master collection levels. Only at these levels are the standard scholarly lexical tools (dictionaries/grammars) for advanced study of the original languages made available. Thus, only beginning with the respective Pro levels of the Greek and Hebrew tracks ($999) does one have access, for example, to the BDAG Greek lexicon and to the BDB Hebrew lexicon.

In addition to the English, Greek, and Hebrew tracks, Accordance also offers a Graphics Collection at the Learner/Discoverer/Pro/Master levels, with various maps, photos, and atlases. They are offered at lower price points than the other collections, with the Graphics Learner starting at $99, going up through Discoverer ($199) and Pro ($399) to Master ($849). Finally, there are "Triple Combos" in the Learner and Discoverer levels that combine the Graphics and Greek/Hebrew resources. These combos come at a discounted price ($100 off) compared to purchasing the collections separately. (See Fig. 8.4).

Version XII marks a significant revision in how Accordance resource collections are purchased. There is more of an emphasis on different kinds of users: some who want primarily English resources, and those with more interest in dedicated study of the Hebrew and Greek texts of the Bible, with varying resource levels. There are also a wide array of add-on "Bundles" offered in Accordance, grouped according to various themes. For example, one can purchase the "Catholic Documents Group" add-on bundle, which consists of the Roman Catholic Catechism, the Code of Canon Law, the Council of Trent, the Order of the Mass, and documents from Vatican I and Vatican II (most in both English and Latin). Accordance regularly sends out emails with offers for Mobile Modules, Clergy Appreciation discounts, and the like.

In keeping with its stated philosophy, Accordance markets its Bible program as "simple, lightning fast, easy to use. . . . Simply Brilliant." The "Simply Brilliant" slogan appears on the opening page of Accordance, featuring a logo of an ancient clay oil lamp with a flame. The simplicity of the program can be seen in how it opens automatically to the text of Genesis 1 on full screen. This is the default workspace, though it can be altered in any number of ways. Other built-in workspaces include "English Study," which opens to three parallel columns featuring an outline of Genesis 1 on the left, the English Standard Version with an interlinear and parsed Hebrew text in the middle, and the right-hand column featuring various commentaries, cross-references, and various topics (beginning, creation, earth, God, gods, heaven, etc.). The "New Testament" workspace opens with four columns: the English text of Matthew 1 on left, the Greek New Testament and "Info for Matt 1:1" in two center columns, and Mounce's Greek Dictionary in the right column. Each of these texts can be changed to other versions, depending on which package one has purchased. Other workspaces include "Theme Sampler," which changes the appearance of the columns, and "Translation Comparison," which starts off with three parallel English translations of Genesis 1, all of which can be changed with ease. Another powerful tool is the "Research" feature, which allows for a quick search of the entire library (bringing up a host of texts, Bible dictionaries, commentaries, lexicons, grammars, etc.). This feature can be combined in a workspace with any other resource in Accordance. One can also easily create and save one's own tailored workspace, which many users of Accordance do. Accordance offers various levels of support, from dozens of "Lighting the Lamp" video tutorial podcasts (in keeping with the theme of the ancient oil lamp), to live webinars, interactive courses, training seminars, forums, blogs, live chat, and more.

The Accordance program opens up to a simple workspace that includes a single screen with Search Text, Instant Details, the Toolbar, and the Library, each of which can be modified in various ways (see Fig. 8.3G). The default toolbar (which can easily be modified) includes buttons for the library, daily reading (for devotional reading), instant details, highlights, user notes and tools, language, an amplify button, workspaces, and help options. The basic search window of Accordance, regardless of workspace, toggles between a Verses, Words, and Flex pane (see top left of Fig. 8.3G). One can add any number of parallels (texts, commentaries, tools) in parallel columns that scroll together with the primary biblical text. A key parallel is the Info Pane, which displays relevant content and quick links for the verses in the search pane. It provides available commentaries, cross-references, topics, and parallel passages, all of which expand out to additional parallels. One can hover over a resource with the mouse and it will open in the Instant Details screen, or one can have the information appear in a scrollable small pop-up window, or click and open it in another parallel frame. One can open new panes in both vertical and horizontal windows. The Info Pane display only shows materials relevant to the passage in question, drawing on resources available in whatever package one has chosen.

Two significant new features of Accordance XII are "stack" and "paper," in addition to more robust analytics throughout (including interactive pie and bar charts). Stack allows the user to collect what amounts to a collection of digital notecards that keeps track of quotations, images, and ideas for later use in writing papers and sermons, or for developing classroom presentations. Stack saves bibliographic information and also remembers the resource one has used and the date of access. Items in "stack" can be organized and reordered according to topic, type of resource, and more. A "stack" is basically a sophisticated notecard that allows users to collect and organize materials on the fly. Stacks can be saved with dedicated file names for ease of storage and editorial access. Adding items to a "stack" is very simple. One simply highlights whatever resource one wishes to add (a commentary passage, a lexicon's definition of a Greek term, a saying from a church father), and then, clicks on the "add to stack" icon in the menu bar at the top of the screen. It is a very cool feature.

"Paper" provides a resource to develop outlines and includes some word processing features. Users can open various outline templates for different kinds of lectures and sermons, into which one can import materials previously collected in a Stack. Users can also create their own templates to create better workflow for their own particular projects. It is also easy to import hypertexted biblical references. One can make full or partial use of the templates in Paper, allowing for the integration of Accordance with its own outlining program without having to go back and forth between different programs. In practice, one might be tempted to think that Paper is a word processing program built into Accordance, but its purpose is far more limited. One can certainly take notes and organize thoughts within the framework of the outlines, but if one wants to do more than this, one would need to copy and paste the material into Word or Pages for more exacting editing.[11] One can also export Paper contents using the RTF feature.

In performing a study of Luke 1:1–4 in Accordance I have selected the "NT Study" workspace using the "Essential" collection in Accor-

. The "Infopane" of Accordance has also been significantly updated and now includes the option of accessing word lists, study Bibles, grammars, manuscripts, and manuscript images.

dance (see Fig. 8.4G). After I type in the verses I want to study (Luke 1:1–4), and have selected an English version I want to use (let us use NRSV for starters), I click on Add Parallel and select Info Pane, which brings up a host of commentaries and other resources. The available commentaries include both newer titles along with much older works in public domain (including Calvin, Luther, and Wesley, along with Matthew Henry). The newer commentaries include both evangelical series (Intervarsity Press Commentary, Tyndale Commentary) and series that have a more scholarly tone (Hermeneia, Anchor, Jewish commentaries). There are plenty of resources from which to choose. I decide to open up the Word Biblical Commentary on Luke by John Nolland, just to have a running commentary along with the primary text. I then open up another parallel, this time adding the Greek New Testament (Nestle-Aland, 28th ed). Next, I open up a Greek lexicon, BDAG, and it goes to whatever word in the Greek text that I click on (three clicks). I decide to see what there might be in the Ancient Christian Commentary on Scripture. It opens up and provides comments from Origen and Ambrose, among others. Interesting. I copy each of these resources to my Stack on Luke 1, and drag some of the materials to my Paper on Luke 1. I'm off and running. I then highlight the name "Theophilus" in Luke 1:3 and click on Research under the Amplify tab. Accordance searches all of the modules in a few seconds and returns 116 hits found in various texts and tools. I drop several of these into my growing Stack on Luke 1. There is an intuitive character to Accordance's interface that drives a focus on the primary text, yet allows for reference to a host of primary and secondary sources, as well as lexical tools. If I wanted to engage Luke 1:1–4 more with a focus on preparing a sermon, Accordance would be a very valuable help in that regard as well.

BibleWorks

BibleWorks began in 1992 as a program for PCs with the express purpose of serving the life of the church, for students, teachers, pastors, and missionaries, along with the goal of providing a robust program to study the Bible in the Hebrew and Greek original languages at an affordable price. Owned and developed by lead programmer Michael Bushell, the slogan for BibleWorks is "Focus on the Text." It advertises itself as "Software for Biblical Exegesis and Research." Like Logos and Accordance, BibleWorks has numerous translations of the Bible (over

200 in 40 languages), along with over 50 original language texts and morphology databases. The most recent version of the program is BibleWorks 10. (Beginning with BibleWorks 9, it was also possible to run the program on a Mac computer.) Rather than having a plethora of different options with different program levels (like Logos and Accordance), BibleWorks comes at one standard price ($389) that is well below most of the packages offered by either Logos or Accordance. For that one-time investment, BibleWorks comes with many language resources to help students, scholars, and pastors engage the Bible in the original languages. It includes the standard lexicons, dictionaries, and grammars for both Greek and Hebrew. Like Logos and Accordance, BibleWorks can be reformatted to whatever the user desires by way of number of windows open and such. It also comes with images of manuscripts, satellite maps, audio Bibles, sophisticated search windows, and the ability to view the Gospels in synopsis parallel columns, among many other features. Much like other Bible software programs, BibleWorks also offers optional add-on modules that can be purchased at additional cost (e.g., Dead Sea Scrolls, Greek and Hebrew grammars and lexicons).

Although one can purchase additional modules for both the Hebrew Bible and the Greek New Testament, the developers of BibleWorks have chosen to include essential tools for working with the biblical text rather than to offer a huge digital library or extrabiblical resources. For those who desire to add electronic books to the program, it is possible to import EPUB titles into BibleWorks from any source they wish. Users can thus craft very finely tuned libraries of additional resources without having to purchase a larger package of materials that they may or may not want.

The BibleWorks program opens up to a screen featuring three parallel windows: a search window, a browse window, and an analysis window (see Fig. 8.5G). It can all be customized and reconfigured in a variety of ways. At the top of the page, there are buttons galore (word and verse lists, sophisticated maps, parallel versions, synoptic tools, and many more). How intuitive a software program is tends to be in the eye of the beholder. As is the case with all Bible programs, different users will have different evaluations of how user-friendly the software interface is. The greatest strength of BibleWorks can be found in its capacity to provide deep analysis of the Hebrew and Greek texts of the Bible. Along with the context menu that provides many help topics, a number of training videos are also available. If one does not really use

Hebrew or Greek, it may not be obvious why one would choose to get BibleWorks. There are, however, a good number of English Bible texts that are easy to compare and that can be searched with quick and powerful tools.

For anyone wanting to study the morphology of the Hebrew or Greek text in very fine detail, BibleWorks offers very sophisticated search mechanisms. The Command Line includes a pop-up Morphology Helper that lists parts of speech, which makes it easier for users to search morphological forms. The content menu in the Browse Window also provides a simple way to search for exact forms or all forms of a word. Simplest of all is the Use Tab in the Analysis Window, which automates a search when the cursor is placed over a word in the Browse Window. There are also more specialized searches that can be conducted using command codes and wildcards. It is possible to drill down quite deep using the program. Let's say you want to find all the occurrences of the Greek verb *agapaō* (to love). Easy enough. But then say you want to find only present indicative forms or aorist subjunctive forms in the second person as part of a conditional clause. You can do that kind of search in BibleWorks, or you can do Greek Semantic Domain Searches linked to the Louw-Nida domain codes (let the reader understand!). Thus, one can conduct anything from a very simple search to an unbelievably complex search of the Bible in the original languages. Some users will find BibleWorks to have a steep learning curve with its vestiges of older-style command codes for PCs, while others will find the program's focused precision on the biblical text proper to be its greatest strength.

Due to the focus on original language research BibleWorks has an amazing array of Hebrew and Greek texts, with most texts coming in two versions—the actual Hebrew or Greek text, and then, a morphological version that allows for incredibly precise searches. One can search dozens of critical editions of Greek texts, including the Griesbach 1805 manual edition of the Greek New Testament, the 1871 Alford Greek New Testament, the Byzantine Greek New Testament, the 8th edition of Tischendorf's Greek New Testament, and a host of others. (Only about twenty-five Hebrew texts are available for detailed searches, though this includes the Leningrad Codex.) For those interested in the history of the Greek text, it is possible to compare (for example) Scrivener's 1894 text alongside Stephanus's 1550 version of the Greek New Testament. Not everyone will want to do this, of course, but should the user be interested in comparing the history of different

NT Greek texts, BibleWorks makes the process fairly straightforward. BibleWorks does not impose any interpretive bias upon the user, so that each user can conduct whatever search one wants with the many tools at hand. Because of its capacity to do very sophisticated searches, some may feel that the program can cross too easily into not always seeing the forest for the trees, or even the trees for the leaves. But the various tabs (e.g., Use, Context, Related Verses, Stats) do allow one to see broad patterns in word usage. It is certainly a powerful program that can provide very detailed analysis especially of the Hebrew and Greek texts of the Bible.

When I used BibleWorks to conduct an analysis of Luke 1:1–4, it provided many different versions and translations in multiple languages, including Greek of course. It also provided detailed analysis of the Greek text in terms of morphology, along with various lexical aids and grammatical helps. Beyond this, however, the program does not seek to provide commentaries or dictionary articles, or any real research beyond intensive study of the text in its original language. The goal truly is to focus on the text per se. (See Fig. 8.6G.)

Olive Tree

Finally, we turn our attention to Olive Tree Software, which first began in 1998 as the program BibleReader for the handheld Palm OS device, then in 1999 for the Pocket PC with the Windows mobile operating system. The company took the name Olive Tree Bible Software in 2000 and expanded its operating system to cover more products in the mobile device market, initially for the once popular BlackBerry, then in 2007 for the newly released iPhone and iPad, and for the Android smartphone. It was not until 2011 that Olive Tree released its Bible study program for desktop and laptop Mac and Windows PC computers. Whereas other companies such as Logos and Accordance started with the desktop computer market, and from there went to mobile smartphones and tablets, Olive Tree took the opposite approach by first being available on mobile devices, coming to the desktop/laptop computer Bible study market much later. In 2014, Olive Tree was acquired by the Christian Publishing arm of the HarperCollins publishing group, which also owns Zondervan. Olive Tree has grown to offer a great variety of translations and resources, with hundreds of digital books available for additional purchase beyond the basic program. (There are also numerous books available for free because they are out of copyright.) The most recent version of Olive Tree Bible Study software is version 6.

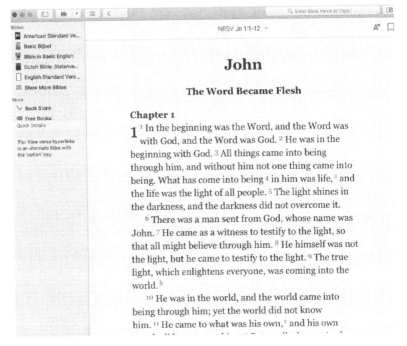

Fig. 8.7. A screenshot of Olive Tree open to Luke 1.

Of all the Bible study programs, Olive Tree has the simplest interface, opening initially to the Gospel of John, with one large text window and an easy toggle between text only and a left-hand pane revealing available Bibles and the Olive Tree store (see Fig. 8.9). There is also a library icon that leads to different categories that may or may not be relevant, all depending on what additional resources one has purchased. There are a number of free books, a textual apparatus, maps, commentaries, devotionals, dictionaries, and study bibles. Many of these are available only as additional purchases. Olive Tree Bible Study software keeps the screen very simple and uncluttered. It is easy to split the screen to have two different Bible versions open at the same time, or a biblical text and a commentary, or a text and study Bible notes. The simplicity of Olive Tree makes it the most intuitive of all the Bible study programs, perhaps because it started as the first mobile Bible app. It is possible to highlight, take notes, do color-coordinated word searches, and more, but this program does not pretend to have the sophistication of the other programs we have surveyed, especially with original language study. Because it is a simple program to use, there are relatively few tutorials, unlike the other Bible software programs, all of which offer extensive (and necessary) tutorial videos and guides.

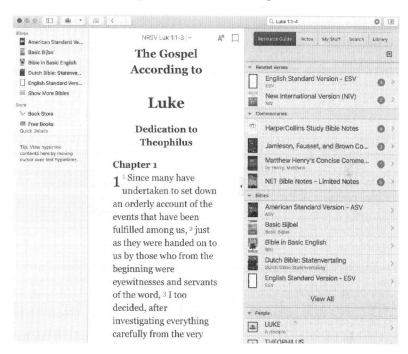

Fig. 8.8. A screenshot of Luke 1 in the Olive Tree app.

One notable feature of Olive Tree Bible Study software is the Resource Guide tab that is context-sensitive. If we repeat our study of Luke 1:1–4 and click on the Resource Guide, Olive Tree provides a list of "related verses," whatever commentaries one has downloaded or purchased, the range of Bibles one can open, any references to "people" in the given text (in this case, Theophilus, which then takes me to *Easton's Bible Dictionary* for a brief article about Theophilus), a brief list of topics, maps, outlines (based on the free download from Matthew Henry's Concise Commentary), Introductions (I purchased *HarperCollins Study Bible Notes*), My Notes (where one can add one's own observations), and an option to "Get More," which takes one to the Olive Tree store to peruse other resources one might wish to purchase. Other tabs beyond the Resource Guide at the top of the page include Notes (personal notes on the text), My Stuff (with Study Helper Categories of Notes,

Highlights, Book Ribbons, Saved Passages, Tags, and Reading Plans), a search window, and Library (listing the resources to which the user has access in alphabetical order). One clear virtue of Olive Tree is its simplicity and ease of use. It is difficult to get a screen that is overly cluttered or distracting, since one can really only have a few resources open at any given time, typically the biblical text along with another resource (a different translation, a commentary, et al.).

Comparing and Contrasting Computer Bible Programs

Having discussed the four major computer-based Bible programs, it is now time to compare and contrast the relative strengths and weaknesses of Logos, Accordance, BibleWorks, and Olive Tree. In a sense, we can conduct a kind of "program parallel" analysis of the four programs (as opposed to Gospel parallel analysis). Several features are common to all of the programs. All of them operate in either a PC or Mac environment. All of them provide modules that give a good number of English translations and tools, as well as solid resources for studying the Hebrew and Greek texts of the Bible. Beyond this, the odd program out is BibleWorks. Unlike the other programs, it does not have an IOS presence that allows it to be used on mobile devices such as smartphones or tablets. Further, BibleWorks is alone in not offering extensive libraries of additional resources that are not strictly geared toward the study of the Bible. This actually seems to be a point of pride for BibleWorks. There are many users who are quite happy with this fixed limit to what the program offers, especially given the depth it offers in its ability to parse and analyze morphological forms to a very fine degree. In one respect, it could be seen as the most academic and least pastorally oriented of all the programs, in that it presumes an ability to work with the original Hebrew and Greek languages—and narrowly so at that.

This leaves us with three other very strong programs in Logos, Accordance, and Olive Tree. As noted above, Olive Tree Software began life on mobile devices, and its elegance as an IOS program for smartphones and tablets remains its greatest strength. It also offers a huge number of Christian e-books for purchase across a wide range of categories along with its Bible resources. But it pales in comparison to the analytical depth of the biblical text offered by the other three programs.

We turn, then, to a comparison of Logos and Accordance, both excellent programs. They match each other extremely well in most regards when it comes to providing tools and resources for analyzing the biblical text in translation or in the original languages. Both allow for a great deal of flexibility on the part of the user to shape templates, have multiple resources open at the same time, and to have anything from a very complex screen, arranged with many modules open, to having a very simple screen with but one large text window open. Both offer different levels of the respective programs for different kinds of audiences at different price points. Both seek to tailor their programs to the needs of their users as best they can. Both provide significant customer support and plenty of training videos. And both continue to develop and improve from one version to the next. Both also seek to make good use of older resources that are now out of copyright, and hence, can be digitized and included as part of larger program packages.

But there are significant differences. One difference has to do with marketing. Logos originally started off as a Bible study program, but it has now morphed into but one component of Faithlife (faithlife.com), a much larger umbrella for a wide array of digital resources that are intended to serve not just students of the Bible, but the devotional and worship life of faith communities, providing a virtual seminary of courses for those wanting to explore far more than the Bible. Because of this broader focus, Faithlife boasts the largest number of digital resources available for any company engaged in distributing the study of the Bible in digital form. But the sheer number of resources tends to overwhelm. Although it appears that Logos is seeking to do a better job of tailoring these vast resources into more discrete sets of focused materials, it remains the case that more is not always more. So this is the downside of being big and providing a large platform for virtually endless resources. But the upside is that if one knows what to look for, it is likely that Logos offers it, and that it offers videos to help make the most of the resources that have been purchased and downloaded.

While the culture of Logos implicitly suggests starting big, and then, utilizing whatever smaller portion of resources one desires, the culture of Accordance explicitly suggests that users start with a smaller set of resources, and then build up to whatever else one needs. Thus, although—like Logos—Accordance offers a very large set of resources, Accordance also seems to get the "less is more" model when it comes to resources for the study of the Bible. The trick, of course, is always one of balance. Both Accordance and Logos (as well as BibleWorks and Olive Tree) can be tuned by the user to have a balance that works for the individual user, and different users will be comfortable with different kinds of balance between complexity and simplicity in studying the Bible. And that's as it should be.

By way of direct comparison between Logos and Accordance, the chart put together by Pedro Cheung is helpful.[12] Here, he compares Logos 7 and Accordance XII in relation to two parallel software packages, Logos 7's "Silver" collection and Accordance XII's "Triple Discoverer" collection.

Category	Logos 7 Silver ($999 list)	Accordance 12: Triple Discoverer ($997 list)
Bibles with Key Number Tagging	ESV, KJB, NASB, NKJV, NIV, NRSV	ESV, KVJ, NASB, NKJV, NIV
Bible Dictionaries	Baker's Encyclopedia of the Bible (4 vols)	International Standard Bible Encyclopedia (4 vols)
		Eerdmans Dictionary of the Bible
	Holman Illustrated Bible Dictionary	Holman Illustrated Bible Dictionary
	Lexham Bible Dictionary	IVP New Bible Dictionary
		IVP Pocket Dictionaries
Commentaries	Tyndale Commentaries (49 vols)	Tyndale Commentaries (49 vols)
	Keil and Delitzsch OT Commentaries (10 vols)	Holman's OT and NT Commentaries (32 vols)
	New Daily Study Bible NT (17 vols)	
		IVP Bible Background OT and NT Commentaries
	Evangelical Commentary on the Bible	Bible Knowledge Commentary
		IVP New Bible Commentary
Greek NT	Greek NT: SBL Edition	Nestle-Aland 28th edition morphology tagged
		Textus Receptus morphology tagged
Greek Lexicon	Liddel and Scott Lexicon	Louw and Nida Lexicon
	Exegetical Dictionary of the NT (3 vols)	TDNT (Little Kittel)

12. http://biblesumo.com/logos-vs-accordance-bible-software-review/.

		LEH Septuagint Lexicon
		Thayer's Lexicon
		Spicq Theological Lexicon of the NT
		Complete Word Study NT Dictionary
	New Strong's Concise Dictionary	Strong's Greek Dictionary; Mounce's Greek Dictionary
Hebrew OT	Lexham Hebrew Bible with morphology tagging	Biblia Hebraica with Westminster Morphology 4 tagging
Hebrew Lexicon	BDB Complete Lexicon	BDB Complete Lexicon
		Complete Word Study OT Dictionary
Study Bible	Faithlife Study Bible	HCSB Study Bible, Life Application Study Bible
Bible Atlas	Holman Bible Atlas	IVP New Bible Atlas

Accordance offers slightly more overall resources than Logos, but they are roughly parallel. Either would serve a student well who was seeking to use original languages in studying the Bible.[13]

Computer Bible Programs and Mobile Devices

Before drawing this chapter to a close, it is important to give some dedicated attention to the shift from desktop computer programs for the Bible to mobile devices and their programs for the Bible. Calling attention to this shift from desktop to mobile acknowledges what is widely seen as the most important development in computers over the last generation—namely, the ways in which computers have been increas-

---

In his comparison of Logos 7 and Accordance XII, Pedro Cheung concludes "If you do not own any Bible software and are looking for a first purchase, Accordance is the Bible software to get. It is more affordable. It is easier to use. It is faster. You will not outgrow the power of Accordance. If you are looking for the ultimate Christian electronic library, you should purchase Logos. Just about every possible digital library resource is available in Logos." (http://biblesumo.com/logos-vs-accordance-bible-software-review/). In the view of Dustin Battles, Accordance holds the slight edge overall, with better user interface, faster speed and less intensive use of computer memory, a less aggressive marketing approach to sales, and greater flexibility overall. (Battles was comparing Logos 6 with Accordance 11; http://rootedthinking.com/2014/12/15/logos-accordance/.) Nathan Parker, in a 2015 review of Logos 6 and Accordance 11, indicates a slight preference for Logos, but sees both as excellent programs. (http://www.stilltruth.com/2015/a-comparison-between-logos-6-and-accordance-11/).

ingly miniaturized and made exponentially faster with each iteration. Nowhere has this been seen more visibly and with greater impact than in the world of mobile devices. The famous ENIAC computer (the Electronic Numerical Integrator And Computer) that was powered on in 1945 was originally intended to calculate the trajectories of artillery shells. It had over 17,000 vacuum tubes, weighed more than 25 tons, took up 1,800 square feet of warehouse space, and could execute 5,000 instructions per second. By contrast, the iPhone 6 (2014) weighs 4.5 ounces and can carry out 25 billion instructions per second. The earliest handheld computer device was the Palm Pilot 1000, introduced in 1996 as the first PDA (personal digital assistant). It came with a monochrome touchscreen and less than one megabyte of memory. Shortly thereafter, as we noted, Bible Reader was introduced in 1998 as the first digital mobile Bible. Palm Bible appeared in 2003, and within a few years, the first iPhone was introduced (2007), followed by the iPad (2010), and the world of mobile apps was in full swing. Whereas desktop computers used to be rather hulking necessities with their large screens and CPUs, the lines between desktops, laptops, tablets, and smartphones have become increasingly blurred.

This has led, in turn, to a blurring of boundaries between digital Bibles designed for desktop computing and mobile computing. As we have just noted, Olive Tree Bible Software actually began life as a program for accessing the Bible on a mobile device. It can now be readily synced with Olive Tree's software for smartphones or tablets and laptop or desktop computers. The same is the case for Logos Bible Software and Accordance Bible Software. (Bible Works remains the one holdout in this regard and, according to Bible Works representatives, currently has no plans to introduce software for the mobile market.) Although made for the smaller screens of smartphones and tablets, both Logos and Accordance offer robust apps for portable devices that can do pretty much the same thing as their standalone software on desktops and laptops. To be sure, there is little incentive to have multiple windows open at the same time on these smaller devices, but the programs, by and large, offer the same kind of computing power in their mobile form as they do in their larger cousins.

But there is far more competition among digital Bibles in the mobile app world than is the case for full-featured programs such as Logos and Accordance. There are hundreds of Bible apps for both smartphones and tablets. None of them really compete with such standalone programs as Logos, Accordance, or Olive Tree in terms of depth of resources, but they are all fairly easy to use and provide dozens or hundreds of ready access translations, reading plans, and audio/video resources for Bible reading and studying the Bible. The most popular is certainly YouVersion, but there are plenty of others. There are also a host of Bible games, children's Bibles, and other niche Bible apps.

On the mobile app scene for smartphones and tablets of all kinds there is a vast array of options, from IOS versions of the standalone desktop programs we have just surveyed, to hundreds of other apps one can download. A quick search of "Bible" on the app store for the iPhone reveals nine categories of programs: bible app, the bible app free, bible gateway, bible verse of the day, bible study, the bible, bible for kids, bible.is, and bible trivia. There are comparable Bible apps at the Android store. YouVersion is the clear leader for both iPhone and Android, but BibleGateway among other apps also comes with many features. Of course, one can get readily overwhelmed with the myriad choices of Bibles, translations, and apps. We do our level best to filter all of the information into some organized patterns that make all things digital work for us and not us for all things digital.

Bible apps have become increasingly popular both in and out of church precisely because mobile devices allow for such easy portability and convenience in accessing the biblical text. They also provide multiple versions of the Bible at the swipe or press of a finger on the touchscreen, where one can adjust for lighting and font size, as well as access the biblical text in various forms—text, video, and audio, all very liquid. The tangibility of such devices is an important factor in their success. They have different haptic aspects than do physical books, but it is hard to deny that there is something quite satisfying about touching an icon and opening a new app, or scrolling with the swipe of a finger, or holding and underlining a text with one's finger. Physical books have their magical appeal, but so do digital screens.

Conclusion

In this chapter, we have explored a snapshot of the current state of computer Bible software. I emphasize that this is merely a snapshot, because if we know anything about computer programs, we know they will continue to change and develop—sometimes in small increments, sometimes in large leaps. The "next thing" is a moving target, though the Biblical text they all seek to study remains basically the same from one generation to the next. The question of course, is to what degree the constancy and unchanging character of the actual biblical text will be perceived in the same way as people make use of digital Bibles and programs that are ever changing and upgrading to new platforms.

9

Biblical Pasts and Digital Futures

Now that we have come to the end of, or at least a pause in, our exploration of digital Bibles, I would like to close with a few reflections that I hope might be helpful as we move ever more into the digital future while seeking to hold on to our biblical pasts.

Faith and Adaptation

If anything is clear about the Christian faith across the centuries, one key component is its ability to adapt to changes of all kinds: social, political, economic, and technological, among other variables. We have been focusing on some of the impacts of the changes brought about by the application of digital technology to the reading and understanding of the Bible. But this technology has affected the Church in so many ways beyond how Christians access and use the Bible. The kind of immediacy that the digital world has brought about, especially in telecommunications and computer applications, has been nothing short of epochal. It rivals the industrial revolution and the introduction of the automobile. Before the digital revolution, we were much more tethered to particular places, times, and communities. We could receive phone calls on our home phones, or use a pay phone in the street. We could clear our schedules to watch a particular television show with our families (I still remember the Wonderful World of Disney in this regard). But cell phones and digital media have changed all of this, so that rather than having to conform ourselves to the limitations of communication, we now find increasingly limitless possibilities so that we can adapt place and time and even community much more to our own personal preferences. In many cases, we can telecommute. Being able to communicate and participate in the information superhighway virtually at will changes so much in our lives. We can and do personalize what we want to see, hear, or watch; how we want to text, talk, or snapchat; with whom we wish to link-in, friend on Facebook, or follow on Twitter. All of these options are made possible by the digital world, a bunch of simple but complex sets of 1s and 0s.

And so, we adapt our faith to this digital world as well. We can download a sermon or a church service or a Bible study. We can follow the latest ecclesial news online and be informed instantly of new developments. As much as we hold on to the older traditions and modes of worship, creeds, and hymns, we also expand out onto the new and changing world that digital technology opens up for our lives of faith. Freshly personalized, perhaps, by a particular reading plan for the Bible, we bring our traditional faith to a nontraditional digital world. We open up virtual Bible programs rather than opening up physical Bibles. We look at the giant screens in church for the scripture reading or for the words of the hymn rather than open the hymnal. We love the convenience provided by all of our gadgets, our flat-things with screens (as comedienne Paula Poundstone of NPR's *Wait Wait Don't Tell Me* calls them).

Personalizing the Bible

When "personal" computers were introduced back in the 1980s, little did we realize just how personal and portable they could and would become.[1] By today's standards, the original personal computers might as well be IBM mainframes that take up an entire room. So-called personal computers anchored us to a desk with a large cathode ray tube screen, further anchored by wires connecting us to this new thing called the internet. But things changed dramatically with the emergence of laptops and wireless. The advent of smartphones and dedicated e-readers in 2007 shrunk our worlds further still, making them

---

1. For a helpful overview of the history and development behind computers and the digital age, see W. Isaacson, *The Innovators: How a Group of Hackers, Geniuses, and Geeks Created the Digital Revolution* (New York: Simon & Schuster, 2014).

far more mobile and interconnected through new forms of social media. While our worlds shrunk, and our Bibles with it, onto initially smaller and smaller screens, at the same time our Bibles both expanded and became increasingly personal. They expanded via social networking and the development of complex Bible programs. They became increasingly personal and individualized through endless versions and reading plans. This all fits well with what Lee Raine and Barry Wellman have called "networked individualism," in their book *Networked: The New Social Operating System*.[2] Increasingly autonomous individuals interact with the network as their fingers tap and swipe across endless screens. As Heidi Campbell and Stephen Garner have noted, while networked individualism encourages interaction and active participation across the network, "such networked individualism also encourages loose, fragmented networks of relationships and can enable individuals to develop multiple social circles rather than investing and being accountable to a single group."[3] Personal boundaries are crafted on an individual basis, rather than by particular groups.[4] Personalized Bibles and interpretation of the biblical text have likewise become a sort of "craft brew" that individuals conjure in an American culture that is all about "me" and "I," iPhones, iPads, iTouch, and now, virtual iBibles or YouVersions. The hundreds of niche Bibles marketed by Zondervan in their personalized NIV Bibles now shift to hundreds of versions of the Bible in digital form that individuals choose according to their own personal preferences. Yes, communities of faith do gather still around the common text, but it is a common text increasingly read on screens and mediated by personalized handheld digital devices, which presents the possibility of myriad translations and versions being consulted at once. Just as a unified sense of the Bible as one unified Book fragmented in the twentieth century into a Bible of diverse books, so have digital Bibles in the twenty-first century continued to fragment into personalized tweets and snippets, from multiple versions of the Bible, representing increasingly individualized voices rather than a communal text.

. Lee Raine and Barry Wellman, *Networked: The New Social Operating System* (Cambridge, MA: MIT Press, 2012), 9.
. Heidi Campbell and Stephen Garner, *Networked Theology: Negotiating Faith in Digital Culture* (Grand Rapids: Baker Academic, 2016), 9.
. The shift from the front porch to the back porch, from physical social networking to personal and virtual social networking has been captured well by Robert Putnam, *Bowling Alone: The Collapse and Revival of American Community* (New York: Simon and Schuster, 2001).

Fast Times and Slow Times

The big family Bibles of the nineteenth century slowly changed into pew Bibles and personal Bibles. Time for devotional Bible reading and prayer has continued, but it has done so in a world that has an increasing addiction to speed and efficiency. It has been no less than astonishing to see how quickly all things digital have increased by way of speed and power. Billions of calculations a second are hard to fathom. Shrinking a far less powerful computer of twenty years ago into a mechanism no larger than a watch is simply amazing. Speed and more speed. While we are all happy that computers have become faster and more efficient, this development has had no small side-effect in compelling us to do likewise. Faster, more efficient, more cost effective.

But in adapting digital technology to the practice of our faith, and adapting our faith to the new realities of the digital age, do we move too fast? This is one growing critique of all things digital. The machines are so fast that we have learned to be impatient with even a few second delay in seeing a website load, or having a phone call break up because the satellite signal gets a little scrambled. The culture of speed to which we have become increasingly acclimated poses a significant problem for a faith that requires reflection, meditation, prayer, and contemplation, even silence. In their book *The Slow Professor: Challenging the Culture of Speed in the Academy*, Maggie Berg and Barbara Seeber challenge professors and the culture of higher education to s l o w d o w n, and to resist the culture of speed.[5] They stress the notion of investing time to engage more deeply with students, with colleagues and with one's own research, in order to ease stress and foster deeper understanding and collaboration. This is part of the "slow movement" seen also in church circles. The book *Slow Church: Cultivating Community in the Patient Way of Jesus,* by Christopher Smith and John Pattison,[6] helps to imagine local church communities as places where individuals are attentive and caring, sharing in the fullness of life's joys and sorrows, all in the shadow of God's grace. Along the same lines, the well-known Hebrew Bible scholar Walter Brueggemann has written *Sabbath as Resistance: Saying No to the Culture of Now,*[7] building on the classic work, *The Sabbath,*

---

5. Toronto: University of Toronto Press, 2016.
6. Downers Grove, IL: IVP, 2014.
7. Louisville: Westminster John Knox, 2014.

by the Jewish sage Abraham Joshua Heschel.[8] This is a call to breathe, reflect, pause, see, taste, r e s t.

Screen Sabbaths

Several years ago, my wife Judy (also an ordained Presbyterian minister and professor of New Testament) and I spent a few weeks for each of two summers as Fellows at the Shalom Hartman Institute in Jerusalem, as part of their Christian Leadership Initiative. Aside from being a wonderful experience in every regard, one of the things that our Jewish hosts invited us as Christians to practice is what they called a "screen Sabbath." As our Jewish hosts were entering into their Sabbath rest from Friday sundown to Saturday sundown, we were invited to participate in a parallel manner. We shared the Sabbath meal with folks, and then, wandered back to where we were staying with the challenge of observing a "screen Sabbath." The notion of a "screen Sabbath" is fairly simple. No screens on the Sabbath! No TV, no cell phones, no computers, no tablets, no screens. Off. After going through a bit of withdrawal when we first tried it, we were amazed at how freeing and liberating it was. It was like allowing blood to rush back into our brains, letting our eyes recover from the constant glow of screens, seeing things fresh, spending time engaged with other human beings, real flesh-and-blood people and not any virtual conversations over email or text message.

Of course, you can guess what happened over the succeeding years upon our return to long-established routines. Yup. Sunday? Church, and then, a perfect day to catch up on those e-mails! A great time to text, to check out Facebook, to . . . screen, screen, screen. Reflecting upon it here inspires me to give the screen Sabbath another try, as it is a wonderful way to create space and time that wards off the urgent and pressing "demands" of our lives. I know my wife would welcome it. Even the thought of it has me breathing deeper.

The Bible in the Marketplace

One further aspect of the digital Bible that has become rather apparent is the role it plays in the marketplace of Bibles. The Bible has ever been the best-selling book, year after year after year. Now, the Bible in digi-

---

Published originally in 1951, this classic has been republished by Farrar, Strauss, & Giroux (2005) with a new introduction by Heschel's daughter and Judaica scholar, Susannah Heschel.

243

tal form, with many additional digital resources, has entered the marketplace in significant ways, accompanying the physical publishing of Bibles. Publishers have markets to target, sales figures to set and meet. None of this should surprise or bother us. Many more Bibles are given away for free every year than are sold. Publishing houses and designers and distributors of Bible computer programs have to survive in the open marketplace in competition with others. But it is a marketplace that is both shaped by the consumer and that shapes the consumer. Even with the unsurprising evangelical leanings of Logos Bible Software, and to a lesser degree, of Accordance Bible Software (among others), it seems clear to me that these companies are striving to serve a broad market of both confessional and academic audiences, recognizing all the while that there is often significant overlap between the two. It will be interesting in the years to come to see what other software developers enter into the market of Bible programming for the different digital platforms that exist, and to see what products they develop.

At the same time, Bible programs on all platforms (smartphone, tablet, computer) increasingly suffer from what might be called "Bible bloat," a malady that—while intended to be helpful to the user by providing nearly endless possibilities and choices—in fact, can paralyze, distract, or so atomize the biblical text that it can become difficult to see the larger picture, to hear to whole story, or parable. It used to be the case that faithful nonacademic readers of the Bible would read a passage, and most questions could be answered by a Bible dictionary, a commentary, a pastor, or a Bible-study leader. (More academic types would inevitably seek to draw on more resources, more commentaries.) But the utter flood of resources now available to consumers of digital Bibles has reached such a level that not only is there a babel of Bibles in terms of the sheer number of translations, but there is also a babel of commentaries, dictionaries, lexicons, morphological tables, and the ability to parse and search so finely that it is now possible to strain out a gnat and swallow a camel, digitally! More is not always more. In fact, more can be much less. The race of Bible study programs to out-resource each other with digital everything is a problem that needs fixing. The answer is not getting rid of all of the resources. But the answer may well be stressing quality of resources over quantity of resources. Just because one can now access anything and everything digitally does not mean that this aids the process of reading and interpreting the Bible.

A Book without Covers

One of the more significant developments with the arrival of digital Bibles is how the Bible as "the Book" has lost its covers. The unified Bible as a bound volume, a single physical volume between two tangible covers, vanishes into the pixels of a screen. No longer does a binding gather the pages together into a sewn and glued-together identifiable book. To be sure, the Bible did not start out as a single bound volume. That form of the Bible only emerged with the codex in the first few centuries CE. Before that, there were separate scrolls. And before that, there was oral tradition along with various written texts, with no two written texts exactly alike. Still, books have been around for nearly two millennia, and the Bible as book has been around since the fourth century. We have no real collective recollection of what the Bible was apart from a book, *The* Book. We can try to imagine what it was like for the earliest Christians who heard scripture read aloud, or for the masses in the late medieval era who relied on stained glass windows rather than on written texts to "read" their Bible. Yet it is not part of our experience. But the digitization of the Bible reminds us that the words were not always written, that the message of the Bible has always been delivered in oral form for an aural experience. It is spoken and heard perhaps even more than it is read by individuals. So while, on the one hand, it does indeed feel like the Bible is losing its covers, on the other hand, we know that the biblical "text" has not always been "text." There is certainly an important comfort in the knowledge that a printed volume exists in physical book form, for this physical text provides authority for the message it contains, its words and ideas, its stories and laws. Apart from the written words, we would have only the words remembered and handed down, surely not the most reliable method of transmission.

So, the Bible in digital form retains the precision of the written word, and a written word than can be copied and transmitted in so many more ways than traditional print text can. But the Bible has, indeed, lost its covers in the digital realm. Not only that, it has lost something of its canonical status. The Bible as book automatically comes with the recognition that it is sacred scripture, it is the official canonical text. It may be a collection of separate writings, but together, these comprise the one and only Bible that faith communities have come to know over the centuries as the Word of God. The book itself is considered holy and worthy of veneration as a representation of the divine Word. But when it is stripped of its covers and placed not on a lectern in a worship service, but on an iPad or smartphone next to God-knows what else, does this association with everything else on the digital device detract in some way from the dignity of the Bible as book? Does it lose something of its authoritative aura? I leave this as an open question, since for some this is clearly the case, while for others, the Bible remains the Bible, no matter its form.

A final matter related to the Bible losing its covers has to do with its very physicality, its tangibility. The Bible is a special book, a book like no other. To those with a very high view of the authority of scripture, the Bible is veritably the Word of God incarnate, even enfleshed. While this may sound (and may be) idolatrous, leading to charges of bibliolatry, there is something to the notion of a tangible book that bears witness to a tangible savior who told the doubting Thomas to touch, see, and feel. The red-letter edition of the Bible serves as but one testament to the special character of the divine speech of Jesus.[9] But what happens if the very tangibility of the book is lost because it has "gone digital"? For some of the faithful, the Word made flesh in Christ (John 1:14) is somehow parallel to, even coterminous with, the Word made text in the Bible as Book. Take that Book away, and somehow, the Word is less tangible, less real. For others, it makes absolutely no difference, as the printed Book and the digital Bible are simply two different forms of exactly the same thing. Such is the power (or lack thereof) held by the *form* of the Bible, with covers or without.

Old Bibles and New Technology

Finally, there is much to celebrate in the age of digital Bibles. There are such obvious things as the ability to adjust screens so that the text of the Bible can be read more easily. The possibility to disseminate the Bible in an instant across thousands of miles via digital downloads is also a huge benefit to those who otherwise would not have ready access to the Bible. YouVersion and the American Bible Society, along with other Bible publishers and translators (e.g., Wycliffe), are taking full advantage of the power of digital technology to translate and circulate Bibles in places where it has been difficult to do so with physical Bibles.

---

9. For those unfamiliar with the "red-letter edition" of the Bible, these Bibles print the words of Jesus in red ink, so they stand out as the most important words in the Bible. The first red-letter edition of the New Testament was published in 1899, in the King James Version. It became a very popular version and is still in much demand today.

Generous individuals and communities of faith are deeply involved in these efforts.

Less obvious, but just as important, the publishers of digital Bible programs, such as Logos and Accordance, have increasingly made older Bible commentaries available to populations who otherwise would have had no occasion to read any of the church fathers, or Calvin and Luther among scores of others (or even Matthew Henry). The kind of democratization that takes place in the digital domain is real and it is very powerful. That I or anyone with a computer can access these kinds of resources for studying the Bible and its interpretation across time and space is sparking new conversations and renewed realizations across denominational boundaries, since the Bible is the one book we all share in common (even with the differences in the make-up of the biblical canon between Catholics and Protestants).

Social media can certainly be both a blessing and a curse. There is great truth in the warning against the culture of superficiality. This kind of superficiality can infect one's approach to and understanding of the Bible as well. But social media can also be a powerful tool in enhancing the depth of Bible study, especially when this is done in concert with other individuals in a dedicated Bible study, and when there is some sure guidance about the many resources that exist for studying the Bible.

The study of the Bible is not a self-contained thing. The biblical witness is large and messy, much like the human population that reads it. It spills out on every side. It bears witness to the joys and sorrows of people whom God has sought out, and who, in turn, continue to seek God. It is the common touchstone of the initial voices of faith with whom we all enter into conversation and dialogue, sometimes debate, all the while pressing ahead, even though we acknowledge we see now but through a glass darkly, a screen darkly.

The digital age is here to stay. The digital Bible is here to stay with it—on our cell phones, on our tablets, on our computers, on our iTunes playlist. Even with some of the cautions that we have encountered, the Bible will continue to proliferate on all manner of digital devices in ever-new forms that move beyond mere text to include more images and sounds as well. As we seek to integrate digital Bibles into our lives and communities of faith, I am reminded of the words by of our technological predecessor, Johannes Gutenberg, with which the book began. Perhaps it would be good to adapt those words to the Bible in the digital world:

"Yes, it is a digital Bible, certainly, a Bible on screens of all kinds, but a virtual Bible from which shall flow, in inexhaustible streams, the most abundant and most marvelous liquor that has ever flowed to relieve the thirst of God's people! Through it, God will spread God's Word."

Bibliography

"25th Anniversary for Bible Software is Celebrated with New Release." 2005. *The Free Library*. Business Wire. https://www.thefreelibrary.com/25th+ Anniversary+for+Bible+Software+is+Celebrated+with+New+Release.-a0137 395881.

Abbott, Kirsten. "Wrestling texts: Hypertext and Biblical Studies." *Stimulus* 12, no. 3 (2004): 49–54.

Abel, Richard. *The Gutenberg Revolution: a History of Print Culture*. New Brunswick, NJ: Transaction, 2011.

Ackerman, Rakefet, and Tirza Lauterman. "Taking Reading Comprehension Exams on Screen or on Paper? A Metacognitive Analysis of Learning Texts under Time Pressure." *Computers in Human Behavior* 28, no. 5 (2012): 1816–28. doi: 10.1016/j.chb.2012.04.023.

Ackoff, Russell. "From Data to Wisdom: Presidential Address to ISGSR, June 1988." *Journal of Applied Systems Analysis* 16 (1989): 3–9.

Adema, Janneke. "On Open Books and Fluid Humanities." *Scholarly and Research Communication* 3, no. 3 (2012): 1–16.

Agger, Ben. "The Book Unbound: Reconsidering One-Dimensionality in the Internet Age." In *Putting Knowledge to Work and Letting Information Play*, 2nd edition, 15–22. Edited by Timothy Luke. Rotterdam: Sense, 2012.

Aichele, George. "The Virtual Bible." In *The Future of the Biblical Past: Envisioning Biblical Studies on a Global Key*, 263–71. Edited by Roland Boer and Fernando F. Segovia. Atlanta, GA: Society of Biblical Literature, 2012.

Aland, Kurt, and Barbara Aland. *The Text of the New Testament: An Introduction to the Critical Editions and to the Theory and Practice of Modern Textual Criticism*. Grand Rapids: Eerdmans, 1987.

Allen, Woody. *Without Feathers*. New York: Ballantine Books, 1986.

Amazon.com. *The Bible Store*. https://www.amazon.com/Bibles-Christianity-Religion-Spirituality-Books/b?ie=UTF8&node=12059.

American Bible Society. *State of the Bible 2011.* 2011. http://www.american-bible.org/uploads/content/2011_analysis.pdf.

_____. *State of the Bible 2012.* 2012. http://www.americanbible.org/uploads/content/2012_analysis.pdf.

_____. *State of the Bible 2013.* 2013. http://www.americanbible.org/uploads/content/State%20of%20the%20Bible%20Report%202013.pdf.

_____. *State of the Bible 2014.* 2014. http://www.americanbible.org/uploads/content/state-of-the-bible-data-analysis-american-bible-society-2014.pdf.

_____. *State of the Bible 2015.* 2015. http://www.americanbible.org/uploads/content/State_of_the_Bible_2015_report.pdf.

Angier, Michael. "Top Ten Reasons Why eBooks are Better Than Printed Books." *SuccessNet.org,* 2013. http://successnet.org/cms/sales-and-marketing/top-ten-reasons-why-ebooks-are-better-than-printed-books.

Bachmann, H., and W. A. Salby. *Computer Konkordanz zum Novum Testamentum Graece.* Berlin: de Gruyter, 1980.

Bagnall, Roger, ed. *The Oxford Handbook of Papyrology.* Oxford: Oxford University Press, 2011.

Barach, Rachel. "What's Technology Really Doing to the Bible?" *OnFaith,* September 7, 2016. https://www.onfaith.co/commentary/whats-technology-really-doing-to-the-bible.

Barna Group. *The Bible in America: 6-Year Trends.* Barna Group, 2016. https://www.barna.com/research/the-bible-in-america-6-year-trends/.

_____. *How Technology is Changing Millenial Faith.* 2013. https://www.barna.com/research/how-technology-is-changing-millennial-faith/.

_____. *Millennials and the Bible: 3 Surprising Insights.* 2014. https://www.barna.com/research/millennials-and-the-bible-3-surprising-insights/.

_____. *State of the Bible 2014: 6 Trends for 2014.* 2014. https://www.barna.com/research/the-state-of-the-bible-6-trends-for-2014/.

_____. *State of the Bible 2017: Top Findings.* 2017. https://www.barna.com/research/state-bible-2017-top-findings/.

Baron, Naomi. *Always On: Language in an Online and Mobile World.* New York: Oxford University Press, 2008.

_____. "How E-Reading Threatens Learning in the Humanities." *The Chronicle of Higher Education,* 2014. http://www.chronicle.com/article/How-E-Reading-Threatens/147661.

_____. *Words Onscreen: The Fate of Reading in a Digital World.* New York: Oxford University Press, 2015.

Barrett, Matthew. "Dear Pastor, Bring Your Bible to Church." *The Gospel Coali-*

tion, 2013. https://www.thegospelcoalition.org/article/dear-pastor-bring-your-bible-to-church.

Bartholomew, Craig, and Scott Hahn, eds. *Canon and Biblical Interpretation.* Grand Rapids: Zondervan, 2006.

Battles, Matthew. *Palimpsest: A History of the Written Word.* New York: W. W. Norton, 2015.

Bauman, Zygmunt. *Liquid Modernity.* Malden, MA: Polity, 2000.

_____. *Liquid Times: Living in an Age of Uncertainty.* Malden, MA: Polity, 2007.

Baym, Nancy K. *Personal Connections in the Digital Age.* Second edition. Malden, MA: Polity, 2015.

Beal, Timothy. *The Rise and Fall of the Bible: The Unexpected History of an Accidental Book.* Boston: Mariner, 2012.

_____. "The End of the Word as We Know It: The Cultural Iconicity of the Bible in the Twilight of Print Culture," in *Iconic Books and Texts,* 207–24. Edited by J. W. Watts. Sheffield: Equinox, 2015.

Bellinger, William, and William Farmer, eds. *Jesus and the Suffering Servant: Isaiah 53 and Christian Origins.* Harrisburg: Trinity Press, 1998.

Ben, Irwin. "Four Modern Versions of the Bible that Are Ruining the Bible." *OnFaith,* 2015. https://www.onfaith.co/onfaith/2014/06/02/four-modern-versions-of-the-bible-that-are-ruining-the-bible/32219.

Benedetto, Simone, Véronique Drai–Zerbib, Marco Pedrotti, Geoffrey Tissier, and Thierry Baccino. "E-readers and Visual Fatigue." *PloS One* 8, no. 12 (2013): e83676. doi: 10.1371/journal.pone.0083676.

Benjamin-Pollak, Noah. "Rant: 10 Reasons to Love E-Books." *National Book Review,* 2015. http://www.thenationalbookreview.com/features/2015/9/24/rant-10-reasons-to-love-e-books-despite-those-new-sales-numbers.

Berg, Maggie, and Barbara Seeber. *The Slow Professor: Challenging the Culture of Speedin the Academy.* Toronto: University of Toronto Press, 2016.

Bergstrom, Jennifer, and Andrew Schall. *Eye Tracking in User Experience Design.* Amsterdam: Elsevier, 2014.

Bernstein, J. H. *The Data-Information-Knowledge-Wisdom Hierarchy and its Antithesis. In Proceedings from North American Symposium on Knowledge Organization,* vol. 2, 68–75. Edited by E. K. Jacob and B. Kwasnik. Syracuse, NY, 2009.

Bibb, Bryan. "Readers and Their E-Bibles: The Shape and Authority of the Hypertext Canon." In *The Bible in American Life,* 256–65. Edited by Philip Goff, Arthur E. Farnsley II, & Peter J. Thuesen. New York: Oxford University Press, 2017.

Bibles, Crossway. *The ESV Study Bible.* Wheaton, IL: Crossway, 2008.

Birkerts, Sven. *The Gutenberg Elegies: the Fate of Reading in an Electronic Age.* Boston: Faber and Faber, 1994.

Blair, Ann. *Too Much to Know: Managing Scholarly Information Before the Modern Age*. New Haven, CT: Yale University Press, 2010.

Boer, Roland, and Fernando F. Segovia. *The Future of the Biblical Past: Envisioning Biblical Studies on a Global Key*. Atlanta, GA: Society of Biblical Literature, 2012.

Bolter, J. David. *Writing Space: Computers, Hypertext, and the Remediation of Print*. Mahwah, NJ: Lawrence Erlbaum Associates, 2001.

_____. *Writing Space: The Computer, Hypertext, and the History of Writing*. Hillsdale, NJ: Lawrence Erlbaum Associates, 1991.

Bombaro, John. "The Book that Isn't Really There: Digital Texts and Declining Discipleship." *Modern Reformation Magazine* 22, no. 3 (2013): 30–35.

Borges, Jorge Luis. *Book of Sand; and, Shakespeare's Memory*. London: Penguin, 2007.

Bottigheimer, Ruth B. *The Bible for Children: From the Age of Gutenberg to the Present*. New Haven, CT: Yale University Press, 1996.

Bradberry, Travis. "Multitasking Damages Your Brain And Career, New Studies Suggest." *Forbes.com*, October 8, 2014. https://www.forbes.com/sites/travisbradberry/2014/10/08/multitasking-damages-your-brain-and-career-new-studies-suggest/#42f2e6256ee6.

Bradbury, Ray. *Fahrenheit 451: A Novel*. New York: Simon & Schuster, 1953.

Bradley, Steven. "3 Design Layouts: Gutenberg Diagram, Z-Pattern, And F-Pattern." *Vanseo Design*, 2011. http://vanseodesign.com/web-design/3-design-layouts/.

Breznau, Michael. "Digital Bible vs. Print Bible." 2012. http://www.jtcochran.com/tag/digital-bible-vs-print-bible/.

Brooks, Mark. *The Digital Church: How to Use the New Tools of Technological and Communication Revolution for Your Church*. Amazon Digital Services, 2013.

Brown, Raymond. *The Community of the Beloved Disciple*. Mahwah, NJ: Paulist, 1979.

_____, and T. A. Collins. "Church Pronouncements." In *New Jerome Biblical Commentary*, 1166–74. Englewood Cliffs, NJ: Prentice Hall, 1990.

Brown, Michele P., ed. *In the Beginning: Bibles Before the Year 1000*. Washington, DC: Smithsonian Institution, 2006.

Brueggemann, Walter. *Sabbath as Resistance: Saying No to the Culture of Now*. Louisville: Westminster John Knox, 2014.

Bryant, John L. *The Fluid Text: A Theory of Revision and Editing for Book and Screen*. Ann Arbor: University of Michigan Press, 2002.

Budiu, Raluca. "The State of Mobile User Experience." *Nielsen Norman Group*, March 22, 2015. https://www.nngroup.com/articles/mobile-usability-update/.

_____. "Mobile User Experience: Limitation and Strengths." *Nielsen Norman Group,* April 19, 2015. https://www.nngroup.com/articles/mobile-ux/.

Bulkeley, Timothy. "Form, Medium and Function: the Rhetorics and Poetics of Text and Hypertext in Humanities Publishing." *The International Journal of the Book* 1 (2003): 317–22.

_____. "Hypertext and Publication in Biblical Studies." *SBL Forum,* May 2004. https://www.sbl-site.org/publications/article.aspx?articleId=261.

_____. *Amos: Hypertext Bible Commentary.* Hypertext Bible. Auckland, 2005.

_____. "Presence and Pixels: Some Impacts of Electronically Mediated Communication on Christian Living." *Review and Expositor* 111, no. 1 (2014): 56–63.

Burdick, Ann, and Holly Willis. "Digital Learning, Digital Scholarship and Design Thinking." *Design Studies* 32, no. 6 (2011): 546–56.

Burk, Denny. "Discerning Corinthian Slogans through Paul's Use of the Diatribe in 1 Corinthians 6:12-20." *Bulletin for Biblical Research* 18, no. 1 (2008): 99–121. https://www.ibr-bbr.org/files/bbr/bbr18a05_burk.pdf.

Burnyeat, M. F. "Postscript on Silent Reading." *The Classical Quarterly* 47, no. 1 (1997): 74–76.

Burroughs, Dillon. "Should Christians Use a Digital Bible Instead of Print Bible?" 2016. http://www.blogos.org/scienceandtechnology/digital-bible.php.

Busa, Roberto. "The Annals of Humanities Computing: The *Index Thomisticus.*" *Computers and the Humanities* 14 (1980): 83–90.

Bush, Vannevar. "As We May Think." *The Atlantic,* July, 1945. https://www.theatlantic.com/magazine/archive/1945/07/as-we-may-think/303881/.

Buttrick, George A., ed. *The Interpreter's Bible,* 12 vols. New York: Abingdon-Cokesbury, 1951–1957.

Caccamo, James. "Let Me Put It Another Way: Digital Media and the Future of the Liturgy." *Liturgy* 28, no. 3 (2013): 7–16.

Campbell, Heidi, and Stephen Garner. *Networked Theology: Negotiating Faith in Digital Culture.* Grand Rapids: Baker Academic, 2016.

Carr, Nicholas. "Is Google Making Us Stupid?" *The Atlantic,* July, 2008. https://www.theatlantic.com/magazine/archive/2008/07/is-google-making-us-stupid/306868/.

_____. *The Shallows: What the Internet is Doing to Our Brains.* Stanford: Stanford University Press, 2010.

Castillo, Stephanie. "Real Books Beat E-Readers: How Your Brain Reads Words On Paper Vs. On A Screen." *Medical Daily,* 2014. http://www.medicaldaily.com/real-books-beat-e-readers-how-your-brain-reads-words-paper-vs-screen-304104.

Caston, Jason. *The iChurch Method.* Caston Digital, 2012.

Challies, Tim. *The Next Story: Life and Faith after the Digital Explosion.* Grand Rapids: Zondervan, 2011.

Chartier, Roger. *Forms and Meanings: Texts, Performances, and Audiences from Codex to Computer.* Philadelphia, PA: University of Pennsylvania Press, 1995.

Chazelle, Celia M. "Pictures, Books, and the Illiterate: Pope Gregory I's Letters to Serenus of Marseilles." *Word & Image: A Journal of Verbal/Visual Enquiry* 6, no. 2 (1990): 138–53.

Chen, Chih-Ming, and Fang-Ya Chen. "Enhancing Digital Reading Performance with a Collaborative Reading Annotation System." *Computers & Education,* 2014. 77:67–81. doi: 10.1016/j.compedu.2014.04.010.

Cheong, Pauline. "Tweet the Message? Religious Authority and Social Media Innovation." *Journal of Religion, Media and Digital Culture* 3, no. 3 (2014): 1–19. https://www.jrmdc.com/journal/article/view/27.

Cherry, Kendra. "Multitasking: A Few Reasons Why Multitasking Reduces Productivity." VeryWell.com, May 22, 2015. https://www.verywell.com/multitasking-2795003.

Cheung, Pedro. "Logos vs. Accordance Bible Software Review and Feature Comparison." 2016. http://biblesumo.com/logos-vs-accordance-bible-software-review/.

Childs, Brevard. *Introduction to the Old Testament as Scripture.* Philadelphia: Fortress Press, 1979.

_____. *The New Testament as Canon: An Introduction.* Philadelphia: Fortress Press, 1984.

_____. *Biblical Theology of the Old and New Testaments: Theological Reflection on the Christian Bible.* Minneapolis: Fortress Press, 1992.

Clark, Andy. *Natural-born Cyborgs: Minds,Technologies, and the Future of Human Intelligence.* New York: Oxford University Press, 2003.

_____. *Supersizing the Mind: Embodiment,Action, and Cognitive Extension.* Oxford; New York: Oxford University Press, 2008.

Clivaz, Claire, A. Gregory, & D. Hamidović, eds. *Digital Humanities in Biblical, Early Jewish and Early Christian Studies.* Leiden: Brill, 2013.

_____. "Introduction: Digital Humanities in Biblical, Early Jewish and Early Christian Studies." In *Digital Humanities in Biblical, Early Jewish and Early Christian Studies,* 1–8. Edited by Claire Clivaz, Andrew Gregory, & David Hamidović. Leiden: Brill, 2013.

_____. "New Testament in a Digital Culture: A Biblaridion (Little Book) Lost in the Web?" *The Journal of Religion, Media and Digital Culture* 3, no. 3: 20–38.

_____. Jérôme Meizoz, François Vallotton, and Joseph Verheyden. *Lire demain. Des manuscrits antiques à l'ère digitale.* Lausanne: PPUR, 2012.

Codone, Susan. "Megachurch Pastor Twitter Activity: An Analysis of Rick Warren and Andy Stanley, Two of America's Social Pastors." *The Journal of Religion, Media and Digital Culture* 3, no. 2 (2015): 1–32.

"Computer Points to Single Author for Genesis." Special To *The New York Times*, 1981. http://www.nytimes.com/1981/11/08/world/computer-points-to-single-author-for-genesis.html.

Cordón, García, José Antonio, Julio Alonso Arévalo, Raquel Gómez Díaz, and Daniel Peter Linder Molin. *Social Reading: Platforms, Applications, Clouds and Tags, Chandos Information Professional Series*. Oxford: Chandos, 2013.

Crosby, Robert C. "The Social Network Gospel: How Interconnectivity Helps Us Better Engage the Bible." *Christianity Today* 56, no. 6 (2012): 36–40.

Danker, Frederick W., Walter Bauer, William F. Arndt, and F. Wilbur Gingrich. *Greek-English Lexicon of the New Testament and Other Early Christian Literature*, 3rd ed. Chicago: University of Chicago Press, 2000.

Darnton, Robert. *The Case for Books: Past, Present, and Future*. New York: PublicAffairs, 2010.

Davidow, William H. *Overconnected: The Promise and Threat of the Internet*. Harrison, NY: Delphinium, 2011.

De Hamel, Christopher. *The Book: A History of the Bible*. London and New York: Phaidon, 2001.

Dehaene, Stanislas. *The Number Sense*. New York: Oxford University Press, 1997.

———, J. R. Duhamd, M. Aarber, and G. Rozzolatti. *From Monkey Brain to Human Brain*. Cambridge, MA: MIT Press, 2003.

———. *Reading in the Brain: The Science and Evolution of a Human Invention*. New York: Viking, 2009.

Denes, Gianfranco. *Neural Plasticity Across the Lifespan: How the Brain Can Change*. Hove, UK: Psychology Press, 2015.

Desrochers, Nadine. *Examining Paratextual Theory and its Applications in Digital Culture*. Hershey, PA: IGI Global, 2014.

Detweiler, Craig. *iGods: How Technology Shapes Our Spiritual and Social Lives*. Grand Rapids: Baker, 2013.

Deyo, Steve. "Cyber-Boost Your Faith: The Latest Bible Study Software Will Empower Your Study at Any Level." *Christianity Today* 42, no. 5 (1998): S15.

Dillon, Andrew. "Reading From Paper Versus Screens: A Critical Review of the Empirical Literature." *Ergonomics* 35, no. 10 (1992): 1297–326.

———, C. McKnight, and J. Richardson. "Reading From Paper versus Reading From Screen." *The Computer Journal* 31, no. 5 (1988): 457–64. doi: 10.1093/comjnl/31.5.457.

Dixon, Patrick. *Cyberchurch: Christianity and the Internet*. Eastbourne, UK: Kingsway, 1997.

"Does the Brain Like E-Books?" The Editors, Room for Debate: A New York

Times Blog. *The New York Times*, October 14, 2009. http://roomforde-bate.blogs.nytimes.com/2009/10/14/does-the-brain-like-e-books/?_r=0.

Doidge, Norman. *The Brain's Way of Healing: Remarkable Discoveries and Recoveries from the Frontiers of Neuroplasticity*. New York: Penguin, 2016.

Dover, Kenneth J. *Greek Homosexuality*. Cambridge, MA: Harvard University Press, 1978.

Drescher, Elizabeth. *Tweet If You You ♥ Jesus: Practicing Church in the Digital Reformation*. New York: Morehouse, 2011.

Dungan, David L. *Constantine's Bible: Politics and the Making of the New Testament*. Minneapolis: Fortress Press, 2007.

Dyer, John. *From the Garden to the City: The Redeeming and Corrupting Power of Technology*. Grand Rapids, MI: Kregel, 2011.

_____. "The History of Bible Software." 2016. http://donteatthefruit.com/2016/09/the-history-of-bible-software-infographic/.

The Economist. "How Luther Went Viral." *The Economist*, 2011. 401: 93–96. http://www.economist.com/node/21541719.

Edwards, Mark. "Webspeak: Hypertext Challenges." *Christian Century* (August 29–September 5, 2001): 4.

Ehrman, Bart D. *Misquoting Jesus: The Story Behind Who Changed the Bible and Why*. San Francisco: HarperSanFrancisco, 2005.

_____. *The Orthodox Corruption of Scripture: The Effect of Early Christological Controversies on the Text of the New Testament*. Updated and with a new afterword. New York: Oxford University Press, 2011.

_____. *The New Testament: An Historical Introduction to the Early Christian Writings*. New York: Oxford University Press, 2015.

Eisenstein, Elizabeth L. *The Printing Press as an Agent of Change: Communications and Cultural Transformations in Early Modern Europe*. Cambridge: Cambridge University Press, 1979.

_____. *The Printing Revolution in Early Modern Europe*. Cambridge: Cambridge University Press, 1993.

_____. "Defining the Initial Shift: Some Features of Print Culture." In D. Finkelstein & A. McCleery, eds., *The Book History Reader*, 2nd ed., 232–54. New York: Routledge, 2006.

Eliot, T. S. *The Rock: A Pageant Play*. New York: Harcourt, Brace, & Co., 1934.

Elliott, J. K. "A New Edition of Nestle-Aland, Greek New Testament." *The Journal of Theological Studies* 64, 1 (2013): 47–65.

Emerson, Lori. *Reading Writing Interfaces: From the Digital to the Bookbound, Electronic Mediations*. Minneapolis: University of Minnesota Press, 2014.

Epp, Eldon J. *The Theological Tendency of Codex Bezae Cantabrigiensis in Acts*. Cambridge: Cambridge University Press, 1966.

Ess, Charles M., ed. *Critical Thinking and the Bible in the Age of New Media.* Lanham, MD: University Press of America, 2004.

_____. "'Revolution? What Revolution?' Successes and Limits of Computing Technologies in Philosophy and Religion." In *Companion to Digital Humanities,* 132–42. Edited by Susan Schreibman, Ray Siemens, and John Unsworth. Oxford: Blackwell, 2004.

Eyal, Nir. "The App of God." *The Atlantic,* July, 2013. https://www.theatlantic.com/technology/archive/2013/07/the-app-of-god/278006/.

Fackler, Mark. "The Second Coming of Holy Writ: Niche Bibles and the Manufacture of Market Segments." In *New Paradigms for Bible Study: The Bible in the Third Millennium,* 71–88. Edited by Robert M. Fowler, Edith Blumhofer, and Fernando F. Segovia. New York: T & T Clark, 2004.

Fea, John. *The Bible Cause: A History of the American Bible Society.* New York: Oxford University Press, 2016.

Fenton, James. "Read My Lips." *The Guardian,* 2006/07/29/. https://www.theguardian.com/books/2006/jul/29/featuresreviews.guardianreview27.

Fields, Leslie Leyland. "People of the Nook: What Bible Smartphone Apps Tell Us about the Book." *Christianity Today* 55, no. 5 (2011): 66.

Finkel, Irving. *The Ark Before Noah: Decoding the Story of the Flood.* New York: Anchor, 2015.

Finkelstein, David, and Allistair McCleery, eds. *The Book History Reader.* London: Routledge, 2006.

Finnegan, Ruth. *Literacy and Orality: Studies in the Technology of Communication.* Oxford: Oxford University Press, 1988.

Finley, Emma. "25 Years of Digital Bible Initiatives at DTS From CDWord to Logos Bible Software." 2013. http://www.dts.edu/read/logos-bible-software-cd-word-project/.

Fischer, Steven R. *A History of Writing: Globalities.* London: Reaktion Books, 2001.

Fish, Stanley. "The Digital Humanities and the Transcending of Mortality." *Opinionator: A Gathering of Opinion from Around the Web,* 2012. https://opinionator.blogs.nytimes.com/2012/01/09/the-digital-humanities-and-the-transcending-of-mortality/.

_____. *Is There a Text in This Class?: The Authority of Interpretive Communities.* Cambridge, MA: Harvard University Press, 1980.

Flew, Terry. *New Media: An Introduction.* 2nd ed. New York: Oxford University Press, 2005.

Flood, Alison. "Readers Absorb Less on Kindles than on Paper, Study Finds." *The Guardian,* 2014/08/19/. https://www.theguardian.com/books/2014/aug/19/readers-absorb-less-kindles-paper-study-plot-ereader-digitisation.

Foasberg, Nancy M. "Student Reading Practices in Print and Electronic Media." *College & Research Libraries* 75, no. 5 (2014): 705–23. doi: 10.5860/crl.75.5.705.

Fortna, Robert T. "Review of A.Q. Morton, *The Genesis of John.*" *Computers and the Humanities* 17, no. 3 (1983): 154.

Fowl, Stephen, and L. Gregory Jones, *Reading in Communion: Scripture and Ethics in Christian Life.* Grand Rapids: Eerdmans, 1991.

Fowler, Robert. "How the Secondary Orality of the Electronic Age Can Awaken Us to the Primary Orality of Antiquity, or, What Hypertext Can Teach Us About the Bible," *Interpersonal Computing and Technology: An Electronic Journal for the 21st Century* 2, 3 (July 1994): 12–46. http://www.helsinki.fi/science/optek/1994/n3/fowler.txt.

_____. "The End of the Bible as We Know It: The Metamorphosis of the Biblical Traditions in the Electronic Age." In *Literary Encounters with the Reign of God,* 341–56. Edited by Sharon Ringe and H. C. Paul Kim. New York: Bloomsbury T & T Clark, 2004.

Frymer-Kensky, Tikva. "What the Babylonian Flood Stories Can and Cannot Teach Us About the Genesis Flood," *Biblical Archaeology Review,* Nov/Dec, 1978. http://cojs.org/what-the-babylonian-flood-stories-can-and-cannot-teach-us-about-the-genesis-flood/.

Fuller, Matthew. *Behind the Blip: Essays on the Culture of Software.* Brooklyn, NY: Autonoma Media, 2003.

Fung, Brian. "A U.S. ambassador was just sworn in on a Kindle." *The Washington Post,* June 2, 2014. https://www.washingtonpost.com/news/the-switch/wp/2014/06/02/a-u-s-ambassador-was-just-sworn-in-on-a-kindle/.

Furnish, Victor Paul. *The Moral Teaching of Paul: Selected Issues,* 3rd ed. Nashville: Abingdon, 2009.

Füssel, Stephan. *Gutenberg and the Impact of Printing.* Burlington, VT: Ashgate, 2005.

Gaille, Brandon. "27 Good Bible Sales Statistics." *BrandonGaille.com,* 2015. http://brandongaille.com/27-good-bible-sales-statistics/.

Galloway, Alexander R. *The Interface Effect.* Cambridge; Malden, MA: Polity, 2012.

Gamble, Harry Y. *Books and Readers in the Early Church: A History of Early Christian Texts.* New Haven, CT: Yale University Press, 1995.

Garber, Megan. "Behold, the Kindle of the 16th Century." *The Atlantic,* February, 2013. https://www.theatlantic.com/technology/archive/2013/02/behold-the-kindle-of-the-16th-century/273577/.

Gass, William. "In Defense of the Book: On the Enduring Pleasures of Paper, Type, Page, and Ink." *Harper's Magazine,* November, 1999: 45–51. http://harpers.org/archive/1999/11/in-defense-of-the-book/.

Gavrilov, A. K. "Reading Techniques in Classical Antiquity." *Classical Quarterly* 47 (1997): 56–73.

Gee, James Paul. *What Video Games Have to Teach Us about Learning and Literacy.* New York: Palgrave Macmillan, 2007.

Genette, Gerard. "Introduction to the Paratext." *New Literary History* 22 (1991): 261–72.

_____. *Paratexts: Thresholds of Interpretation, Literature, Culture, Theory.* New York: Cambridge University Press, 1997.

_____. *Palimpsests: Literature in the Second Degree.* Translated by Channa Newman and Claude Doubinsky. 8th ed. Lincoln: University of Nebraska Press, 1997.

Geyer, Miklós. "Spreading the Word of God Through Apps." United Bible Societies, 2015. https://www.unitedbiblesocieties.org/spreading-the-word-of-god-through-apps/.

Gilmont, Jean-Francois. "Protestant Reformations and Reading." In Guglielmo Cavallo and Roger Chartier, eds., *A History of Reading in the West*, 213–37. Translated by Lydia G. Cochrane. Amherst: University of Massachusetts Press, 1999.

_____. *John Calvin And the Printed Book.* Kirksville, MO: Truman State University Press, 2005.

Glickman, Mark. *Sacred Treasure, The Cairo Geniza.* Woodstock, VT: Jewish Lights, 2011.

Goff, Philip. "The Bible in American Life: A National Study by The Center for the Study of Religion and American Culture (IUPUI)." Indianapolis: Indiana University-Purdue University Press, 2014.

Gold, Penny Schine. *Making the Bible Modern: Children's Bibles and Jewish Education in Twentieth-Century America.* Ithaca, NY: Cornell University Press, 2004.

Goldman, Shalom L. *God's Sacred Tongue: Hebrew and the American Imagination.* Chapel Hill, NC: University of North Carolina Press, 2004.

Gomez, Jeff. *Print is Dead: Books in Our Digital Age*: New York: Macmillan, 2008.

Goody, Jack. *The Interface between the Written and the Oral.* New York: Cambridge University Press, 1987.

Gorman, Michael J. *Elements of Biblical Exegesis*, Revised & Expanded. Grand Rapids: Baker Academic, 2010.

Gould, Meredith. *The Social Media Gospel: Sharing the Good News in New Ways*, 2nd ed. Collegeville, MN: Liturgical, 2015.

Graber, Adam. "Review of 'From the Garden to the City: The Redeeming and Corrupting Power of Technology' by John Dyer (Kregel Publications, 2011)." *The Journal of Religion, Media and Digital Culture* 2, no. 2 (2013).

Grafton, Anthony. *Christianity and the Transformation of the Book: Origen, Eusebius, and the Library of Caesarea.* Cambridge, MA: Harvard University Press, 2008.

Greenfield, Susan. *Tomorrow's People: How Twenty-first Century Technology is Changing the Way We Think and Feel.* Harmondsworth, UK: Penguin, 2004.

Groot, Esther de. "Problematic Screen Reading: Is it Caused by Our Brain?" *TXT: Exploring the Boundaries of the Book* 1, no. 1 (2014); 96–104. Leiden, NL https://openaccess.leidenuniv.nl/handle/1887/30047.

Group Publishing. *Jesus-Centered Bible, NLT.* Loveland, CO: Group Publishing, 2015.

Gruenewald, Bobby. "The Engagement Economy." In *Book: A Futurist's Manifesto: Essays from the Bleeding Edge of Publishing*, 229–36. Edited by Hugh McGuire and Brian O'Leary. Boston, MA: O'Reilly Media, 2012.

Gryboski, Michael. "Are Digital Bibles as Holy as Paper Bibles?" *The Christian Post*, July 15, 2014; http://www.christianpost.com/news/are-digital-bibles-as-holy-as-paper-bibles-123342/.

Guillory, John. "How Scholars Read." *ADE Bulletin*, 8–17. 2008. doi: 10.1632/ ade.146.8. https://ade.mla.org/bulletin/article/ade.146.8.

Gumbrecht, Hans Ulrich. *Production of Presence: What Meaning Cannot Convey.* Stanford, CA: Stanford University Press, 2004.

Gutjahr, Paul. *An American Bible: A History of the Good Book in the United States, 1777-1880.* Stanford, CA: Stanford University Press, 1999.

_____. "From Monarchy to Democracy: The Dethroning of the King James Bible in the United States." In *The King James Bible after 400 Years: Literary Linguistic, and Cultural Influences*, 164–80. Edited by Hannibal Hamlin and Norman W. Jones. Cambridge: Cambridge University Press, 2010.

Haines–Eitzen, Kim. *Guardians of Letters: Literacy, Power, and the Transmitters of Early Christian Literature.* Oxford; New York: Oxford University Press, 2000.

Hall, David D. *Cultures of Print: Essays in the History of the Book.* Amherst: University of Massachusetts Press, 1996.

Hall, Gary. "Fluid Notes on Liquid Books." In *Putting Knowledge to Work and Letting Information Play*, 33–53. Edited by Timothy W. Luke and Jeremy W. Hunsinger. Blacksburg, VA: Center for Digital Discourse and Culture, 2009. http://www.cddc.vt.edu/10th-book/putting_knowledge_to_work.pdf.

Hallo, William W., and Bruce William Jones. *The Bible in the Light of Cuneiform Literature: Scripture in Context III.* Lewiston, NY: Edwin Mellen, 1990.

Hamilton, Edith, and Huntington Cairns, eds. *The Collected Dialogues of Plato.* Princeton: Princeton University Press, 1973.

Harris, William V. *Ancient Literacy.* Cambridge, MA: Harvard University Press, 1989.

Harris, W. Hall, III. "Bible Software History 101," *Bible.org Blogs*, 2008. http:// blogs.bible.org/netbible/w._hall_harris_iii/bible_software_history_101.

Hatch, W. H. *The Principal Uncial Manuscripts of the New Testament.* Chicago: University of Chicago Press, 1939.

Hauerwas, Stanley. *The Peaceable Kingdom: A Primer in Christian Ethics.* Notre Dame, IN: University of Notre Dame Press, 1991.

Hay, David M. *Glory at the Right Hand: Psalm 110 in Early Christianity.* Nashville: Abingdon, 1973.

Hayles, N. Katherine. "Translating Media: Why We Should Rethink Textuality." *The Yale Journal of Criticism* 16, no. 2 (2003): 263–90. doi: 10.1353/yale. 2003.0018.

_____. *Electronic Literature: New Horizons for the Literary.* Notre Dame, IN: University of Notre Dame Press, 2008.

_____. "How We Read: Close, Hyper, Machine." *Association of Departments of English Bulletin* 150 (2010): 62–79. http://nkhayles.com/how_we_read.html.

Hays, Richard. *Echoes of Scripture in the Letters of Paul.* New Haven: Yale University Press, 1993.

_____. *Echoes of Scripture in the Gospels.* Waco, TX: Baylor University Press, 2016.

Heschel, Abraham Joshua. *The Sabbath.* Republished with a new Introduction by Susannah Heschel. New York: Farrar, Strauss, & Giroux, 2005.

Hess, Mary. "What Difference Does it Make? Digital Technology in the Theological Classroom." *Theological Education* 41, no. 1 (2005): 77–91. http://digital-commons.luthersem.edu/cgi/viewcontent.cgi?article=1012&context=faculty_articles.

Hey, Jonathan. "The Data, Information, Knowledge, Wisdom Chain: The Metaphorical Link." 2004. http://fliphtml5.com/zobq/ysge.

Hillesund, Terje. "Digital Reading Spaces: How Expert Readers Handle Books, the Web and Electronic Paper." *First Monday* 15, no. 4 (2010). http://first-monday.org/article/view/2762/2504.

Hindley, Meredith. "The Rise of the Machines: NEH and the Digital Humanities, The Early Years." *Humanities: The Magazine of the National Endowment for the Humanities* 34, no. 4 (2013); July-August Issue. https://www.neh.gov/humanities/2013/julyaugust/feature/the-rise-the-machines.

Hipps, Shane. *Flickering Pixels: How Technology Shapes Your Faith.* Grand Rapids, MI: Zondervan, 2009.

_____, and Brian McLaren. *The Hidden Power of Electronic Culture: How Media Shapes Faith, the Gospel, and Church.* El Cajon, CA: Zondervan/Youth Specialties, 2006.

Hockey, Susan. "The History of Humanities Computing." In *A Companion to Digital Humanities,* 3–19. Edited by S. Schreibman, R. Siemens, & J. Unsworth. Oxford: Blackwell, 2004.

Holmes, Michael W., and Bart Ehrman, eds. *The Text of the New Testament in Con-*

temporary Research: Essays on the Status Quaestionis. Grand Rapids, MI: Eerdmans, 1995.

Holtz, Barry, ed. *Back to the Sources: Reading the Classic Jewish Texts.* New York: Simon & Schuster, 1992.

Honoré, Carl. *In Praise of Slow: How a Worldwide Movement is Challenging the Cult of Speed.* San Francisco: HarperSanFrancisco, 2004.

Howard, R. G. *Digital Jesus: The Making of a New Christian Fundamentalist Christian Community on the Internet.* New York: New York University Press, 2011.

Hsu, Jeffrey, Kermit Allen Ecklebarger, and Terri A. Gibbs. *Computer Bible Study: Up-To-Date Information on the Best Software and Techniques.* Dallas: Word, 1993.

Hubbard, Thomas K. *Homosexuality in Greece and Rome: A Sourcebook of Basic Documents.* Berkeley, CA: University of California Press, 1989.

Hughes, John Jay. *Bits, Bytes & Biblical Studies: A Resource Guide for the Use of Computers in Biblical and Classical Studies.* Grand Rapids, MI: Academie Books, 1987.

_____. *Speaking the Truth in Love: The Theology of John M. Frame.* Phillipsburgh, NJ: P & R, 2009.

_____, and W. D. Mounce, eds. *God's Word Complete Concordance.* World Publishing, 1996.

Hurtado, Larry W. "The Early Christian Preference for the Codex," in *The Earliest Christian Artifacts: Manuscripts and Christian Origins,* 43–93. Grand Rapids: Eerdmans, 2006.

Hutchings, Tim. "Studying Apps: Research Approaches to the Digital Bible." In *Digital Methodologies in the Sociology of Religion,* 97–108. Edited by Sariya Cheruvallil-Contractor and Suha Shakkour. New York: Bloomsbury Academic, 2016.

_____. "Creating Church Online: Networks and Collectives in Contemporary Christianity." In *Digital Religion, Social Media and Culture: Perspectives, Practices and Futures,* 207–26. Edited by Pauline Hope Cheong and Peter Fischer-Nielsen. New York: Peter Lang Publishing, 2012.

_____. "Network Theology: Christian Understandings of New Media." *The Journal of Religion, Media and Digital Culture* 1, no. 1 (2012): 1–14. https://www.jrmdc.com/journal/article/view/8.

_____. "I Am Second: Evangelicals and Digital Storytelling." *Australian Journal of Communication* 39, no. 1 (2012): 71–86. https://search.informit.com.au/documentSummary;dn=775177112022985;res=IELHSS.

_____. "The Dis/Embodied Church: Worship, New Media and the Body." In *Christianity in the Modern World.* Edited by Giselle Vincette. Farnham, UK: Ashgate, 2014. https://www.academia.edu/8287907/The_Dis_Embodied_Church_Worship_New_Media_and_the_Body.

_____. "Digital Media and the Future of Religious Education." In *The Future of Education and Society Through the Eyes of Social Researchers*, 177–84. Edited by Michal Kwiatkowski, Anna Odrowaz-Coates, (Polish). Warsaw: Wydawnictwo Akademii Pedagogiki Specjalne, 2014.

_____. "Now the Bible is an App: Digital Media and Changing Patterns of Religious Authority." In *Religion, Media and Social Change*, 143–61. Edited by Kennet Granholm, Marcus Moberg, and Sofia Sjö. New York: Routledge, 2014.

_____. "Real Virtual Community." *Word and World* 35, no. 7 (2015): 151–61.

_____. "Christianity and Digital Media." In *The Changing World Religion Map: Sacred Places, Identities, Practices and Politics*, 3811–30. Edited by Stanley D. Brunn; Heidelberg, Germany: Springer Netherlands, 2015. DOI: 10.1007/978-94-017-9376-6.

_____. "E-Reading and the Christian Bible." *Studies in Religion/Studies Religieuses* 44, no. 4 (2015): 423–40. DOI: https://doi.org/10.1177/0008429815610607.

IndependentBaptist.com. "Is a Digital Bible Still the Word of God?" 2014. http://www.independentbaptist.com/is-a-digital-bible-still-the-word-of-god/.

Irwin, Ben. "Four Modern Versions of the Bible that Are Ruining the Bible." *OnFaith*, 2014. https://www.onfaith.co/onfaith/2014/06/02/four-modern-versions-of-the-bible-that-are-ruining-the-bible/32219.

Isaacson, Walter. *The Innovators: How a Group of Hackers, Geniuses, and Geeks Created the Digital Revolution*. New York: Simon & Schuster, 2014.

Jabr, Ferris. "The Reading Brain in the Digital Age: The Science of Paper versus Screens." *Scientific American*, April 11, 2013. https://www.scientificamerican.com/article/reading-paper-screens/.

_____. "Why the Brain Prefers Paper." *Scientific American* 309, no. 5 (2013): 48–53. DOI: 10.1038/scientificamerican1113-48

Jackson, Amy. "A Review of Logos 6 Bible Software." *ChristianityToday.com*, 2016. http://www.christianitytoday.com/biblestudies/articles/bibleinsights/review-of-logos-6-bible-software.html.

Jackson, Maggie. *Distracted: The Erosion of Attention and the Coming Dark Age*. Amherst, NY: Prometheus Books, 2008.

Jantzen, Jean. "The Bible: The Original Hypertext." 2011. http://cogwebcast.com/articles/the-bible-the-original-hypertext/.

Jeffrey, David L., ed. *A Dictionary of Biblical Tradition in English Literature*. Grand Rapids: Eerdmans, 1992.

_____, ed. *The King James Bible and the World It Made*. Waco, TX: Baylor University Press, 2011.

Jerome. *Letter to Damasus*. Printed in *Nicene and Post-Nicene Fathers of the Christian*

Church, 2nd series, 6:487–88. Edited by P. Schaff & H. Wace. Grand Rapids: Eerdmans, 1890.

Jobes, Karen, and Moises Silva. *Invitation to the Septuagint.* Grand Rapids: Baker Academic, 2015.

Johns, Adrian. *The Nature of the Book: Print and Knowledge in the Making.* Chicago, IL: University of Chicago Press, 1998.

Johnson, William A. *Readers and Reading Culture in the High Roman Empire: A Study of Elite Communities, Classical Culture and Society.* New York: Oxford University Press, 2010.

Jones, James Earl. *The Complete Audio Holy Bible: King James Version.* Renton, WA: Topics Entertainment, 2009.

Jones, Steven E. *Roberto Busa, S. J., and the Emergence of Humanities Computing: The Priest and the Punched Cards.* New York: Routledge, 2016.

Jordan, Mark. *The Invention of Sodomy in Christian Theology.* Chicago: University of Chicago Press, 1998.

Kalvesmaki, Joel. "Canonical References in Electronic Texts: Rationale and Best Practices." *Digital Humanities Quarterly* 8, no. 2 (2014).

Katz, William A. *Cuneiform to Computer.* Lanham, MD: Scarecrow Press, 1998.

Kauffman, Richard A. "Holy Digital: the Bible on iPad." *The Christian Century* 130, no. 9 (2013): 11. https://www.christiancentury.org/article/2013-04/holy-digital.

Kaufman, G., and M. Flanagan. "High-Low Split: Divergent Cognitive Construal Levels Triggered by Digital and Non-digital Platforms." In *Proceedings of the 2016 CHI Conference on Human Factors in Computing Systems,* 2773–77. 2016.

Keck, Leander, ed. *The New Interpreter's Bible.* 10 vols. Nashville: Abingdon, 1994–2004.

Kelly, Kevin. "Nerd Theology." *Technology in Society* 21 (1999): 387–92.

_____. "Scan This Book!" *The New York Times,* 2006/05/14/. http://www.nytimes.com/2006/05/14/magazine/14publishing.html.

_____. "Becoming Screen Literate." *The New York Times,* 2008/11/23/. http://www.nytimes.com/2008/11/23/magazine/23wwln-future-t.html.

Kenyon, F. G. *The Chester Beatty Biblical Papyri: Descriptions and Texts of Twelve Manuscripts on Papyrus of the Greek Bible.* London: Emery Walker Ltd, 1933–1937.

Kim, Larry. "Multitasking Is Killing Your Brain." *Inc,* 2015. https://www.inc.com/larry-kim/why-multi-tasking-is-killing-your-brain.html.

Kissane, Dylan. "5 Most Important Trends for Blogging in 2016." *DOZ Marketing Software,* 2016. http://www.doz.com/content/trends-in-blogging-2016.

Kitada, Ryo. "The Brain Network for Haptic Object Recognition." In *Pervasive*

Haptics: Science, Design, and Application, 21–37. Edited by H. Kajimoto, S. Saga, & M. Konyo. Tokyo: Springer, 2016.

Klauck, Hans-Josef, ed. *Encyclopedia of the Bible and Its Reception*. Berlin: Walter de Gruyter, 2009–present.

Klingberg, Torkel. *The Overflowing Brain: Information Overload and the Limits of Working Memory*. New York: Oxford University Press, 2009.

Kraft, Robert. *Barnabas and the Didache*. The Apostolic Fathers: A Translation and Commentary, vol. 3. Edited by R. M. Grant. New York: Thomas Nelson & Sons, 1965.

_____. "In Quest of Computer Literacy." *Bulletin - Council on the Study of Religion* 15, no. 2 (1984): 41–45.

_____. "The Use of Computers in New Testament Textual Criticism." In *The Text of the New Testament in Contemporary Research: Essays on the Status Quaestionis. A Volume in Honor of Bruce M. Metzger*, 268–82. Edited by Bart D. Ehrman and Michael Holmes. Leiden: Brill, 1995.

_____. "How I Met the Computer, and How it Changed My Life." *SBL Forum*, 2004. https://www.sbl-site.org/publications/article.aspx?ArticleId=246.

_____. "Para-mania: Beside, Before and Beyond Bible Studies." *Journal of Biblical Literature* 126, no. 1 (2007): 5–27.

_____, Emanuel Tov, and John Abercrombie. *Computer Assisted Tools for Septuagint Studies (CATSS), Volume 1, Ruth*. Septuagint and Cognate Studies 20. Atlanta: Scholars Press, 1986.

Krugg, Steve. *Don't Make Me Think, Revisited: A Comon Sense Approach to Web Usability*. 3rd ed. Berkeley, CA: New Riders, 2014.

Krupp, Michael. "Manuscripts of the Mishna. The Three Complete Mishna Manuscripts." In *The Literature of the Sages I*, 253–54. Edited by Shmuel Safrai. Philadelphia: Fortress Press, 1987.

Kubo, Sakae, and Walter F. Specht. *So Many Versions? 20th Century English Versions of the Bible*. Grand Rapids: Zondervan, 1983.

Kurlansky, Mark. *Paper: Paging Through History*. New York: W.W. Norton & Co., 2016.

Lanier, Jaron. *You Are Not a Gadget: A Manifesto*. New York: Alfred A. Knopf, 2010.

Lapowsky, Issie. "Don't Multitask: Your Brain Will Thank You." *Inc.com*, 2013. http://business.time.com/2013/04/17/dont-multitask-your-brain-will-thank-you/.

Lazar, Michael. "Study Finds Difference In Recollection From Screen Reading Vs. Paper Reading." *The Huffington Post*, May 30, 2016. http://www.huffingtonpost.com/michael-lazar/study-finds-difference-in_b_10210036.html.

Lebert, Marie. *A Short History of EBooks* (1971–2008). NEF, University of Toronto, 2009. http://www.gutenberg.org/files/29801/29801-pdf.pdf.

Legaspi, Michael C. *The Death of Scripture and the Rise of Biblical Studies*. New York: Oxford University Press, 2010.

Levy, David M. *Scrolling Forward: Making Sense of Documents in the Digital Age*. 2nd ed. New York: Arcade, 2016.

Lewis, Bex. "Review of "@StickyJesus: How To Live Out Your Faith Online" by Tami Heim & Toni Birdsong. Abingdon Press, 2012." *The Journal of Religion, Media and Digital Culture* 1, no. 2.

Lewis, Naphtali. *Papyrus in Classical Antiquity*. Oxford: Oxford University Press, 1974.

Leyva, Elsa Margarita Ramírez. "The Impact of the Internet on the Reading and Information Practices of a University Student Community: The Case of UNAM." *New Review of Libraries and Lifelong Learning* 4, no. 1 (2003): 137–57. doi: 10.1080/1468994042000240287.

Life Application Study Bible NIV, Personal Size. New International edition. Carol Stream, IL: Tyndale, 2012.

LifeChurch. *The Bible App for Kids Storybook Bible*. Pompano Beach, FL: OneHope, Inc., 2015.

Linville, James. "Book Review: Tim Bulkeley, Amos: Hypertext Bible Commentary." *Catholic Biblical Quarterly* 69 (2007): 316–18.

Liu, Ziming. "Reading Behavior in the Digital Environment: Changes in Reading Behavior over the Past Ten Years." *Journal of Documentation* 61, no. 6 (2005): 700–712.

_____. *Paper to Digital: Documents in the Information Age*. Westport, CT: Libraries Unlimited, 2008.

Lloyd-Jones, Sally. *The Jesus Storybook Bible: Every Story Whispers His Name*. Grand Rapids, MI: Thomas Nelson, 2007.

Maclean, Marie. "Pretexts and Paratexts: The Art of the Peripheral." *New Literary History* 22 (1991): 273–79.

Madrigal, Alexis C. 2010. "Is Google Making Us Stupid?" *The Atlantic*, 2010/09/15/. https://www.theatlantic.com/technology/archive/2010/09/is-google-making-us-stupid/62964/.

Mak, Bonnie. *How the Page Matters*. Toronto: University of Toronto Press, 2012.

Maloney, Jennifer. "The Rise of Phone Reading." *The Wall Street Journal*, August 14, 2015. https://www.wsj.com/articles/the-rise-of-phone-reading-1439398395.

Man, John. *The Gutenberg Revolution: How Printing Changed the Course of History*. London: Bantam Books, 2002.

Mangen, Anne. "Hypertext Fiction Reading: Haptics and Immersion." *Journal of Research in Reading* 31, no. 4 (2008): 404–19. doi: 10.1111/j.1467-9817.2008.00380.x.

_____, Bente R. Walgermo, and Kolbjørn Brønnick. "Reading Linear Texts On Paper Versus Computer Screen: Effects on Reading Comprehension." *International Journal of Educational Research* 58 (2013): 61–68. doi: 10.1016/j.ijer.2012.12.002.

Manovich, Lev. *Remixing and Remixability*. 2005. http://remixandremixability.blogspot.com.

_____. *Software Takes Command*. New York: Bloomsbury Academic, 2013.

Margolin, Sara J., Casey Driscoll, Michael J. Toland, and Jennifer Little Kegler. "E-readers, Computer Screens, or Paper: Does Reading Comprehension Change Across Media Platforms?" *Applied Cognitive Psychology* 27, no. 4 (2013): 512–19. doi: 10.1002/acp.2930.

Martens, John. "The Word Made Digital: Who to Follow and What to Watch for While Engaging the Bible Online." *America*, 12/18/2013. http://www.americamagazine.org/faith/2013/12/18/word-made-digital-who-follow-and-what-watch-while-engaging-bible-online.

Matlock, Michael D., and Jason R. Jackson. "Accordance 8 Bible software: Scholars collection." *Asbury Journal* 66, no. 1 (2011): 134–37.

McGann, Jerome J. *Radiant Textuality: Literature after the World Wide Web*. New York: Palgrave, 2001.

McLuhan, Marshall. *The Gutenberg Galaxy: The Making of Typographic Man*. Toronto: University of Toronto Press, 1962.

_____. *The Medium is the Massage*. New York: Random House, 1967.

_____. *Understanding Media: The Extensions of Man*. Critical edition, edited by W. Terrence Gordon. Berkeley, CA: Gingko, 2003.

Mellinkoff, Ruth. *The Horned Moses in Medieval Art and Thought*. Berkeley, CA: University of California Press, 1970.

Merkoski, Jason. *Burning the Page: The Ebook Revolution and the Future of Reading*. Naperville, IL: Sourcebooks, 2013.

Metzger, Bruce Manning. *The Canon of the New Testament: Its Origin, Development, and Significance*. New York: Oxford University Press, 1987.

_____. *A Textual Commentary on the Greek New Testament*, 2nd ed. Stuttgart: Deutsche Bibelgesellschaft, 1994.

_____. *The Bible in Translation: Ancient and English Versions*. Grand Rapids: Baker, 2001.

_____, and Bart D. Ehrman. *The Text of the New Testament: Its Transmission, Corruption, and Restoration*, 4th ed. New York: Oxford University Press, 2005.

Meyer, Joyce. *The Everyday Life Bible: The Power of God's Word for Everyday Living*. New York: FaithWords, 2013.

Minard, Tomothée. "Accordance, Bibleworks, Bible Parser, Logos: Speed Test." 2015. https://www.youtube.com/watch?v=-zQkG72utr4.

Mitchell, Matthew W. "Biblical Studies on the Internet." *Religious Studies Review* 32, no. 4 (2006): 216–18. doi: 10.1111/j.1748–0922.2006.00124.x.

Morton, A. Q., and James McLeman. *Christianity in the Computer Age*. New York: Harper & Row, 1964.

_____, and Alban D. Winspear. *It's Greek to the Computer*. Montreal: Harvest House, 1971.

_____. *A Critical Concordance to the Acts of the Apostles (The Computer Bible)*. Biblical Research Associates, 1976.

_____. *The Genesis of John*. Edinburgh: Saint Andrew Press, 1980.

_____. "The Annals of Computing: The Greek New Testament." *Computers and the Humanities* 14, no. 3 (1980): 197–99.

_____. *The Gathering of the Gospels: From Papyrus to Printout*. Lampeter: Mellen Press, 1995.

Morville, Peter. *Ambient Findability: What We Find Changes Who We Become*. Sebastopol, CA: O'Reilly, 2005.

Mullins, Phil. "Sacred Text in an Electronic Age." *Biblical Theology Bulletin* 20 (1990): 99–106.

Nasselqvist, Dan. *Public Reading in Early Christianity: Lectors, Manuscripts, and Sound in the Oral Delivery of John 1-4*. Leiden: Brill, 2015.

National Telecommunications and Information Administration, and Economics and Statistics Administration. *Exploring the Digital Nation: America's Emerging Online Experience*. Washington, DC: U.S. Department of Commerce, 2013. http://www.esa.doc.gov/reports/exploring-digital-nation-americas-emerging-online-experience.

Naughton, John. *From Gutenberg to Zuckerberg: disruptive innovation in the age of the Internet*. New York,: Quercus, 2014.

Neff, David. "How the Physical Form of a Bible Shapes Us." *Christianity Today* 56, no. 1 (2012): 60. http://www.christianitytoday.com/ct/2012/january/almostlooks.html.

Neumann, Kenneth J. *The Authenticity of the Pauline Epistles in the Light of Stylostatistical Analysis*. SBLDS 120. Atlanta: Scholars Press, 1991.

Nicolás, Fr. Adolfo, S.J. "Challenges to Jesuit Higher Education Today," *Conversations on Jesuit Higher Education* 40, no. 5. 2011. Available at: http://epublications.marquette.edu/conversations/vol40/iss1/5.

Nicolson, Adam. *God's Secretaries: The Making of the King James Bible*. New York: HarperCollins, 2005.

Niebuhr, Reinhold. *The Nature and Destiny of Man*. 2 vols. New York: Charles Scribner's Sons, 1964.

Nield, David. "A Brief History of the Amazon Kindle: The Gadget That Changed

Reading." *The Gadget Website,* August 6, 2015. http://www.t3.com/features/a-brief-history-of-the-amazon-kindle.

Nielsen, Jakob. "F-Shaped Pattern for Reading Web Content." *Nielsen Norman Group,* April 6, 2006. https://www.nngroup.com/articles/f-shaped-pattern-reading-web-content/.

_____. "How Little Do Users Read?" *Nielsen Norman Group,* May 6, 2008. https://www.nngroup.com/articles/how-little-do-users-read/.

_____, and K. Pernice. *Eyetracking Web Usability.* Berkeley, CA: New Riders, 2010.

Nielsen, Michael. *Reinventing Discovery: The New Era of Networked Science.* Princeton, NJ: Princeton University Press, 2011.

Nissenen, Martti. *Homoeroticism in the Biblical World: A Historical Perspective.* Minneapolis: Fortress Press, 1998.

NIV Study Bible. Grand Rapids, MI: Zondervan, 2011.

NIV Life Application Study Bible. Grand Rapids, MI: Zondervan, 2011.

NIV Boys Bible. Grand Rapids, MI: Zonderkidz, 2012.

Novelli, Michael. *Shaped By the Story: Discover the Art of Bible Storying.* Grand Rapids: Zondervan, 2013.

Nyce, James M., and Paul Kahn. *From Memex To Hypertext: Vannevar Bush and the Mind's Machine.* San Diego: Academic Press Inc., 1992.

O'Leary, Amy. "In the Beginning Was the Word; Now the Word Is on an App." *The New York Times,* 2013/07/26/. http://www.nytimes.com/2013/07/27/technology/the-faithful-embrace-youversion-a-bible-app.html.

Oborne, David J., and Doreen Holton. "Reading from Screen Versus Paper: There Is No Difference." *International Journal of Man-Machine Studies* 28, no. 1 (1988): 1–9. doi: 10.1016/S0020–7373(88)80049–X.

Occhipinti, Lisa. *The Repurposed Library: 33 Craft Projects That Give Old Books New Life.* New York: Stewart, Tabori and Chang, 2011.

_____. *Novel Living: Collecting, Decorating, and Crafting with Books.* New York: Stewart, Tabori and Chang, 2014.

O'Keefe, Evin. "How Multitasking is Killing Your Brain." *High Performance Blog,* July 8, 2015. https://www.teamwork.com/blog/the-myth-of-multitasking/.

Olsen, Ted. "Hacking the Bible." *ChristianityToday.com.* http://www.christianitytoday.com/ct/2014/march/bible-in-original-geek.html.

_____. "The Bible in the Original Geek: Inside the World of the New Bible Coders––and How They Will Change the Way You Think about Scripture." *Christianity Today* 58, no. 2 (2014): 28–35.

Olson, David R. *The World on Paper: The Conceptual and Cognitive Implications of Writing and Reading.* New York: Cambridge University Press, 1994.

Ong, Walter. *Interfaces of the Word: Studies in the Evolution of Consciousness and Culture.* Ithaca, NY: Cornell University Press, 1977.

_____. *Orality and Literacy: The Technologizing of the Word.* New York: Methuen, 1982.

Ophir, Eyal, Clifford Nass, and Anthony Wagner. "Cognitive Control in Media Multitaskers." *Proceedings of the National Academy of Sciences* 106, no. 37 (2009): 15583–87.

Orgel, Stephen. *Books and Readers in Early Modern England: Material Studies.* Philadelphia, PA: University of Pennsylvania Press, 2001.

Paget, James Carleton, ed. *The New Cambridge History of the Bible*, 4 vols. Cambridge: Cambridge University Press, 2013–2015.

Palfrey, John, and Urs Gasser. *Born Digital: How Children Grow Up in a Digital Age.* Revised ed. New York: Basic Books, 2016.

Palmer, Michael. "Scripture Study in the Age of the New Media." In *Critical Thinking and the Bible in the Age of New Media,* 237–66. Edited by Charles Ess. Lanham, MD: University Press of America, 2004.

Parker, David C. "Through a Screen Darkly: Digital Texts and the New Testament." *Journal for the Study of the New Testament* 25, no. 4 (2003): 395–411.

_____. "The Oldest Bible." British Broadcasting Corporation, October 6, 2008. http://www.bbc.co.uk/radio4/theoldestbible/.

_____. *An Introduction to the New Testament Manuscripts and Their Texts.* Cambridge: Cambridge University Press, 2008.

_____. *Codex Sinaiticus: The Story of the World's Oldest Bible.* Peabody, MA: Hendrickson, 2010.

Parker, Nathan. "A Comparison Between Logos 6 and Accordance 11." 2015. http://www.stilltruth.com/2015/a-comparison-between-logos-6-and-accordance-11/.

Perkins, Pheme, ed. *The New Oxford Annotated Bible with Apocrypha: New Revised Standard Version.* 4th ed. New York: Oxford University Press, 2010.

Pfeiffer, Cara. "The Contour Methodology: Teaching the Bible in the Digital Age." *Conversations with the Biblical World* 31 (2011): 204.

Philipps, Peter. "The Bible as Augmented Reality: Beginning a Conversation." *Theology and Ministry* 1, no. 2 (2010): 1–10.

Piper, Andrew. *Book Was There: Reading in Electronic Times.* Chicago: University Of Chicago Press, 2013.

Pontifical Biblical Commission. *The Interpretation of the Bible in the Church.* Rome: The Pontifical Biblical Commission. 1994.

Posner, Miriam. "Think Talk Make Do: Power and the Digital Humanities." *Journal of Digital Humanities* 1, no. 2 (2012). http://journalofdigitalhumanities.org/1-2/think-talk-make-do-power-and-the-digital-humanities-by-miriam-posner/.

_____. "What's Next: The Radical, Unrealized Potential of Digital Humanities." Personal blog, 2015. http://miriamposner.com/blog/whats-next-the-radical-unrealized-potential-of-digital-humanities/.

Pui–lan, Kwok. "Holy Bible 3.0: Scripture in the Digital Age." *Reflections: A Magazine of Theological and Ethical Inquiry from Yale Divinity School,* 2008. http://reflections.yale.edu/article/between-babel-and-beatitude/holy-bible-30-scripture-digital-age.

Putnam, Robert. *Bowling Alone: The Collapse and Revival of American Community.* New York: Simon & Schuster, 2001.

Radday, Yehuda Thomas. "Isaiah and the Computer: A Preliminary Report." *Computers and the Humanities* 5, no. 2 (1970): 65–73.

_____. *Analytical Linguistic Key-Word-In-Context Concordance to the Book of Exodus.* Wooster, OH: Biblical Research Assn., 1985.

_____, and Heim Shore. *Genesis: An Authorship Study in Computer–Assisted Statistical Linguistics.* Analecta Biblica, vol. 103 Rome: Gregorian & Biblical Press, 1985.

Radosh, Daniel. "The Good Book Business." *The New Yorker,* 2006. http://www.newyorker.com/magazine/2006/12/18/the-good-book-business(12/18/2006).

Raine, Lee, and Barry Wellman. *Networked: The New Social Operating System.* Cambridge, MA: MIT Press, 2012.

_____. *The Rise of e-reading.* Pew Internet and American Life Project, 2012. http://libraries.pewinternet.org/files/legacy-pdf/The%20rise%20of%20e-reading%204.5.12.pdf.

Rakow, Katje. "The Bible in the Digital Age: Negotiating the Limits of 'Bibleness' of Different Bible Media." In *Christianity and the Limits of Materiality.* Edited by Minna Opas and Anna Haapalainen. London: Bloomsbury, 2017.

Reventlow, Henning Graf. *History of Biblical Interpretation,* 4 vols. Leiden: Brill, 2010.

Riding, Jon. "Bible in the Raw." *Fulcrum Anglican,* 2014. https://www.fulcrum-anglican.org.uk/articles/bible-in-the-raw/.

Ritchie, Rene. "iPhone to iPhone 6: History in Specs." imore.com, September 23, 2014. http://www.imore.com/iphone-iphone-6-history-specs.

_____. "History of the iPhone: Apple Reinvents the Phone," *iMore,* August 31, 2015. http://www.imore.com/history-iphone-original.

_____. "History of iPhone 3G: Twice as Fast, Half the Price," *iMore,* September 1, 2015. http://www.imore.com/history-iphone-3g.

Roberts, Colin H., and T. C. Skeat. *The Birth of the Codex.* New York: Oxford University Press, 1987.

Rosen, Christine. "People of the Screen." *The New Atlantis: A Journal of Technology and Society,* 2008. Pages 20–32. http://www.thenewatlantis.com/docLib/ 20081020_TNA22Rosen.pdf.

Rosenwald, Michael S. "Why Digital Natives Prefer Reading in Print. Yes, You Read that Right." *The Washington Post,* February 22, 2015. http://tiny url.com/lj9kf92.

Ross, Martha. "Audio Books: Is Listening as Good as Reading?" *The Mercury News,* June 20, 2016. http://www.mercurynews.com/bay-area-living/ ci_30054295/audiobooks-is-listening-good-reading.

Rowley, Jennifer. "The Wisdom Hierarchy: Representations of the DIKW Hierarchy." *Journal of Information Science* 33 (2007): 163–80.

Rowsell, Jennifer, and Anne Burke. "Reading by Design: Two Case Studies of Digital Reading Practices." *Journal of Adolescent & Adult Literacy* 53, no. 2 (2009): 106–18. doi: 10.1598/JAAL.53.2.2.

Runnel, Pille, Pille Pruulmann-Vengerfeldt, Piret Viires, & Marin Laak, eds. *The Digital Turn: User's Practices and Cultural Transformations.* Frankfurt am Main: Peter Lang, 2013.

Ryken, Leland. *The Legacy of the King James Bible: Celebrating 400 Years of the Most Influential English Translation.* Wheaton, IL: Crossway, 2011.

Saenger, Paul Henry. *Space Between Words: The Origins of Silent Reading.* Stanford, CA: Stanford University Press, 1997.

Salvucci, Dario D., and Niels A. Taatgen. *The Multitasking Mind.* New York: Oxford University Press, 2010.

Sanner, Kent. "Bible Study Software Put to the Test: Logos 6 in Review." *LogosTalk,* 2014. https://blog.logos.com/2014/11/bible-study-software-put-to-the-test-logos-6-in-review/.

Santoro, Anthony, and Daniel Silliman. *Religion and the Marketplace in the United States.* New York: Oxford University Press, 2015.

Scheiffele, Walter. *The Digital Turn: Design in the Era of Interactive Technologies.* Chicago: University of Chicago Press, 2013.

Schreibman, Susan, Ray Siemens, and John Unsworth, eds. *Companion to Digital Humanities* Oxford: Blackwell, 2004.

_____. *A New Companion to Digital Humanities.* 2nd ed. Oxford: Wiley-Blackwell, 2015.

Schwartz, Tony. "Addicted to Distraction" – The New York Times, 11/28/2015. https://www.nytimes.com/2015/11/29/opinion/sunday/addicted-to-distraction.html?_r=0.

Sharma, N. "The Origin of the 'Data Information Knowledge Wisdom' Hierarchy." 2008. http://tinyurl.com/m8644d6.

Shier–Jones, Angela. "From Transmission to TXT: The Bible in a Digital Age." *Epworth Review* 37, no. 3 (2010): 32–49.

Shifman, Limor. *Memes in Digital Culture*. Cambridge, MA: MIT Press, 2013.

Siegenthaler, Eva, Pascal Wurtz, Per Bergamin, and Rudolf Groner. "Comparing Reading Processes on e-ink Displays and Print." *Displays* 32, no. 5 (2011): 268–73. doi: 10.1016/j.displa.2011.05.005.

Siker, Jeffrey S. "Disciples and Discipleship in the Fourth Gospel: A Canonical Approach." *Studia Biblica et Theologica* 10 (1980): 199–225.

_____. *Disinheriting the Jews: Abraham in Early Christian Controversy*. Louisville, KY: Westminster John Knox, 1991.

_____, ed. *Homosexuality in the Church: Both Sides of the Debate*. Louisville: Westminster John Knox, 1994.

_____. *Scripture and Ethics: Twentieth-Century Portraits*. New York: Oxford University Press, 1997.

_____. "President Obama, the Bible, and Political Rhetoric." *Political Theology* 13, no. 5 (2012): 586–609. doi: 10.1558/poth.v13i5.586.

_____. "Jewish/Christian Relations at 25: Retrospect & Prospect." *Ancient Jew Review*, 2014. http://www.ancientjewreview.com/articles/2014/12/9/jewishchristian-relations-at-25-retrospect-prospect.

_____. "Digital Turns and Liquid Scriptures." *Reflections: A Magazine of Theological and Ethical Inquiry from Yale Divinity School*, 2015. http://reflections.yale.edu/article/new-voyages-church-today-and-tomorrow/digital-turns-and-liquid-scriptures.

_____. *Jesus, Sin, and Perfection in Early Christianity*. New York: Cambridge University Press, 2015.

Skeat, Theodore Cressy. "The Length of the Standard Papyrus Roll and the Cost-Advantage of the Codex." *Zeitschrift für Papyrologie und Epigraphik* 45 (1982): 169–75.

Small, Ian. "Why Audio is Better than Print." 2016. http://www.digitalbookworld.com/2016/why-audio-better-print/.

Smith, Christopher and John Pattison. *Slow Church: Cultivating Community in the Patient Way of Jesus*. Downers Grove, IL: IVP, 2014.

Smith, Julien. "Bible Software Review." *Perspectives in Religious Studies* 35, no. 3 (2008): 325–28.

Sneed, Annie. "Everything Science Knows About Reading On Screens." July 8, 2015. https://www.fastcodesign.com/3048297/evidence/everything-science-knows-about-reading-on-screens.

Stack, Liam. "Emoji Bible Translates Scriptures Into Smileys." *The New York Times,* June 2, 2016. http://tinyurl.com/l7rl2ju.

Stallybrass, Peter. "Books and Scrolls: Navigating the Bible." In *Books and Readers in Early Modern England: Material Studies,* 42–79. Edited by Jennifer Anderson and Elizabeth Sauer. Philadelphia: University of Pennsylvania Press, 2001.

Starre, Alexander. *Metamedia: American Book Fictions and Literary Print Culture after Digitization.* Iowa City: University of Iowa Press, 2015.

Stewart, Emily. "The Torah in Transition: Imitative Aspects from Codex to Database." *The Journal of Religion, Media and Digital Culture* 3, no. 3 (2015): 107–28.

Stoop, Judith, Paulien Kreutzer, and Joost Kircz. "Reading and Learning from Screens versus Print: A Study in Changing Habits. Part 1." *New Library World* 114, no. 7/8 (2013): 284–300.

_____. "Reading and Learning from Screens versus Print: A Study in Changing Habits. Part 2." *New Library World* 114, no. 9/10 (2013): 371–83.

Stroman, Patrick W. *Essentials of Functional MRI.* Boca Raton, FL: CRC Press, 2011.

Striphas, Theodore G. *The Late Age of Print: Everyday Book Culture from Consumerism to Control.* New York: Columbia University Press, 2009.

Taylor, Annette Kujawski. "Students Learn Equally Well From Digital as From Paperbound Texts." *Teaching of Psychology* 38, no. 4 (2011): 278–81.

Taylor, Jim. "Technology: Myth of Multitasking," *Psychology Today,* March 30, 2011. http://psychologytoday.com/blog/the-power-prime/201103/technology-myth-multitasking.

Taylor, Mark. *Speed Limits: Where Time Went and Why We Have So Little Left.* New Haven, CT: Yale University Press, 2014.

Thayer, Alexander, Charlotte Lee, Linda Hwang, Heidi Sales, Pausali Sen, and Ninad Dalal. "The Imposition and Superimposition of Digital Reading Technology: The Academic Potential of E-readers." *Proceedings of the SIGCHI Conference on Human Factors in Computing Systems,* 2011. 2917–2926.

Thieme, Richard. "Entering Sacred Digital Space: Seeking to Distinguish the Dreamer and the Dream." In *New Paradigms for Bible Study: The Bible in the Third Millennium,* 49–70. Edited by Robert M. Fowler, Edith Blumhofer, and Fernando F. Segovia. New York: T & T Clark, 2004.

Thompson, Jason. *Playing with Books: The Art of Upcycling, Deconstructing, and Reimagining the Book.* Beverly, Mass: Quarry Books, 2010.

Thorpe, James. *The Gutenberg Bible: Landmark in Learning.* Huntington Library Press, 1997.

Tov, Emanuel. "Computers and the Bible." *Bible Review* 4 (1988): 38–42.

_____. _Textual Criticism of the Hebrew Bible._ 3rd revised and expanded edition. Minneapolis: Fortress Press, 2012.

Trachtenburg, Joshua. _The Devil and the Jews: The Medieval Conception of the Jew and Its Relation to Modern Anti-Semitism._ New York: Jewish Publication Society, 1993.

Treat, Jay Curry. "Computing and the Religious Studies Department at Penn." 1996. https://www.sas.upenn.edu/~jtreat/rs/rscpuhx.html#offline.

Trepel, Simon. "Multitasking Is Not Killing Your Brain." _Medium,_ 2016. https://medium.com/@SimonSaysPsychStuf/multitasking-is-not-killing-your-brain-99d8ffee338a.

Tucker, Gene. "Book Review: Amos: Hypertext Bible Commentary, Tim Bulkeley (Auckland: Hypertext Bible Project, 2005)." _Colloquium_ 39, no. 1 (2007): 103–6.

Turkle, Sherry. _Alone Together: Why We Expect More from Technology and Less from Each Other._ New York: Basic Books, 2011.

Turner, E. G. _The Typology of the Early Codex._ Philadelphia: University of Pennsylvania Press, 1977.

United States Conference of Catholic Bishops. _Catechism of the Catholic Church,_ 2nd ed. Washington, DC: United States Catholic Conference, 1994.

Vaca, Daniel. "Selling Trust: _The Living Bible_ and the Business of Biblicism." In _The Bible in American Life,_ 169–82. Edited by Philip Goff, Arthur E. Farnsley II, and Peter Thuesen. New York: Oxford University Press, 2017.

van der Weel, Adriaan. "Is a Book Still a Book When It is not a Printed Artifact?" _Logos: The Journal of the World Book Community_ 12, no. 1 (2003): 22–26.

_____. _Changing Our Textual Minds: Towards a Digital Order of Knowledge._ New York: Manchester University Press, 2011.

van Peursen, Wido. "Is the Bible Losing its Covers? Conceptualization and Use of the Bible on the Threshold of the Digital Order." _HIPHIL Novum_ 1, no. 1 (2014): 44–58. http://ww.see-j.net/hiphil/ojs-2.3.3-3/index.php/hiphil/article/view/53.

_____, Ernst Thoutenhoofd, and Adriaan van der Weel, eds. _Text Comparison and Digital Creativity: The Production of Presence and Meaning in Digital Text Scholarship._ Leiden: Brill, 2010.

Vandendorpe, Christian. _From Papyrus to Hypertext: Toward the Universal Digital Library._ Urbana & Chicago: University of Illinois Press, 2009.

Vander Stichele, Caroline, and Hugh S. Pyper, eds. _Text, Image, and Otherness in Children's Bibles: What Is in the Picture?_ Atlanta: Society of Biblical Literature, 2012.

Varner, William. "Review of Logos Bible Software 3. Libronix Digital Library

System. 2000–2006." *The Master's Seminary Journal.* https://www.logos.com/press/reviews/tmsj18-2007.

Vermes, Geza. *An Introduction to the Complete Dead Sea Scrolls*, rev. ed. Minneapolis: Fortress Press, 1999.

Vogt, Brandon, ed. *The Church and New Media: Blogging Converts, Online Activists, and Bishops Who Tweet.* Huntington, IN: Our Sunday Visitor, 2011.

Walsh, Maureen, Jennifer Asha, and Nicole Sprainger. "Reading Digital Texts." *Australian Journal of Language and Literacy* 30, no. 1 (2007): 40.

Weaver, John B. "Accordance Bible software in reading and teaching: the difference a digital text makes." *Advances in the Study of Information and Religion* 1 (2011): 227–33.

_____. "Transforming Practice: American Bible Reading in Digital Culture." In *The Bible in American Life*, 249–55. Edited by Philip Goff, Arthur E. Fransley II, Peter J. Thuesen. New York: Oxford University Press, 2017.

Weinberger, David. *Everything is Miscellaneous: The Power of the New Digital Disorder.* New York: Times Books, 2007.

_____. "The Problem with the Data-Information-Knowledge-Wisdom Hierarchy." *Harvard Business Review,* 2010. https://hbr.org/2010/02/data-is-to-info-as-info-is-not.

_____. *Too Big to Know: Rethinking Knowledge Now That the Facts Aren't the Facts, Experts Are Everywhere, and the Smartest Person in the Room Is the Room.* New York: Basic Books, 2011.

Weizenbaum, Joseph. *Computer Power and Human Reason: From Judgment to Calculation.* New York: W.H. Freeman, 1976.

Westera, Wim. *The Digital Turn: How the Internet Transforms Our Existence.* Bloomington: AuthorHouseUK, 2012.

Wheeler, Dale M. "Push–Button Bibles: How to Compare Computer Software for Bible Research." *Christianity Today* 34, no. 15 (1990): S3–S13.

Wilson, Walter. *The Internet Church.* Nashville: Thomas Nelson, 2004.

Wise, Justin. *The Social Church: A Theology of Digital Communication.* Chicago: Moody, 2014.

Wiseman, Karyn L. "Click 2 Save: The Digital Ministry Bible." *Homiletic (Online)* 39, no. 1 (2014).

Witman, Paul, Kapp Johnson, and Nicole Sparkman. "The Church Online – The Impact of Online Social Networks on Church Congregations." 2010. *SAIS 2010 Proceedings Paper 2.*

Wolf, Maryanne. *Proust and the Squid: The Story and Science of the Reading Brain.* New York: HarperCollins, 2007.

Wosh, Peter J. *Spreading the Word: The Bible Business in Nineteenth-Century America.* Ithaca: Cornell University Press, 1994.

Würthwein, Ernst, and A. A. Fischer. *The Text of the Old Testament: An Introduction to the Biblia Hebraica*, 3rd ed., revised and expanded. Grand Rapids: Eerdmans, 2014.

Yates, Frances A. *The Art of Memory*. Chicago: University of Chicago Press, 1966.

Zaupan-Jerome, Danielle. *Connected Toward Communion: The Church and Social Communication in the Digital Age*. Collegeville, MN: Liturgical, 2014.

Zax, David. "This Is Your Brain on E-Books." *MIT Technology Review*, April 12, 2013. https://www.technologyreview.com/s/513766/this-is-your-brain-on -e-books/.

Zeleny, M. "Management Support Systems: Towards Integrated Knowledge Management." *Human Systems Management* 7 (1987): 59–70.

Zoba, Robert V. "Cruising the Electronic Bible." *Christianity Today* 39, no. 12 (1995): 21–21.

Zylstra, Sarah. "Fifty Shades of the Good Book." *Christianity Today* 57, no. 1 (2013): 15. http://www.christianitytoday.com/ct/2013/january-february/ fifty-shades-of-good-book.html.

_____. "Sorry Again, John 3:16: The World's 10 Most Popular Bible Verses of 2014." *Christianity Today*, 2014. http://www.christianitytoday.com/gleanings/2014/december/worlds-10-most-popular-bible-verses-youversion-2014.html.

_____. "The Most Popular and Fastest Growing Bible Translation Isn't What You Think It Is." *Christianity Today*, 2015. http://www.christianitytoday.com/gleanings/2014/march/most-popular-and-fastest-growing-bibletranslation-niv-kjv.html.

Scripture Index

Name Index

Subject Index